Y0-CPD-703

The Correspondence of Daniel O'Connell
Volume III
1824–1828

THE CORRESPONDENCE OF DANIEL O'CONNELL

Editor: Maurice R. O'Connell, Ph.D.
Assistant Editor: Gerard J. Lyne, M.A.
Editorial Assistants:
Hugh C. McFadden, M.A. *and* Elizabeth M. O'Connell

THE CORRESPONDENCE OF DANIEL O'CONNELL

Volume III

1824-1828

Edited by

Maurice R. O'Connell

Professor of History

Fordham University

IRISH UNIVERSITY PRESS
Dublin Ireland

BARNES & NOBLE BOOKS · NEW YORK
(a division of Harper & Row Publishers, Inc.)

for the Irish Manuscripts Commission

ISBN 06–495234–7

Published in the U.S.A. 1974

by Harper & Row Publishers, Inc.
BARNES & NOBLE IMPORT DIVISION

PRINTED IN THE REPUBLIC OF IRELAND BY
CAHILL & CO. LIMITED, DUBLIN

Contents

The preface acknowledgments and list of manuscript and published sources for *The Correspondence of Daniel O'Connell* are to be found in Volume I.

Abbreviations

BLG	*Burke's Landed Gentry*
BM	British Museum
Boase	Boase, Frederic. *Modern English Biography . . .*
CMC	*Cork Mercantile Chronicle*
CMP	*Carrick's Morning Post*
DEM	*Dublin Evening Mail*
DEP	*Dublin Evening Post*
DNB	*Dictionary of National Biography*
Ency. Brit.	*Encyclopaedia Britannica*
FJ	*Freeman's Journal*
Gillow	Gillow, Joseph. *A Literary and Biographical History . . . of the English Catholics . . .*
LEP	*Limerick Evening Post*
MC	*Morning Chronicle*
MR	*Morning Register*
NLI	National Library of Ireland, Dublin
PRO	Public Record Office
SNL	*Saunders' News-Letter*
Times	The London *Times*
UCD	University College, Dublin

Fagan, *O'Connell*	Fagan, William. *The Life and Times of Daniel O'Connell.* 2 vols. London 1888.
Fitzpatrick, Corr.	FitzPatrick, William John. *Correspondence of Daniel O'Connell.* 2 vols. London 1888.
Hall, *Bank of Ireland*	Hall, Frederick G., *The Bank of Ireland, 1783-1946.* Dublin 1949.
Inglis, *Freedom of the Press*	Inglis, Brian St. J., *The Freedom of the Press in Ireland, 1784-1841.* London 1954.
Macintyre, *The Liberator*	Macintyre, Angus. *The Liberator: Daniel O'Connell and the Irish Party, 1830-48.* London 1965.
Reynolds, *Emancipation Crisis*	Reynolds, James A. *The Catholic Emancipation Crisis in Ireland, 1823-29.* New Haven 1954.

In the footnotes the journals of the House of Lords and House of Commons are usually not cited when they are the sole authority for a statement. They are always cited when combined with other authorities.

1072

To Henry Brougham

Colonnade Hotel, Charles Street, Friday
[16 January 1824]

My dear Sir,

You have tempted me to remain tomorrow. I am so desirous to talk more to you and to *know* Mr. Abercrombie [*sic*]. I think I have much to say to you both. I will therefore take my fish with you tomorrow as we say in Ireland. Will you let me know your hour? I wish you could know how very fervid the gratitude is which my wretched countrymen entertain for your exertions on their behalf.

SOURCE : Brougham MSS, University College London

1073

To his wife, Southampton

Colonnade Hotel, Charles St., Haymarket
[London], 16 January 1824

My darling Heart,

. . . After I left you and my darling girls and sweet, sweet boy I felt inclined in the street to burst into tears. It would have relieved [me] if I could have done so as my heart swelled almost to suffocation. I was *too* happy with you, darling. I do not deserve so much happiness. . . . Oh, what a scoundrel I am to have made it necessary to separate from you, my *own*, own heart's dearest, sweetest, darling Mary. . . .

I picked up at Winchester two gentlemen, one a supercargo or factor from China, the other a great city radical. They made me spend the journey more pleasantly than I expected. Yesterday I saw Charles Butler and looked for Brougham and dined at O'Meara's where I met Kit Hutchinson and General L'Allemand[1] and had a most splendid entertainment including some beautiful champagne. I stayed there till near one in the morning listening to some fine singing and conversing. I have this day seen Brougham and have had an hour's talk with him. I like him exceedingly. We discussed Irish and English affairs at great length and I repeat, darling, that I am greatly pleased with him. . . .

SOURCE : Fitz-Simon Papers

1 Baron Charles François Antoine L'Allemand (1774-1839); general in French army, 1814-39. See *Nouvelle Biographie Générale.*

1074

To his wife, Southampton

London, 18 January 1824

My own darling Love,

. . . I had taken my place in the coach on Saturday but I was induced to change my plan in order to dine yesterday with Mr. Brougham. We were tête-à-tête for three hours. He had an elegant dinner and *some* fish which I stuck to as you may imagine perhaps to his surprise. We talked for three hours on many a subject. It was an opportunity which I did not miss to give him my views on various topics. We have arranged, that is, Charles Butler and I have arranged that the Catholics should be heard this sessions by counsel. This will give me a *loud* and *long* speech at the Bar of the House about the 20th of April next. . . . I also had a long consultation yesterday on law business with Lord Headley's brother.[1] I found him an intelligent man and a good lawyer. I believe he thinks favourably of me. I leave with Bric for Maurice £52 exclusive of the sum to be paid to Morgan's tailors. He will have £32 to pay at Gray's Inn, and thus will be able to lay out ten or twelve pounds in clothes. . . . I leave with Bric for him letters of introduction to Charles Butler, to a Mr. Lynch,[2] a barrister, and to the Hon. Mr. Winn, Lord Headley's brother, who is also a barrister. Do you introduce him to Mrs. Langdale.[3] . . .

SOURCE : Fitz-Simon Papers

1 Hon. George Mark Arthur Way Winn, B.L. (1785-1827), son of first Baron Headley; M.P. for Maldon, 1826-27.

2 Andrew Henry Lynch, only son of Patrick Lynch, Moycullen, Co. Galway. M.P. for Galway town 1832-41. Called to the English bar, 23 January 1818; appointed master in chancery (England) 1838. Married Theresia, daughter of Charles Butler, one of the English Catholic leaders.

3 Mary (died 1857), daughter of Marmaduke William Constable Maxwell, Everingham, Yorkshire, and sister of tenth Baron Herries. Married 1821 Hon. Charles Stourton Langdale.

1075

From his brother James to Merrion Square

19 January 1824

My dear Dan,

. . . He [Hunting-Cap] desired me tell you he would allow your son Maurice £200 a year until he was called to the Bar, and as that sum would *be punctually paid him* he thinks it will be quite sufficient for his support and indeed with prudence I also think it will. If Maurice can be persuaded to exert those talents which God has blessed him with he will, I am convinced, succeed in his profession, but should he fancy he has an independent fortune it will be a most fatal delusion and he will when too late find what *an unimportant* gentleman he will be *with a few* hundred pounds a year in Iveragh. . . .

SOURCE : O'Connell MSS, UCD

1076

From his wife to Merrion Square

Southampton, 19 [and 20] January 1824

[No salutation]

My own love will be pleased to hear the old gentleman[1] has most willingly complied with the General's request of allowing Maurice £200 a year while he remains at the Temple. The General communicated this good news in a most affectionate letter to Maurice which he got by this morning's post. I hope my dear Maurice will justify the good *character* given of him to his uncle. If he has no motive for exertion but gratitude to each of his kind uncles he should leave nothing undone to follow in the footsteps of his father. For his success I have no fears if he will only properly apply himself. You will smile at *this*, love, though in this remark I lay all partiality aside. Your girls have prevailed upon me to take places at the theatre for this evening. Kean makes his first appearance here in *Richard the Third*. How provoking that it was not this day week his engagement commenced. You never saw Kean in the character of Richard and you would have so much enjoyed accompanying your girls anywhere that could afford them the least amusement. The only thing I *fancy* that could annoy *you* would be the presence of a *certain little woman* who *you* seem to have a great *antipathy* to. Danny insists on going to the theatre. He remembers seeing Cobham[2] in *Richard* and he wishes to see if Kean is a better Richard. . . .

Tuesday the 20th.

. . . I am delighted that you dined with Brougham and quite alone which was a greater compliment as it evidently showed how much he wished to know you. I flatter myself his expectations were not disappointed and that you have made an acquaintance equally as prepossessed in your favour as you seem to be in his. I greatly like the idea of having the Catholic cause heard by counsel. *It* is the only dignified manner for *them* to proceed. *They* have too long continued their *humble* petition for the sake of the cause. I hope the nasty envy and prejudice of the Irish Catholics may not lead them to appoint any other counsel before you. But where have they one to uphold their cause as you would? I need not, therefore, be afraid for self-interest must prevail. What a pity you were not present when those English Catholics made such ninnys of themselves at your Association. I am quite obliged to Mr. Sheil for the dressing he gave them. How much better he is getting on since he gave up his useless and foolish opposition to you. . . . We were greatly pleased with Kean last night. He is a most delightful actor. It is impossible he can do any character better than Richard. *Danny* gives him *unqualified* praise. You never saw anything like his attention and, as for questions, they were innumerable. The people in the boxes at each side of us were quite astonished at him, particularly an old gentleman who asked Kate his age and what his name was. . . . How proud was the Mod of her sweet little boy. How often did she say, 'Would to God your father was looking at you.' . . . May the great God preserve and spare you to your happy wife and family, happy as belonging to the best of husbands and of fathers. . . . In my next letter I must give you an account of my introduction to an old schoolfellow at St. Omer's. His name is Richard Hill.[3] He knew your brother Maurice better than he knew you, but he had also a brother at the same time at St. Omer's who knew you better. . . .

SOURCE : O'Connell Papers, NLI 13651

1 Hunting-Cap.

2 Thomas Cobham (1786-1842), Shakespearean actor. See *DNB*.

3 *Recte* Frederick Hill (see letter 1079).

1077

To his wife, Southampton

Merrion Square, Tuesday, 20 January 1824

My darling Heart,

Here I am in my solitary house having left London only on Sunday night. I travelled in the mail the whole way. I left London with one companion, a northern attorney, and took up a Col. Gore[1] of the Castle and his son at Birmingham on Monday morning. He and I debated religion and politics a good deal, especially the former. He is a rude Calvanist without, I think, the resolution to avow it. We were, however, excellent travelling friends. We arrived this morning in Holyhead about five and left it at half after six. . . . I arrived here at four o'clock this afternoon, much less that 48 hours since I left London. And I assure you, my love, that I am not one bit fatigued. I went down in a hackney coach to Murphy's baths[2] so that after this night's sleep I shall be as fit for business in the morning *as ever*. . . .

You will be glad to hear that I met in London Col. Lyster who you remember with Devereux. He is in excellent health, quite delighted with everything and came home on leave of absence with plenty of money. Devereux is hourly expected. I think he will go down to visit you. I also found on my table here before me a letter from Major Somerville[3] who you may remember came in the first visit with Devereux. He wrote to send me a book he has published upon the state of France. I have not as yet been able to form any opinion of it as *this* is the only job I do this day. . . .

SOURCE : Fitz-Simon Papers

1 Hon. William John Gore (1767-1836), son of second earl of Arran. Master of the horse to the lord-lieutenant.

2 The public baths of Thomas Murphy, Irishtown, Dublin.

3 William Clark Somerville.

1078

To his wife at Southampton

Merrion Square, 21 [22, 23 and 26]
January 1824

My darling Mary,

. . . I sent off your Kerry letters. I *sent* to Miss Gaghran and to Mr. L'Estrange their letters. . . . The other death is that of Lord Ventry. He has behaved tolerably well to his eldest son[1] but shockingly to his grandson[2] whom you may remember to hear spoken of as an officer much wounded in several actions. . . .

Thursday, the 22d January.

. . . Nic Mahon was here to invite me to dine with him and his son-in-law[3] tomorrow. I believe I will go because I like the son-in-law. He has, do you know, some of the right sort of agitation. . . .

Friday, 23 January.

. . . I began my early rising near six o'clock. I was *obliged* to dine at Nic Mahon['s] with his daughter and son-in-law. We had *quality* there, a Lady May,[4] and got three beautiful bottles of champagne. It is now near eleven o'clock. . . . Sheil and Curran dined at Mahon['s]. We had a fine turbot, but you could have got your fish *rare* or *well* done whichever way you liked. You see the champagne has made me gay. . . . There is no kind of Irish news. The country is rather quiet. The prices *hold* but I fear rather from scarcity than any other cause. . . .

Monday 26th January.

. . . Yesterday I dined with young Sympson.[5] We had the new Lord Ventry and Capt. Mullins, the grandson, and his wife.[6] She is a mild, lovely looking woman, very big in the family way. . . .

SOURCE : Fitz-Simon Papers

1 William Townsend (Mullins), second Baron Ventry (1761-1827), succeeded 11 January 1824.

2 Thomas Townsend Aremberg Mullins (1786-1868), captain, 7th Regiment; on half-pay from 1817. Succeeded as third Baron Ventry, 1827.

3 Nicholas Mahon Power (1787-1873), Faithlegg, Waterford, son of Nicholas Power, J.P., Snowhill, Co. Kilkenny; married 1818 Margaret, only daughter of Nicholas Mahon, Dublin. M.P. for Co. Waterford, 1847-59.

4 Probably the wife or widow of a member of the May family of Mayfield, Co. Waterford. Their genealogical records are confusing (see Cokayne, *Complete Baronetage V*, 367-70).

5 Richard A. Simpson, attorney, 2 Lower Gloucester Street, Dublin. Law agent to Lord Ventry; a Catholic.

6 Eliza Theodora (died 25 Oct. 1879), second daughter of Sir John Blake, tenth baronet, Menloe Castle, Co. Galway; married 1821 Capt. Thomas Townsend Aremberg Mullins, later third Baron Ventry.

1079

From his wife to Merrion Square

Southampton, 23 [and 24] January [1824]

[No salutation]

. . . Maurice, before he left this, wrote a letter of thanks to each of his grand-uncles. He did not say anything to your Uncle Maurice of your being here at Christmas as the General gave Maurice the exact words in your uncle's letter: '. . . I am very happy to hear from you so favourable an account of our grand-nephew Maurice. I will contribute two hundred pounds a year to his support at the Temple which sum I think with prudence will be quite sufficient. Was there occasion for an advocate to induce me to do this there could not be one, my dear brother, so powerful and persuasive as you.' The General says his health improves every day. . . .

I must now tell you of my introduction to Mr. Frederick Hill[1] who lives here. I was sitting quietly looking at my son and daughters dancing at *the* ball when a gentleman accosted me in the following manner: 'Excuse this liberty, Madam, is not your name O'Connell?' 'Yes, Sir.' 'Your husband's name Maurice?' 'No, Sir, Daniel.' 'Yes, I recollect there were two brothers, one very studious and the other something like myself, very wild. I had also a brother with me at the same period at St. Omer's. Your Mr. O'Connell will recollect him better and be glad to hear he is now a Catholic bishop and this same time at the head of the College at Washington. He was in the army, was married but had no family. By mutual consent his wife and he separated, she to a convent and he to a Catholic college. In a very few months he was ordained, being a very clever man and now a great divine.' The Mr. Hill here is married and has a family. They live at the Polygon but I fear he is a bad Catholic and his wife and children Protestants. This introduction took place ten days since and strange to tell neither Mr. *Frederick* Hill nor his wife have visited me. I was introduced to her by Mrs. Conway.[2] So much for English manners. They are to be sure the coldest people in the world. . . .

Saturday the 24th.

. . . I do so hate the sea and dread the sickness. Will you be surprised, love, when I tell you I went with my girls to see *Hamlet* last night, our only beau our little Danny. My poor Ellen and Kate set their hearts so much on seeing Kean in *Hamlet* I could not resist their entreaties. . . . We were greatly delighted with Kean. He is a bewitching actor but I should only like to see him in tragedy. Danny cannot *decide* which *he* admires Kean most in, the character of Richard or Hamlet. Believe me, heart, your little boy enjoyed his acting much more than many of the John Bulls that were at the theatre last evening. The Southampton people don't seem to have much taste for theatricals even in the upper rank. . . . My poor Charles,[3] I trust, will get a situation. He is a most excellent creature and will, I think, give his employer every satisfaction. Our poor friend, Maurice O'Connell,[4] would to God he was as fortunate as Colonel Lyster. It is sinful for me to make the remark, but I fear fate is against his branch of the O'Connells. God help his good mother. . . .

SOURCE : O'Connell Papers, NLI 13651

1 Unidentified.
2 Widow of Col. Conway, a cousin of O'Connell.
3 Charles Connor.
4 Died in South America 2 April 1822 (see letter 828, note 3).

1080

To Henry Brougham

Merrion Square, 26 January 1824

My dear Sir,

Very many thanks for your kindness towards my friend[1] —not succeeding cannot lessen his gratitude or mine.

The plan the Catholics intend to adopt for their parliamentary campaign is twofold. 1st we mean to pour in a volley of petitions on various topics of local grievance, and 2dly a *grand* petition praying the repeal of the declaration against Transubstantiation, etc., and praying to be heard in evidence to support our right to that relief and also by counsel. This is the species of petition which Mr. Charles Butler suggested after his interview with Lord Colchester. Upon the entire plan any advice or suggestion which you may be pleased to give will be thankfully received as it is anxiously requested. We are indeed desirous to conduct the cause in the manner which should meet the approbation of our *sincere* friends in the House amongst whom *on every account* you hold the first place.

There is at present a moment of repose in this wretched country. The Lord-Lieutenant[2] is going on in the same foolish, foppish, useless way and Goulburn as rancourous a supporter of all the abuses in the Church and in the Corporations and, above all, in the Orange Lodges which are abuse personified as any *governor* your country has imported hither since the days of the second Henry. He is a man of miserable intellect and only the more virulent on that account. There are materials prepared and in preparation to perpetuate all our moral evils, and our sapient government is the prime manufactory of present and future discontent.

I have reason to think that I was not warranted in telling you that the French Government had *already* begun to form a party in Ireland. I now believe that it has not yet been done, but it is plain that the present system will give them as it has already afforded former governors of that country the most ample means to organize a French party in this country and a party which may become too strong for British control. The danger upon this point is I verily believe much more imminent than any of our statesmen can conjecture. There are sympathies of various sorts between the discontented Irish and the French which, when brought into action by circumstances, may separate these islands after a conflict of blood. You will perhaps think lightly of my apprehensions but they are founded on local knowledge which gives me means not within the reach of persons resident out of Ireland or of many within this country.

SOURCE : Brougham MSS, University College London

1 Possibly Richard Newton Bennett.

2 Marquis Wellesley.

1081

To his wife, Southampton

Merrion Square,
26 [27, 28 and 29] January 1824

My own darling Love,

. . . How I wish you were settled anywhere else in Ireland where you were well and happy, and where you could often have your husband with you. A couple of years is the utmost that it would be at all necessary for you to be out of Dublin. . . . Darling, I make no doubt I would have earned £200 if I had not gone to England this vacation. I do not regret the money in the least. I only mention this to you to show you what an interest I have in remaining in Ireland. Think of this subject for me, my own love, and be assured I will never ask you to go anywhere to risk your health or unless you most fully, most cordially approve of it. . . .

I just wrote a letter to Brougham.[1] The Lord-Lieutenant had a grand *levée*.[2] I did not go near the old dotard[3] [about two words illegible] will do any good for Ireland and I do [about two words illegible] throwing away my *countenance* upon him.

Tuesday 27 January.

How monotonous my life is. The history of one day is the story of all. I rose today at soon after five. I worked till a quarter after eight by the town. Then breakfast. I eat two fresh eggs every day which is making me fat. Working then till a quarter before eleven. Then to court. There until near four. I spoke but in two courts this day. I made 'an argument' in the King's Bench. At four on my way home call at Milliken's,[4] read the morning papers *for nothing,* then home. Strip off my *day dress,* put on night-shirt, morning gown, *old* wig and so work until a quarter after five by the town. Then dine. In my study again before half after six for I read as I sit after dinner, and so work till this hour, half after nine. Thus in one day you have the history of the entire. But I omit to say that the business is increasing and the fees coming in fast. . . .

All the Kerry attornies are come up and few Kerry lawyers. Good night, my own heart's darling love. Write to me *often,* darling. Why do you not write to me often, my own dearest, sweetest, darling love?

Wednesday the 28th.

. . . The Munster judges are Vandeleur[5] and Torrens,[6] both quiet and gentlemanly men. . . . I just heard from James.[7] My uncle[8] is about to buy another lot of Maglass. I did not hear how he means to dispose of it. I suppose in common between us three. . . .

Thursday, 29th.

. . . Then went to court, spoke in three courts, succeeded against the Bishop of Cork, Dr. St. Lawrence,[9] to compel him to levy a debt due of his son out of the son's livings. . . . I remember the Hills. They were Protestants. The elder brother I knew best and had reason to think that he would become a Catholic. I recollect his speaking to me of going to Germany and throwing out something that showed me he was convinced of Catholic truth. I recollect his brother also, your acquaintance. They were in the second class, one might have been in the third. [? I am] getting a great deal of money, darling, and it cheers me, not as you may imagine because I love it but because I love you and your sweetest, dearest best of girls. . . .

SOURCE : Fitz-Simon Papers

1 Letter 1080.
2 At Dublin Castle, 26 January (*FJ*, 27 Jan. 1824).
3 The lord-lieutenant, Marquis Wellesley.
4 Richard Milliken, bookseller and stationer, 104 Grafton Street.
5 Thomas Burton Vandeleur (1767-1835), son of Crofton Vandeleur, Kilrush, Co. Clare. Justice of the king's bench, 1822-35.
6 Robert Torrens.
7 His brother.
8 Hunting-Cap.
9 Rev. Hon. Thomas St. Lawrence (1755-1831), son of the twenty-seventh baron and first earl of Howth, had three sons in holy orders.

1082

From his wife to Merrion Square

Southampton, 27 [28 and 29] January 1824

My dearest Love,

Not a single line have I got from Maurice[1] since he left me. Was I not aware of his disposition for putting off I should indeed be not a little uneasy at his silence. There is nothing, in my opinion, less pardonable than this neglect of friends when you are absent from them. It is, however, darling, a charge I can't bring against you for with all your business you never forget those you love. . . . Not one of *those* introduced to us by Mrs. Conway[2] have as yet paid us a visit. We are Irish Catholics. This is against us. From every inquiry I have made, I find Ryde in the Isle of Wight the most desirable place for a summer residence, lodgings cheap and good, society most excellent and markets reasonable. If there is a Catholic chapel in the town or neighbourhood it will be our best plan to spend the summer months there. As soon as the weather permits after Maurice returns we will go in the steam packet to Cowes. From thence we can easily get to Ryde and be able to ascertain everything necessary for us to know; we got three Irish papers this morning, one of them the new paper.[3] The only mention of your name that I could see was in the advertisement for the charity sermon in Townsend Chapel.[4] . . .

Wednesday the 28th.

This morning, love, I got from Ireland four papers and the *Times* franked by the Knight of Kerry. I don't know to whom I am indebted for this last paper. It is entirely taken up with Lord Byron's *Vision of Judgment*.[5] We shall therefore preserve it. . . . I admire your letter on the subject of the dinner[6] to Lord Clanricarde[7] very much, and I perceive by a paragraph in the *Herald* that you purpose to bring forward at the Catholic Association the resolution[8] formed by you and Mr. Butler respecting the Catholic cause. I shall be very curious to read the debate on this question. I expect a great deal of opposition though I hope I may be disappointed.

Thursday the 29th.

. . . I hope you continue to wear your warm night-shirts. Independent of the comfort of them, let the recollection of who they were made by be a sufficient inducement to prevent them from being thrown by. James[9] may not think them sufficiently fine for you, but coarse linen is now recommended for sleeping in. . . . Your girls will write to you in turn beginning the latter end of next week. . . .

SOURCE : O'Connell Papers, NLI 13650

1 O'Connell's eldest son.

2 See letter 1079, note 2.

3 The *Dublin Evening Express,* which commenced publication 2 January 1824.

4 An annual sermon in aid of the general free school (of the Irish Christian Brothers), Hanover Street, East, Dublin. O'Connell is listed among those to whom donations may be sent (*FJ,* 22 Jan. 1824).

5 In the court of king's bench on 15 January, John Hunt was indicted with libelling George III, and thus doing injury to George IV, by his publication in 1822 of Byron's poem, 'The Vision of Judgment'. The jury found Hunt guilty (*Times,* 16 Jan. 1824).

6 On 19 January 1824 a public dinner was given in Galway town to Lord Clanricarde in honour of his coming of age the previous month. O'Connell was unable to attend but he sent a congratulatory letter of a conventional kind. Judging by the newspaper account, the dinner was frowned upon by the Galway corporation (*DEP,* 27 Jan. 1824, quoting the *Connaught Journal*).

7 Ulick John (de Burgh), second earl of Clanricarde (I) (1802-74), created 1825 marquess of Clanricarde (I); 1826 Baron Somerhill (U.K.). Under-secretary of state for foreign affairs, 1826-27; lord lieutenant of Co. Galway 1831-74; married 1825 Harriet, sister and sole heir of John, Earl Canning, and only daughter of George Canning, later prime minister.

8 At a meeting of the Catholic Association on 24 January 1824 O'Connell suggested that the Catholics should petition parliament to repeal the oath of abjuration (an oath or, more correctly, oaths provided for Ireland by an English act of 1691—3 Wm. and Mary c. 2—which stated that no foreign prelate had any spiritual authority in Ireland, that the sacrament of the Lord's Supper did not involve transubstantiation and that the Mass was idolatrous). He suggested further that Catholic barristers rather than Protestant be employed to plead the Catholic case at the bar of the House of Commons. He attributed both these suggestions to Charles Butler, the English Catholic barrister (*DEP,* 27 Jan. 1824).

9 Man-servant.

1083

From Bishop Doyle (J.K.L.) to Merrion Square

Old Derry, Carlow, 27 January 1824

Private

My Dear Sir,

I had a letter this day from Sir H. Parnell who desires I would request some person competent to draw up a bill relative to C[atholic] Charities to call upon him at 25 Merrion Square,

North, as he, in the event of obtaining leave, intends to introduce it to the House of Commons.[1]

Being fully satisfied of your competency, knowing the interest you take in whatever concerns our body and having heard that in the last year you were engaged in preparing such a bill as Sir Henry has in contemplation, I take the liberty of pressing on your time already too much engaged, that our zealous co-operation may not be wanted to a man who in all times and vicissitudes has been our steady and uncompromising friend.

Sir Henry desires to know my opinion of the details of the measure, but of this opinion, if it were of any value, he is already in possession, and it is the same as that which he himself entertains.

The substance of it is that the R[oman] Catholics should be enabled to take legally lands or houses to a limited extent, whereon to build places of worship, of education, of refuge for the poor, sick or infirm and to endow the same with lands to an extent also to be limited, and with money to be vested in the public securities to a greater but yet limited extent. The lands above mentioned are supposed to be bestowed or bequeathed by will or purchased as the case might be.

The trustees, the mode of preventing abuses or correcting them in the several institutions are details which I do not understand but which must be very obvious to you.

I perceive that I have omitted in the above enumeration 'residences for the clergy', and hence I begin to suspect that I have lost somewhat of that holy selfishness which generally attends upon Churchmen. This, however, you will be kind enough to excuse as well as the liberty I take in troubling you. . . .

SOURCE : Fitz-Simon Papers

1 In the House of Commons on 9 March 1824 Sir Henry Parnell stated that it had been his intention to bring in a bill to enable Catholics to endow their religious and charitable institutions in the same manner as Protestant dissenters. He had recently been informed by the attorney-general (for Ireland) that in a case in the (Irish) court of chancery the lord chancellor had ruled that such an endowment could legally be made. The attorney-general had now assured him (Parnell) that this decision left in no doubt the fact that (Irish) Catholics stood in the same situation legally as Protestant dissenters and 'could build and endow schools, chapels, hospitals and residences for their clergy'. See letter 1108.

1084

From his wife to Merrion Square

Southampton 30 [31 January, 1 and 2 February] 1824

[No salutation]

Never, my own dearest love, should I be able to bear our separation but for the frequency of your affectionate and cheerful letters. The letter I got this day is one of the sweetest I ever received, so truly affectionate and gay and so flattering to the little old woman who, believe me, darling, is not a little vain of still retaining her *place* in the heart of her beloved husband. How often and how sincerely on my knees do I thank the Almighty for the many blessings he has bestowed upon me, but for none do I feel more grateful than for being blessed with such a husband. From you, darling, every happiness comes to me, and you are dearer to my heart than you will *ever* believe. If I could convince you on one *point* I should be *too* happy. . . .

Saturday, January the 31st. . . .

Sunday, February the 1st.

Your girls, my love, were at Communion this morning and tomorrow I purpose going. How fervently will I pray for my darling husband. I must now give you a piece of intelligence which, I know, will give you great pleasure. This morning I got a letter from poor Charles Connor telling me of his disappointment of the situation he expected. . . . I will transcribe exactly his words: 'I bear this disappointment with resignation. The fact is I do not regret it as I have entertained very seriously the notion which you intimated to me my uncle formed of my entering the Church. Believe me I am in perfect earnest. If I have your opinion that it would be wise I shall forthwith set off for Dublin, thence with my uncle's recommendation to Maynooth as soon as he pleases.' Now, love, I will tomorrow write to Charles and strongly advise him to this step as I am fully convinced he possesses everything necessary for embracing a clerical life. He is truly religious and extremely well disposed, and I have not a doubt should it be the will of God to call him to his ministry, he will be an ornament and acquisition to the Church. . . .

Monday February the 2d.

I prayed for you, my own love, this morning. God be thanked, you have little necessity for my prayers. Will you, my heart, do what is necessary for me about the Ladies Charitable Society established in Kerry? Last week I got an unsealed letter from Lady Godfrey[1] announcing that I was appointed one of the Lady Patronesses and that Miss Gallwey[2] of Killarney was to receive subscriptions. Is it necessary for me to write to Lady Godfrey? . . .

The newspapers of which we get a reasonable number are a great source of amusement to us. I admire your friend Dr. England's letter[3] very much. How will Lord Fingall and Killeen like the *truths* he tells them so publicly? What a pity he can't get as many priests as he wants. If there were a few Irish clergymen scattered through England what an immense good they would do. . . .

SOURCE : O'Connell Papers, NLI 13651

1 Lady (Eleanor) Godfrey (died 1852) wife of Sir John Godfrey, second baronet, Co. Kerry.

2 A member of the Gallwey family who were land agents to the earls of Kenmare.

3 Letter 1052.

1085

From Thomas Sutton to Merrion Square

86 Pill Lane [Dublin], 31 January 1824

Sir,

You may perhaps think it rude of a person not known to you, to address a few lines to you relative to his circumstances in life. . . .

I joined the standard of General Devereux as Captain and First Assistant Commissary and would not since have returned to my native land were I not compelled to do so from my ill state of health . . . seeing an advertisement from the Chamber of Commerce for an head porter . . . and being aware of your powerful influence on *some members* of that body I flatter myself that you will use your interest in my behalf. . . .

SOURCE : O'Connell MSS, UCD

1086

To Denys Scully

Merrion Square, Tuesday [3 February 1824]

My dear Scully,

I am not to blame in breaking my appointment *this* day because I was detained in the King's Bench. . . . If I can do no more I can certainly pledge myself to this, to make every month a deposit of some part of your debt for you at Latouche's beginning with this month. I solemnly and deliberately pledge myself to you to begin within a week and make my payment for February and then every month to make another until the entire sums I owe you are discharged. To this I pledge my most solemn word of honour. I will make no payment of a *less sum* than £50 and it shall be as much more as I can compass.

SOURCE : Scully Papers

1087

From his wife to Merrion Square

Southampton, 4 February 1824

My dearest Love,

On the principal subject of your last letter I feel quite at a loss how to decide. My inclinations would lead me to acquiesce with your wish of fixing *our* residence in Ireland but there are so many objections. I will give them to you in detail. First, my health, which unfortunately is of that nature that requires a dry climate. To Killarney I have an inveterate objection and the constant discusses [*sic*] that rage there justifies [*sic*] my dislike. You are aware, love, that latterly Kerry did not agree with me. I never went there that I was not laid up by illness. *Then it* was not so injurious to my children as I had a governess for them, but who is to take care of them at present should my health render me incapable of attending to my family? Dublin is the only part of Ireland where I enjoyed good health for a long period and even there you know how often I suffered. Here I am obliged to be most cautious of exposing myself to cold. I cannot make as free as I did in France and most sensibly do I feel the difference of the two climates. Indeed, my own heart, there is no happiness I could enjoy equal to being near you, but in a bed of sickness how could I enjoy your society?

The second objection is the disadvantage to your girls. They are now at that age when it is necessary they should not appear in Ireland until they can do so as your daughters ought. The society of a country town in Ireland is not the most advantageous for young girls educated as they have been and, from a conversation I had with Ellen and Kate last night, I am convinced they would rather live in the greatest obscurity anywhere than live in any of the country parts of Ireland in our present circumstances. This objection, however, would give way if they thought my health would not suffer. *This* is the chiefest bar to a compliance with your wishes as well as with our own.

I also am of opinion there would be little saving in our living in Kerry. Your doors could not be kept shut to your connections or to mine. There would be an eternal *relay* of *cousins*. I am surprised *James*[1] does not think more or think as he did before our trip to France was decided on. He is certainly a very bad judge of the necessary advantages for a family such as yours except in the pecuniary way. His family or John's[2] family could live in any place or in any way they liked, but you have a respectability to keep up for yours which it is impossible to have until you are out of your difficulties and able to have them as they ought to be in Dublin. The world is unkind, and *they* would delight to think your embarrassments were such as to oblige you to send your family to live separate from you in the same kingdom with you, whereas the delicacy of my health and the necessity of having Maurice in England for a few years is a sufficient reason for our living here. To Maurice I am convinced our residing in England will be of essential benefit. He is naturally of a domestic disposition but without his family I fear he would to kill time give up to dissipation where there is such temptation to it in London. I had a letter this morning from him acknowledging the receipt of the £20 out of which he paid his tailor £17.16.6. He had just returned from spending three days at Windsor with Dr. Looby.[3] He writes in rapture with the place and expresses a wish I should *live there*. It would be so convenient to him. Dr. Looby told him he could get me a furnished house for two guineas a week, that the markets were reasonable and every necessary of life more reasonable (as being near London) than where we are at present, the situation delightful, the air good and a most excellent chapel with a resident clergyman.

You have asked me, darling, for my unbiassed opinion. *That* opinion I have given you with many a pang because I am aware it will give you as much pain to read it. I have a hard part to act between my love for the best of husbands and my duty towards my children. Self I put entirely out of the question as I would willingly make any sacrifice to be where I could see so frequently him who is as dear to me as my existence. May God direct me to the best. I am sure, darling, when you reflect on what is for and against our living in Ireland you will say, 'Mary is right. We must make a sacrifice for our children though to both it is equally as painful. I know Mary loves me and I am convinced her heart feels as sore as mine at being obliged to differ in opinion with me.' When I think, my own Dan, on the solitary life you lead, I ask myself is it possible any consideration can keep me from being in the same kingdom with you. The power rests with myself but if I avail myself of that power what will be the consequence? *Thus* do I argue and with a heavy heart fear you may think your wife and children do not love you as much as they ought. But, my own love, should such thoughts occur to you banish them at once and believe that absence instead of weakening our love for you has only increased it tenfold. Never was there a father or husband so loved. I am, darling, incapable of saying more than I feel. The fact is I can never give you an idea of the sincerity and purity of the love I ever had and still have for you. Write to me, my darling, in reply to this letter as soon as you receive it. My mind will be in a constant state of agitation until your letter arrives. Tell me what part of Ireland beside Kerry or has any other part occurred to you for a residence for your family? Tell me exactly what you think of those objections I have stated to you, and let not *James'* opinion influence you. . . .

[P.S.] Take care where you put up all my letters.

SOURCE: O'Connell Papers, NLI 13651

1 O'Connell's brother.
2 O'Connell's other brother.
3 Unidentified.

1088

To his wife, Southampton

Merrion Square, 5 [and 6, 7] February 1824

My darling Love,

. . . On Tuesday I worked as usual and our Shamrock Club[1] dined together. I sat till near ten and took some wine, not however so as to be in the slightest degree tipsy. We discussed politics *learnedly*. Yesterday, Wednesday, I dined out also at a Mr. Staines,[2] an attorney who entertained Spring Rice and a mercantile party. We were dull enough but there was something interesting in the style of conversation. What an immense advantage it is to be a member of parliament! There is a natural and necessary importance about a member which cannot belong to any other person. This day, darling, I did not rise until seven, very late for me. . . . Darling, you can satisfy me on the *one point,* but if you think of doing it do it *my way* and then be assured it is gone for ever. But do not do it [at] all unless it be perfectly voluntary. It would relieve my mind of a source of sinful thought. I will not say more on this subject than, sweetest darling, that all I desire is to know literally the fact and whatever that be, a knowledge of it will increase my tenderness and devotedness and anxious affectionate respect. Be quite certain of that, my own and only love. Be quite certain of that.

Your letter delights me about Charles Connor. May the great God guide him for his holy service. It is pure unmixed delight to me that he should *so* determine. Tell him from me to consult his conscience and his God and if he feels strength to dedicate himself entirely to the sweet yoke of religion let him do so. My darling, I will cheerfully pay his expenses to Dublin and will write to Dr. Sugrue[3] about him to get him on the establishment at Maynooth, that is, when he has quietly made up his mind to the sacrifice for the love of *Him* who died in agony to show *His* love. Tell my dearest Charles that he shall ever be a child of my heart. . . . Your letter with respect to Maurice alarms me much. How can he spend his money? He had nothing to do with paying Morgan's[4] tailor. I left that money with Bric, and he ought not to have put that forward to you as a reason for his wanting money. Oh, darling, he afflicts me very very much. Not one line will he condescend to write me, not one line. There is gratitude for you, sweetest. I left him money enough. Indeed I did. . . . Poor fellow, my heart bleeds at his weakness. I know how you love him, Mary, and yet you see he did not write you until he wanted money. . . .

Friday, 6 February.

Darling, I have seen Mr. Burke,[5] the friend of my poor Morgan. He is just arrived from South America and has given in a *twist* gold chain for you a yard in length. I will send it to you by the first possible opportunity. He tells me positively that Devereux[6] is actually worth one hundred and fifty thousand pounds. He, Devereux, must now be daily expected. . . . I have just got a letter from James. My uncle[7] is again unwell, poor man. He has lived a good long time of it. Dr. Hickson and John[8] have gone off to him. His present complaint is gravel or stone. May the great God bestow on him eternal happiness. His danger, however, cannot be pressing. James[9] *now* thinks you ought to come home, darling. How the blood thrills in my veins at that word. Yes, darling, the best way is to come home. Surely we can live quietly, and after all, darling, we are actually supporting two establishments at present. You could come here, sweetest, in the end of April and living in the house as we are till I go circuit, you could take a place near Dublin for the summer and paint and paper and get ready for the winter. . . . James's letter has filled me with pleasing anticipations. . . .

Saturday the 7th.

. . . You may imagine how anxious I am to have you home. We surely should not want Mrs. Shiel.[10] I have, darling, a horror of her expensiveness. I should hope Hannah[11] would be able to assist you sufficiently and my girls should begin to take the housekeepership week about. . . . We will however act with deliberation, and if you come home we will not go in debt for any one article. There is great economy in buying everything at ready money.

SOURCE : Fitz-Simon Papers

1 Probably the Irish club (see letter 907).
2 Henry Staines, attorney, 88 Abbey Street, Dublin.
3 Charles Sugrue, bishop of Kerry.
4 O'Connell's son.

5 Sergeant-Major William Burke.
6 General John Devereux.
7 Hunting-Cap.
8 O'Connell's brother.
9 O'Connell's brother.
10 The housekeeper.
11 Maidservant.

1089

From his brother James to Merrion Square

Killarney, 5 February 1824

My dear Dan,

. . . I fully agree with you in thinking there is no true way of surmounting any difficulty but by boldly looking it in the face. . . . I find you now form a real, rational estimate of the amount of your embarrassments. Heretofore you were *much too sanguine* as to the means you possessed of getting out of debt, but *I now* have little doubt a few years of persevering prudence will not only enable you to do so but also to provide for the junior members of your family. As you must bring your family to Ireland, I really think Dublin, where you have a house, is after all the cheapest place they can be in. £1500 a year with economy ought to cover the expenses of your establishment and between what *they now spend* and what it costs you it can at the end of the year want little of that sum. . . .

I will take care that any offer made for Maglass must first come through your hands. I regret to tell you that my dear Uncle's disorder has rather increased . . . and at his great age any malady becomes very dangerous indeed should he not get much better. . . .

SOURCE : O'Connell MSS, UCD

1090

To his son John, Clongowes Wood College, Co. Kildare

Merrion Square, 6 February 1824

My dearest child,

I ought to have written to you sooner but you may imagine that I have been a great deal hurried since my return from

England. Your mother and sisters are quite well. . . . I heard yesterday from your dear mother. He[1] had not then returned to Southampton. I also heard from Morgan since my arrival from England. He is still at Vicenza and as gay as it is possible. He is fit to be a soldier but it is a trade of which men soon tire. I hope he will shortly turn himself seriously to the literary part of his profession which requires considerable study. If he do not, he will all his life remain in a subordinate situation. I am, my dear child, very anxious to see you and talk to you. You have discretion and good sense beyond your years and you are and always have been a great treasure to my heart. . . . Do exert yourself at present and you will find labour hereafter a pleasure. I will contrive to see you before circuit. You may rely on that. Keep up your spirits and attend to your business. Above all things, my own John, remember always that we are in this world only *on trial* and that there is no happiness hereafter without genuine religion nor indeed, my child, any true happiness here without it. I must not, however, preach to you. . . .

SOURCE : Fitz-Simon Papers

1 Maurice.

1091

From his wife to Merrion Square

Southampton, 6 [7 and 8]
February 1824

[No salutation]

. . . Do you, darling, recollect the letter you wrote to me to Tours last May[1] on the subject of my *then* objecting to quit France. In my memory it is still fresh. I cannot forget the melancholy strain in which *that* letter was written or the effect it had upon me, 'your wife, your children cared not for you. Absence had estranged their affections from you.' Let not this idea now occur to you. . . .

To be near you, my darling husband, is the first wish of my heart, but when I recollect what I have suffered by illness latterly in Kerry I dread again encountering the damp air of that country. Your girls bid me tell you with their fondest love, though their objection is very great to a country residence in Ireland for the present, yet they would most willingly waive every objection could they believe my health would not suffer or they would have more of their [? father's] society in Kerry. They say you were always so much engaged with business they scarcely enjoyed any of your company. In this country they would have you all to themselves. Would to God the advantages to your profession were the same.

I am grieved to find Maurice has not written to you. This omission, I am quite certain, does not proceed from want of affection but I cannot further excuse him. . . . My Danny observed, 'Fado is very good to write so often.'

Saturday the 7th.

. . . I suppose, love, you were not disappointed in the King's Speech. He seems much more interested for the liberty of the West Indies slaves than for those of that part of his United Kingdom called Ireland.[2] Mr. Weld[3] and *I* have *agreed* in opinion that the Catholics must emancipate themselves. Their assistance, believe *me,* before many years will be wanting to the government. The different sects that are starting up every day will at length endeavour to destroy both church and state, and what is to prevent them if the Catholics of Ireland do not come forward which I trust they will not do without getting more than promises. . . .

Sunday the 8th

. . . long before this reaches Dublin you will have received a letter from Maurice. I had one this day from him. . . . His money is not *all* gone. . . . Maurice tells me that Charles[4] seems quite determined on becoming a minister of the Church and that he strongly advises him to do so as he is quite certain his vocation is sincere. . . .

SOURCE : O'Connell Papers, NLI 13651

1 Not extant.

2 At the opening of parliament on 3 February 1824 the king's speech expressed satisfaction with the improved condition of Ireland but dealt at much greater length with the amelioration of the conditions of Negro slaves in the West Indies (*FJ,* 6 Feb. 1824).

3 James Weld (1785-1855), son of Thomas Weld, Lulworth Castle, Dorset. Married 1812 Juliana Anne Petre, daughter of tenth Baron Petre.

4 Charles Connor.

1092

To his wife, Southampton

Merrion Square, 7 [and 11] February 1824

My darling Heart,

. . . 'Mary is right,' I always said so and I say so still. The scheme of going to any part of Ireland save Dublin is at an end, quite at an end, sweetest. It was superceded before I got your letter, and that letter would have crushed it effectually in spite of *the world*. Do not for one moment imagine that any human being can lessen the influence you possess over me. Darling, that influence is founded on a conviction of your strong good sense and your still stronger love. . . . Well, darling, all we have now to canvass is whether you return this summer or the next to Ireland, I mean to Dublin, to Dublin only, sweetest. . . . I want to have you here, but I want also to get out of debt. We will, darling, at our leisure talk of it. I confess I like your Windsor scheme for a twelvemonth. *That* would completely bring me round, and besides we may then be able to show our girls off better. Let us take time to consider, but all schemes of coming anywhere else to Ireland save to Dublin are at an end. I got a letter while ago from our sweet John and another from Mr. Esmonde.[1] John is become a great favourite. He is head of his class. I always said my John would be a comfort to his father's heart. How delighted I should be if it pleased God to give him a powerful vocation to His holy service. May the great God bless our child, darling. I would like to hear his Mass. Esmonde speaks highly of him. I have heard nothing further of my Uncle Maurice. . . . Maurice has certainly spent a furious deal of money in London, . . . a very foolish and unreasonable expenditure and one which, I must fear, marks his incompetence to be left to his own control in respect to pecuniary matters. . . . Darling, I had a very, very busy day of this, and have the pleasure to tell you that the order for a criminal information was this day made absolute against Lord Farnham,[2] Col. Barry that was, for flogging a boy in execution of a sentence which as a magistrate he and another magistrate passed on the boy for cutting a tree of his, Lord Farnham's. This is a great blow to the faction. He, you know, was the great Col. Barry of the House of Commons last year.[3] Good night, sweetest, dearest, darling Mary. *Mary is right!* You taught me to say that, darling. God bless you.

11 February

. . . [Describes the attempted duel[4] between Thomas Spring Rice, M.P., and Waller O'Grady] the entire demonstrating what an absurd as well as criminal thing duelling is. . . . I now only think of being out of debt. . . .

SOURCE : Fitz-Simon Papers

1 Rev. Bartholomew Esmonde, S.J., rector of Clongowes Wood College, 1820-21 and 1830-36.

2 John (Maxwell-Barry), fifth Baron Farnham (1767-1838), M.P. for Co. Cavan, 1806-23. Succeeded to the peerage, 1823. On 24 January 1824 a conditional order was granted by the court of king's bench charging Lord Farnham with an abuse of magisterial authority. The charge was made on the affidavit of Michael Lynch on behalf of his son, Michael, the boy who had been flogged (*FJ*, 26 Jan. 1824). On 7 February 1824 the order was made absolute by the court after counsel had argued on both sides, the case to be tried at the spring assizes in Cavan. The arguments were reported at great length in the press (*FJ*, 9 Feb. 1824). O'Connell does not appear to have figured in the court proceedings. The case seems to have been dropped since it was reported in the *Dublin Evening Post* of 16 March 1824 that it would not be tried, at least not in Cavan. The fact that Farnham was in 1825 elected a representative peer for Ireland suggests that he had not been convicted on any such charge.

3 Several debates took place in the House of Commons in April-May 1823 on the conduct of the Dublin city sheriff, Charles Thorpe, when the 'Orangist' grand jury threw out the charges brought against the men accused of having assaulted the lord-lieutenant in the notorious 'bottle-throwing' incident of December 1822 (see letter 982). Lord Farnham, when John Maxwell-Barry, M.P. for Co. Cavan, was prominent in defending the sheriff and, thereby, the grand jury, in several Commons debates, notably on 22, 24 April and 2 May (*DEP*, 26, 29 April, 6 May 1823).

4 See letter 1095, note 3.

1093

From his wife to Merrion Square

[Southampton], 10 [and 11] February 1824

My dearest love,

The post of this morning brought Ellen a letter from our dear Morgan . . . written in his usual spirits. He is still at Vicenza. . . . Morgan desires Ellen to tell his Mama that he and all the officers are obliged to go to confession with the men and, if he understood the German or Italian languages, he would go more constantly. Does not this intelligence delight you, darling? How I rejoice my dear child is in this service in preference to the British! There is some report of withdrawing the Austrian troops from Italy but *Morgan* is quite certain, if such was the case, the Emperor would *write to him* on the subject. Through the whole of his letter there is an air of gaiety and content that is truly gratifying to his mother. . . .

I perceive they are trying to put down the Association, I hope without any prospect of success.[1] Danny has just informed me it is his intention, as soon as he is able to write well, to write an account of his life since he was five years of age and to continue it as long as he lives. At present he is very busy making a scrap-book. His selection consists chiefly of murders and highway robberies. Since Saturday the girls have not been able to take a walk. Only they have so much to occupy their time I don't know what I should do for them as there is neither private nor public amusement going forward in this stupid, prejudiced place. Neither your schoolfellow nor his family, the Hills, have condescended to pay us a visit. . . . Do you know, heart, I have some notion that Betsey is thinking of becoming a nun. Really, I suspect as much but this between you and me.

February the 11th.

My own darling, you can alone judge of my feelings (by your own) on reading that part of your letter concerning our return home.[2] I do indeed, love, think it our very best plan. The separate establishments would, I am certain, united be quite sufficient for us until it will be perfectly convenient for you to extend the establishment. . . . We would of course live very differently from what we did before. Therefore two men-servants, that is, a footman with James, and two women servants would be quite enough to have. As to getting horses, until you are quite out of debt I don't at all approve of. When I want horses I can get job [ones] and it is only now and again in winter that I shall ever want them. Everything we get either for the use of the house and all kinds of clothing to be paid for at once. Now, love, I think it would be expensive to take a country house. My plan would be as follows, for you to send for Boylan[3] and to tell him you want to have the house *plainly* painted from the top to the bottom, the walls of the lower part of the house cleaned and whitewashed, the bedrooms papered of the two storeys with a cheap dark paper (including the dressing-rooms attached to the bedrooms) on the two floors. Maurice's late apartments would also want to be painted and papered *cheaply*. The ceilings of the rooms should be all cleaned and whitened and great care should be taken of the paper in the drawing-room. While *this* was doing you should particularly tell Boylan you do not want any papering or painting that would be expensive for the present but what is absolutely necessary for the preservation and cleanliness of the house. . . . On your return from the spring circuit the house will be ready for us to go home, and until then I think it would be better for us to stop here. . . . I gave the girls a hint of what was in prospect for them and they are quite beside themselves with joy. Our dear Maurice returned last night, looking extremely well. I am sorry you think he has been extravagant. He assures me and so does Charles[4] that he did not spend unnecessarily a pound. . . . Charles will write to you in a few days. He seems quite determined to become a minister of the Church. When should he set out for Dublin? Would not an application to Dr. Murray be sufficient to entitle him to go to Maynooth? I don't like any application to Dr. Sugrue. He has, in my opinion, behaved very haughtily to my brother[5] respecting the burse. Surely it is no compliment for him to give a signature to any of the immediate descendants of the founders of the burse. I don't consider it a compliment for *any one* to sign for my brother's son. It is only his right he is asking for. . . .

SOURCE : O'Connell Papers, NLI 13651

1 The particular event or report on which Mary O'Connell based this statement is not identified.
2 See letter 1088.
3 P. Boylan, house painter, 102 Grafton Street, Dublin.
4 Charles Connor.
5 Rickard O'Connell. See letter 1121, note 8.

1094

From Henry Brougham

Lincoln's Inn [London], 12 February 1824

My dear Sir,

After the best consideration I have been able to give the important subject of the petition, I remain of my first opinion, that it will be very beneficial to the Catholic question if the House of Commons allows you both to be heard by Counsel and to give evidence at the Bar.[1] This evidence will be especially useful in showing the practical operation of the Penal Laws, and of the state of division upon religious grounds which those laws have in part created and almost entirely keep up. I do not say that the mere hearing by counsel, without evidence, would be of no importance but it is from the inquiry carried on by examination of witnesses that I expect the most salutary consequences, both to the question itself and to the interests of the Irish people generally.

Almost everyone with whom I have conferred upon this matter agrees in this opinion.

SOURCE : O'Connell Papers, NLI 13647

1 See letter 1082, note 8. 'Both' refers to O'Connell and, probably, Richard Lalor Sheil.

1095

From his wife to Merrion Square

Southampton, 12 [13, 14 and 15] February 1824

My dearest love,

Since I last wrote to you I have been thinking a great deal on the delightful prospect of returning home and the more I consider, my darling, the more convinced I am that it is our best and wisest plan. We are at present living retired and economically but with the bitterness of separation. If it is necessary for us to retrench even still more, surely, my own heart, the delight and happiness of being together is worth any sacrifice where the interests of our children are not injured. What think you, love, of my suggestion about the necessary repairs of the house? . . . Boylan would not take a long time to paint the house and paper those rooms I mentioned to you, by your telling him that you only wanted what was useful and necessary done to the house in its present state. In two years more I hope we shall be able to furnish it handsomely and then it will also want papering and painting. . . .

February the 13th.

. . . We went to *our* last ball last night. The girls only danced one set but they consoled themselves by the recollection they would *soon* be where they could have more partners than they wished for. Your eldest son danced every set. He seems to be in great favour with the ladies here. He is every day improving in his appearance and manners. He is certainly a very fine young man. He will, I think, darling, resemble what you were when first I knew you. I am sorry you are displeased with him. He will for the future be more economical but you wrong him by saying he did not write to me until he wanted money. . . .

Saturday the 14th.

The post of this morning only brought us an *Evening Express*[1] in which there is honourable mention made of you. I am delighted with your success for Grace.[2] How it must annoy the Corporation! . . . I am sorry to perceive there is almost a certainty of Mr. Rice, the Member's, being engaged in duel with O'Grady.[3] How I feel for his wife from my own experience! . . .

SOURCE : O'Connell Papers, NLI 13651

1 Not extant. *Recte Dublin Evening Express.*

2 On 7 February 1824 O'Connell obtained from the court of king's bench a conditional order for a mandamus against Dublin corporation on behalf of Richard Grace (a printer, bookseller and stationer of 3 Mary Street, Dublin), a Catholic, who required to be admitted as a freeman, 'having served seven years apprenticeship to a Free Printer' (*SNL,* 10 Feb. 1824).

3 On 8 February Waller O'Grady, a barrister, and Thomas Spring Rice attempted to fight a duel near Ballsbridge, Dublin, but were apprehended and bound to the peace. O'Grady later apologized to Spring Rice. The challenge had been issued because O'Grady had made an insulting remark about Spring Rice's father-in-law, Lord Limerick (*DEP,* 10 Feb. 1824). This quarrel arose from an inquiry by the House of Commons into the legality of certain fees charged by chief judges in Ireland in which O'Grady's father, Standish O'Grady, chief baron of the (Irish) exchequer, was subjected to hostile criticism. Spring Rice had taken a prominent part in attempting, though unsuccessfully, to have Chief Baron O'Grady's conduct investigated, (see especially *Commons Journal,* LXXVIII, 466-7, 470; *DEP,* 15 July 1823).

1096

To his wife, Southampton

Merrion Square, 13 [14 and 15]
February 1824

My own darling Love,

. . . I had to dine with Mr. Curtis,[1] a stock-broker nephew to Dr. Curtis, the Archbishop. He and Dr. Murray dined there and a very large and wealthy party of Catholics with Major Edgeworth[2] whom you remember in Tralee *when we were young*. He is now one of the Paving Board. We had *not* a pleasant party, it being over-crowded, and I was sorry I went there because I could have done more good by staying at home to earn money. I was also thereby detained in bed till six this morning. The [Lord] Chancellor[3] condescended twice to laugh at *points* I made this day. He has not smiled on me so for some time. . . .

I do not take any wine or punch and yet I am growing daily more and more corpulent. I do not know, darling, what to do with myself to keep this propensity in order. I rise early, keep on my legs and walk very fast through the streets. Yet I get fat. I ought not, I believe, to eat so much. . . .

I go specially on that day [8 March] to Trim in the County of Meath on a heavy cause upon a will between two parties of the name of Dopping.[4] I next go specially to Wexford and from Tralee I go to Galway. Three special retainers in one circuit is *not bad*. . . . I travel on these occasions with no small rapidity. . . . Good night, sweetest.

Past ten.

Saturday 14th February.

. . . I had a long speech in a wrangling cause[5] before Lord Norbury. It is really shocking to do business before him because, in addition to all his other unfitness, he is grown cruelly deaf and one is obliged to roar at the top of the voice to make him hear an occasional sentence. Then the counsel must be perpetually squabbling because there is no person to decide the disputed points. I went from court to the Association where we had a full meeting. I read a long 'Report' on the subject of the subscription. All I ask is one farthing a week from one-sixth of the Catholics.[6] Who is it that cannot afford a farthing a week? Yet it would make more than £50,000 if collected. We are to have a county meeting on Monday at Kilmainham to attack the Corporation who want to get an act to legalize their tolls.[7] It is cruel of that miserable Mr. Goulburn to support the wretches. Do you know, love, that the English papers are abusing me at a great rate?[8] . . . I wish I could go to see my darling, darling John.[9] He is a great pet of mine. . . .

Sunday the 15th February.

Darling, this too has been a busy day with me. I heard the 8 o'clock Mass and was about half after ten at Mr. Lube's in James' Street Chapel House to breakfast and *talk* about Ribbonmen surrendering to Government which is shortly to be before parliament.[10] I then went to Gardiner Street to meet Dr. Doyle to talk upon an act of parliament respecting Catholic Charities.[11] I then went to the Commercial Buildings and drew several wicked resolutions against the Corporation of Dublin on the subject of tolls.[12] I then went to Townsend Street [Catholic chapel] and assisted to arrange to have a new chapel in Pembroke Street close to us here which will be a great object to our family when you come home. And then, darling, I came here to finish my letter and take it to the post office, telling you that you are most fondly loved by

Your own,

Daniel O'Connell

SOURCE : Fitz-Simon Papers

1 Patrick Curtis, stock-broker, 42 Dame Street, Dublin.

2 Major Thomas Newcomen Edgeworth (1778-1857), Kilshrewly, Co. Longford, and Gardiner Street, Dublin. High sheriff, Co. Longford, 1814 and 1815; major, Royal Limerick County Militia. Member of the paving board, 1823-27.

3 Lord Manners.

4 See letter 1109, note 4.

5 Not identified.

6 This is the famous Catholic rent launched this year. See letter 1110.

7 See letter 1097, note 2.

8 At the meeting of the Catholic Association on 14 February much mention was made of attacks on Catholicism by the two English newspapers, the *Morning Chronicle* and the *Globe and Traveller* (*DEP*, 17 Feb. 1824). At the Catholic meeting of 4 February O'Connell had attacked the London papers, the *Courier*, the *Morning Chronicle* and the *Times* as prejudiced (*FJ*, 5 Feb. 1824).

9 His son at school in Clongowes.
10 A select committee was appointed by the House of Commons on 12 May 1824 to inquire into disturbances in Ireland (*Commons Journal*, LXXIX, 349). In June a bill was introduced and enacted for dealing with Irish disturbances (5 Geo. IV c. 105).
11 See letter 1083.
12 See letter 1097, note 2.

1097

To his wife at Southampton

Merrion Square, 16 [and 17] February 1824

My own Mary,

A short letter and I hope a sweet one. I believe, darling, you are quite right as to coming home. I say I believe only in order to be safe in any assertion because, darling, I cannot consult my judgement where my affections overpower me. Yes, darling, it is decided. Not one word more of deliberation. I am more convinced than ever I was of anything of its fitness. Yes, darling, it is the only plan and never was blooming bride so welcome to her husband's arms as my own own Mary to mine. I promise you, darling, to make it my constant study to compensate to you and your girls for the banishment I have made you suffer. . . . The middle of the garden is in a grass plot. I will get the exterior border, that is, near the wall, dug up for my sweet, sweet girls to work into flower knots. . . . I hope to be with you by Easter Sunday which this year falls on the 18th of April. This would enable us to leave Southampton after Mass on Easter Monday and go that evening to Salisbury and the next day to Bristol where the finest steamboats in the world will ply this next season. . . . My poor uncle[1] continues to suffer but is, thank God, not dangerously ill at present.

We had this day a great meeting at Kilmainham of the County of Dublin.[2] As usual I had almost all the business done. I made a long and loud harangue against the Corporation. The object was to prevent them from getting an act of parliament to legalize their tolls. Col. Talbot brought me back in his carriage to the courts. Everything went off perfectly well. Even some high flyers of the opposite party set about praising me as I am told. . . .

Tuesday the 17th.

Darling, I wish to finish this letter so as to send it this day to the post because some of my last letters wavered as to your coming home and approved of going to Windsor. . . . Tell Maurice I hope he sometimes thinks of work.

SOURCE : Fitz-Simon Papers

1 Hunting-Cap.

2 On 16 February 1824 a Dublin County meeting was held to protest against an attempt by the Dublin city corporation to have a bill enacted giving legal sanction to the levying of certain tolls (*FJ*, 17 Feb. 1824). The meeting approved a petition which was presented to the House of Commons on 13 April (*Commons Journal*, LXXIX, 288). The bill was introduced and received its first reading on 22 March but was not proceeded with.

1098

From Denys Scully to Merrion Square

Merrion Square, 16 February [1824]

Dear O'Connell,

. . . You pledged yourself solemnly and deliberately to me in writing that you would begin within a week from Tuesday the 3d inst. to make a payment for me at Latouche's . . . and yet you have not paid one halfpenny. Still I will not *put you to the sword,* but will give you another week to do what is right, although I see clearly that it is idle to rely upon your performance of your promises and pledges. I expect, however, that you will now do something towards redeeming your pledges. . . .

Your professional receipts must easily enable you to do this and to pay off the whole debt in the way already pointed out.[1]

SOURCE : O'Connell Papers, NLI 13647

1 See letter 1086.

1099

To John Primrose, Jr., Hillgrove

Merrion Square, 17 February [1824]

My dear John,

. . . I also heard from you on the subject of the Cahirciveen fields. You must not allow the parson[1] to build. Do not permit it. The church is always griping and I believe their claim to till those fields is one which ought to be resisted but we will not do so for the present, but do not let him build.

. . . I hope that this year will give a great clearance to all minor debts in the vicinity of the city of Cahirciveen. How are they off as to potatoes in Iveragh? Are there any returns of more comfort from the increased prices?. . .

I have as to yourself to say that nothing can exceed the satisfaction I feel at the manner you manage for me. . . . How is my poor Uncle[2] getting on? I wish you to have an eye to his state and say whether you think anything that could be done for him is neglected. This in *strict* confidence. . . .

SOURCE : O'Connell MSS. UCD

1 Rev. Barry Denny (c. 1782-1862), nephew of Sir Barry Denny, first baronet; rector of Cahirciveen, 1806-62.

2 Hunting-Cap.

1100

To Denys Scully

Merrion Square, 18 February 1824

My dear Scully,

All the indulgence I now ask is not to proceed against me if I make a lodgement each month. I am the most unfortunate of human beings about your debt. I thought it impossible that I should not have paid it before now and have been prevented by most unexpected accidents. I believe it never occurred to any person to be disappointed as I have been. In the instance of the first lodgement, that which I was to make according to my last letter to you, I was to wait for the arrival of Mr. Hickson[1] from London here. He has necessary documents of mine to get money from a friend of mine. . . . He was suddenly taken ill and will not be here before Friday. The moment he arrives I will make my first monthly lodgement and every month make another till you are paid. . . .

It is quite true that my Bar resources are great, exceeding £5,000 per annum,[2] but everybody is pouring on me at once and I apply every shilling to paying them off. This year will see me perfectly clear. I made arrangements for this and the next month which at the moment cripple me, and you happen to be treading on my heels at this unfortunate moment. . . . I may be able to pay you with more rapidity. My uncle, who is in his 96th year, has a physician attending him for some weeks, and he has hitherto been an healthy man. His complaint is a strangury. But in any event you shall have monthly payments.

SOURCE : Scully Papers

1 Probably John C. Hickson, formerly of College Green, Dublin.

2 O'Connell's fee book shows that he earned £6,045 in 1824 (James A. Reynolds, *The Catholic Emancipation Crisis in Ireland, 1823-1829* [New Haven, 1954], p. 38 n.).

1101

To his wife, Southampton

Merrion Square, 18 [24 and 25] February 1824

My own Mary,

. . . Darling, you are quite right, you are always right. It would indeed be worth our while to make any sacrifice in order to be together. Surely there is nothing we would not do to promote the interest of our darling children. And we may as well economize together as separately. Being together will make every economy sweet and consolatory. Enough said. The thing is determined. . . . What I propose to get done before your arrival—*first* I will get all the lower part of the house cleared and cleaned. *Secondly,* the parlour and stairs up to the top painted. *Thirdly,* the upper rooms of all plainly papered. *Fourthly,* all the windows painted externally and all but our bedroom and my study painted internally. . . . Sweetest, you will be surprised to hear that the [Lord] Chancellor[1] at the last dinner given by the Lord-Lieutenant in the presence of nine of the judges spoke of *my talents* in strong language. He said that in a cause before him of *O'Neil* v. *Harriet* I had made one of the best arguments he had heard since he came to Ireland. What think you of *that,* darling?

We are working hard for Emancipation. It would be of some use to me. Blessed be the great God who gives me something to suffer for—His holy religion—and thrice blessed be His name for giving me that religion. Darling, I promise you immediately to attend to Charles Connor's wishes.[2] They do indeed give me unfeigned delight.

24th Tuesday.

I will detain this letter no longer [which] I kept, darling, in consequence of your *two* letters in which you are *wild* to go to Windsor. No, darling, no. You must come home. We do not want to puff off our daughters by splendour and show, and if we keep for a year or so in the background, why they will only come forward with more effect and pleasure when the temporary privation is over. . . . Oh, I am sorry we thought of Windsor at all. I would have liked that you had continued of your first opinion. Do then, sweetest, endeavour to reconcile my girls to Ireland and their father for I have made up my mind on the subject. The truth is I cannot live without you and, darling, be assured we can live cheaper together than separate. Oh, Mary, you little know how cruel it is to be separated from *all, all* our loves. If Danny and your girls and Maurice were removed from you, *how* would you feel? I am, however, not selfish but I am quite convinced that without denying my sweet girls any reasonable gratification we can economize quite as much here as being in different places. Besides I certainly lose a couple of hundred pounds at the very least during a vacation spent out of Ireland. My health though good requires your *petting* and, darling, I promise you the most unremitting tenderness. . . .

Wednesday, 25th February.

I enclose you a note for £20. I left you in October £80. I sent you £70 in two notes. I gave you £200 and this note will make £370 British in four months which would make full £1,100 a year British and upwards. Now certainly, darling, by adding to that about £300 a year, which is the least my living *here* and my journeys to you cost, we will be able to support the family and a pair of horses on the money. . . .

SOURCE : Fitz-Simon Papers

1 Lord Manners.

2 See letter 1084.

1102

From his wife to Merrion Square

Southampton, 19 [and 20] February 1824

[No salutation]

. . . As your letter this morning contains nothing on the subject of our going home, I suppose you have given up all idea of it which, I am sure, after all, darling, is the most prudent and sensible plan for us to adopt, at all events for another year. Taking your family home would inevitably bring on expenses we could not avoid. *It* is therefore better be out of the way of temptation, more particularly should the King make his promised visit to Dublin this summer. During the next autumn the house can be painted and papered. . . . I wrote about the house at Windsor which for the present I will only take by the month. I can then at my leisure please myself. Maurice is all anxiety for us to go to Windsor, and I am of opinion that his family living near him for some months will be of essential service to him in a moral as well as in a pecuniary way. He is at present free from every vice. How long he may continue so was he constantly to reside in London, '*that* is the question '.

I perceive, darling, that *trade* is succeeding well with you. Three special retainers is what I believe very few barristers get for one *circuit*. It was, I know, long ago considered a great thing to get one but, as Danny says, ' it is not everyone that is so clever as Fado.' As to the newspaper attacks, I think they get as much as they give. Who is the proprietor of the *Dublin Express*?[1] I feel partial to him for his defence of you. I read the attack of Mr. Black[2] and your answer.[3] Charles Connor smiled when I said how I should like to have it in my power to chastise Mr. Black, Mrs. Black having said to Bric something of a similar nature when she read your attack on her husband. I think, were she and I to meet, something *serious* might be the consequence. I do, darling, dislike these English more than ever. They are a nasty, selfish lot. . . . Danny is making a great progress. He has commenced Mrs. Trimmer's *History of England*[4] which I got for him from London. . . .

Friday the 20th.

. . . In one of my late letters I mentioned [? to you] my suspicion of Betsey's inclination to become [one or two words illegible]. I must now tell you I don't know what to make of her. Her temper, if possible, is every day becoming less bearable. For a week before and after she goes to Communion she is quite *good*. She is now at that age that punishment, such as is suitable, she takes more as an indulgence. She makes me very unhappy but she has no feeling. How cruelly has Miss Gaghran kept me in the dark respecting this child's disposition and temper! She is in every sense of the word different from her sisters and brothers and really, heart, I am often puzzled to think why we should have such a child. May God convert her. Pray for her, love. The happiest thing that could occur for her in this world and ensure her happiness in the next would be a sincere and true vocation to become a nun. May the great God give her that grace. Our other children have their faults but none to equal any of Betsey's. It is impossible, love, to give you a just idea of her. Indeed, you had some opportunity of judging for yourself. What would you think of writing to her? Perhaps a feeling and *determined* letter from you may have a good effect. I was sorry to hear that *Miss* [? Finn], Mr. L'Estrange's friend, is as bad as ever. It is well her case was not published. I hope you may succeed about the Chapel but when I left Dublin, Mount Street[5] close to us was the street spoken of for the Chapel, the ground to be given *gratis* by Mr. Corballis, to whom all that street belongs. Even in Pembroke Street the chapel would be a great convenience to us. Such a one as that *we* could have a pew to ourselves [in]. . . .

SOURCE : O'Connell Papers, NLI 13651

1 The proprietor was Joseph Blundell. Issues of this newspaper (*recte* the *Dublin Evening Express*) for February 1824 are not extant.

2 John Black, editor of the *Morning Chronicle*.

3 Black's attack is not identified. O'Connell was reported by the *Globe and Traveller* of 7 February 1824 as having described Black as 'a sour sectarian from Scotland'.

4 Mrs. Sarah Trimmer, *A Concise History of England, Comprised in a Set of Easy Lessons* . . ., 2 vols. Probably the 1820 edition.

5 Upper Mount Street, Dublin.

1103

From his wife to Merrion Square

[Southampton], Saturday, 21
[22 and 23] February 1824

My own dearest Love,

Our letters this time back have been so wavering on one subject, I feel quite at a loss just now what reply to give to the letter I got from you this morning. My inclination would lead me one way and my prudence the other. And how to decide is the question. I wish I could be with you for *one* hour in the study after my letter of the 17th reaches you. The point, I think, would be soon settled between us. However, as this can't *be,* I think I had better wait *in silence* until your opinion on that letter reaches me. You will, my own love, in the meantime consider well if your present circumstances are such as to allow you to bring your family home. Should another year be sufficient to pay all your debts it would be a pity during that year to incur any additional expenses. May God direct us to the best. The contents of your letter this post I have not mentioned to your girls. I think it is better say nothing more to them until everything is decided upon. At present they only imagine [that] if anything occurred to your Uncle Maurice you would at once take them home.

Sunday the 22d.

. . . The post brought us this morning only the *Globe and Traveller,*[1] I presume from Bric, as it contains a defence of you, evidently written by him. Poor fellow [he] leaves nothing undone to *vindicate* you but, in my opinion, the only way to treat *those* people is with silent contempt and I am glad to perceive, darling, that you act in this way. . . . Maurice studies every day. I assure you I run him well when I perceive he is at all inclined to be idle. I hope you approve of his learning the German language together with Ellen. Their master seems much pleased with their progress.

Monday the 23d.

. . . I am up every morning at eight o'clock and nothing can go on more regularly than my establishment. . . . The only objection I have to go[ing] home at once is the fear of doing away the good that has been done. Should you still continue to think it best to have your family return, you have only to say the word because you must be the best judge. The enclosed *liberal* article I took out of the *Southampton Herald* this morning.[2] . . .

SOURCE : O'Connell Papers, NLI 13651

1 Issue unidentified.

2 Unidentified.

1104

From his wife to Merrion Square

Southampton [England], 25 [and 26] February 1824

My dearest Love,

. . . I perceive by the papers this post you are so much taken up with law business as not to have time to attend to your *duty* at the Catholic Association.[1] Is it possible that *you* will again give Mr. Plunket[2] another petition[3] to present? Surely, love, it would be only throwing away money and merely giving that gentleman an opportunity of displaying his eloquence and certainly without the smallest service to the cause. *Wait patiently* for a few years and, believe me, what is now refused you as a boon will be then given to conciliate and secure your assistance for strengthening the *throne*. You will laugh, darling, at my politics but you will yet acknowledge 'Mary was right.' I perceive you were not at Mr. Blake's[4] grand dinner. It amuses me much when I think of the many efforts that gentleman made to *catch* you. He now sees you are not to be bought, and therefore his civilities are at an end. It is, I think, the greatest compliment he could pay you not to ask you amongst such a corrupt *set*.

February the 26th.

Why, darling, have you let so many days pass without sending a letter for Southampton? The aggregate meeting is put off.[5] *That* could not be the reason, and Sunday you do no law business. What have you to say, love, in your *defence*? . . . Peter[6] is this moment come upstairs with his eyes and his mouth wide open to tell me there is a most beautiful speech[7] of the Master's in the paper. 'How do you know, Peter?' 'Mr.

Arnold[8] told me so and he said, "this master of yours is a terrible man. He spares nobody, not even the Duke of York." ' And I told him the master thought as little of dukes as he did of Orangemen. So far I think Peter is right. . . . Charles[9] hopes, should he not reach Dublin before you leave it, that you will have arranged everything necessary for his immediately going to Maynooth and leave letters of introduction for him to Dr. Murray and the President of the College. . . . *She* [Betsey] is just going on in her usual way. It is useless for me to speak to her. I will pray for her. She is a most extraordinary child. May God convert her. Our sweet little Danny is a great comfort to me. . . . Maurice, between his German and his other studies, has his time occupied. He is improving very much in his appearance, becoming every day more like what you *were*. . . .

[P.S.] We have leave for meat here during Lent three times in the week.

SOURCE : O'Connell Papers, NLI 13651

1 O'Connell obviously did not attend the meeting of 23 February since his name is not recorded in the report of it (*FJ*, 24 Feb. 1824).

2 William Conyngham Plunket.

3 It had obviously been decided already to draft a petition to parliament but to entrust it to Earl Grey (Lords) and Henry Brougham (Commons) (*FJ*, 26 Feb. 1824). See letter 1116, note 5.

4 On 16 February Anthony Richard Blake gave a dinner at his house in Merrion Square, North, in honour of the lord-lieutenant. The attendance included the lord chancellor and the other chief judges, attorney-general, solicitor-general, the provost of Trinity College, Dublin, and William Gregory (*FJ*, 18 Feb. 1824).

5 At a meeting of the Catholic Association on 18 February it was decided to postpone the holding of an aggregate meeting from 20 to 27 February (*FJ*, 19 Feb. 1824).

6 Man-servant.

7 At the Catholic Association meeting on 21 February (*FJ*, 23 Feb. 1824).

8 The owner of the house being rented by O'Connell's wife.

9 Charles Connor.

1105

To his wife at Southampton

Merrion Square, 27 [and 29] February
[and 1 and 2 March] 1824

My heart's darling,

. . . The workmen began yesterday with the garret rooms and are this day at Maurice's. They are very attentive and everything is proceeding with great rapidity. I am to pay as we go along. . . . My earnings this month will exceed, I hope, £700 so that, although my debts are still enormous, we will, please God, work them off by another year of prudence and strict economy, and then the year after we will, please God, be able to enjoy ourselves more. Darling, this has been a very hard-working week with me and this, you will perceive, was the day of the aggregate meeting. Sir Thomas Esmonde took the chair. I never saw any meeting go off better in every respect. Stephen Coppinger made an excellent speech, so did Sheil. I spoke for full two hours. Billy Murphy attended the meeting and was quite zealous. I read various Orange documents.

Sunday, 29th.

Darling, you will have read *all* the debates before you get this letter. You may imagine what a paltry account of *the debate* when my speech of two hours is compressed in so very small a space. . . . James Sugrue dined with me on a beautiful turkey I got from a County Wexford client. Darling, there is leave for meat this Lent in Dublin and I suspect that a certain cocknosed woman of my acquaintance, not a thousand miles from Netley Abbey,[1] wrote to a priest at Townsend Street Chapel. I only suspect it, darling, because I certainly did not get the least hint that it was so, but I strongly suspect her of being *malicious* enough to do so. Do you know who I mean? . . .

Monday, 1st March.

. . . Darling, how delighted I shall be if your next letter *rejoices* at the prospect of being once more at home and if my sweet, sweet girls concur in that sentiment. . . . My Uncle Maurice is considerably better. He underwent a surgical operation which gave him immediate relief, and you may judge of the strength of his constitution from his appetite having continued quite good even when he was in considerable danger. There is every probability that he will get completely over this attack. Darling, I had a busy day of this too. I rose soon after four, was employed in a heavy cause in Chancery and a successful one there and in the King's Bench[2] and went lastly to preside at a Charity dinner where I met Finlay and remained until near ten. I go on Sunday next to Navan to the residence of the Catholic bishop, thence the next morning to Trim. I will be in Wexford on the following Thursday and thence the following Saturday to Limerick.

2nd March.

. . . The workmen are busy preparing for you. They arrive soon after six in the morning, and I have this day the pleasure to make the first payment on account of the work which is a symptom of my Mary's return. I perceive, indeed, by your letter that you have *no objection* to come home. . . . My uncle is decidedly better. He is a wonderful man. He is now anxious to buy the Sealy estate of Maglass. It would cost about £8,000 and he has that sum idle. Give my tenderest love to my girls, to Maurice and to Dan. I am glad they are learning German.

SOURCE : Fitz-Simon Papers

1 A monastic ruin near Southampton.

2 *Stourgeon* v. *Douglas,* a case that involved much discussion in court on the privileges of the bar (*DEP,* 4 Mar. 1824).

1106

From his wife to Merrion Square

Southampton, Friday, 27 [28 and 29] February 1824

My own dearest Love,

. . . I borrowed the last *Courier*[1] containing your *attack* on the Duke of York which, I assure you, has created no small sensation here. Only Maurice tells me there is not the slightest fear, I should very much dread that you would be prosecuted. He tells me there is not the slightest word *they* could lay hold of, but as my dear Maurice is yet too young a lawyer I shall not be quite satisfied on this subject until I hear from you. . . . Mr. Weld was just here to ask me to lend him any papers containing your *speeches* or the proceedings of the Association. He seems gratified by your attack on the Duke and highly approves of the noise the Catholics are at present making in Ireland. He speaks of the wrongs of that country as if he belonged to it. He told me that a gentleman said in his presence the other day 'he wished Ireland was in the bottom of the sea.' Mr. Weld answered him by remarking he thought Ireland had more reason to wish England at the bottom of the sea. Are you aware, love, that Mrs. Fitzherbert[2] is sister to the late Mr. Weld[3] of Lulworth Castle?

Saturday the 28th.

How often, love, have you faithfully promised that nothing should prevent you from writing at least once in every week, and what can you say when I call to your recollection that *this* is the eighth day since I got your last letter? Indeed, my own love, I can see no excuse, for your Sundays are your own and when you can't write during the rest of the week you should not let Sunday pass without writing. There are many reasons why you should have written to me. The first, to give me your final determination respecting our future plans. To tell you what I feel when I do not hear from you is impossible. It has even an effect on my temper. I am as cross as a cat and inclined to *wish* the Catholic Association at the bottom of the sea. . . . How I wish I was near you! What a *scolding* I would give for thus *forgetting* me. Even your girls allow you deserve to be scolded. . . . At no period of my life was I more anxious to hear from you than I am at present. I can't help being uneasy when I think there may be a chance of your being prosecuted for that article of yours respecting the Duke of York which I read in the *Courier*.

Sunday, February the 29th.

At length I have got from you a letter. . . . I must now, darling, tell you I am a little hurt at one expression in your letter, 'I see you are *wild* to go to Windsor.' *This* may be applied to me if [I] was young and fond of pleasure, but the case being quite the reverse I am sure, heart, you were not aware of what you wrote or you would not make use of such an expression to me, but I forgive you from my heart. It was wrong of me to say anything against our going home. I was only led to do so from the letter you wrote to me immediately after you spoke of taking us home. From that letter I was convinced you had given up all intention on the subject for another year and, recollecting I had made the General a promise in Paris that I would not return home until all the debts were paid, I was not sorry when the letter above alluded to arrived from you. Those were the motives that induced me to change my mind and not any wish to remain in England, the country of all others I dislike most, but there is now an end to every objection and home, sweet home, I must now go to. Say what you will to the *contrary,* I wish, love, to have my room papered and painted. Winter is no time for doing it and while you are on circuit it can be done. I don't think Kelly's estimate high if you consider the house has not been painted for some years, but there is no harm in getting another estimate. . . . He [Kelly] is an excellent painter and he is a Catholic. So is Boylan. . . . You are mistaken to suppose your girls wished to go to Windsor. Home, their father and Miss G[aghran] is the first wish of their heart. I should have put Father before home. . . .

SOURCE : O'Connell Papers, NLI 13651

1 The *Courier* of 25 February 1824 denounced O'Connell for his attack on the duke of York at the Catholic Association meeting of 21 February. The *Courier* added that if the Catholics wished to obtain Emancipation they would have to prove that the incendiary language of such advocates as O'Connell was alien to their own sentiments.

2 Maria Anne Fitzherbert (1756-1837), daughter of Walter Smythe, Brainbridge, Hants. Married 1775 Edward Weld (died 1775), married 1778 Thomas Fitzherbert (died 1781) and in 1785 married George IV when Prince of Wales. See *DNB*.

3 *Recte* sister-in-law of Thomas Weld of Lulworth Castle who died in 1810.

1107

From his wife to Merrion Square

Southampton, 2 [3 and 4] March 1824

My dearest love,

. . . I am quite out of patience with the opposition to you from *Nick* Mahon and his honoured nephew.[1] The latter, I am convinced, is influenced by no motive but that of envy, and instead of succeeding he makes himself still more ridiculous. I am quite obliged to you for what you said in reply to Nick at one of the late meetings. It is exactly such mean, paltry Catholics as he is that have kept the Catholics as they are these years back. Sheil, I perceive, is now always with you. Kate and I quiz my poor Nell about him. We say he is trying to make interest with you against Ellen's return. You can form no idea of the delight of your girls since I informed them of your intention of taking us home this spring. The only person that feels any regret on the occasion is Maurice, but my poor fellow says he should not regret what he is aware will confer such happiness on his father and poor little Mod. As to our Danny it is quite right to take him out of England. In the street he can hardly forbear abusing the English. Such a little patriot as he is. . . .

Wednesday the 3d.

This is a black day with us all but doubly so, I fear, with you should you observe it as strictly as you did last year. Indeed, my own heart, you fast much more strictly than you ought, but should Mr. Coleman[2] have no influence on you, there is still less chance of my having any on this subject. This is a wretched bad day. The morning was bitter, particularly in the Chapel. On our return we got two papers by the post wherein *honourable* mention is made of you. I hope tomorrow's post will bring the papers containing your speech at the Aggregate. . . . How I long, darling, to get another long letter from you. The last was a *half* angry one but I forgive it because I know it was written without reflection and in the bitterness of disappointment at my supposed preference to Windsor. I see, heart, that you know me very little when you allow yourself to suppose for one minute that in my objection to go home I was influenced by any motive but the sole advantage of my family. To this feeling I was certainly sacrificing my own happiness and be assured, my own Dan, there is no happiness for me but where you are. It is quite impossible for any person to form a notion of what I have suffered since our separation. Thank God, it is now nearly at an end, and we shall be as happy as it is possible for mortals in this world to be. I heard this morning from Kerry. All our friends there are well with the exception of my dear Rickarda. She is immediately to undergo a course of mercury which Leyne thinks necessary for her.

March the 4th.

When I was in France I heard [from you] nearly as often as I do in England. Why, love, let Sunday pass without writing? I feel greatly disappointed, and to add to *it* this morning a letter directed in your hand to Kate was from Mr. L'Estrange and no papers of any kind. Really, I wish Mr. L'Estrange would contrive to get a frank. His letters this week cost me 4s. 8d. and, after all, contained nothing either interesting or amusing. I am as angry as possible. I can't bear to be eight days without a letter from you. It completely sours my temper. I am also very uneasy about Charles Connor. I fear he was at sea yesterday which was with us a terrific day and *night,* and then the passage from Bristol to Dublin is so dangerous. He should have written from Bristol as he promised. I gave Charles Connor five pounds to bear his expenses. Poor fellow had not one shilling and you desired me tell him in a former letter that you would bear his expenses to Dublin. . . . The servants I pay every month. . . .

SOURCE : O'Connell Papers, NLI 13651

1 Nicholas Purcell O'Gorman.

2 Rev. Patrick Coleman.

1108

To Bishop Doyle (J.K.L.),[1] Carlow

Merrion Square, 5 March 1824

My Lord,

I prepared the draft bill[2] the Sunday I promised and now send it. I have been quite unable to send it sooner because I could not accompany it by a letter, and I wanted to tell you that I have on the fullest deliberation returned to the opinion I originally entertained that it would be injudicious to press this bill at present. The fact is that I have no hesitation in pledging myself that the law, as it stands at present, permits and would enforce such a trust as this bill recognizes or creates. I wish you to understand me distinctly. I say as a lawyer that at present the law allows everything which this act would sanction. See, therefore, whether it would be right *quieta movere*. Whatever decision your Lordship comes to, it will give me the greatest pleasure to contribute if possible to carry into effect. But if Sir H[enry] Parnell be not *certain* of carrying this act through *both* Houses, it strikes me that its rejection would plainly do mischief. Do you, however, decide. I have a great propensity to submit to the Church—and, prelate or layman, I would greatly confide in the powers of your mind.

I beg leave next to submit the foregoing report[3] to your Lordship. . . . I do not, of course, think of committing any portion of our clergy in the carrying on or approval of my plan. I would, however, be very apt to give it up if it met with your disapprobation. On the other hand I do not think it *ought* to succeed unless the clergy give it just so much countenance as will prevent frauds in the collection and the obtrusion of improper persons or improper objects amongst the collectors or subscribers. I would also venture to ask from each of the Catholic bishops to enable me to procure a list of the parishes in his diocese and the name and address of each incumbent. I gladly avail myself of this opportunity to express the deep and conscientious conviction I entertain if your Lordship's eminent services to the Catholic Church. . . .

SOURCE : MSS IV Misc., Trinity College, Dublin

1 The letter seems to have been sent on to Sir Henry Parnell since the back of it bears his name and address (94 Jermyn Street, London) in a handwriting other than O'Connell's.

2 See letter 1083.

3 The report concerning the organizing of the Catholic rent (see letter 1110).

1109

To his wife at Southampton

[probably Trim, Co. Meath]
8 [9 and 10] March 1824

My own love,

. . . I never was *worked* so hard. I remained out of bed on Saturday night till near twelve and, although I did scarcely any court business for the preceding week, I could not get through *one half* of what lay on my table. . . . I could not help smiling at your *attack* on me for saying you were *wild* to go to Windsor.[1] Oh, my Mary, sure you ought to know I said it only in joke and out of the exuberance of animal spirits which I felt at your being so soon to be at home again. . . .

My poor Charles[2] came in to me half starved on Friday. I have written by him in the strongest terms to Dr. Murray but do not yet know the result. I calculate that it must be favourable. I left Dublin yesterday. . . .

Tuesday, 9 March 1824.

Darling, on Sunday I travelled to Navan in this county and [? spent] the day with the bishop, a very fine old gentleman of the age of 86,[3] and met a large party of his clergy. I made a harangue to the people in the Chapel and set the penny a month subscription agoing. It will succeed. I had on the whole a delightful day of it. I came here early yesterday morning and we began the trial. It lasted until past eight in the evening but I was not one bit incommoded because I 'by permission' took a sufficient quantity of breakfast before the trial began. It was the most cruelly cold court I ever was in. I never felt anything at all like it, and I therefore got my great cloak, a warm ruff round my neck and my fur cap and so completely escaped taking cold. We began again this day at rather an early hour, and as we were closing the case the opposite party gave up and left my clients in possession of about £7,000 a year. I got £140, pretty well for one trial.[4] I now write while I prepare to return to Dublin where I mean to sleep this night, first sending off this letter. . . . Believe me, I never for one moment doubted the sincerity of your wish to come home. I only quizzed, darling, when I spoke of your being *wild* for Windsor. I *know* that your heart and soul are with your husband, and when you can have your husband and children together you do not desire more. . . . I trust my poor Maurice will begin to read law with some attention. I wish I had time to write to him. . . . The work [on the house] is going on admirably well. I paid £1.10.0 for the garden. It looks very gay. Everything will be perfectly ready for you. . . .

10th March.

. . . I am now just starting for Wexford. I slept last night in the back room, our room being painted. . . . I will get a pair of fine fresh young horses in the County of Clare for your carriage. Old John is here. You must look out for a footman for yourself. When we are at home you *shall* be commander-in-chief. When were you otherwise? With tenderest love to our children. I have all their pictures about me here in my study. . . .

SOURCE : Fitz-Simon Papers

1 See letter 1106.

2 Charles Connor.

3 Patrick Joseph Plunkett (1738-1827), born Kells, Co. Meath; educated Paris, 1752-64; bishop of Meath, 1779-1827.

4 This was a case at Trim assizes on 8 and 9 March in which the will of Samuel Dopping, deceased, of Lowtown, Kinnegad, Co. Westmeath, was contested by his sisters, Dorothea and Catherine Dopping, but unsuccessfully. The property involved was said to be worth more than £200,000 (*FJ,* 11 Mar. 1824).

1110

To Archbishop Laffan[1]

Merrion Square, 10 March 1824

My Lord,

I take the liberty of transmitting to your Grace the copy of a Report and of Resolutions[2] upon the latter of which it is intended to found a general subscription of the Catholics of Ireland. I anxiously hope that our objects may be found deserving of your sanction and countenance. It is, however, very far from my wish to commit any portion of the Catholic clergy in the responsibility attached to our proceedings, but I should not wish those proceedings to be successful if they did not deserve your Grace's approbation.

May I respectfully request to know in what way I could procure an accurate list of the parishes in your archdiocese with the name of each incumbent and his address?

SOURCE : Cashel Diocesan Archives

1 Robert Laffan (c. 1767/8-1833); educated at Salamanca; archbishop of Cashel, 1823-33.

2 At a Catholic Association meeting on 4 February 1824 O'Connell stated his plan for a national subscription to be raised at the parish level, each subscriber to pay one penny a month (*DEP,* 5 Feb. 1824). At the association's meeting on 14 February O'Connell read a report from a committee appointed to consider the plan (*DEP,* 17 Feb. 1824). This report, which was published in the *Dublin Evening Post* of 19 February 1824, contained fourteen resolutions. The first

called the subscription 'The Monthly Catholic Rent'; the eleventh stipulated that each subscriber must pay not less than one penny a month and not more than two shillings; the fourteenth appointed O'Connell as secretary for subscriptions and James Sugrue as assistant secretary. At their meeting on 3 March the Catholic Association decided to circulate the report (*DEP*, 4 Mar. 1824). The above letter to Archbishop Laffan is obviously one of a kind that O'Connell sent to all the Irish prelates.

1111

From Denys Scully, Merrion Square, 10 March 1824, to Merrion Square

Requests payment of part of the money O'Connell owes him.

SOURCE : O'Connell Papers, NLI 13647

1112

To his wife, Southampton

Wexford, 11 [and 12, 13, 15] March 1824

My darling Heart's Love,

I am very sorry I was so pressed as to have left so many days pass without sending a letter to you, but I think *it* will be to you *a proof* of the extreme state of hurry I was in. I have no greater pleasure, darling, than in writing to you. Indeed I have not. Darling, I stayed in Dublin yesterday till near two, busy at work. I then started for this and arrived before one in the morning at Enniscorthy. I went to bed and got five hours in it, rose after six and came in here. Mr. Coleman[1] came to the house yesterday to press on me to take milk in my tea which I have accordingly done this day. I now must get through the Lent without the slightest inconvenience as I take a good round of the loaf in dry toast, in fact, very nearly as much bread as I usually eat for breakfast. I assure you therefore that *in fact* I do not fast at all. Darling, I have just touched my 100 guineas for coming here, and I am about to send fifty pounds to James Sugrue to turn into English notes in order to send them to you. . . .

12th March, Friday.

Darling, I had a very busy day of this. I dined yesterday with Mr. Talbot[2] and got an excellent *bottle* of claret. There was a large party of gentlemen. I stayed until near ten but made up for lost sleep by not rising this day till after eight. I then took *breakfast* with a large party of priests at a wealthy Catholic's house. The trial[3] commenced soon after and lasted till after five. We then adjourned till tomorrow. At an early hour in the day James[4] brought me your *sweet* letter of the 7th. It was truly cheering to me. I knew, sweetest, you wished to come home and no *blame* to you, darling. You will find your home made as sweet to you as your husband possibly can make it. . . . The trial is a dull and stupid one but my client has as yet the better of it and shall keep his advantage if I possibly can. The jury are very favourable to him. The Chief Justice[5] tries the cause. I think it will be over before two tomorrow. If I can get to Waterford I am to be at a public dinner there got up in honour of me. There is no kind of spirit in this miserable town. Every attempt to get up a public meeting has miserably failed. . . .

I believe I did not tell you that Dr. Murray received Charles[6] very kindly. He found, however, that he was not sufficiently prepared in Latin and Greek, and Charles goes to Tralee to devote himself for a few months to those languages. He will then get on the establishment at Maynooth. He is a sweet, darling fellow, the greatest possible favourite to me. . . .

Saturday, March 13.

The Chief Justice is not very well and here I am, I fear, detained longer than I could wish. The trials will scarcely allow me to go to Waterford this day which will be a disappointment to others as well as to myself. The trumpet however is actively sounding and so *to battle*.

Darling, I spent the rest of Saturday in court until past seven in the evening and left the Chief Justice charging very strongly in our favour and the jury very favourable. I have no doubt but my client got a verdict. I arrived that night at New Ross, about nineteen miles from Wexford which I left at eight. I slept till past seven in a very cold room, heard Mass at [New] Ross and came on to Waterford where they had got up a public

Monday, March the 15th, Limerick.

dinner[7] for me *the day before,* expecting my coming; from Waterford to Carrick-on-Suir where, in spite of me, the people sent away the horses and drew me in triumph through the town, and I then got out, stood on the front board and made them a speech[8] against *Stavey* [?][9] *and Lord Castlereagh*, as my Nell had it. I arrived here this morning at one and am now preparing for many and many a battle. Sweetest, I am in perfect health and spirits, doating of my children and of you, darling Mary.

SOURCE : Fitz-Simon Papers

1 Rev. Patrick Coleman.

2 Probably either John H. Talbot, Bettyville, Wexford, or William Talbot, Rockview, Wexford.

3 *Shelton* v. *Ball* (*Waterford Mirror,* 13 Mar. 1824).

4 His servant.

5 Charles Kendal Bushe.

6 Charles Connor.

7 A dinner held by Catholic inhabitants in the schoolroom of the orphan house in John Street. Thomas Meagher, Jr., presided and Richard Lalor Sheil was present (*Waterford Mirror,* 13, 17 Mar. 1824). From Limerick on 16 March O'Connell addressed a public letter of apology to Meagher for non-attendance (*Waterford Mirror,* 20 Mar. 1824).

8 O'Connell was recognized at De Courcy's Hotel in Carrick-on-Suir and events took place as he describes in the above letter (*Waterford Mirror,* 17, 20 Mar. 1824).

9 Unidentified.

1113

To his wife, Southampton

Limerick, 18 [and 19] March 1824

My own Love,

. . . The records were few. There was only one in the city and that was for £8 and yet it was the cause which created most noise and made a greater sensation than any other.[1] I made a brilliant harangue which brought upon the applauses of one party and the abuse of the other. The question was whether Mr. Rice's[2] advertisements were to pay one shilling a line in the Orange newspaper here or only seven pence as other advertisements did. The jury was almost all Orange and found against us, but this paltry cause gave me an occasion to introduce all the heart-stirring topics connected with the battle for independence in this city. Yesterday I had a great row with that snivelling Serjeant Lefroy who, in the criminal court when I was defending two men for their lives, interrupted my cross-examination. The entire bar were with me on the point and I did not spare the *learned* Serjeant. The matter would be heard of in parliament but that the jury saved all trouble by acquitting the prisoners who are gone home to their families merry and happy.[3]

This day I have been at home all day arranging business and writing letters on the subject of the Catholic Rent. It will certainly succeed to our heart's content. The effect will be truly formidable. It will secure the press in *both* countries. . . .

I have the pleasure to tell you that the house is finished in point of painting, etc., and will be cleaned out early next week. . . . I will, I think, get a capital pair of young sound bays for your carriage, for you must have horses. . . . As to religion, darling, surely it has not made any of us gloomy. Mr. Coleman's maxim is—*beaucoup de piété, beaucoup de gaieté*. . . . For my part I would not think any religion sincere that did not make the person more affectionate and considerate. Tell me, sweetest, candidly if you have any apprehensions of the contrary. If you have, darling, I will endeavour to dissipate them. . . .

Friday 19 March.

. . . Lefroy had a row yesterday with Serjeant Goold and treated him with great insolence. What weakness of intellect it must be which blinds the creature and makes him so totally to forget himself. . . . There is a great dinner getting up for me in Cork—the first compliment they paid me since I was chaired in the year 1811—but I should not boast of this before it is actually given. The Waterford Catholic meeting took place yesterday.[4] Here it will be held on Monday. It is more unanimous than I ever before knew it to be. . . .

SOURCE : Fitz-Simon Papers

1 *Limerick Chronicle* v. *Joseph Harvey, Jr.* (*Patriot,* 25 Mar. 1824).

2 Thomas Spring Rice, M.P.

3 See letter 1114, note 3.

4 The Catholic meeting for the county and city took place in the Great Chapel in Waterford. Patrick Power of Bellevue, Co. Waterford, was in the chair, and Richard Lalor Sheil spoke to an enthusiastic audience.

1114

To Richard Newton Bennett, Clonmel

Limerick, 21 March 1824

(*Private*)

My dear Bennett,

There was nothing in my communications with Plunket of which any use could be made. They were strictly confidential and were confined to a *testimonial* of character. I took no part myself in the proceeding and, indeed, cautiously avoided everything that could mix my name with it. I believe you know that if that name could possibly be of the least use to you it is altogether at your service, but certainly I cannot, from the nature of the transaction, afford you any aid as between you and Plunket. By Plunket, of course, I mean the Att[orne]y-General, not he[1] who so insanely interposed in the matter.[2] I examined the debate on *your* question to see if there was anything to affect your name or character, and I solemnly assure you I did not find anything of *that* kind. I therefore cannot advise you to take any further proceedings, but if you once determine to proceed let me know that I may assist you in any way I can.

Serjeant Lefroy has disgusted the entire Bar. He has been extremely rude to Serjeant Goold. We have signed a requisition to the father for a Bar meeting although Goold would be better pleased we let the matter rest. Lefroy stopped me in a most important cross-examination of the single *identification* witness. *All* the Munster Bar joined in condemning his conduct. It would have gone before Parliament and government but fortunately the jury acquitted the prisoners.[3] It is astonishing what a miserable creature he is, eaten up with the worst of all pride—spiritual pride—and totally devoid of feeling or judgement. He is a strange instance of what puffing will do to exalt, even in a difficult profession, a being of little intellect and no heart.

SOURCE: NLI, MSS 837

1 Unidentified.

2 Possibly one of O'Connell's many attempts to obtain an appointment for Bennett.

3 This case is treated of in the *Patriot* 25 March, and the *Morning Chronicle,* 30 March 1824. Serjeant Lefroy was the judge.

1115

To his wife, Southampton

Limerick, 22 [25 and 26] March 1824

My darling Love,

. . . The parlour and everything else is painted of the same colour as before. . . .

Tralee, 25 March 1824.

. . . On the 24th after doing some business I went to sleep to Adare, eight miles from Limerick, where there really is a good inn. I started very early the next morning and came here yesterday about one o'clock to attend a consultation with Lord Headley, etc., on an act of parliament for dividing Castleisland among the *six gentlemen* of whom *Lady* Headley,[1] his mother, *is one*.[2] . . . He [Judge Torrens] has just asked me to dine with him *on the ground* that Lefroy is not to be in town and I accordingly am to dine with him. . . . I am to leave this after Mass and the Catholic meeting on Sunday. I go that night I hope as far as *Adare,* at all events to Tarbert, and the next day, please God, to Galway. I will remain there only two days, Tuesday and Wednesday, and be back to Cork on Thursday for, darling, *I fly* from one end of the Kingdom to another in a day. We had a glorious meeting at Limerick.[3] There was a strong vote of thanks to the Association and to me, at the latter of which I suppose you will be surprised. At Waterford there were similar votes.[4] . . . These judges are cruelly slow[5] and I cannot promise myself that happiness [of coming to you] so soon. . . . What you please is *law* and so it ought, my own Mary. James and John[6] are here quite well. My poor Uncle is still suffering but has dismissed Hickson[7] who got 25 guineas from him, the highest fee he ever received. The old gentleman is in a precarious way but in full possession of his intellect.

26 March.

I am able to write to you only by snatches. . . .

SOURCE : Fitz-Simon Papers

1 Jane (died 1825), daughter of Arthur Blennerhassett, Ballyseedy, Co. Kerry. Married 1783, as his second wife, first Baron Headley.

2 On 20 February 1824 a petition was presented to the House of Commons on behalf of Jane Lady Headley and William Meredith, Dicks-

grove, Co. Kerry, as part owners with Henry Arthur Herbert, a minor, Muckross, Co. Kerry; David Crosbie, a minor, Ardfert Abbey, Co. Kerry; William James Crosbie, Florence, Italy; and Richard Boyle Townsend, Castle Townsend, Co. Cork, of the town of Castleisland, Co. Kerry, and adjacent lands, comprising 1,022 acres. The petitioners sought an act of parliament for the division of this property among them. Eventually a bill was introduced to the Commons on 22 March and, after much alteration, received the royal assent on 17 June 1824 (5 Geo. IV c. 31, private). The act stated the owners of the property to be Henry Arthur Herbert, Frances and Mary Anne Crosbie, Jane Lady Headley, William Meredith, Richard Chute of Chutehall, Co. Kerry, and William Townsend (Mullins), second Baron Ventry. The act does not appear to have aroused any public interest.

3 The Limerick Catholic meeting was held in St. Michael's chapel on 22 March, William Roche in the chair (*DEP,* 27 Mar. 1824, supplement).

4 See letter 1113, note 4.

5 Robert Torrens and Thomas Lefroy (prime serjeant).

6 His two brothers.

7 Dr. Robert Hickson, New Street, Killarney.

1116

From his wife to Merrion Square,

Southampton, 27 [and 28] March 1824

[No salutation]

When I have not the happiness of hearing from you, my own love, it is the greatest delight to me to read of you. The *Express*[1] of the 22d contains a sweet letter of yours to the chairman presiding at the dinner given for you at Waterford.[2] I read it twice over and had my children laughing at my vanity in insisting there was no person could either write or speak like you. Really, darling, this is my most impartial opinion. I wish the speech prefacing the drinking of your health was reported. It is always such a gratifying feeling to me to have your private virtues spoken of in any public meeting. They little know how numerous those virtues are. It is only from your wife they could have them justly described. . . . He [James Weld] seems greatly pleased with the Catholic politics, particularly with your success on the [Catholic] rent speculation. The necessity of keeping the press at each side of the water in pay appears to him most necessary. He told me that during Mr. Jerningham's[3] secretaryship the press was always paid well, but since his death the English Catholics are nothing. His dependence rests entirely on the Irish Catholics and *Captain*.[4] I leave you to guess the rest. . . .

Sunday the 28th.

I have again read of you this day, darling, and I am very much pleased that Mr. Conway should have succeeded in retaining the sentence Catholics of Ireland instead of Roman Catholics. I can't tell you how much annoyed I was at the debate that occurred on the question since your departure from Dublin. I said to the girls it would not have occurred were you on the spot, and I now perceive it was your influence that carried the point against the cringing set who at the Association opposed it.[5] . . .

We like greatly the idea of going by Liverpool for two reasons. We shall see more of England and have a shorter passage than we could by Bristol. . . .

[P.S.] Take *good* care where you put my letters. Leave them not on your table when you are out or when you go to bed.

SOURCE : O'Connell Papers, NLI 13651

1 *Dublin Evening Express.*
2 See letter 1112, note 7.
3 Edward Jerningham.
4 O'Connell.
5 At this time the Catholic Association was organizing a petition on the general state of Ireland to be presented to both Houses of parliament by Earl Grey and Henry Brougham. At the association's meeting on 13 March 1824 (O'Connell being away on circuit) it was decided, despite Frederick W. Conway's opposition, to describe the petition as signed by *Roman* Catholics rather than Catholics since the latter terms might be objected to by parliament (*DEP*, 16 Mar. 1824). At the association's meeting on 20 March, this decision was rescinded in favour of the designation *Catholic,* a letter from O'Connell being mentioned by Conway at the meeting as a reason for doing so (*DEP*, 25 Mar. 1824).

1117

To his wife, Southampton

Galway, 29 [and 31] March 1824, Monday

My own Love,

. . . I was asked to a public dinner in Tralee on Saturday.

31st March, Wednesday

. . . If I could have remained on Saturday the dinner in Tralee would have been, I believe, splendid. Col. Crosbie, Ponsonby, etc., etc., had announced their intention of attending it. The Catholic meeting for Kerry was to have taken place on Sunday. I hope it went off well,[1] but on Saturday morning an express came to Tralee for me from this town to announce that the trial here would be one day sooner than I expected. I was therefore obliged to leave Tralee on Saturday evening and I got that night to Tarbert. I started thence next morning soon after three and reached Limerick before nine. I then heard Mass and breakfasted on *four* fresh eggs and reached this place about eight in the evening. On Monday morning the trial commenced.[2] I spoke yesterday morning for three hours and the entire was closed about eleven o'clock last night, but as yet I have not heard what the verdict *is*. I expect to hear it every moment and am sure it must be for my client. I remain here to attend a Catholic meeting[3] at twelve this day and will, I hope, get at least as far as Newmarket[4] this night and to Cork by a reasonable hour tomorrow. . . . Hurrah. Victory! We got a verdict easily so that all my *specials* were triumphant this time, and, thank God, they are now all over and I am on *my way* to my sweet darling and her dearest children. . . . The letter you wrote Mr. Milliken I approve of in the very highest degree. . . . There is about you, Mary, a most happy and ready application to what ought to be said and done on every occasion, and it comes to your mind at once naturally and without study or effort. I believe, darling, that it was this excellent perfection that made me first fall in love with you. . . .

SOURCE : Fitz-Simon Papers

1 The Kerry Catholic meeting was held in the chapel in Tralee on 28 March. O'Connell's brother John presided and a petition to both Houses of parliament was passed (*DEP*, 3 April 1824).

2 Unidentified.
3 The Galway Catholic meeting was held on 31 March in the New Parish chapel, the Hon. Gonville ffrench in the chair. O'Connell spoke, and it was decided to organize an Emancipation petition to parliament (*Dublin Evening Express,* 5 April 1824; it erroneously gives the date of the meeting as 1 April).
4 That is, Newmarket-on-Fergus, Co. Clare.

1118

From his wife to Merrion Square

Southampton, 30 [and 31] March
[and 1 April] 1824

My own dearest Love,

. . . It is an *age,* love, since I heard from you. However, I am quite aware it is not your fault. I read again of you this day, an article taken from the Galway paper.[1] . . . You mentioned to me having the row with the judge.[2] . . .

Wednesday, March the 30th [*recte* 31st]

. . . Ally[3] tells me your uncle, the General, is in perfect health and all his family quite well. He is sending you his picture by Bordeaux. He found out you had given directions to have a copy taken from the one we all admired so much in Madame's saloon, and he insisted on being at the entire expense of having it done and forwarding to Dublin. Your Kate and I cried over your speech or, rather, the curtailed report of one delivered by you at the aggregate meeting in Limerick. It is, love, mutilated, as it is a most feeling and delightful speech, and William Finn says it is exactly the kind of speech most calculated to make an impression on the lower orders.[4] He is quite indignant with North.[5] In my opinion there is not either in England or Ireland a *real* Protestant anxious for the emancipation of the Catholics. They are a horrid bigoted set. The *Herald* of *this* morning contains an article upon what occurred in Limerick between you, Serjeant Lefroy and Goold.[6] Whatever is to be the nature of the Bar meeting on this subject I am very very anxious to hear.

Thursday, April the 1st.

. . . I shall be as economical as I possibly can be, but we

should either here or in Dublin lay out money for the girls and things here are much cheaper than with us. . . .

SOURCE : O'Connell Papers, NLI 13651

1 Unidentified.

2 See letter 1113.

3 O'Connell's sister Ally Finn.

4 See letter 1115, note 3. In this speech O'Connell condemned Whiteboy activities, proselytism and the dispersal of a local Catholic funeral by the military at the behest of a Church of Ireland clergyman.

5 John Henry North (died 1831), 31 Merrion Square (next door to O'Connell's house), B.L.; M.P. for Plympton-Earl, 11 March 1824-26; judge of the high court of admiralty (Ireland), 1830. This is a reference to his maiden speech in the Commons on 29 March when he defended the Kildare Place Society for the Education of the Poor and attacked the Irish Catholic clergy for obstructing its efforts (*Hansard*, N.S., X, 1479-84).

6 See letter 1114.

1119

To his wife, Southampton

Cork, 5 [7, 8 and 9] April 1824

My own Love,

. . . I left Galway in great triumph after the aggregate meeting on Wednesday last.[1] We defeated the *lousy* aristocracy there in great style. I beat them fairly out of their opposition, and at length everything was carried unanimously.[2] I spoke for near two hours and gave both members[3] a great dressing. Daly[4] had the full benefit of the sermon as he was present in the Chapel, although I affected not to know he was in the room. I left Galway on the evening of the 31st, Wednesday, at about 5 and went to Gort 18 miles where I slept. I left that soon after 4 next morning and travelled before *breakfast* 35 miles to Limerick and 51 here to dinner, about 86 miles or upwards of 110 English miles, but that is a journey I think nothing of. The assizes were opened the day of my arrival, Thursday the 1st., but no business was done until the 2d. . . . I have already received something approaching on £200 so that the delay will be greater here than one could wish, but the business, you know, is a compensation to a certain extent

7 April, Wednesday . . .

8 April, Thursday

. . . We had a great aggregate here on Monday.[5] The greatest I ever saw. I spoke for two hours and made, they say, a *beautiful* speech, but we have, you know, no kind of reporters. You will see a miserable edition of my speech, but to console you there will reach you a wicked letter of mine on Plunket's burial bill.[6] It is, in fact, a rascally bill.[7] . . . I am *asked* to a great public dinner on Easter Monday. I will therefore leave this on Easter Tuesday and then Mass at Southampton the following Sunday, please God. I have some expectation of going for a week to London as counsel to oppose the Corporation of Dublin jobbing bills.[8] My heart bounds at that hope because, sweetest, if I do I will have *my family* in London that week. . . . I got two letters from Cornelius McLoghlin, a most respectable Catholic merchant, on the subject, but there can be no determination until we hear from Mr. Spring Rice. . . .

Friday the 9th

Darling, my brother James will send to Maurice[9] £100 from this on account of the annuity given him by the old gentleman.[10]. . . The newspapers tell you of me continually. I hope you will like my letter on Plunket's bill. Indeed, *you* will like it because it is *mine*. . . .

SOURCE : Fitz-Simon Papers

1 See letter 1117, note 3.

2 Christopher Dillon Bellew, Mount Bellew, Co. Galway, appears to have been the spokesman of the ' lousy aristocracy ' at this meeting (*DEP,* 6 April 1824, supplement).

3 James Daly and Richard (' Humanity Dick ') Martin, Galway County representatives in parliament.

4 James Daly (1782-1847), Dunsandle, Co. Galway; M.P. for Galway borough, 1805-11; for Co. Galway, 1812-30 and 1832-34. Created Baron Dunsandle, 1845.

5 The chairman, Jeremiah Murphy, Hyde Park, Cork, was requested by this meeting to write letters to Hon. Christopher Hely-Hutchinson, M.P., Lord Lansdowne and Earl Grey, protesting against the Catholic Burial Bill (*CMP,* 9 April 1824).

6 A public letter, dated 7 April 1824, which O'Connell addressed to ' the Chairman of the Committee of the Catholic Association appointed to report on the Subject of " the Burial Bill " ' (*DEP,* 13 April 1824).

7 On 25 March 1824, Plunket, the attorney-general, introduced to the Commons a bill to make further provision for the burial of ' persons in Ireland dissenting from the Established Church '. The bill was amended in the Lords and received the royal assent as 5 Geo. IV c. 25 on 15 April (*Commons Journal,* LXXIX, 207, 300).
8 One such bill concerned tolls (see letter 1097, note 2). Possibly the Dublin Coal Bill was another. It met with strong opposition and was defeated in the Commons on 13 April (*MC,* 14 April 1824).
9 O'Connell's son.
10 Hunting-Cap.

1120

To his wife, Southampton

Cork, 10 [and 19] April 1824

My own Love,

. . . Three men were convicted this day for the murder of the Franks family.[1] I am not satisfied with their conviction. I defended them. If they be really guilty twenty hangings would be too good for them. It is a wretched profession when one has the agony of playing for the human life. Darling, are you not glad that Lent is so near being over? I have got through it perfectly well. I have taken my full and usual quantity of milk in my tea or coffee five mornings out of the seven and on *all* mornings eat heartily of dry toast. In short, sweetest, I have felt no kind of effect whatsoever from the Lent save continuing to grow fat.

19 April 1824

I have *thus* allowed nine days to elapse without finishing my letter. . . . [the cause of my not writing] was simply, darling, *the security* I felt at being so soon with you and the hurry of the assizes also interfered, but I had no notion that I was so long in arrears. . . . This *you know* is the day of the great dinner[2] to me. It has succeeded admirably and when I finish this letter I set about *dressing* myself for it. I have sent off my luggage to Dublin and have everything quite ready to start at six in the morning. I hope to reach Kilkenny tomorrow and Dublin rather early the next day. . . . I perceive you are disposed to come by Bristol, and I will settle for your passage on as cheap terms as possible. I have got through the Lent famously and eat my beefsteak yesterday and today with a *ferocious* appetite. I breakfast always with Aunt Nagle and we have large parties at breakfast. It is a great delight to her, poor woman. She always speaks of you with the most sincere affection, and Maurice is an idol of hers. Darling, this has been a famous assizes to me. I never had better here. I received very near £340 in Cork alone, more than any other counsel made on any entire circuit except those who may have got public money. Besides, *my reputation* as an advocate has certainly increased. I may say this to you, darling, without the imputation of any other person calling it vanity. The dinner this day is a most grand affair. You will read of it in all the papers. Tell my children that I doat of them, my darling Nell, my sweetest Kate, my dearest Betsey, my own Maurice and the sweet of sweets, my Danny. . . .

SOURCE : Fitz-Simon Papers

1 On 9 September 1823 Thomas Franks, his wife and their son Henry, Lisnagourneen, Kildorrery, Co. Cork, were murdered (*CMC,* 15 Sept. 1823). On 10 April 1824 three brothers, Patrick, Maurice and John Cremin, were convicted of the murder and were executed on 12 April. They protested their innocence to the end (*DEP,* 15 April 1824).

2 A public dinner in honour of O'Connell took place at the Chamber of Commerce Hotel, Cork, on 19 April, Denis R. Moylan presiding (*FJ,* 23 April 1824).

1121

From his wife to Merrion Square

Southampton 14 [and 15] April 1824

My own dearest love,

Had I not received a letter from you this morning I should have considered you were on the road to Dublin. It is, my love, no small disappointment to us all to find you will be detained so much longer than we were led to expect, but [it] is some consolation that in a pecuniary way you will be compensated for this delay. I trust there is every chance of your being sent to London.[1] You will not, of course, make this your way as we could arrange matters so as to meet you in London accompanied by Maurice, who bids me tell you with his fond love he is much obliged for your present of twenty pounds which in your present circumstances he considers more than he would, at any other period, a much larger sum. He will leave his money in my hands until he is going to London. He does not, I assure you, spend any money here. He is quite domestic in his habits and very good in every sense of the word. . . . I am greatly pleased you have written on the subject of the burial bill.[2] Mr. Plunket is, in my opinion, as bad as any of the King's ministers. I really think, love, the Orangemen are getting afraid. Dawson's and Brownlow's[3] speeches look a little like it,[4] and Judge McClelland's charge to the jury is quite unlike *himself*.[5] I admire the spirit with which the *Dublin Express* is carried on. The Editor does not seem at all afraid to speak out.[6] If the unfortunate peasantry would keep quiet and the press and the agitators *pull* together I am convinced the Catholics would be soon emancipated and the Union repealed. You perceive, love, what a politician I am, but I could not be your wife without feeling interested for everything concerning Ireland. May we live, darling, to see your exertions crowned by success. You are at this moment, and most justly, the idol of the people.

Thursday, 15 April.

. . . How we shall rejoice when we turn our backs on Southampton. My six months' residence here have confirmed the dislike I ever felt for the English. Such a nasty selfish prejudiced set! . . . How I wish you may be sent to London. It would be such a treat to the girls to see that city before they left Ireland [*sic*]. . . . I am every moment expecting Dan O'Connell.[7] . . . Rick should lose no time in sending the child. Your uncle is quite anxious for him to be put on the burse,[8] and the Bishop cannot now plead any excuse for refusing to sign for Dan O'Connell. He has had from Mr. Kenney the *official* communication he required.

SOURCE : O'Connell Papers, NLI 13651

1 See letter 1119.

2 See letter 1119, note 6.

3 Charles Brownlow (1795-1847), Lurgan House, Lurgan, Co. Down; M.P. for Co. Armagh, 1818-33; created 1839 Baron Lurgan.

4 On 30 March George Robert Dawson presented a petition from certain Freemasons in Ireland asking that Freemasons be exempted from the provisions of 4 Geo. IV c. 87 (1823) which was designed for the more effective suppression of oath-taking in secret societies. In his speech Dawson suggested that processions of both Orangemen and Ribbonmen be prohibited (*MC*, 31 Mar. 1824). Charles Brown-

low presented a similar petition and spoke to the same effect as Dawson.

5 On 20 March Judge McClelland addressed the Co. Antrim grand jury on the evil of Orange and Ribbonmen processions (*DEP*, 27 Mar. 1824).

6 This newspaper (*recte Dublin Evening Express*) published in its issue of 24 March 1824 an outspoken editorial condemning 'the attempt made by the King of England to " conciliate " the Orange faction '.

7 Daniel O'Connell (1808/09-46), son of Capt. Rickard O'Connell, Tralee, and nephew of O'Connell's wife. Second lieutenant, Royal Marines, 1831-42, when he retired on half-pay.

8 The O'Connell family had the right of nomination to members and relatives of the family to burses in Paris for both clerical and secular studies. In evidence before the House of Lords select committee on the state of Ireland on 11 March 1825, O'Connell said: ' The largest foundation in Paris was one made by my family several years ago [before the French Revolution], that would give us at present, if there had been no revolution, something more than twenty burses. My two brothers and I have three at present: it is regulated that the three principal persons of the name in the County of Kerry should nominate to those burses. We have at present three or four establishments in the University of Paris; the young men we have sent there are not educating for the priesthood. . . . Our presentation, I may call it, is a right to be received in the University of Paris unless there be particular objection to the individual. We consider in ourselves vested the right of presentation ' (*Minutes of Evidence taken before the Lords' Select Committee appointed . . . to examine into the nature and extent of the Disturbances which have prevailed in . . . Ireland . . .*, 1825 (200) VII, 501.

1122

To Denys Scully

Merrion Square, 22 April 1824

My dear Scully,

I enclose you £50, my March deposit. I also send you the first voucher. I have underlined two passages for your consideration. I made no payment to *your* account at Latouche's, the payment was to account Denys and James Scully Esqrs. I never passed any notes *to you.* I passed two notes of £1,000 each to Leonard Doherty[1] for money lent by you. I also executed a mortgage to him for the same money of my house.

Since then on a settlement of £1,000 you gave me up one of the notes. There remains another in your hands and a bond of mine for *about* £240, both counter-secured by the mortgage. I am thus particular merely that the voucher may be, on the face of it, like the transaction itself. I know that Mr. Doherty's name was that of a mere trustee and as long as you and I both live there could be no difference of opinion, but I am sure you will think it right to have the matter stated as it really is, namely, as payments at foot of the mortgage and collateral securities the principal and interest of which I am thus reducing at £50 a month *at the least*. Give me a written direction how I shall make the deposits in your absence, whether in your own name or in those of D[enys] and J[ames] Scully.[2]

[P.S.] . . .

SOURCE : Scully Papers

1 Denys Scully's attorney, 91 St. Stephen's Green, Dublin.

2 James Scully (1777-1846), Shanballymore and Tipperary; married 1806 Margaret, daughter of John Wyse of the Manor of St. John, Co. Waterford. Chairman of the Tipperary Bank, later the Tipperary Joint Stock Bank. Brother of Denys Scully.

1123

From Denys Scully to Merrion Square

Merrion Square, 22 April 1824

Dear O'Connell,

I cannot say whether I gave up one of the notes for a £1,000 to you or not, and I am now not able to make a search for it amongst my papers. I send you . . . my receipt [for £100] . . .

SOURCE : O'Connell Papers, NLI 13647

1123a

To William Conyngham Plunket

Merrion Square, 1 May 1824

My dear Sir,

The Catholic petition[1] is now ready and I hope to be able

to send you tomorrow a copy of it. I am one of a deputation of the petitioners appointed to wait on you to request you will be so good as to present it to the House of Commons and to entreat that you will be pleased to procure as speedy a discussion on its merits as can be done. Be so good as to say at what hour on Monday we may be able to have the honour of waiting on you.

SOURCE : Mrs. Nicholas Shorter

1 At a meeting of the Catholic Association on 1 May it was decided that O'Connell, Mathias J. O'Kelly, Frederick W. Conway and another should wait on Plunket with the Emancipation petition and request that he should present it to the Commons (*DEP,* 4 May 1824). At a meeting of the Association on 12 May it was decided to ask Lord Donoughmore to present the petition to the Lords. In proposing this motion O'Connell said that Donoughmore's father (John Hely-Hutchinson) ' was the first man to bring in a bill in favour of the Catholics ' (*DEP,* 13 May 1824).

1123b

From William Conyngham Plunket

Draft

London, 10 May 1824

My dear Sir,

I have this moment received your letter of the 8th inst., enclosing the draft of a petition[1] for the repeal of the laws which aggrieve His Majesty's Roman Catholic subjects in Ireland, and stating that the original, with signatures, will be sent to me in a few days with the hope that I will present it and procure a discussion on its merits this session. I shall have great satisfaction in presenting the petition immediately on receipt of it, and in stating my sense of its importance but, at such a period of the session, I apprehend it would be hopeless to look for the accomplishment of any legislative measure for the relief of the R.C. and under such circumstances to move on the subject would be not only useless but injurious, as a great portion of the friends of the measure, especially of the English representatives, will not vote or attend when the object is merely discussion.

SOURCE : Mrs. Nicholas Shorter

1 See letter 1123a.

1124

From his brother James, Paris, 9 June 1824, to Merrion Square

'Our Catholic Association makes a great noise among the English and Irish in Paris, but I fear from Mr. Plunket's letter to Conway[1] that *Othello's occupation is gone*.'

SOURCE: O'Connell MSS, UCD

1 A reference to a letter dated 26 May 1824 from Plunket, the attorney-general, to Frederick W. Conway which was read at the Catholic Association on 29 May. In it Plunket maintained that his recent letter had been to O'Connell as a private individual and not as a member of the Catholic Association. He had agreed to present a petition to parliament from 'undersigned Catholics' but had no connection with the Catholic Association. In a discussion of the matter by the meeting O'Connell suggested that it would be unwise for Catholics in the future to have as their advocate one (Plunket) whose political interests and views were so opposed to theirs (*FJ*, 31 May 1824).

1125

To his wife, Merrion Square

Wexford, 4 August 1824

My darling Love,

Do not be angry with me for writing only a short letter. I cannot do more. I am perfectly well, thank God, in excellent spirits, full of business, with a great dinner[1] this day before me and a long speech to make at the sitting of the court in the cause[2] which brought me down. Of course it is as yet undetermined. . . .

SOURCE: Fitz-Simon Papers

1 On 4 August this dinner in honour of O'Connell was held in St. Peter's College, Sir Thomas Esmonde in the chair. O'Connell and Sheil were among the speakers. The college grounds were crowded and there was a display of fireworks (*Waterford Mirror*, 7 Aug. 1824).

2 *Hedges Eyre* v. *Glascott*. O'Connell's client (probably Rev. William Glascott, J.P., Pilltown, Co. Wexford) lost the case (*Waterford Mirror*, 7 Aug. 1824).

1126

To his wife

Tralee, 15 August 1824

My darling Love,

. . . I got to Waterford on Tuesday about five and was dragged by the people from the new bridge at Waterford to my lodgings, about half a mile, along the finest quay imaginable. The next day the record[1] came on—my client was defeated, but *ought not.* The Chief Justice[2] was astounded at the verdict, but it was occasioned altogether by the Orange feeling which prevents Catholics from getting justice. My client was a Catholic, and not a single Catholic was left on the jury. I never was more disgusted by the vileness of the bigotry which crushes the Catholics in every step and situation in life. I got a great dinner[3] on Wednesday. The company was respectable and very numerous. I did not get to bed till near two in the morning. I was up again at or, rather, before six and travelled that day, *Thursday,* to Killarney, 104 miles, but I was not there until near three in the morning. I was obliged to be up again at six or soon after, and came here on Friday morning before the Court sat. Butler's fishery case[4] was postponed for me, and we succeeded in it gallantly. Butler is very grateful, and so, darling, he ought. . . .

Spring Rice has been here on the grand jury. He would have had a public compliment paid to him if I had not interfered. I am quite dissatisfied with him and his politics. . . .

SOURCE : *Irish Monthly,* XII (1884), 215

1 *Osborne* v. *O'Shee.* The case concerned the validity of a lease of lands executed in 1702 and held by Richard Power O'Shee and Arnold O'Shee from the Protestant Osborne family, baronets (*Waterford Mirror,* 14 Aug. 1824).

2 Charles Kendal Bushe.

3 This dinner in honour of O'Connell was held in the Great Town Hall, Richard Power O'Shee, J.P., Gardenmorris, Co. Waterford, in the chair. Richard Lalor Sheil and Rev. John Sheehan were among the speakers (*Waterford Mirror,* 14 Aug. 1824).

4 O'Connell's friend James Butler owned the salmon weir on the channel between Lough Currane and the sea at Waterville, Co. Kerry.

1127

To his wife, Merrion Square

Cork, 17 August 1824

My own darling love,

. . . With respect to the gas, darling, see whether the gasometer be up, and let Maurice go down and learn how it makes the quantity of gas because it is by the quantity we are to pay for it. This should therefore be attended to at once. See that somebody learns the proper mode of ascertainment as it is, alas, quite uncertain whether Maurice will give himself the trouble to procure even so much useful knowledge. . . . On Sunday after I wrote to you we left Tralee and came to dine at James's.[1] It would delight you to see his boys, especially his eldest baby. It is indeed one of the loveliest creatures I ever saw and is in great *training*. Only think of his grandmother[2] torturing him with the sight of custard pudding and refusing him a little of so innocent a thing. If he was mine I would soon stop his weeping. . . .

Tuesday night [19 August 1824] . . .

SOURCE : Fitz-Simon Papers

1 His brother James's home, Kenmare Place, Killarney.
2 James's mother-in-law, Madame O'Donoghue.

1127a

From Lord Westmeath

Clonyn [Delvin, Co. Westmeath, 17 August 1824]

Sir,

I saw a letter[1] addressed to you [? in the] *Freeman's Journal*[2] of yesterday on the subject of the proposed contribution [of] a Catholic rent in the parish of C. T. Delvin.[3] My name happens to be introduced in it, and though if it had not been addressed to you I should have taken no notice of it, yet for this reason it caught my attention. I mean that your name being thus coupled with the subject was sufficient to claim my attention, which no publication referring to it, otherwise circumstanced, should do from me.

I am glad in the first place that it gives me the opportunity of saying to you I have often dwelt with pleasure upon the manly and uncompromising sentiments you have used when treating the subject of the former governments of Ireland, and the ungenerous spirit which appears to have often actuated them in times and ages past. Indeed the natural independence of your mind first riveted my respect for the powers of it, and having that quality as eminently as I think you have, it is plain you cannot dislike the same property in another.

I have long thought the abuse of religious distinctions the bane of Ireland. [? I] presume the ordinary intercourse and [about one word illegible] of society and all the duties of its members *might* be [about one word illegible] in this island without the absurd [one word illegible] which we usually find is made in this country, as to the peculiar creed of an individual, before any other question is entertained respecting him; and which of itself perpetuates prejudices which prejudices make us the laughing stock of nations, and confine the Irish people in poverty and degradation whilst the inhabitants of even the newest countries are rising into importance and into power. Such prejudices, however, have existed and are still strongly rooted in the breasts of the majority of our population, and in my view of the country's welfare the sooner they expire the better. On the promulgation of the Catholic rent I spoke my sentiments to some of my tenants, and openly, because I thought it at the outset calculated to draw a strong line of distinction between the Protestants and Roman Catholics; and the avowed motives of the subscription being such as I would not approve in my comprehension of them.

I neither can nor do admit that the actual government of Ireland exercises any pernicious distinctions but if the *law* still maintains some political disabilities over the Roman Catholics, the continuance of which I regret as much as any man, I for one am [half a line illegible] *distinctions* among the [about one word illegible] which upon similar principles I think [about one word illegible] hurtful, and I therefore have declared to my tenants that the subscription proposed to be raised has within it the seeds of lasting mischief for the peasantry and ought to be discouraged. The principle of reciprocal duty demands from the tenant first, that he shall perform his contract with the proprietor of the land he lives on, and to his own family, that he shall not alienate any share of those funds which are theirs next in order until all domestic duties are acquitted; and where in Ireland upon the *best* managed estates, are the peasantry in a state of commercial prosperity to enable them to pledge themselves to the continuance of a political subscription? As to me, Sir, I have no interest separate from that of my tenantry. I feel we must stand or fall together. I have nothing but the inheritance which I possess from my Roman Catholic ancestors,[4] and who were proudly connected enough with everything good and honourable in the past history of Ireland to [about three words illegible] opinion and to give it too for these reasons, that I yield to no man in good will for my country. Without domestic tranquillity the country must remain a reproach to herself; and though I admire your talents and think you find your account (as every honest man must) in being incorruptible, yet I think the subscription on foot ill judged, calculated to make politicians of ploughmen, and to make Irishmen savage against one another to the end of the chapter.

SOURCE: O'Connell Papers, NLI 13647

1 A letter to O'Connell dated 12 August 1824 from P. Sheridan, Crow Park, in support of the collection of the Catholic rent in the united parishes of Castletown Delvin, Killulagh, Killough and Crowinstown, Co. Westmeath, and diocese of Meath. Reference is made to 'the puny yet persevering hostility' of Lord Westmeath.

2 Of 16 August 1824.

3 Castletown Delvin or simply Delvin, Co. Westmeath.

4 The sixth earl, grandfather of the writer of this letter, had become a Protestant, 1754/5.

1128

To his wife, Merrion Square, Dublin

Cork, 19 August 1824

My own Love,

. . . Well, sweetest, are you ready to start for your husband? Am I to have the happiness of seeing you here? Say, darling, if I am. . . . If you come I will have rooms for you at the hotel[1] belonging to the *Chamber of Commerce* where you will be perfectly comfortable. . . .

Darling, give direction that the *Evening Herald*[2] should

be sent to me regularly, that is, a second copy of it if you or my girls wish also to have it. I like that paper extremely, indeed, it is the only honest paper in Dublin and I hope we will yet be able to assist in getting a morning paper as an addition to the present establishment. At least it is very much my wish that it should be *so*. Aunt Nagle was quite delighted at the prospect of seeing you and is very anxious to see Maurice. . . . Give my tender love to Maurice, my dear idle Maurice. . . . How delighted I shall be if your letter announces your determination to pay Kerry a visit. . . .

SOURCE : Fitz-Simon Papers

1 104 Patrick Street.

2 *Dublin Evening Herald,* a pro-Catholic paper.

1129

From General John Devereux[1]

London, 22 August 1824

My dear and valued friend,

Accept this small token of regard from one who can neither flatter nor deceive his friends. Receive it not merely as the pledge of personal esteem, but as a mark of the high sense which I entertain of your valuable and unwearied exertion in the great cause of Colombian Independence, to which my heart has been long and ardently devoted.

The prayers and the arms of free men have at length prevailed:—Colombia is no longer in bondage. . . .

In that awful and perilous struggle for a nation's rights, much obloquy was cast upon many who had embarked in the sacred cause: I could not therefore, expect that *my* name should remain exempted from the general slander. . . .

I cherished the delightful hope of coupling the glories of the country of my birth with the new-born liberties of the country of my adoption: but to no man did I ever hold out a delusive prospect, or lure him forward with promises which I could not realize. To each and all who joined my standard, I frankly explained the hardships which awaited them, and that our way to success must be fought through sickness, perils and fatigue.

In the midst of the discontents that followed, and calumnies which disappointment had engendered, that one sincere and constant friend who boldly defended my reputation against its assailers . . . has ever been found the firmest and most faithful in private life. Believe me, my friend, your manly and intrepid conduct, at that period, has sunk deep into my heart. . . . Its design will be answered, if whilst it serves occasionally to make you look back with complacency on the course you have pursued, it shall also sometimes recall to your remembrance the high regard and unalterable attachment of your obliged and devoted friend,

J. Devereux

of the Order of Liberators,
and General of Division of the Armies of Colombia, etc.

[P.S.] I embark immediately for France[2] and Holland.

SOURCE : O'Connell MSS, UCD

1 This letter was probably written shortly after Devereux's return from South America.

2 Devereux's visit to France was in connection with Colombian gold mines. He was jailed when he got to Italy in 1825 and returned to London on being released.

1130

To his wife, Merrion Square, Dublin

Cork, Tuesday, 24 August 1824

Darling,

I am come in late. I did not leave court until after seven *long*. I have been defeated in two causes and my heart was sore, but I found your letter, sweetest, before me. Shall I attempt to describe my sensations? No, my Love, my own sweet, sweet Love. No, my Mary, I will not attempt to tell you. Darling, I will remain here till you come. Write to me from Kilkenny or, rather, make Maurice write the instant you arrive there. You are to stop in this town darling at the 'Chamber of Commerce'.[1] It is *not* the commercial buildings, take notice, sweetest. It is the Chamber of Commerce in Patrick Street. . . .

SOURCE : Fitz-Simon Papers

1 Chamber of Commerce Hotel.

1131

From his son Morgan to Merrion Square

Vincenza, 7 September 1824

My dear Father,

. . . I wrote also to my uncle the General in order that he might [about two words illegible] H. E. Baron Vincent[1] my intention of leaving the service. I told everyone here it was on account of family affairs. I also wrote to Baron O'Connell at Vienna in order to let him know of my departure, and I received his answer a few days ago in which he wishes me to pass through Vienna that, according to his own words, he may have the satisfaction of embracing before he dies the grandson of his beloved cousin Morgan. . . .

[P.S.] With respect to my unfortunate rupture I have had myself treated according to your wishes and [at] Vienna I intend to get the opinion of the first surgeons there.

SOURCE : O'Connell Papers, NLI 13645

1 Karl Freiherr von Vincent (1757-1834), cavalry general; ambassador-extraordinary in Paris, 1815-25.

1132

To his wife, Merrion Square

Killarney, 11 September 1824

Darling,

. . . I am a vile rascal to write such a letter as I did to you and to have it find you ill. So, darling, you are ill again and my cure for you is a vile letter. My own, own Mary, my poor darling Mary. Oh take care of yourself, sweetest, dearest, darling. I intended to have written again to you from Cork, but on Thursday we discovered by accident that there was to be a bible meeting in the court-house. We accordingly broke in upon them. Bric, Sheil and I spoke.[1] Sheil made an admirable speech. I spoke for about an hour with some effort, and we prevented them from passing one single resolution and made them adjourn to the next day. Accordingly I remained until Friday. The dinner to Sheil was on Thursday and it was got up delightfully. Everything went off in the best possible way.

About 130 sat down to dinner.[2] Toasts, speeches, etc., in great style. Do not feel the slightest jealousy, darling. Believe the fact that it is the greatest compliment to me that he is thus treated. Whilst he differed with me he was totally disregarded and indeed, darling, you would wrong those who entertained him sadly if you thought that they did not feel kindly towards me, most kindly, most affectionately. Darling, on Friday we went again to the bible meeting. It was the most crowded meeting I ever attended. The thing had been got up by an Englishman and a Scotchman.[3] We had several speeches. A priest, a Mr. Falvey,[4] spoke inimitably well. Mr. England[5] also spoke delightfully. I spoke for *three hours*. I had the *entire* meeting laughing at the mummers for at least an hour and a half of the time. We finally routed them completely. . . .

Now, darling, to our quarrel as to which I have first to tell you that I will do anything you please about Maurice. *You* shall regulate my conduct to him in every respect. . . .

There are great schemes on foot for Iveragh. Our slate quarries and salmon fisheries are in great demand and I believe that the steam vessel company will certainly be arranged. What a difference to Iveragh to have every foot of ground valuable. Darling, it is quite certain that *some* great changes will take place in that country from the many schemes on foot. Darling, I never had the least notion of asking any person to our home, not the least, and if I had, your letter would be of course quite decisive against my doing so. . . .

SOURCE : Fitz-Simon Papers

1 A meeting of the ladies auxiliary of the Munster Hibernian Society of the County and City of Cork in the county court-house on 9 and 10 September 1824. Baptist Wriothesley Noel (1798-1873, see *DNB*) and Lieut. James Edward Gordon, R.N., were the principal speakers as representatives of the London Hibernian Society. Sheil, O'Connell and Bric were among those who spoke in opposition to them. The meeting was conducted in an orderly manner. O'Connell proposing a vote of thanks at the end to the chairman of both days, Joseph Deane Freeman, Castlecor, Kanturk, Co. Cork (*FJ*, 14, 15 Sept.; *DEP*, 18 Sept. 1824).

2 The Cork dinner in honour of Richard Lalor Sheil was held on 9 September, Francis McCarthy, B.L., in the chair (*Waterford Mirror*, 13 Sept. 1824).

3 Noel and Lieut. Gordon, R.N.

4 Rev. John Francis Falvey, P.P., Glanmire, Co. Cork.

5 Rev. Thomas England.

1133

To his wife, Merrion Square

Carhen, 26 September 1824

Darling,

I write merely to tell you that I am off in the morning. I much fear that our darling Morgan has been detained *still* at Vicenza. There must have been some continued [contrived ?] mistake. Nic Mahon was convinced he had given a *general* credit, and although I spoke to James Sugrue twice on this subject I could not get the idea out of their heads. Go off, darling, to Mr. Mahon's, and if he did not write a *fresh* letter to his London bankers on this subject, get it done at once. This was also one of the things Maurice neglected and I now much fear my darling fellow is still detained. Oh, how bitterly I regret that I did not myself attend to my sweet, darling boy.

We leave this in the morning for Grenagh.[1] There is to be a rascally stag hunt on Wednesday but, darling, between you and me I will, I hope, give it the slip and be that day on the road, that is, *if possible*. . . . I left the old gentleman[2] quite well for his time of life but he is a great deal broken. He parted with me with the greatest affection and sent his love to you and my children in the warmest terms. He gave me £100 for Maurice. He made every arrangement with respect to his tomb and made me write his epitaph[3] and had it read to him distinctly least, as he said, it should be fulsome. His firmness is really extraordinary. May the great God bless him. . . .

SOURCE : Fitz-Simon Papers

1 Near Killarney, home of O'Connell's brother John.

2 Hunting-Cap.

3 The inscription on the tomb (in which lie Hunting-Cap, his parents, and O'Connell's wife, Mary) in Abbey Island cemetery near Derrynane, is as follows:

DOM

Sacred to the Memory of
Daniel O'Connell Esq.,
Formerly of Derrynane
Who departed this life in the Month
of September 1770
Full of years and of Virtues

and of
Mary his Wife
She also was of an ancient race
of the House of O'Donoghue
She survived her husband 22 years
and was a Model for Wives and Mothers
to admire and to imitate
Requiescant in Pace

Here also are deposited the Mortal remains
of
Maurice O'Connell Esq.,
their son who erected this Monument
the chief ambition of his long and Prosperous Life
was to elevate an Ancient Family from unmerited
and Unjust Oppression
his allegiance was pure and Disinterested
his love of his native land sincere and avowed
and his attachment to the ancient Faith of his Fathers
to the Church of Christ
was his first Pride
and his Chiefest Consolation
he died on the 10 day of February
in the year 1825
in the 97 year of his age
they loved him Most who knew him best
May his Soul rest in
Eternal Peace

The third last line ('they loved him Most who knew him best') was obviously inserted by O'Connell since it lacks the eighteenth-century style of the rest and, if written by Hunting-Cap, would certainly have been 'fulsome'.

1134

To his wife, Merrion Square

[postmarked Kilkenny, 21 October 1824]

Darling,

I am kept *here* on Thursday by Major Bryan. I could not possibly get off from him. I will leave his house at 5 on Friday morning and be in Townsend Street certainly before the meeting.[1] I write this, sweetest, in a hurry in the room with Major Bryan, Col. Butler,[2] etc.

SOURCE : Fitz-Simon Papers

1 A public meeting of the parishioners of St. Andrew's in Townsend Street chapel, Dublin, on 22 October, Thomas Kirwan in the chair. Resolutions to forward the collection of the Catholic rent were passed. O'Connell does not appear to have been present (*FJ*, 23 Oct. 1824).

2 Pierce Butler (1774-1846), Ballyconra, Ballyragget, Co. Kilkenny, fourth son of eleventh Viscount Mountgarrett; M.P. for Co. Kilkenny, 1832-46; colonel in Co. Kilkenny Militia.

1135

From Emelia Hamilton, Annadale Cottage, Phillipsburgh Avenue, Dublin, 21 October 1824, to Merrion Square

Seeks £100 from the Catholic Association for the publication of her husband's[1] work, *School for Patriots.*

SOURCE : O'Connell Papers, NLI 13647

1 Joseph Michael J. G. Hamilton, a prolific writer of pamphlets. Was praised by O'Connell for his *School for Patriots* (Dublin 1824) in the 1828 edition of this pamphlet. Dismissed from his position in the *Waterford Chronicle* (c. 1827) for his political views.

1136

From Rev. S. Walsh[1]

R. Catholic Chapel, East Lane, Bermondsey,
London, 23 October 1824

Sir,

The place you hold in the estimation of your countrymen, the interest you feel and the prominent part you take in Catholic politics in Ireland will be, I hope, a sufficient apology for the liberty I, an utter stranger, take in thus addressing you. I shall take leave to hope that you will turn your mind a little to the subject of this letter which has nothing for its object but the good of religion in Ireland, and I have hopes that, if it meet your approbation and if you take the matter in hands, it will succeed under your auspices. For, from the respect which I know the Catholic clergy have for you and their grateful acknowledgments of your exertions in the Catholic cause, and more particularly for one of the grandest political measures that has been ever devised to promote and, as I trust, eventually to effect Catholic freedom, I am confident through your suggestion they will promote the object I have in view and which I shall presently explain. But before I do so, Sir, permit me to congratulate you on the present posture of Catholic affairs in Ireland.

A new era has commenced for the people of Ireland, as I must call them emphatically. I mean by this the extraordinary and important change you have caused in the sentiments, in the opinions and in the feelings of the Catholic gentry, and this I consider of more importance in a religious point of view than the Catholic Rent itself. The Catholic Rent is a political matter, but from your example the respectable Catholics all over the kingdom are beginning to study and to know their religion, and the easy consequence will be that they'll practise it too. In fact, Sir, the knowledge of the attachment to and the defence of the religion of Ireland is now become fashionable among respectable Catholics. I rejoice at this exceedingly because I know it has not been the case some years ago. I have myself beheld some skulking from an avowal of their religion and others declaring their disapprobation of some of its principal tenets and condemning the doctrine of exclusive salvation as unchristian and uncharitable, but now it is not the case. It has been reserved for our times and for your name (which by the by I am glad has an O to it) to make a perfect knowledge and defence of Catholic principles fashionable and a matter of pride. I have been delighted, Sir, to hear of the defeat of the Bible missionaries in Ireland, and I have been more delighted to see them defeated by the zeal and talent of the laity as well if not more than that of the clergy. The political horizon and the religious too is manifestly brightening over our country (for I too am an Irishman). Your political affairs are assuming an important and encouraging appearance, but I feel a peculiar gratification as a clergyman fond of my religion to see the interest which the respectable Catholics feel for their religion [and] the zeal and talent they have shown in defending it from the unhallowed encroachments of Bible men and reformers.

This important change you certainly have been the principal instrument in effecting, and you have done so by means of the popularity which a steady, undeviating course of manly remonstrance and patriotic exertion to promote the freedom of millions of your fellow-countrymen, have deservedly acquired for you. The people saw you expose your life—and your eternal life too—to repel an insult offered your religion through you. They saw your sincerity and admired your spirit. These are, in my opinion, the just causes of your popularity and to that popularity is Ireland and its religion indebted for the important improvement I have mentioned.

I hope Sir, you'll pardon this digression. I need not, I am sure, apologize for the freedom of this letter, the principal object of which is to solicit your attention to a few reflections that have occurred to me on the mischievous exertions of the Bible societies in England and Ireland. In the first place, Sir, their principal object, which is confessedly proselytism, the means they employ, the industry and zeal with which they pursue that object, I consider in the light of a dangerous persecution. The noble personages and high characters they have not only to patronize them but to share cheerfully in the drudgery of business, the enormous sums of money which are daily poured into their funds, the union of people of different creeds, their simultaneous and unceasing exertions, all seem to me a combination not only to resuscitate a morient [*sic*] cause but to assail in all possible ways the reviving cause, that of our holy religion. This combination seems to me to be tolerably evident, and no matter who may be its original promoter, whether mundane or otherwise, every Catholic should use all his influence, talent and exertion to frustrate their dangerous designs. My reason for insinuating a supernatural assistance is their deep-laid plan of circulating the Bible in the Irish language among the poorer Catholics of Ireland, for a more dangerous scheme could not be devised. Some may say there can be no danger to religion, that few people can read the Irish language, but I shall say to the one, if there be even a possibility of danger to our religion, as in the Veto for instance, we should use our endeavours to guard against it, and I shall answer the other by appealing to any man who knows the poorer class of Catholics in the country parts of Ireland, for the truth of the assertion that the Irish language is the only language spoken in many parts of the south and that almost every man who can read at all, reads Irish. There are even schools in some parts of Munster for teaching Irish, as I have been told. We all know how fond Irishmen in general are of their own language, even such as cannot speak it, and this attachment is peculiarly discernible among the poorer classes, perhaps not having anything else literary to occupy their minds at leisure hours. A respectable clergyman in the County

Tipperary told me that he offered a poor labourer in his parish 10 guineas for an old manuscript which he indignantly refused though he was at the same time in the greatest indigence. The Bible in the native language is in greater circulation in Ireland than most people are aware of. I have been myself a Catholic missionary in the County of Kilkenny for some years in which county the Irish is by no means so generally known as in others in the south and yet there is scarcely a village in half that county which I knew but had one or other in to read an Irish book for the neighbours on Sundays and winter's nights. I have found Irish bibles in many poor cabins there which were there many months unknown to me or to any other priest, and the very reading a Protestant bible without leave in Ireland renders a man liable to ecclesiastical censures. And yet they were read with more pleasure and more frequently than the Catholic prayer books because they were Irish. You'll be surprised perhaps when I tell you that here in London, where I reside at present, they have distributed thousands of their bibles amongst the poor Irish labourers, and in the discharge of my duties as a clergyman I have found in the house of a poor Irishman 10 copies of an Irish bible which could not be printed under 10s. or 15s. each, and they were given gratis. I have known Irishmen here who never read their own language at home and learned [it] here for the purpose of reading the Bible. I have heard that 2 Protestant clergymen and 2 Methodist preachers have learned the Irish merely for the purpose of preaching to the poor Irish here in their own language.

Now, Sir, in my opinion the most effectual way to meet and defeat this dangerous combination is to get the sanction of the Irish bishop[s] to get the Old and New Testament, but particularly the new, translated into Irish and circulate the parts of it which they deem fit for the perusal of the unlearned, as much as possible amongst the poor. An Irish Catholic version of the Bible is certainly a great *desideratum*. We have a Catholic edition of the Bible, I believe, in every language but our own, and if our own were a barbarous jargon I should not wonder, but [it is] a language to which General Vallancy,[2] and I should say, many European languages are much indebted, a language which all allow is ancient and which every Irishman knows or ought to know, is remarkable for copiousness, strength and poetical elegance. I need not say much to you in its praise for its critical knowledge is, I understand, hereditary in your family. Ireland is indebted to your granduncle, Dr. J. O'Connell,[3] for one of the finest and most pathetic historical poems that has been written in any language. I need not tell you, Sir, that the want of a Catholic bible in our own language is a national disgrace but which you, in my opinion, will be able to remove by representing to the bishops the utility and above all the practicality of the undertaking. There is, I understand, a doubt if Catholic clergymen could be found sufficiently versed in the language. This is a groundless apprehension. Many could be found through the kingdom. There is a professor of the language in Maynooth College who has taught several clergymen, particularly a Mr. S.[4] who translated *Thomas à Kempis* into Irish, a book more difficult to be translated than many other, and the style of which comes nearer to that of the scripture than perhaps any other human composition.

I fear I have trespassed too much on your patience but as the subject is national and religious I hope you'll pardon the intrusion and overlook the trouble I give. . . .

Your very obedient and very humble servant,

S. Walsh

SOURCE : O'Connell Papers, NLI 13647

1 Rev. Simon Walsh, an Irishman from the diocese of Ossory. He went on the London mission 24 May 1824 at East Lane, Bermondsey. He later petitioned to be removed on account of bad health. An Irish language scholar.

2 Charles Vallancey (1721-1812), general in the army and director of corps of Royal Engineers in Ireland, 1803-10; author of many antiquarian works on Irish history, language and literature. See *DNB*.

3 John O'Connell (c. 1700), Gaelic poet; author of *Dirge of Ireland* and *John O'Connell's Confession*.

4 Rev. D. O'Suilloibhain (Sullivan).

1137

From Eneas MacDonnell

15 Duke St., Adelphi, London,
30 October 1824

Sir,

[Thanks O'Connell for complimenting him publicly and making a conciliatory statement about the interruption of their friendly intercourse.[1]] . . .

There is a society here entitled 'the Protestant society for protection of Religious Liberty'. It is the mouthpiece and practical agent of all the discontents and complaints of the Dissenters of every denomination. It is right that you should be apprised that some of its members are very clamorous in their bigotry: others, particularly of the numerous and increasing sects of Independents and Unitarians, are more tolerant and liberal. The chairman of their meeting last year was Lord Dacre[2] and this year, Lord Holland, both eminently liberal.

[MacDonnell suggests that the Catholic Association should give a donation[3] to the above-mentioned society, which could be done] without compromising a particle of principle or an inch of station; but *purporting* to be founded upon your desire to support . . . the great principle of universal religious toleration. . . . I use the word '*purporting*' to be influenced by such disinterested motives because, in fact and truth, I never originated any proposition so entirely selfish in a political point of view. . . .

[MacDonnell then lists the beneficial results which he considers would accrue from making such a donation. They include: 'A probable ground for arguments of defence in Parliament by the Dissenters, particularly the many Unitarians having seats in both Houses'. The Irish in England would be assisted by the moral effect of the donation 'in inducing further contributions to the charitable institutions here to which our poor exiled countrymen are compelled to look up, in many instances, particularly for the education of their youth. . . . There are one hundred and thirty thousand Irish Catholics or descendants of such in London and its vicinity and . . . 110,000 of these are dependent on daily labour for sustenance.'] . . .

SOURCE : O'Connell MSS, UCD

1 At the Catholic Association meeting on 27 October, O'Connell proposed that Eneas MacDonnell be appointed general agent in London of the Catholic Association. In doing so O'Connell mentioned that he had not been on terms of intimacy with MacDonnell for some time (*FJ,* 28 Oct. 1824). At the meeting on the following day the appointment was made (*FJ,* 29 Oct. 1824).

2 Thomas (Brand), twentieth Baron Dacre (1774-1851); M.P. for Helston, 1807; Herts, 1807-19. Succeeded to peerage, 1819.

3 A donation of £20 was forwarded. See letter 1150.

1138

From Edward John Fitzsimons,[1] *39 Mary St., Dublin, 5 November 1824*

(Copy)

Asks O'Connell to censure the editor of his newspaper[2] for libelling the writer's father.

SOURCE : Peel Papers, BM Add. MSS 40,370, ff. 229-30

1 Edward John Bourke Fitzsimons: called to the bar, 1810. Only son of John Bourke Fitzsimons, Dublin.

2 The (Dublin) *Morning Register,* founded by Michael Staunton (first issue 29 Oct. 1824). It was erroneously believed to be owned or conducted by O'Connell and the Catholic Association (Brian Inglis, *The Freedom of the Press in Ireland,* 1784-1841 [London 1954], pp. 167-9).

1139

To Edward John Fitzsimons

Merrion Square, 5 November 1824

Sir,

My opinions upon what are called points of honour are avowed. I never entertain any subject of that kind and most heartily wish I never had.

[Concerning the newspaper][1] in which I have no kind of concern, which is not mine in any sense of the word and for which I cannot possibly incur any kind of responsibility . . .

. . . I would not discuss the point on the score of duelling as I am convinced there is a higher duty than any worldly notions which forbids that practice. . . .

SOURCE : Peel Papers, BM Add. MSS 40,370, f. 231

1 See letter 1138.

1140

From Count O'Connell to Merrion Square

Paris, 15 November 1824

My Dear Daniel,

I heartily congratulate you on the satisfactory prospect the exertions of the Catholic Body of Ireland in vindication of their just claims now exhibit, and I fondly trust the period is not far distant when religious prejudices and jarring interests will melt into an universal feeling for the happiness and prosperity of the country.

I have read in the account of the finance committee of the 3 Nov. that Mr. MacDonnell[1] has been appointed agent to the Association in London, and it has occurred to me that Mr. Baldwin[2] may be employed under him as an *assistant* with some advantage. Some claims he certainly has, nor is he destitute of talents. His acquaintances in London are numerous and I firmly believe his *subordinate* adjunction to Mr. MacDonnell may prove useful. You know he is in want, so much in want that without my assistance he must have starved ere now. If you can procure him any relief without injuring the sacred cause you advocate, let me request you will do so.

Pray what is become of your son Morgan? . . . Indeed, he has taught me not to trouble myself about him. . . .

SOURCE : Fitz-Simon Papers

1 At this meeting the question of what remuneration should be paid to Eneas MacDonnell was discussed (*DEP,* 4 Nov. 1824).

2 Walter J. Baldwin, J.P. (1774-1835), eldest son of James Baldwin, Clohina, Co. Cork, and first cousin of O'Connell. Author of pamphlet, *An Appeal to Common Sense and to Religion on the Catholic Question with a Word on Tithes* (London 1823).

1141

To John Primrose, Jr.

Merrion Square, 9 December 1824

My dear John,

. . . I have been obliged to settle for three years fine to the College[1] amounting to £921.4.2. . . . The year 1823 was so bad that we did not renew and this has been the means of throwing an additional load upon our shoulders at present. . . . The prices have continued high and you ought to be able to make *much* of the lands this year. . . .

SOURCE : O'Connell MSS, UCD

1 Trinity College, Dublin.

1142

To John Primrose, Jr., Hillgrove

Merrion Square [Saturday] 18 December 1824

My dear John,

. . . I would write *first* to my brother James if I had time but I am going '*on the Mission*'[1] to England next Tuesday week at daybreak. . . .

. . . The Catholic rent will surely emancipate us. Press it as much forward as possible, but a repetition of small payments are better than one large one.

SOURCE : O'Connell MSS, UCD

1 The meeting of the Catholic Association on 16 December appointed a deputation consisting of O'Connell, Sheil and Bric (Bric to act as secretary) to proceed to London to bring the Catholic question before parliament. The deputation were instructed to make contact with the Liverpool and London Catholic Associations (*FJ*, 17 Dec. 1824). The deputation did not go (see letter 1151).

1143

From George Ensor[1] *to Merrion Square*

Ardress, Loughall [Co. Armagh, December 1824]

[No salutation]

I am ashamed to *assault* you [about two words illegible] but the people think they have a right to your [? legal services] gratuitously. In their case perhaps my [? friend, Mr. Peter Coleman], P.P.[2] may be excepted. He manfully proclaimed the good tidings from the altar and called on the people to subscribe to the Catholic Rent. Now I hold that to be a *quid pro quo* for an opinion. This is the centre of the fever of Orangism, and so much is my priest in terror that a few days ago when he dined with me he made a circuitous course home and had a guard from my house. I did not know this till the next morning else I should not have let him have gone [*sic*] out that night.

The parish is very willing to go to law and they must do so as the ejectment has been served, but if they have no prospect of success some arrangement must be made with the Orange proprietor. This is one of the chapels which suffered in the confusion. It is now in good order but in the next parish the chapel was prostrated and the people attend the priest in the open air at present.[3] I wish you success on your apostolic tour.[4]

SOURCE : O'Connell Papers, NLI 13647

1 George Ensor (1769-1843), author of many works on politics and religion. See *DNB*.

2 Rev. Peter Coleman, P.P. of Derrynuse, Keady, Co. Armagh.

3 Attached as part of this leaf is a letter dated 18 (?) December 1824 from Rev. Peter Coleman, P.P., to Ensor on the right of the Catholics to the tenancy of the chapel and its grounds.

4 See letter 1142, note 1.

1144

To John Primrose, Jr., Hillgrove

Merrion Square, 21 December 1824

My dear John,

The Attorney General[1] has instituted a *footy* prosecution[2] against me which I think I [*sic*] will blow him to powder but I do not wish my uncle to hear one word of it. . . . Read the [*Dublin*] *Evening Post* for my uncle, taking care to leave out everything connected with this prosecution, and make arrangements with Julia[3] and your uncle[4] that not one word should be said on the subject till you hear further. . . .

SOURCE : Fitz-Simon Papers

1 William Conyngham Plunket.

2 On 20 December O'Connell was charged with having uttered seditious language at the Catholic Association meeting of 16 December. The charge was based on the report in *Saunder's News-Letter* (17 Dec. 1824) of O'Connell's statement: 'He hoped Ireland would be restored to her rights—but, if that day should arrive—if she were driven mad by persecution, he wished that a new Bolívar may be found—may arise—that the spirit of the Greeks, and of the South Americans may animate the people of Ireland!!!' On 3 January 1825 the attorney-general presented bills of indictment to the Dublin city grand jury. The press reporters questioned refused to co-operate, and when Samuel Nolan Elrington, the reporter for *Saunder's News-Letter,* was questioned, he replied that he had been asleep during O'Connell's speech and only wrote what another person had told him. By a majority of 15 to 8 the grand jury

threw out the bills of indictment (*FJ*, 3 Jan. 1825; Fagan, *O'Connell*, I, 319-21).

3 Julia O'Connell, daughter of John Jeffry O'Connell, Ballybrack, Waterville, Co. Kerry. Her mother was of coloured stock. She acted as housekeeper to Hunting-Cap and continued to live at Derrynane until her death about 1890.

4 John Charles O'Connell, whose sister Honoria married John Primrose, Sr.

1145

From Lord Cloncurry to Merrion Square

Torquay, Devon, 24 December 1824

My dear O'Connell,

I have received a letter from London to say that some friends of Ireland of high rank wish to meet you in London and they pay me the compliment of asking me to be of the party. Tell me when you are likely to be in that city and nothing shall prevent my meeting you. Perhaps you will visit Devon. The Cliffords,[1] Carys,[2] etc., of this county are amongst the oldest and most respectable Catholic families of England and have truly Irish feelings.

SOURCE : Dublin Diocesan Archives

1 The Barons Clifford of Ugbrooke Park, Chudleigh, Devon.

2 The Carys of Torr Abbey, Torquay.

1146

From William Cobbett to Dublin

183 Fleet Street, London, 28 December 1824

My dear Sir,

Let me not waste precious time in expressing feelings, in which I only partake with a good *four-fifths of all England*, of admiration of your talents and exertions and of indignation and loathing at the conduct of your malignant, mean and mercenary foes. But let me at once say to you what I hope you will not think impertinent; namely, that I am decidedly for an address 'from the Catholic Association of Ireland to their fellow-subjects, the Protestants of England', but that, for reasons that would make you think with me in a moment, if I could state them *here*, which I cannot, I am very anxious that it should not appear in print *until the Parliament has just met*; and I am equally anxious that I may *see* it before it appear. It should be *short*; it should appear in *every newspaper in England*; and it should appear in all *at one time*. I would give a hundred guineas to *see you* before this thing goes forth. . . . The effect if this thing be done properly will be *prodigious*. You remember the effect of the *Queen's Letter*![1] What we want, and all we want, is to have with us that weighty body the *middle class* in England; and have them we shall if this thing be judiciously done.

God bless you and protect you against your dastardly foes.

W. Cobbett

SOURCE : *NLI, MSS* 15473

1 The letter of 16 March 1820 which Queen Caroline addressed from Italy to the British public demanding to be accorded her rights as queen (*Annual Register*, pp. 129-31).

1147

To Eneas MacDonnell, 15 Duke St., Adelphi, London

Merrion Square, 30 December 1824

My dear MacDonnell,

I am greatly obliged to you for your very kind letter. . . .

I approve highly of your notion of getting a draft of the address to the people of England, and the name of the writer shall remain in just such silence as he himself desires.[1] Apropos, Cobbett has appointed a *beginner* of the name of Scully[2] his agent in Dublin. I believe the creature honest but he looks poor, and it would be cruel to let our valuable, our most valuable friend run any risk of his property amongst us. He will not deem me officious if I interfere on this subject. Find out from him to what extent in value he trusts Scully and I will then ascertain beyond any doubt whether he ought to do so. Take that opportunity or some other of expressing to him my unfeigned respect for his great intellect and deep gratitude for the use he has made of his powers. The only mode I have of showing that gratitude is punishing any attempt at piracy of his works in this country.

The aspect of affairs here is good. We watch every attempt to create Ribbonism or riot and will, I think, secure general tranquillity in spite of our enemies, aye and in spite of our *able friends*. Plunket is detested by everybody in so much that you must not be surprised if the bills are thrown out.[3] I will take your advice and defend myself. I think I will do it coolly. I certainly will do it *strongly*. I am turning in my mind a thousand and one hits at Plunket. It may, I think it *will*, do the cause good to expose him thoroughly. The Grand Jury will be sworn on Saturday but the trial cannot be on before Wednesday or Thursday next. Moore[4] and Vandeleur are the judges, weak men both, but Vandeleur's brother[5] is a candidate for the county of Clare which may check his propensities. Moore affects popularity but has a son *ripe* for *provision*, and in the Church. I can therefore only look to his weakness. There are very many Catholics summoned on the Grand panel but in what order I know not. You may be quite sure I will not flinch. I look upon it that the selection of this foolish prosecution is greatly favourable to us as it shows that they would do more *if possible*. I look upon your being in London as one great cause of the tone of the London papers on this subject. It has had a powerful effect here. We will certainly be before parliament the first day of this sitting. The main petition will be powerfully signed. You will write to me as often as you think I can be of use. I am a bad correspondent but you shall not complain.

SOURCE : Fitz-Simon Papers

1 This 'Appeal of the Catholics of Ireland to the People of England' was drafted by Cobbett and published in his *Political Register* in February 1825. It was signed by Nicholas P. O'Gorman as secretary to the Catholics of Ireland (*Selections from Cobbett's Political Works*, 6 vols. [London 1835], VI, 464-9).

2 Joseph C. Scully, bookseller and stationer, 35 Upper Ormond Quay, Dublin.

3 Bills of indictment. See letter 1144, note 2.

4 Arthur Moore (c. 1764-1846), 7 Henrietta Street, Dublin; M.P. for Tralee, 1797-1800, 1801-02; justice of the common pleas, 1816-39.

5 John Ormsby Vandeleur.

1148

To Eneas MacDonnell, 1 January 1825, from Merrion Square

'I have the pleasure to tell you that the bills[1] *are thrown out* after a deliberation of three hours. So much for my friend, Plunket.'

SOURCE : Fitz-Simon Papers

1 Bills of indictment. See letter 1144, note 2.

1149

From Eneas MacDonnell

London, 4 January 1825

My dear O'Connell,

I rejoice at the termination of the proceedings against you[1] as tending most powerfully to the preservation of the public peace in our country.

I called at the *Globe and Traveller* Office, also at the *Morning Chronicle* office, and on Cobbett. He was quite delighted. . . .

Again and again I implore you to discontinue the proceedings against the *Courier*[2]. . . . I have reason to know that the most fatal consequences would follow your rejection of this advice.

I attended the B[ritish] Catholic Committee, produced your letter and handed it to the Chairman, the Hon. Mr. Clifford,[3] to read. It was received with acclamation. I suggested to Kernan[4] the propriety of passing a vote of congratulation which he immediately did, and it passed with cheers, and will be forwarded to you by Blount.[5] . . .

SOURCE : O'Connell MSS, UCD

1 See letter 1144, note 2.

2 On 16 December 1824 the (London) *Courier* published an editorial attack on the Catholic Association and on Maynooth College. At their meeting on 23 December the Catholic Association decided to institute an action for criminal libel against the *Courier* or the author of the editorial if the newspaper should name him. The action would be brought in an Irish court. They further resolved that in order to gain an acquittal it would be sufficient for the defendant to prove

the truth of the charges against the college (*FJ*, 31 Dec. 1824). The matter on which the action would be based was 'the many *misstatements* respecting the Catholic Clergy and Laity of Ireland, and especially respecting the Royal College of Maynooth' (*FJ*, 12 Jan. 1825).

3 Very probably Hugh Charles Clifford (1790-1858); attended Cardinal Consalvi to the Congress of Vienna, 1814. Succeeded as seventh Baron Clifford, 1831. See *DNB*. The reference *could* be to Charles Thomas Clifford (1797-1870), brother of the seventh Baron Clifford.

4 —— Kiernan, member of the scripture committee of the English Catholic Board. Possibly James Kiernan, a London lawyer.

5 Edward Blount (1769-1843), Bellamore, near Rugeley, Staffs.; second son of Sir Walter Blount, sixth baronet; secretary of Catholic Board from 1822 and later of British Catholic Association. M.P. for Steyning, 1830-32.

1150

To John Smith, London

Merrion Square, 11 January 1825

Sir,

Pursuant to a vote of the Catholic Association of Ireland, I have the honour to transmit to you £20 as a donation from that body to the 'Protestant Society for the Protection of Religious Liberty'.[1]

The amount is small but it strikes me that it derives an importance from the principle on which it was voted. It was voted by Catholics to maintain the rights of Protestant fellow-Christians and upon the principle that conscience ought to be free and that neither force nor fraud should be allowed to interpose to prevent the exercise of that faith which is conscientiously and sincerely believed.

I have always felt a pleasure in the assertion of this principle, and I am, indeed, delighted at the opportunity of communicating with you upon such a principle—with you, whose name is cherished with ardent affection by the people of Ireland. That fine people want, as is admitted, food and fire, clothing and hospitable dwellings—but they do not want kindly dispositions or generous sentiments; and so long as human hearts can throb or the human voice utter words, so long shall your name be repeated amongst us with affection and gratitude. Allow me to say that there is not one who participates more strongly in those feelings than he who has the honour to be, etc.,

Daniel O'Connell

SOURCE : FitzPatrick, *Corr.*, I, 533

1 See letter 1137.

1151

To Eneas MacDonnell, 15 Duke Street, Adelphi, London

Merrion Square, 11 January 1825

My dear MacDonnell,

I enclose you a letter to ' John Smith ' with a £20 bill to his order for an object originally proposed by you. Call on him with it as speedily as you can and let me have *his answer* as soon as possible.

I also enclose you the list you asked for respecting the King's Counsel. It is curious enough. I have made it more extensive than you suggested. I think it would be fair to include the men of my own standing although not my senior—because the silk gown places them now at such an immeasurable distance from me. Every man put over my head has this double disadvantage to me, first in being himself put before me, and next in removing to a greater distance from me everyone who has already been a King's Counsel. For example, I formerly moved and spoke next to Edward Pennefather.[1] Now he moves *hours* before me. His advantage was formerly slight and I could compete with him easily. Now the competition is all to his advantage and yet he is the only man who has more business than me *if* even he does more.

The deputation[2] to England is given up. It was scarcely possible for me to have gone even if the Attorney-General had not interposed,[3] but at present it would be utterly impossible. He was to have been [one word illegible] in great triumph in *the North*. You have no notion of the enthusiasm which the letters contain on this subject. Believe me, the deputation would have been greatly useful. The telling our own story our own way with truth and justice at our side and follo[three or four words missing] the London newspapers [three or four words missing] must have done good. The peers Lord Cloncurry alluded to were Protestant, not Catholic, peers.[4] It is now over but, believe me [one word illegible] must have been greatly useful. With respect to the prosecution against the *Courier*[5] that was in a state not to be given up *at once* when your [? letter] arrived. But the game is in my hand. I can easily get rid of it. In fact, the proprietors of that paper have a full opportunity of avoiding it if they please. They will either take that opportunity or not. If they do, all is well. If not, then they naturally put themselves in the wrong, but in any event I can easily draw off, either in obedience to your advice or by reason of a request *to be made* from Maynooth. In short, the game is in our hands either way. We will have the petitions[6] ready for the first day of the Sessions. On this subject O'Gorman ought to have written to you long since. But you have no notion of the miserable and unnecessary jealousy that I met with on this and other points, but, depend on it, the petitions will be ready for the first day of the Sessions. Your last publication[7] is calculated to do good. Write as often as you can.

SOURCE : Fitz-Simon Papers

1 Edward Pennefather (1774-1847), second son of Maj. William Pennefather, Knockevan, Co. Tipperary. Solicitor-general, January-April 1835, September-November 1841; chief justice of the queen's bench, 1841-46. Presided at O'Connell's trial, 1844.

2 See letter 1142.

3 The charge of seditious utterances. See letter 1144, note 2.

4 Apparently a reference to those 'of high rank' who wished to meet O'Connell in London. See letter 1145.

5 See letter 1149, note 2.

6 Emancipation petitions for presentation to parliament.

7 Probably MacDonnell's (undated) letter to the *Morning Chronicle* of 29 December 1824, in which he defended the Irish Catholic clergy from charges of inciting the laity to acts of violence.

1152

From his brother James to Merrion Square

Derrynane, 13 January 1825

My Dear Dan,

I am sorry to tell you that my poor uncle has been very severely attacked with erysipilas. He is now rid of that complaint but is reduced to a great state of debility, so much so that Dr. Hickson thinks he will be very soon bedridden. In fact in a few days unless his appetite returns which has of late completely failed him, we intend tomorrow to have his bed brought to the large parlour as it is very difficult to carry him upstairs. He is not at present confined to his bed. He is in the most perfect possession of his faculties though he does not seem to think his situation so alarming as it really is. Indeed I regret the parish priest here is not a man very likely to rouse him to a sense of his situation. Dr. Hickson says *at the present* he does not think his life is in any immediate danger. . . .

SOURCE : O'Connell MSS, UCD

1153

From his brother James to Merrion Square

Derrynane, Friday night, 14 January 1825

My Dear Dan,

Though I wrote to you last night and said I would not write again unless there was some change in my uncle's health, I am obliged to do so for the following reason. About an hour ago he sent for me to his room and said he wished to have his will read as he had *some trifling changes to make in it.* I opened his desk and read the will. He then said he wished to leave John Goold,[1] who has been at Derrynane for the last five weeks, an annuity of twenty-five pounds a year during Goold's life and a sum of one hundred pounds, and that he would leave John Charles O'Connell a sum of £100 which was to be in discharge of any claim he had on him for salary as clerk, and a sum of £100 to Julia O'Connell, his housekeeper, which was to be in full discharge of any balance of wages due to her. Goold's annuity is to be charged on John, you and me, *£8.6.8 each.* I told him I would not venture to add any codicil to his will without having legal advice and promised to write to you to send me the copy of a codicil to *merely contain these latter bequests.* He said you were so occupied you probably may delay sending me the draft of this codicil *until it was too late.* I have therefore to entreat of you on receipt of this letter to write to me and to send me a copy of the necessary codicil. However inclined you may be on other occasions to neglect the legal business of your family, I am convinced you will not give *this document a moment's delay.* Indeed it would be unpardonable of you to do so. *My uncle's will* was executed in December

1822. . . . Mr. Tehan,[2] the priest, spent the greater of this day with him, and there never was a human being more resigned than my dear uncle or in more perfect possession of all his faculties. . . . Pray, ought not I recommend to my uncle to forgive the greater part of the arrears due of *his cotter tenants*? Could not this be done by its being marked *as forgiven* in his Rent Book by his directions? Perhaps he would not consent to have this done but I wish to have your opinion.[3] . . .

SOURCE : O'Connell MSS, UCD

1 Unidentified.

2 Rev. Denis Teahan or Tehan (died 1830), P.P. of Cahirdaniel, Co. Kerry, from 1816.

3 Whether O'Connell tendered his opinion is not known. Presumably Hunting-Cap either refused to write off the arrears or, as seems more likely, O'Connell advised taking no action until after the old man's death. The total arrears were then calculated at upwards of £8,000, and O'Connell and his two brothers agreed to remit the bulk of them and collect only £2,500 (this information is contained in an account of Hunting-Cap's assets, O'Connell MSS, UCD). It is very probable that in this way James's proposal to have the cotter tenants treated generously was implemented.

1154

From John Bric to Merrion Square

Cavan, 14 January 1825

My Dear Sir,

Cavanagh[1] has written to you by this night's post and therefore it is not necessary for me to trouble you with what that letter contains. My Lord Farnham and all 'the Gang'[2] are on their best manners—the sensation my very appearance has excited coming as I do from 'the Seditious Assembly'[3] is considerable. I had a hit at the police yesterday. Nothing could be more frank than Lord F. save this, that he wanted me to send up bills of indictment. You'll see the matter[4] reported and please to say whether I ought to urge any and what proceeding.

Mayne,[5] the C[lerk] of the Peace, has spoken to Cavanagh, I presume on authority. It looks as if they were frightened. Deering[6] has been sent for and the case postponed till Monday. There are a number of distinct cases and, notwithstanding the exertions of Chs Cavanagh, the proofs and facts are not as clear and as complete as I would wish, owing to the folly and ignorance of the poor people themselves. The Parish Priest of Killeshandra[7] is strongly for having all parties shake hands after a lecture he read to them. He thinks it may promote the peace of the country, our common object. The police, however, must be excepted, and it strikes me that the cause to be pursued ought to be this. Let all the prosecutions at all sides be withdrawn on this understanding, that as far as the police are concerned, a magisterial inquiry be instituted (settling the time and place) into their conduct in order to ascertain whether they are persons that ought to be kept in the establishment. Mr. Southwell[8] is greatly respected and confided in by the people. He has attended the Bench. Such a bench of magistrates has never been known at Cavan. Mr. Southwell has been just with me. He [one or two words missing] an honest man and a patriot. As to the subject-matter of trial, of course we did not enter into it, he being a mag[istrat]e, but the suggestion we talked on and he agrees with me that if the proposition came from *the parties* themselves it might do much for the peace of the country, but that it ought to come from them. The investig[atio]n of the police to be settled for a certain day. You will perceive the importance of sending even a line in answer by return of post, or Dwyer will write.

SOURCE : Fitz-Simon Papers

1 Charles Cavanagh, attorney, probably of 2 Upper Dominick Street, Dublin. Died 20 October 1862.

2 Presumably the Protestant magistrates.

3 The Catholic Association.

4 The Catholic Association sent Charles Cavanagh (as attorney) and John Bric (as barrister) to the quarter sessions at Cavan to defend some Catholics charged as the result of a riot at a fair at Killeshandra, Co. Cavan, on 8 November 1824. In addition Bric demanded that bills of indictment be sent to the grand jury against police constables for assaulting Nicholas Brady at the fair and for preventing him from attending court to lodge information (*FJ*, 15, 17, 20, 24 Jan. 1825). One Protestant being found guilty and five Catholics acquitted, 'gave unqualified satisfaction to all parties' according to the *Freeman's Journal* of 20 January 1825. Bric stated that, since the (Protestant) bishop of Kilmore and the parish priest of Killeshandra urged conciliation, and since he had received a letter from O'Connell to the same effect, he would not seek any further prosecutions. The *Freeman's Journal* of 24 January 1825 concluded its account of the court proceedings with the statement:

'The prisoners on both sides were now discharged and we understand they left the town as one friendly party on their way towards their respective homes.' Whether legal proceedings were taken against the police is not known. In reporting on the matter to a meeting of the Catholic Association Bric praised the magistrates for their handling of the trials (*FJ*, 21 Jan. 1825).

5 Sedborough Mayne (1777-c. 1828), 9 Belvedere Place, Dublin. A native of Co. Meath; assistant barrister and clerk of the peace for Co. Cavan.

6 John Deering (born c. 1773), 25 Temple Street, Dublin. Called to the bar, 1796.

7 Rev. Patrick McCabe (died 4 Nov. 1840).

8 Robert Henry Southwell (born 1789), Castle Hamilton, Killeshandra, Co. Cavan, only son of Robert Henry Southwell. Called to the bar, 1814. Married 1839 Charlotte, daughter of Rt. Rev. George de la Poer Beresford, bishop of Kilmore, 1802-41.

1155

From Eneas MacDonnell to Merrion Square

London, 14 January [postmarked 1825]

My dear O'Connell,

. . . I did not receive your letter till this moment (4 o'c). I called immediately on Black.[1] You will find in *very few* days a friendly notice of the list you sent. . . . I am most anxious for a discontinuance of the pros[ecutio]n of the *Courier*.[2] Black knows the parties and says nothing would delight them more than its continuance. . . . It would be a feather to me, that might be *of public advantage* to have the discontinuance attributed to me; and whoever else is to be the ostensible party in the matter, I would recommend that you do not introduce Maynooth at any stage of it. I have many reasons for this advice. . . .

SOURCE : O'Connell MSS, UCD

1 John Black, editor of the *Morning Chronicle*.

2 See letter 1149, note 2.

1156

From Eneas MacDonnell to Merrion Square

London, 15 January 1825

My dear O'Connell,

I have been to Kensington this morning. It is most essential that I should be furnished, *as speedily as possible*, with a list of the offices, etc., from which the Irish Catholics are excluded, and setting forth the Act of Parliament upon which each is founded. . . .

I am every day more pleased with my advice that you should not leave Ireland while the Paddy McKew[1] plots are going on. . . . This counteraction and exposure of such machinations[2] has been the greatest triumph over faction ever experienced by the Irish Catholics. It has a most powerful influence here. . . .

The British Catholic Meeting has been fixed for Monday. . . . No peer has made his appearance as yet.

SOURCE : O'Connell MSS, UCD

1 Another name for a Whiteboy or Ribbonman.

2 At the Catholic Association meeting on 8 January O'Connell spoke on 'those strange conspiracies that have agitated the public mind and disturbed the country for some time past'. He saw these activities as the work of *agents provocateurs* employed by opponents of the Catholics (*FJ*, 10 Jan. 1825).

1157

[Very probably] *From William Cobbett*

22 January 1825

My dear Sir,

The *first mode* proposed by you is the best. I will take care that it[1] shall be *in your hands* before the *tenth* of February. For reasons which along with it you shall receive from me, the middle of February or a little later will be the proper time for *effect*. *Rely* upon having and be assured that all will be done in perfect accordance with *every part of your* wish.

SOURCE : *Irish Monthly*, XI (1883), 395-6

1 The draft of a public address. See letter 1147.

1158

From Sir John Sinclair,[1] *Edinburgh, 22 January 1825, to Merrion Square*

Informs O'Connell that he drew up a plan for Catholic Emancipation some years ago which Lord Fingall and Henry Grattan considered sound. Though times have changed since then, he thinks his plan is still substantially sound and will readily send it to O'Connell if he should wish to receive it.

SOURCE : O'Connell Papers, NLI 13647

1 Sir John Sinclair, baronet (1754-1835), son of George Sinclair, of Ulbster, Caithness, Scotland. M.P., 1780-1811. Created baronet, 1786. Prolific writer of pamphlets. See *DNB.*

1159

From his brother James to Merrion Square

Derrynane, 27 January 1825

My Dear Dan,

I received your letter covering the copy of the codicil which has not been executed. John Goold is here and my brother John and I satisfied him we would carry my dear uncle's intentions into effect without giving him the trouble in his weak state of executing any new will. Since I wrote to you, my uncle said he would make the annuity for Goold £40. . . . He desired that his servant man, Michael Dowd, should get £10 a year during his life, all to be paid out of his personal property by us three.

. . . Nothing can be more truly edifying than his [Hunting-Cap's] conduct is. He has Mass celebrated in his room every day. He this moment sent for my brother John and gave directions that his coffin should be made of the oak tree he had cut for that purpose many years ago. We are, of course, determined to have his wake private. That barbarous custom of public wakes is exploded even in Iveragh. My dear uncle's remains will be put into a shell of *the oak*, and that put into a handsome mahogany coffin. The inscription for his tomb has been put on a fine marble flag, everything but the time of his death and age which can be added to it when that melancholy event takes place.

Your third of his personal property will amount to about fourteen thousand pounds, including interest money and rents now due to him, the value of his cows, sheep, etc. Out of this *you must* fast discharge the money I am security for, which is little short of three thousand pounds. I do not in this sum include about £1,050 you owe John and me of the General's money. I think you ought not to set any part of the demesne of Derrynane, Farraniaragh or Scariff.[1] Those lands as dairy farms will be very productive, and having a residence at Derrynane will give you a strong claim for a renewal from Lord Cork, in fact, ensure a renewal to your son as all great landed proprietors set to resident tenants.

SOURCE : O'Connell MSS, UCD

1 These lands, including the residence at Derrynane, were held by the O'Connell family on lease from the earls of Cork.

1160

To the Knight of Kerry

Merrion Square, 28 January 1825

My dear Knight,

We are determined to have railways as well as our neighbours, and the utility of them seems to me so obvious that I have consented to be a director of the *Northern* line.[1] I think this line free of all objection because it does not interfere with the property already *sunk* in the canals. Whatever be the policy of protecting the canals, it is preferable, at least in point of good feeling, not to interfere with them.

This will be handed to you by my particular friend Mr. Roose[2] who goes to London on this business. I beg to recommend him to you in the strongest terms. I have ventured to promise him your kind assistance. I am almost ashamed to tell you how *much* I have told him you would do for him. Of course I would not ask you to do anything but what your own judgement perfectly approved. But there are a thousand helps thro' the House which, if you have leisure to give him some of, will certainly be conferring a most particular and personal favour on me.

SOURCE : FitzPatrick, *Corr.*, I, 92-3

1 Probably the 'Leinster and Ulster Rail Company'. Several railroads were proposed about this time but none was established (Kevin Murray, *The Great Northern Railway (Ireland), Past, Present and Future* [Dublin 1944] p. 1).

2 David C. Roose.

1161

To Eneas MacDonnell, 15 Duke St., Adelphi, London

Merrion Square, 31 January 1825

(Private and confidential)

My dear MacDonnell,

Pray excuse me, I have not *half* a moment to write. There is a *lousy jealousy* about O'G[1] and his friends that mars your utility. I had the thing so settled that O'G would not be able to interfere but you would have had full discretion if he—O'Gorman—remained one week more in the country. But it is vain to talk of regrets.

The petition[2] will be *presentable* by the 10th of February. O'G wrote to Sir Francis Burdett some time ago, a kind of *hurtoturmbo* letter which made no request and required no answer. I was under the necessity of dictating another enclosing a copy of the petition with *a request* that Sir Francis would consent to present it as early as possible in the Session. We will afterwards pour in a volley of petitions on lesser topics. . . .

You must write to somebody, and yet to whom? I cannot reply. O'G would be under the necessity of reading your letter publicly. But I think you had best write to me whatever you intend for our Committee, and to O'G what you intend for the Association at large.

I wish to God I had time to write to you. I have one thousand things to say. The country never was so quiet. If they will allow us we will keep it so. There never was a moment when such a disposition to forgiveness and good feeling to the Protestants existed in the Catholic mind. A perfect conciliation could easily be arranged at this period. It is singularly propitious for grace and harmony. If the ministry were not so foolish as to imagine that dissensions were necessary to the *good government* of Ireland.

[P.S.] We have not yet heard from Sir F. Burdett. See him or write to him.

SOURCE : Fitz-Simon Papers

1 Nicholas Purcell O'Gorman.

2 A petition for Catholic Emancipation.

1162

From Thomas Spencer Lindsey[1] *to Merrion Square*

Hollymount [Ballinrobe, Co. Mayo,
—February 1825]

Private

My dear Sir,

I should long ere this have availed myself of your kind permission of [about six lines illegible] . . . Mr. Domk. Browne,[2] one of our representatives, having written to me and put his name to the requisition, I had a confidential communication with him on the subject and made use of the County political connection there is between him and the [about ten lines illegible] Browne or of his family who at present rule with despotic sway here. I believe from all the information I could collect that their determination was to have met my requisition with a counter one and this by way of ingratiating themselves with what is called the High Protestant Party. I mentioned to you the manner in which I had prepared the plan with Mr. Eneas MacDonnell in London. I wrote to him shortly after [? my] arrival here as soon as I could collect [one or two words illegible] to go upon, what my fears [two or three words illegible] results, and I got a letter from [? him requesting] me to proceed and that the names of all his clients would be cheerfully signed to the requisition and their best endeavours given to have as general and unanimous a petition[3] signed as possible. The very day after I received his letter I found that the Right Honble Denis Browne[4] and his son Mr. James Browne[5] had taken their departure from the country for England. You will perceive immediately that this is a novel mode of giving energy to the requisition, and you will also perceive how secret and studied their plan must have been when they even kept Mr. Eneas MacDonnell in the dark as to the true nature of the result they contemplated, which certainly was not one favourable to the cause we had in view or they would not have absented themselves. I shall not trespass any longer upon your valuable time at present than to say that Lord Lucan[6] and his son Lord Bingham's[7] names with their friends and supporters will appear even at the time agreed upon with Mr. Domk Browne and the requisition, and they have been only hitherto withheld by me, for the reasons above mentioned, from a fear of injuring instead of benefitting a cause which they have much at heart. . . . [about two lines illegible] Lord Bingham will certainly give the electors of this county an opportunity at the next election of exercising their franchises, and I trust and, indeed, hope that *they* will seize it in such a manner as to show their hatred and contempt for empty professions of liberality at the other side of the water, as well as the grossest bigotry and oppression on this.

SOURCE : O'Connell Papers, NLI 13647

1 Thomas Spencer Lindsey (1799-1867), Hollymount, Ballinrobe, Co. Mayo; high sheriff, 1822.

2 Dominick Browne (1787-1860), M.P. for Mayo, 1814-26, 1830-36. Created 1836 Baron Oranmore and Browne (I).

3 On 19 April 1825 Dominick Browne presented to the Commons a petition in favour of Catholic Emancipation from the high sheriff, nobility, gentry and clergy, etc., of the Co. Mayo.

4 Denis Browne (1763-1828), second son of second earl of Altamont and brother of first marquess of Sligo; M.P. for Mayo, 1783-1818; Mount Browne, Westport, Co. Mayo.

5 James Browne (1793-1854), M.P. for Mayo, 1818-31.

6 Richard (Bingham), second earl of Lucan (1764-1839).

7 George Charles (Bingham), third earl of Lucan (1800-1877), styled Lord Bingham until 1839. M.P. for Mayo, 1826-30.

1163

From Earl Fitzwilliam[1]

Grosvenor Sq. [London], 1 February 1825

Sir,

Be so good as to put my name as a Subscriber of ten pounds to the Catholic Association Rent. I will direct my Agent, Mr. Haigh,[2] to remit the sum to you.

SOURCE : Dublin Diocesan Archives

1 William (Wentworth-Fitzwilliam), second Earl Fitzwilliam (1748-1833). Lord-lieutenant of Ireland, December 1794-March 1795. Married July 1770 Lady Charlotte Ponsonby, second daughter of second earl of Bessborough.

2 Haigh was agent on Fitzwilliam's Co. Wicklow estate at Shillelagh, Co. Wicklow.

1164

To John Primrose, Junior

Merrion Square, 3 February 1825

My Dear John,

. . . Place yourself for me entirely at the disposal of my dear brothers. Tell them my wish is to keep plate, linen, furniture, cattle on the demesne, etc., at Derrynane. I feel a peculiar anxiety that I should get all in and about the house at a valuation. My family intend to spend four months of the summer there. See and arrange with your uncle John[1] to stay in charge of everything. . . .

SOURCE : O'Connell MSS, UCD

1 John Charles O'Connell.

1165

From Eneas MacDonnell to Merrion Square

London, 4 February [1825]

Private and Confidential

Dear O'Connell,

. . . You can tell the fastidious O'G that I did not know where to address him, seeing by the papers that you had given up the rooms in Capel Street.[1] Believe me that with *union, temperance and firmness* we will triumph. You will perceive I do not name Sheil. I tell you confidentially I do not think he would do the thing well. His voice, person and poetry would not answer for an exhibition at the Bar.[2] If Lord Liverpool should not answer the enclosed,[3] I will have the matter tried another and less agreeable way. If he answers, you shall immediately hear. *Trust not C. Butler.*[4] *Don't believe one word he says.* He is at this moment endeavouring to make himself acceptable to Canning with whom he was last Sunday morning. He does not know that I know him. I give you this caution because I know that he is endeavouring to entrap you into correspondence for his own purposes. Write but *very briefly* to him and *refer him to me* for information. Send me a copy of whatever letter you write him, for *he will most cer-*

tainly misrepresent you. I shall dine with the rascal tomorrow. He is the falsest, meanest fellow I ever heard of, but *he thinks he is playing me*; time will tell. I have taken two parlours near the club houses, where I see persons on business, at 25 shillings a week. Sir F. Burdett is not to be in town till Sunday. . . . I spent an hour with Lord Clifden,[5] an honest man; I am to meet him in the Lords at 5 to give him an extract from your letter. I wish *you* would read my letter[6] at the Association instead of O'G[orman], and if my conduct were approved it would be of public use to say so. I will demolish the Archbishop of Tuam.[7]

[P.S.] You cannot praise Brougham too much.

SOURCE : O'Connell MSS, UCD

1 In January 1825 the Catholic Association completed the transfer of its headquarters from 4 Chapel Street to the former Corn Exchange Tavern on Burgh Quay.

2 At the bar of one of the houses of parliament in arguing the case for Emancipation or in answering questions before a parliamentary committee.

3 Unidentified, perhaps a letter.

4 Charles Butler.

5 Henry Welbore (Ellis), second Viscount Clifden (1761-1836).

6 MacDonnell's letter to the Catholic Association of 4 February which Nicholas Purcell O'Gorman read to the meeting of 9 February (*FJ*, 10 Feb. 1825).

7 This he had attempted to do on 2 February by writing a verbose public letter to the editor of the *Morning Chronicle* (not published until 16 August 1825) censuring the Protestant archbishop of Tuam, the Hon. Power Le Poer Trench, for his unwillingness to entrust a Catholic priest, the Rev. Peter Daly of Galway, with the distribution of £100 raised by the London Tavern Committee for Relief of the Irish Poor.

1166

From the Knight of Kerry

London, 5 February 1825

Private

My dear O'Connell,

I have received your letter[1] about Mr. Roose and shall attend

I am considerably *mis*reported in the papers as to my speech last night.[2] I can only say that I took the course which appeared to me most judicious [a short word illegible] to Catholic cause, and though misrepresented in the newspapers (unintentionally no doubt) I have the satisfaction to learn that my cause was opposed by Government's zealous friends in the House and that which has proved most embarrassing to Ministers.

SOURCE : O'Connell Papers, NLI 13647

1 See letter 1160.

2 The speech as reported in *Hansard* (XII, N.S., 117-119) is strongly pro-Emancipation, but certain statements, if noted carelessly and out of context, could seem hostile to the Catholic Association.

1167

From William Cobbett

Kensington [London], 12 February 1825

My dear Sir,

. . . Your Association was to send *us* an *address*.[1] NOW is the time for it. The enemy shakes in his shoes. . . . *Certain* it is that the *people* here are dead against the Orangemen. And this thanks to *you* and *me* and *nobody else*. If the whole body of Catholics were to give us golden coaches to ride in and golden plates and dishes to eat off from, they would not do more than we deserve.

But pray send us your promised address. Have it here before the Bill[2] can get half through. I think it can be circulated all over the country *without any expense to you* if your agent manage well; and this would save a great sum. Let 50 copies of it be printed VERY CORRECTLY on *slips of paper* and sent over to him. He ought instantly go in person and deliver one copy to *each daily paper in London,* apprising the editor of each that he has *done this* with regard to *all* the daily papers. They will *all* publish it: they *must.* If they should not (which is next to impossible) you shall see what a game *I will play with the vagabonds*. . . . Then . . . *ten* of *each* of the daily papers [should be sent] to my shop in Fleet Street. Thence *I will have them dispatched to every country newspaper in England and Scotland*. . . . As to the *Register*[3] it is most likely that it cannot have the address *till it has been out a week or more*. . . .

I have heard and from *good authority,* that even many of the great *Orange Proprietors* are not only for Emancipation but for a total putting down of the *Church Establishment in Ireland*. One of them . . . said 'That it would be *better for them* if the *present incumbents* had half the value of their benefices *settled on them for life* for that they would really *get more* than they now get and that the *estates* would all be secure and the country at peace and *fit to live in.*' . . .

I cannot conclude without beseeching you to be *bold in your address to us.* For God Almighty's sake do not suffer your thoughts to be *castrated*! More depends upon this one circumstance than you have any idea of. The people are *now* just in the mood *to hear you.* The THING trembles at the *brewings* of the French and the Holy Alliance. Hit the THING hard while it is soft.

SOURCE : Fitzpatrick, *Corr.,* I, 94-5.

1 See letters 1147 and 1157.

2 The bill for the suppression of the Catholic Association (see letter 1173, note 4).

3 His (weekly) *Political Register.*

1168

To his wife

Shrewsbury, 16 February 1825

My darling Heart's Love,

We had rather a rough passage to Holyhead. We slept at Bangor. Started this morning at five, and arrived here before seven this evening. We had eight in and on the Landau. Our party consists of Sir Thomas Esmonde, Hugh O'Connor, Mr. McDonnell[1]—a young gentleman of fortune from Sligo or Mayo—Mr. Sheil, Mr. Kirwan[2]—the gentleman who speaks at the asso-*she*-ation—Fitzsimon[3] and myself, with my servant James. . . . We have *at present* no account of the division against us but the numbers who support us *will* be small. We have read Monday's debate, and if you get Sir Jas. MacIntosh's speech with the Latin quotation at length,[4] get Maurice to translate it for you as there is a compliment in it for a certain little cocknosed woman of my acquaintance whom, after all, I most sincerely love. Our neighbour North[5] made a virulent speech against us, so did that long blockhead Doherty.[6] Nothing could be more indecent than Brownlow,[7] Dawson[8] and the rest of the gang. We have little to expect from such a crew of miscreants. However, it is not in their power to injure us much. We intend to have a recess in London and to make speeches *at* those who speak against us in Parliament. We will, I think, make a sensation and I hope in God do some good. Of course you know that I risk nothing in point of personal encounter. I say this to dissipate any apprehension which you in former times would entertain; and as to any prosecution, there is not in England the least possible danger of that. It is not possible at present to say how long we shall be detained in London. It *will* be as short as I can make it without injuring or deserting the business which has at present torn me from you, my own sweetest, dearest darling. It is a sacrifice—certainly a great sacrifice—and you must not be angry if I meet nothing but ingratitude in return. No man should ever expect gratitude from the public. I wish to God I could make my motives so pure and disinterested as to care little for gratitude or applause. Write to me, sweetest—you whom I do care for—write to me every day, and get my girls and my son *also* to write to me. Beg of Maurice[9] to attend to Catholic affairs—to get forward as many petitions as possible and from as many counties. Let him announce every day at the committee of the Association that he must make to me a daily return of the number of petitions. Let a book be got, and in it the names inserted of five or six to manage the petitions of each county; and let those persons be called on every day to make a report of what they have done to send forward petitions. If there be zeal enough in petitioning, we shall yet be safe. At all events, our motto is 'God and our native Land'.

SOURCE : FitzPatrick, *Corr.* I, 94-5

1 Unidentified.

2 Thomas Kirwan.

3 Christopher Fitz-Simon (1793-1856), Ballinamona, Co. Wicklow, and Glencullen House, Co. Dublin; M.P. for Co. Dublin, 1832-37. Called to Irish bar, 1821. Clerk of the crown and hanaper, 1837-56. Son of Thomas Fitz-Simon (1760-1800), Glencullen House, and Margaret, daughter of Bartholomew Callan, Osberstown House, Naas, Co. Kildare (she later married Thomas O'Mara, 1806). Married 1825 Ellen, eldest daughter of O'Connell.

4 Sir James Mackintosh, Knt. (1765-1832), M.P. for Nairn, 1813; Knaresborough from 1818. See *DNB*. In the Commons debate on the bill to suppress the Catholic Association he praised O'Connell

with the phrase *summi honores, res familiaris amphissima, uxor probatissima* (the highest honours, the more suitable domestic arrangement and a highly approved wife).

5 John Henry North.

6 John Doherty (1783-1850); M.P. for New Ross, 1824-26; Kilkenny city, 1826-27; Newport, Cornwall, July-December 1830. Solicitor-general, 1827-30. Chief justice of the common pleas, 1830-50.

7 Charles Brownlow.

8 George R. Dawson.

9 His son.

1169

To his wife

London, 18 February 1825

My darling Love,

. . . This day we arrived here at half after one. . . . On our arrival we dressed and proceeded to Sir Francis Burdett with whom we had a long conference. He is an elegant gentleman but there is an English coldness about him. I have since had half an hour's conference with Mr. Denman. I like him much. We then went to the House of Commons, *into which* and under the gallery Kit Hutchinson conducted us with the permission of the Speaker. I saw him, the Speaker,[1] measure me with his glass. Many of the members shook hands with me, amongst the rest Tom Ellis. After sitting a short time we have come out to dinner. There is a smart debate expected on presenting several petitions this evening. My opinion of *the honourable house* is greatly lessened by being in it. I do not suppose we shall be heard as counsel. It is said that if we are heard it will principally be from a motive of curiosity. The fact is, they are always careless about Ireland till they want us. I wish the time were come when they wanted us, the scoundrels! . . . Alderman Wood[2] got himself introduced to me; he has the air of an honest man, cordial and frank.

SOURCE: *NLI, MSS* 15540

1 Charles Manners-Sutton (1780-1845), speaker of the House of Commons, 1817-34. Son of archbishop of Canterbury. Created 1835 Viscount Canterbury.

2 Alderman Mathew Wood.

1170

From his wife to care of Colonel Fitz-Simon, No. 18 Bury St., St. James's, London

Dublin, 18 February 1825

My dearest love,

I trust before this time you and your travelling companions are arrived quite safe and well. You have had most delightful weather, the good wishes and prayers of your country, and I trust and hope you will return triumphant to us. I hear you are to be met on landing here with banners borne by some of the most respectable of the citizens followed by the people. . . .

You will of course have some communication with Colonel Fitz-Simon.[1] You should ascertain exactly what he will do for his nephew[2] and I must again impress on you, darling, that I will retract my consent if a jointure of £400 a year is not settled on Ellen and £500 in case she has no children. I also consider £5,000 a very handsome fortune with such a girl as my Ellen, and no sacrifice should be made by her family inconsistent with their interest or her establishment in the world. In short, darling, should matters not appear to you as you expected or as you think I would approve of, be careful not to commit yourself beyond the power of *redemption*. Ellen has a good deal of good sense and, though she likes Mr. F., should anything occur to put a stop to the business, she would be quite satisfied to accede to your wishes and mine. In truth she would not do anything but what we should approve of. . . . Tell me how you like [Maurice's] speech.[3] *Tell* me candidly. Forget I am his mother. Your bust is finished. Mr. Summerville[4] asked me to allow him to publish it under my patronage but without your consent I told him I could not act. He also asked me to take a bust gratis from him. To this I also referred for your permission but I could not get off from putting my name at the head of the list of subscribers (of which there are many) for the bust. You must, my own love, answer for me to Mr. S who sets out for London early in the next week. Take care of my letters but, above all, take care of yourself. . . . Is it possible you will be away a month?

SOURCE : O'Connell Papers, NLI 13651

1 Lt. Col. James Henry Fitz-Simon (1767-1829), Bury Street, St. James's, London, son of Christopher Fitz-Simon (1735-1812), Glen-

cullen, Co. Dublin. A sous-lieutenant in Dillon's Regiment in France he transferred during the revolution to Pitt's 'Irish Brigade' and remained in the British army (65th Foot) until his retirement.

2 Christopher Fitz-Simon.

3 At the Catholic aggregate meeting in Townsend Street chapel, Dublin, on 15 February, Maurice denounced the bill for the suppression of the Catholic Association and made a strong personal attack on John Doherty, M.P. for New Ross, for his speech in the Commons in support of that bill on 10 February.

4 Unidentified.

1171

From his daughter Kate to London care of Colonel Fitz-Simon, 18 Bury St.

Merrion Square, 20 February [postmarked 19] 1825

My dear Father,

As Mama has not time to write to you she has kindly consented to let me be her secretary and I hope you will be content with me. . . . How very interesting the debates have been but how clearly our friends are in the right! Such a foolish display as Brownlow made! I hope you won't take Brougham's advice and give the petition back to Plunket. . . . Mama desires me tell you that she *commands* you as you love her to write to the poor General (if you have not done so already) to tell him of his brother's death. . . . Maurice made a very good speech at the meeting which I suppose you have heard.[1] He desires me tell you he will attend to your directions. He was at the Association yesterday and got the five pounds for the child[2] as her uncle is content to pay the rest: she is to go to the convent in a few days. He also desired me say they were getting on very fast with the petitions. . . .

Are not you very glad we have one week of Lent over? I hope you won't fast too much, remember your life and health are not only precious to us but to your country. How I envy those who travel with you on my chosen seat, the box, but I hope we shall travel many a merry mile this summer. I have been laid up ever since with my strained foot. . . .

SOURCE : Kenneigh Papers

1 See letter 1170, note 3.

2 Unidentified.

1172

To his wife

Cooke's Hotel, Albemarle Street [London],
21 February 1825

My darling Heart,

You are before this apprised that we are not to be heard at the Bar of the House. We were in the House under the gallery during the debate of Friday. It was dull and prosy enough in all conscience. Peel was civil but very malignant to the Catholics. He made a powerful use of the letter[1] to Hamilton Rowan, but certainly we enabled Brougham to have much the better of it in his reply. It was an able speech but to tell you, darling, the honest truth, *you* would prefer certain orators, one of whom shall be nameless, to the talkers of the great house. The Solicitor-General is a blockhead.[2] Mr. Attorney-General[3] *no great things*. Mr. Wynn,[4] who belongs to the Cabinet, is just one of the worst speakers I ever heard. He somewhat resembles McNamara[5] of the county of Clare, who 'forgot to omit' something. You have no notion of what a stupid set they are altogether, and even our friends are not as zealous as we did expect. There is an English coldness; and after all, what is it to them if we are crushed? We yesterday waited on Sir Francis Burdett who met us in company with Brougham, Hobhouse,[6] Abercrombie, Sir John Newport and Jas. Grattan.[7] They have resolved to present the grand petition this night and to fix a day for its discussion.[8] We are to dine to-day at half after three and to be in the house till late. Sir Francis Burdett improves much on acquaintance. Brougham is a manly plain man; Abercrombie is a Chancery lawyer in great business and represents the high Whigs; Hobhouse appears to me to be a direct-minded, honest man. I spent an hour with Cobbett and was greatly pleased with him. He is a bold clear-headed fellow, and his views are distinct and well intentioned. I confess, darling, I have been pleased altogether with this trip. Mr. Sheil, McDonnell and I went this morning with Lord Althorp,[9] who is son to the Earl Spencer, one of the wealthiest and most influential peers. We receive every compliment imaginable. Crowds of peers and parliament men pouring in upon us. I am made the 'spokesman' of every meeting. I have no doubt but this visit will do 'the cause' some good if it were in nothing else but in showing us what a base and vile set the House of

Commons is composed of. Darling, this is a long dissertation on politics. Be assured I will take care of my Nell,[10] my sweet Nell. Do leave that to me.

SOURCE : FitzPatrick, *Corr.*, I, 97-8

1 This was a letter of appreciation to Archibald Hamilton Rowan from the Catholic Association in acknowledgement of his subscription of £5 and congratulatory letter (*FJ*, 25 Nov. 1824; A. H. Rowan, *Autobiography* [Dublin 1840], pp. 400-13). In the Commons on 18 February Peel described this letter to Rowan, an attainted traitor in 1798, as an example of the seditious inclinations of the association (*Hansard*, N.S., XII, 567-75).

2 Sir Charles Wetherell (1770-1846), solicitor-general, 1824-26; attorney-general, 1826-27, 1828-29, but dismissed from office because of his opposition to Catholic Emancipation; knighted, 1824; M.P. almost continually, 1812-32. See *DNB*.

3 Sir John Singleton Copley, Kt. (1772-1863), attorney-general, 1824-26; master of the rolls, 1826-27; created April 1827 Baron Lyndhurst; lord chancellor, 1827-30, 1834-35, 1841-46; chief baron of the exchequer, 1831-34. M.P. for Yarmouth, March-June 1818; Ashburton, 1818-26; Cambridge University 1826-27. See *DNB*.

4 Charles W. W. Wynn (1775-1850), M.P. for Montgomeryshire, 1799-1850. President of the board of control, 1822-28; secretary of war, 1830-31. See *DNB*.

5 Probably Major William Nugent McNamara.

6 Sir John Cam Hobhouse, second baronet (1786-1869), M.P. for Westminster, 1820-31; secretary for war, 1832-33; chief secretary for Ireland, March-May, 1833; president of the board of control, 1835-41, 1846-52; friend and executor of Byron; created Baron Broughton, 1851. See *DNB*.

7 James Grattan (1783-1854), Tinnehinch, Co. Wicklow, eldest son of the statesman, Henry Grattan. M.P. for Co. Wicklow, 1821-41. See *DNB*.

8 Owing to illness Sir Francis Burdett was unable to present the Catholic petition (a petition of the Roman Catholics of Ireland) for Emancipation to the Commons on 21 February (*FJ*, 25 Feb. 1825). He presented it on 1 March and proposed a motion that the House take into consideration the laws against Catholics and whether it would be expedient to alter them. The motion, which was seconded by Lord Duncannon and opposed by Goulburn, the chief secretary for Ireland, was carried by 247 to 234. In consequence, it was ordered on the same day that a bill to effect this purpose be brought in (*Commons Journal*, LXXX, 142-5).

9 John Charles (Spencer), styled Viscount Althorp (1792-1845); M.P. for St. Albans, 1806; Northamptonshire, 1806-35; leader of Whig opposition, 1830. Succeeded as third Earl Spencer, 1834. See *DNB*.

10 His daughter.

1173

To his wife

London, 22 February 1825

My darling Love,

. . . The Duke of Norfolk, Lord Stourton[1] and some others were with us this day to arrange a public meeting on Saturday next where all the talkers are to declaim, amongst the rest your humble servant, whom you must call the worst of all. I was for an hour with the 'sour Sectarian'[2] of the *Morning Chronicle* and had a most pleasant conversation with him. The deputies this day unanimously resolved to invite over the bishops at once. I was commissioned to write to them, and did so accordingly. They will be here before the debate on our petition.[3] We were in the house last night during the debate on the second reading of the bill.[4] It was the most dull and stupid thing imaginable. One scoundrel—a Sir Edward Knatchbull[5]—said that he voted for the bill because I had by my influence *quieted* a district in Ireland which he said was dangerous!!![6] I did not get to bed till after one this morning, and was not up this day until after ten. Only think of that, sweetest!—but rejoice, my darling, cocknosed, sweetest, saucy, best of women—there is a long name for you!—but rejoice, for every member of the House says 'asso-she-ation'.[7] Mr. Brougham says it most distinctly, and at both sides it is the universal pronunciation. So you triumph over us all. We are to get a great dinner from Brougham on Sunday; the Duke of Devonshire[8] is to entertain a batch of *us*; we are to get a great dinner from 'the friends of civil and religious liberty'. There will, I think, be a great aggregate meeting of Westminster and probably another in the city of London. My own opinion is that the Catholic Cause has gained ground greatly and that all it requires is an active perseverance. It is vanity to be sure, but *we,* darling, are equal to the rascals in everything, to say the least of it. I rejoice at your victory about asso-she-ation, but I confess I cannot help being sorry that my darling girls are defeated.

Maurice *did* make a good speech but he should not imitate his father's faults by being so personal.[9] Let me know if there be anything which I ought to write about and which I do not. I wish I could be more detailed. I will endeavour in future to send you a regular journal. Tell me what says my sweet Dan to the world. What does he think of his father's absence? I promise you, darling, not to be so long in bed of a morning in future; but it will console you to know that I never was in better health or in better spirits.

SOURCE : FitzPatrick, *Corr.*, I, 99-100

1 William Joseph (Stourton), eighteenth Baron Stourton (1776-1846); a contemporary of O'Connell at Douai.

2 John Black.

3 See letter 1172, note 8.

4 The bill to suppress the Catholic Association, its official title being 'A Bill to amend certain Acts relating to unlawful Societies in Ireland'. It was introduced by Henry Goulburn, the chief secretary, on 15/16 February and received the royal assent on 9 March as 6 Geo. IV c. 4.

5 Sir Edward Knatchbull, ninth baronet (1781-1849), Mersham Hatch, Kent; M.P. for Kent, 1819-31, 1832-45; succeeded as ninth baronet, 1819.

6 Knatchbull argued that it was dangerous that any man should be able to exercise such power through an organization (*FJ*, 25 Feb. 1825).

7 His wife's pronunciation of the word.

8 William George Spencer (Cavendish), sixth duke of Devonshire (1790-1858).

9 See letter 1170, note 3.

1174

To his wife

Cooke's Hotel, Albemarle Street, London
22 [and 23] February 1825

My own and only Love,

. . . Yet, sweetest Mary, I could have wished to see one line also in that handwriting which gives me recollections of the happiest hours of my life and still blesses me with inexpressible sweetness and comfort when we, darling, are separate. All the romance of my mind *envelopes* you, and I am as romantic in my love this day as I was twenty-three years ago when you dropped your not unwilling hand into mine. Darling, will you smile at the *love letters* of your *old* husband? Oh no—my Mary —my own Mary will remember that she has had the fond and faithful affections of my youth and that, if years have rolled over us, they have given us no cause to respect or love each other less than we did in early life. At least, darling, *so* think I. Do not smile either at the mere circumstance of not getting a letter making me somewhat melancholy. It is *so* cheering to my heart to hear from *you*—it is *so* delicious to me to read what you write that indeed I cannot but feel lonely when I do not read your words.

23 February 1825

I was hurried out yesterday before I could finish my letter to you—I mean this letter—I wrote, however, from the tavern where we dine. I yesterday went to the House of Commons after dinner but, finding from Sir Francis Burdett that he would present the petition on Tuesday next when he makes his motion on its merits, I left the house and soon came home. This morning *soon after eight* I was called by James[1] to see young Mr. Cobbett,[2] and accompanied him to his father. I found the family at breakfast. Cobbett has got the Westminster folks to bestir themselves, and we shall have a meeting, an aggregate meeting in the open air, to which I will have a chance of expressing my sentiments fully. There is also to be a meeting of the Livery of London. No person can attend but a Livery man, and therefore I am to become a Livery man—in other words, a freeman of London. I believe I am already a Pattenmaker of this City. Only think that you are a Pattenmaker's wife. I will make Pattens, I suppose, all the rest of my life. It will be a great opportunity to harangue on Ireland's want and woes. The Catholic meeting is to take place on Saturday in the Freemasons' Hall. Sheil and I are to speak. I am sorry to tell you that I must speak badly. After I came in from Cobbett's we attended in St. James's Street for two or three hours—we *meet* all inquirers there in a room at the Thatched House Tavern, it is called. We had a deputation of the English Catholics to settle with us as to the form of the petition to be presented to the House of Lords.[3] We dine on Saturday at Lord Stourton's. On Sunday at Brougham's to meet the Dukes of Sussex and of Devonshire, &c. We are asked for Sunday, the 6th of March, by the Duke of Norfolk. There is a better chance of Emancipation certainly by our having come over. We are certainly working on the English mind. I calculate on opening an agitation shop here quite exclusive of my pattenmaking! Believe me, darling, I would soon carry the question if I did. Tell my children, my darling children, how tenderly I love them. Tell Maurice I trust to his prudence and care of everything. A little law reading and a little earlier rising would do him no harm.

SOURCE : FitzPatrick, *Corr.*, I, 100-2

1 His man-servant.

2 William Cobbett (1798-1878), eldest surviving son of the celebrated journalist, William Cobbett.

3 See letter 1175, note 3.

1175

To his wife

London, 24 February 1825

My darling Heart,

Every arrangement is made for the English Catholic meeting on Saturday. The Bishop of Norwich[1] sent Sir Henry Parnell to me to beg I would let myself to be introduced to him. Of course I complied and will see the bishop tomorrow. I am to be examined before the Committee on Irish affairs[2] on Tuesday next. I can tell them some facts and give them more theory. I was working all day to get up a meeting of the Livery of London, and I am myself now a freeman of that City. We are getting on pretty well amongst ourselves, but Finn seems to me to be more easily displeased than anybody else. I believe I will go to *the House* this night although the interest is nearly lost in that quarter. I have determined to make a long speech at the Catholic meeting, but my anxiety is great so that I have every reason to fear that I may not speak well. I am obliged to go to the House of Lords to see Lord Donoughmore.[3]

SOURCE : FitzPatrick, *Corr.*, I, 102

1 Henry Bathurst.

2 On 17 February the Commons set up a committee to inquire into Irish affairs. It included Goulburn, Peel, Thomas Spring Rice, Sir Henry Parnell and William Wrixon Becher (*Commons Journal*, LXXX, 72).

3 On 24 February Lord Donoughmore presented the petition from the Catholics of Ireland for Emancipation to the House of Lords (*FJ*, 28 Feb. 1825).

1176

To his wife

London, 25 February 1825

My darling Heart,

I wrote part of a letter at the hotel this morning but unfortunately was summoned before the Committee for Irish Affairs[1] where I spent the far greater part of the day. I was examined on various points: increase of the peasantry in numbers, state of the peasantry, titles to lands, registry of freeholds, freehold tenures, expenses of law proceedings, civil bill courts, manor courts, civil bill ejectments, and I am to be examined again on Tuesday. It consumed a great part of the day and was *therefore* inconvenient. I was this morning with Sir H. Parnell to visit the Bishop of Norwich.[2] A fine, lively old gentleman he is. He is full of his anxiety for Catholic Emancipation, and I pray God he may live to be a Catholic himself. Nothing else has occurred to tell you, darling, and I believe you have more regular information on the subject of Catholic affairs than anyone else. The fact is, darling, that the Catholic cause has certainly advanced in spite of its enemies. It is daily gaining ground and gaining it in the best way upon the popular mind. The people are becoming better informed on the subject of the Catholic claims and Catholic religion. Depend on it, darling, that the fact is as I tell you. Peel was in the room during a great part of my examination this day. Sir Henry Parnell was the principal person who examined me, next to him Spring Rice. Vesey Fitzgerald asked me several questions, Lord Ennismore[3] a few, Capt. Maberley[4] a few. It is probably vanity but I thought they were struck with my evidence. Lord Milton[5] asked me some pertinent questions. He is eldest son to Lord Fitzwilliam. Lord Althorp also asked me questions. Nothing could be more civil and polite than they were all of them to me. You will smile when you see my evidence. . . . How sorry I am that you and my family are not here about me, my own, own darling love. I heard from Primrose this day. All well in Iveragh. I think I will have an excellent habitation for you at Derrynane. The back part of the house was rebuilt about five years ago and is quite capable of being raised one storey which will easily give three additional bedrooms.

SOURCE : NLI, MSS 5759

1 See letter 1175, note 2.
2 Henry Bathurst.
3 Richard (Hare) (1773-1827), eldest son of first earl of Listowel (created 1822). Styled Lord Ennismore from 1822. M.P. for Co. Cork, 1812-27.
4 William Leader Maberly (1798-1885), son of John Maberly, M.P., Shirley House, Surrey; M.P. for Westbury, 1819-20, Northampton, 1820-30; Shaftesbury, 1831-32; Chatham, 1832-34. Surveyor-general of the ordinance, 1831-32; commissioner of the customs, 1834-36; married 1830 Catherine Charlotte (novelist), daughter of Hon. Francis Aldborough Prittie, M.P., of Corville, Co. Tipperary.
5 Charles William (Wentworth-Fitzwilliam) (1786-1857), styled Viscount Milton until 1833 when he succeeded as third Earl Fitzwilliam. M.P., 1806-33.

1177

To James Sugrue

London, 25 February 1825

My dear James,

I suppose O'Gorman[1] has sent his dispatches regularly. He is certainly very attentive and from MacDonnell[2] we have constant and great assistance.

I wish to communicate to you and to my friends who are many in the Committee my notions on the present posture of our affairs, not, however, to be printed but to be used in their discretion. In the first place the Parliament—the packed Parliament—is quite and irretrievably against the Association partly owing to the English hatred of everything Irish and partly arising from the ignorance of the English members and the shameless audacity of those from Ireland in stating all manner of lies. In the next place much of the English press . . . has assailed us with all manner of ribaldry. Sterling,[3] who writes the leading article in the *Times,* the man who wrote letters under the signature of *Vetus* some time ago in defence and praise of the Wellesleys both at home and abroad. *His nephew*[4] is in office in Ireland under Lord Wellesley. I tell you these facts that the Committee may not imagine that the English mind is against us merely because that paper which in general is indicative of public feeling is against us. *Thirdly* the opposition generally and in particular the leaders of it are greatly and warmly with us. There is a good deal of manoeuvring in *other* ranks in order to postpone and put off the discussion. I believe and indeed am convinced that if I was not here the discussion of our petition would have been postponed till *after* Easter. I suppose you are already apprised of the details, and if Mr. O'Gorman has not sent them, you yourself can learn them from my wife to whom I write of course daily, and communicate them to the Committee. Fourthly, *the people are with us*, believe me they are. I have been hard at work in the City and in Westminster to stir up the popular feeling. I saw Cobbett soon and have seen him often and privately. . . . I believe Plaice[5] and Nicholson[6] and others who stir up the City of Westminster and a strong party in the City of London are working for our benefit. It will cost me probably £40 to bring about one great public meeting, and I have found that by paying £39.19.0 I could be a Liveryman of London which I am at this moment, being a most excellent 'Patten Maker'. If I had been able to go into the City again this day I should have completed everything for the meeting of the Livery of London to petition for us. I have gone to several of the workingmen of a middle class and, while others of the deputation were complimenting—as they ought to do—great folks, my study has been directed towards the middling classes. . . .

The men I reason with the moment I get over their prejudices so as to be able to shove them off the stage, become sincere friends. I am quite vain of my success and I think I may venture to promise greater. It is, however, *here* that the great battle is to be fought. I must take a missionary trip to England every year until Emancipation is achieved, if indeed it can possibly be deferred. Canning's friends are most anxious for the postponement of the discussion. He first threatened to send home North, Doherty and many Irish *friendly* members. That has not succeeded. He next sowed dissension amongst our supporters in the Commons. That also has failed although a powerful ally of the Grenvilles spent an hour with me this evening to get me to consent to a postponement. My reply was why postpone till [Remainder of letter missing]

SOURCE : Dublin Diocesan Archives

1 Nicholas Purcell O'Gorman.

2 Eneas MacDonnell.

3 Edward Sterling (1773-1847), educated Trinity College, Dublin; cor-

respondent of the *Times* under signature of 'Vetus', later 'Magus' and 1830-40 as 'The Thunderer'. See *DNB*.

4 Unidentified.

5 Francis Plaice (1771-1854), 'the Tailor of Charing Cross Road'; radical reformer and agitator; very active in Westminster elections. See *DNB*.

6 Unidentified.

1178

To his wife

Cooke's [Hotel], Albemarle Street, London,
28 February [1825]

My own, own Love,

I have succeeded, love. I was sincerely afraid of a failure: I know well that you were not; but, darling, my mind is at ease. I have, I may tell you, succeeded. I had the meeting[1] as cheering and as enthusiastic as ever a Dublin aggregate could be. Lavalette Bruce[2]—the Bruce who assisted at the escape of Lavalette—was there. He is a fastidious but fashionable person and has carried my fame through the fashionable clubs. In short, the thing has gone off infinitely better than I did or could expect.

On Thursday I was in the House of Lords an object of some curiosity. The Duke of Leinster was civil to me but not in the manner mentioned in the newspapers.[3] Indeed, he was very civil. I wrote to you on Friday. I take up the Journal with Saturday. On that day the meeting was held; it was full but not crowded: you have seen the report of the proceedings. Write a line to Staunton[4] to tell him that the best report of my speech is in the *Morning Herald* of this day. . . . I beg of him to print that report. We dined on Saturday at Lord Stourton's. He contrived, by asking me to help him in carving, to place me between him and the Duke of Norfolk, where I was feasted and flattered to the highest degree. Lord Stourton said that neither Pitt nor Fox was my equal. Charles Butler said that since the days of Lord Chatham[5] he had heard nothing like me. So, darling, I was vain enough, and I thought of the sweet little woman I belong to and what a sweet kiss she owes me.

After Mass yesterday . . . we had a meeting with Sir Francis Burdett, Mr. Brougham, Lord Milton, Mr. Abercrombie, Sir John Newport, the Knight of Kerry and Spring Rice. A long discussion arose on the petition,[6] and everything was arranged for its presentation and debate tomorrow. There was displayed the greatest zeal and anxiety for our success by all the members. I am quite satisfied with their sincerity. We are in great expectation of carrying the measure in the Commons.

I then dined with Mr. Brougham. There were of our deputation present Lord Killeen, Sir Thomas Esmonde, Hon. Mr. Preston, Sheil and myself. We had four Dukes—the Duke of Sussex, of Devonshire, of Norfolk and of Leinster; Sir Francis Burdett, Sir Henry Parnell, Mr. Scarlett[7] and the leading Whig lawyers; Alderman Wood and Mr. Lambton, son-in-law to Earl Grey. I was placed between the Dukes of Devonshire and Leinster, and opposite to the Duke of Sussex. He (the Duke of Sussex) is certainly very zealous in our cause, but, darling, I do not like him although he was very kind and courteous to me. He has a great deal of the German trooper about him, and yet his star and single golden garter have an air that strikes one. I was again most flattered, and Brougham spoke to me warmly of the reports that reached him of my speech.

This day I spent principally with Plunket. Lord Killeen and I were with him twice and had much conversation with him on the great question. He was much for the Veto but I believe we beat him a good deal out of that and carried him the unanimous protest of the deputies against that measure. He spoke of my being able to do immense good, and I assured him that I was as much disposed as man could be to use that power in order to do good. Darling, you will think that my head is half turned with all these flatteries. But the cause, the sacred cause, certainly gains ground daily. We are winning our way with the people and with the House, in spite of Peel and the Orange faction. I am glad I came over, at all events, because I feel that we have accomplished much towards exciting a proper sentiment in England, and with the blessing and assistance of God we will do much more.

Darling, direct to me here and while I remain send Maurice[8] to get the papers directed to me here. I am proud of my Maurice. Let him, however, check his propensity to personality, which in him is the more dangerous because it has an hereditary source. I am proud of him, notwithstanding. My sweet fellow will do, if he pleases to exert himself.

SOURCE : FitzPatrick, *Corr.*, I, 103-5

1 On 26 February a Catholic meeting was held in Freemason's Hall to consider petitioning the House of Lords against the bill for the suppression of the Catholic Association, the duke of Norfolk in the chair (*MC*, 28 Feb. 1825).

2 Michael Bruce (1787-1861), grandson of Sir Michael Bruce, sixth baronet. With John Hely-Hutchinson (later third earl of Donoughmore) and Robert T. Wilson he rescued Marie Chamans de Lavalette on 20 November 1816 from prison in Paris. A supporter of Napoleon during the Hundred Days, Lavalette was under sentence of death.

3 'Mr. O'Connell's appearance below the Bar of the House of Lords last evening excited a good deal of attention. . . . Lord Liverpool went round to the Duke of Leinster, apparently for the purpose of having Mr. O'Connell pointed out to him. His Grace took a very conspicuous mode of acceding to the request which caused no trifling sensation, for shortly after he walked down the Bar and shook the learned gentleman by the hand in the most cordial and affectionate manner' (*MC*, 25 Feb. 1825).

4 Michael Staunton, now editing the (Dublin) *Morning Register*.

5 William Pitt, the Elder, earl of Chatham (1708-1778).

6 The Emancipation petition presented on 1 March by Burdett. See letter 1172, note 8.

7 James Scarlett (1769-1844), son of Robert Scarlett, Duckett's Spring, Jamaica. M.P. for Peterborough, 1819-30; Malton, 1830-31; Cockermouth, 1831-32; Norwich, 1832-34. Knighted, 1827; chief baron of the exchequer, December 1834-44. Created Baron Abinger, January 1835. See *DNB*.

8 His son.

1179

To James Sugrue

Cooke's Hotel, Albermarle St., London,
2 March 1825

My dear James,

I believe I may venture to say that *we are to be emancipated*. The tide has turned in our favour, and the reaction of the injustice done us has contributed much to our *promised* success.

I cannot write more today on politics but I am in the highest hopes. I *believe* Lord Liverpool will take up the question. More tomorrow. I got your letter yesterday but could not answer it till now. Tomorrow I will write to you again, and at length. . . .

SOURCE : John O'Connell, *Recollections,* II, 102

1180

To his wife

4 March 1825

My own darling Heart,

I am now writing to you from the Committee room of the House of Commons where I am waiting to be examined.[1] I am literally more harried here than in Ireland, because I dine out and, being kept much longer out of bed, I cannot rise until after eight. Sheil was examined yesterday at great length, and a most comical examination I am told it was. You cannot, love, see the examinations in the newspapers until after they are published by the House—that will not be for some weeks. Now, my love, I have the happiness to tell you that Emancipation is, I believe, at hand. The opposition to it is, I believe, dissolving fast. Indeed, I am *sure* it is. Yesterday I spent principally between Sir Francis Burdett on the one hand, and Mr. Plunket on the other. Plunket has been very kind in his manner and language to me, and I believe and am sure he is quite sincere in his desire to emancipate the Catholics in the most conciliatory manner possible. He will have no veto—no arrangements but what our own prelates desire. A provision will be made for our Clergy[2] which, by the by, will be so much the better for the friars as it will leave almost all the individual donations *free*.

Darling—darling, since I wrote the word ' free ' I have been under examination. Call my children together—tell Danny to fling up his cap for old Ireland. I have now no doubt but that we shall be emancipated. A great Orangeman from the north—Sir George Hill[3]—but his name should not appear in print—has just announced that a number of the English supporters of the Ministry are going in a body to Lord Liverpool *to insist* that he should no longer oppose Emancipation. Tell Maurice to go off with this information to James Sugrue and to Cornelius McLoghlin. Let him not name Sir George Hill because he is not the only member of Parliament to whom the intelligence may be traced. But he should announce *the fact.* I am tomorrow free to write to both those persons and I will fully. How anxious I am that the bishops were here! Doctor Murray has not an hour to lose. Darling, go to him yourself in your carriage and tell him I respectfully solicited his immediate coming. I wrote to him myself yesterday. In short, we have won the game. May I thank Heaven that it was your husband, sweetest, that won it. If I had not been here, nothing would have been done. I *forced* Sir Francis Burdett to bring on his motion. My examination this day related to everything connected with the Catholics in Ireland—the people, the Church, the friars, the priests, the Jesuits, &c. Colonel Dawson, the brother-in-law of Peel, again assured me I had done away many prejudices of his. My own, own heart's love, I am sorry to remain away from you but, darling heart, it is necessary. Blessed be the great God for it all will be right. The suppression of the Association will work wonders. Own darling, I am in the greatest spirits, and I love you the better for that. I forgot to speak of the great charity dinner[4] yesterday. I presided, and you cannot *think* what a shaking of hands I got from the ladies after I came out of the chair. Do not be jealous, darling, you have, *I believe,* no occasion. Lent agrees with me admirably. I have got an old Douay acquaintance as my *story bearer.*

SOURCE : FitzPatrick, *Corr.,* 106-8

1 By the Commons committee on Irish affairs (see letter 1175, note 2).

2 A reference to the proposed legislation for the state payment of the Catholic secular clergy in Ireland. On 29 April the Commons resolved by 205 to 162 to make such a provision. The resolution was not implemented. On 22 April Edward John Littleton presented to the Commons a bill to regulate the exercise of the elective franchise in counties at large in Ireland, that is, for the disenfranchisement of the forty-shilling freeholders. The bill was withdrawn by Littleton on 27 May.

These two measures were known as the 'wings' and were intended as qualifications of the Emancipation bill. They were no longer of relevance once the Emancipation bill was rejected.

3 Sir George Fitzgerald Hill, second baronet (1763-1839), M.P. for Londonderry city, 1802-30. Appointed a lord of Irish treasury, 1806· vice-treasurer of Ireland, 1817. Governor of St. Vincent, 1830, and later governor of Trinidad where he died. Married 1788, Jane, daughter of John Beresford, M.P., commissioner of revenue.

4 The anniversary dinner of the East London Catholic Institution a Freemason's Hall, O'Connell in the chair (*FJ,* 8 Mar. 1825).

1181

From Wm. Hickie[1] to Dublin

Lisbon, 5 March 1825

Dear Sir,

Enclosed you will find a Draft on London for £93.11.4 being the amount of subscriptions to the 'Catholic Rent' paid in this city.

The annexed list of subscribers comprises nearly all the British subjects here, professing the Roman Catholic Religion, amongst whom are several gentlemen of high respectability and great wealth.

Their object was not so much to add to a fund, likely to be extensive, as to mark their confidence in the 'Catholic Association' and their sympathy with its honourable exertions for the attainment of equal Rights. . . .

[A part of the letter is the list of subscribers—some fifty—virtually all being Irish names.]

SOURCE : Dublin Diocesan Archives

1 William Hickie (died 9 April 1855) of Cork and Lisbon. Married 6 November 1813 Bridget (first cousin of O'Connell), fifth and youngest daughter of James Baldwin of Clohina, Cork, by Mary, daughter of Donal Mor O'Connell of Derrynane.

1182

To his wife, Merrion Square, Dublin

'Cookes', Albermarle Street [London, 7 March 1825]

My own darling,

Only think that I *this day only* got your letter of the 3d of March. Darling, you *ought* to write to me every day. While I am here I implore of you to do so.

Yesterday we dined at the Duke of Norfolk's. We had four Dukes — Sussex, Norfolk, Devonshire and Leinster — four Earls, Fitzwilliam, Grey, Shrewsbury and Donoughmore, four barons, Clifford,[1] Stourton, Arundel[2] and Nugent,[3] two lords by courtesy, Killeen and Duncannon, two baronets, Burdett and Esmonde. I was placed between the Duke of Devonshire and Earl Grey. I had no notion of such splendour. There were from two to three thousand pounds worth of new plate purchased for the occasion besides all the old family gold and silver plate. The house[4] is magnificant. Splendid suite of rooms, splendidly furnished, and one of the dining-rooms, that in which we dined, is said to be as handsome as any in England. It was the house in which George the 3d was born. It was impossible to have everything more *majestic* altogether but your husband is lost *by flattery*. You cannot think how everybody says that it is *I* who am carrying emancipation, that it will be carried this sessions I look on as nearly certain.

Tomorrow, darling, I will write to the General,[5] please God. Depend on my making an arrangement complete with Col. Fitzsimon. Every day I like his nephew[6] more and more. The bracelets will, I understand, cost upwards of £50, that is, sixteen guineas each for the setting and about seven guineas for the drawing the miniature. That makes *close* on fifty pounds Irish, but, darling, if I possibly can I will do what you wish about them. Perhaps if I could get my picture painted here we could get them set cheaper in Ireland. I have, darling, no political news to give you this day. The Duke of Sussex was particularly attentive to me yesterday, and I liked him better perhaps on that account than I did the first dinner. Earl Grey is a cold man in his manner but of high principle. To descend from him to Jack Lawless, we have your friend Jack Lawless foaming upon two things, first that there is nothing really to *complain* of about securities in point of religion and secondly that the 40s freeholders are likely to be extinct. Jack affects great patriotism on this subject, and although Sir Francis Burdett's opinion is against him, he would hardly allow Sir Francis to speak on the subject. You cannot well conceive any thing so rude as his manner was to Sir Francis. . . .

SOURCE : Fitz-Simon Papers

1 Charles (Clifford), sixth Baron Clifford of Chudleigh (1759-1831); educated at Douai, St. Omer, Bruges and Liège.

2 James Everard (Arundell), tenth Baron Arundell (1785-1834), married 1811 Mary Anne, only daughter of first marquess of Buckingham. The only Catholic peer who voted against the 1832 Reform Bill.

3 George (Nugent-Grenville), second Baron Nugent of Carlanstown (I) (1789-1850). M.P. for Buckingham, 1810-12; Aylesbury, 1812-32, 1847-50. Lord of the treasury, 1830-32.

4 Norfolk House, St. James Square, London.

5 His uncle, Count O'Connell.
6 Christopher Fitz-Simon.

1183

To his wife

Cooke's, Albemarle St. [London],
8 March 1825

My own love,

. . . I have just been with Cobbett. I walked out to him about a couple of miles and back. I never was out on a finer day—just verging on being too hot but delightful. How my girls would have relished the walk with their fond father if my Kate's, my sweet darling Kate's foot was quite well. I wish I had that foot in my bosom to warm it into health for she is the sweetest, tenderest child that ever blessed a fond father. I had an agreeable *talk* with Cobbett. He talks well and manfully. Perhaps you think that your husband also talks well but that is all vanity in you, sweetest darling. You like to be thought the wife of *a great man*. And now to feed that wish I tell you I dined yesterday with Mr. Frederick[1] and Lady Barbara Ponsonby[2] in St. James Square. She is the lady whose popish ponies Tom Moore in the *Twopenny Postbag* talks as leading the late Princess Charlotte[3] into the horrors of popery.[4] We had *only* one duke—of Norfolk—only two earls, Grey and Bessborough, but then we had a Marquis of Lansdowne, the senior peer sitting in Parliament being, I believe, the 35th Baron of Lixnaw, Sir Francis Burdett and the Knight of Kerry were there. I spent a pleasant evening talking to Sir Francis. Only think that earls are now become so familiar to me that I left out Earls Fitzwilliam and Sefton.[5] I like the latter much. He is a manly, honest, ugly man. Ask Betsey[6] whether he be not an earl. We had members of the Commons like garnish to a dish to complete the table. I dine this day with a rich Popish merchant, Mr. Lonergan,[7] and tomorrow with Mr. Wilks, the Secretary of the Protestant Dissenters.[8] On Thursday with the Duke of Devonshire. I have not as yet drawn our act of parliament[9] but I will finish it for tomorrow, I hope. I am just going to the House of [Remainder of letter missing.]

SOURCE : Kenneigh Papers

1 *Recte,* Hon. William Francis Spencer Ponsonby (1787-1855), son of

third earl of Bessborough, created 1838 Baron de Mauley; married 1814 Lady Barbara Ashley-Cooper.

2 Lady Barbara, wife of Hon. William Francis Spencer Ponsonby and daughter of fifth earl of Shaftesbury.

3 Princess Charlotte Augusta (1796-1817), daughter of George IV and Caroline of Brunswick.

4 Thomas Brown the Younger (i.e., Thomas Moore), *Intercepted Letters or The Twopenny Post-Bag* (London 1813), pp. 1-5.

5 William Philip (Molyneux), second earl of Sefton (I) (1772-1838), M.P. for Droitwich, 1816-31. Radical in politics. Created 1831 Baron Sefton of Croxteth (U.K.).

6 His youngest daughter.

7 Probably of the firm of Lonergan & Co., 3 Austin Friars, London.

8 John Wilks (1776-1854), M.P. for Boston, Lincoln County, 1830-37. Hon. secretary of Protestant Society for Protection of Religious Freedom for twenty years. See *DNB*.

9 The Emancipation Bill which Burdett introduced to the Commons on 23 March (*Commons Journal,* LXXX, 253). In a public letter to the Catholic Association on 7 March 1825 O'Connell said it had been 'permitted to me to draw the rough draft of this Bill, in which I am engaged and hope to have it ready on Wednesday next' [9 March] (*FJ,* 10 Mar. 1825). This bill was passed by the Commons but on 17 May rejected by the Lords.

1184

To his wife

Cooke's Hotel, Albemarle Street
[London, 10 March 1825]

My own darling Love,

I got this day your letter of Monday and an excellent one from my dear Maurice.[1] I am, love, greatly pleased with his exertions. He is doing well and manfully but should avoid altogether personal attacks to which he has unfortunately an *hereditary* propensity. I am indeed proud of our dear fellow and hope he will make a distinguished and patriotic Irishman and above all a *good* Catholic. I wish my sweet fellow would think of that now in his bloom of life. It would for many reasons afterwards *come easy to him*. Darling, I was yesterday examined by the House of Lords[2] on many points and I believe I have made an impression there also. Indeed I am told I have. Only think that somebody said I was the only person fit to be

Lord-Lieutenant of Ireland!!!, I knew so much of everything. Lord Liverpool would be *pleased*, I think, at Emancipation. His examination of me was very courteous, and you will be surprised to hear that the Duke of Wellington[3] was even kind. I was examined for four hours at least and they say that they have not gone through one half of the examination nor probably one third. If so I am [? in] for two days more, Friday and Tuesday.

I dined yesterday at a Mr. Wilks'. He is the agent of *all* the liberal Dissenters, if liberal I can call them. We had Bowring[4] who was imprisoned a short time ago in France bringing over letters to members of the opposition. Buckingham[5] who was driven out of India for daring to print his thoughts. Dr. Collyer,[6] a dissenting clergyman of the first rank. Dr. Morrison,[7] a Protestant missionary to China. Parkes,[8] who wrote the Chemical cathecism, and some others of the high Dissenting party. Today we dine with the Duke of Devonshire. I hear from all quarters that my examination before the Lords has done great good already. Indeed, love, we are fast winning our way. It is scarcely doubted even by our enemies and not at all by our friends that Lord Liverpool and the Duke of Wellington will support us. Mr. Peel threatens to resign and it is said he will carry his threat into effect, but Lord Eldon not only sticks fast himself but very strongly urges Peel to continue in office voting against the measure to be sure but submitting dutifully to the wisdom of Parliament. What a triumph! What a prospect of doing good to poor Ireland! Oh, if we had English wealth pouring in upon us as it ought to do, what comforts would our poor people enjoy compared to their present misery. Darling, it would be a proud thing to be instrumental in doing so much good. Brownlow,[9] Dawson[10] and I are great friends, personal hostility is totally ceasing and I think a general Irish peace may soon be proclaimed. I have written to the poor General by a Mr. Bellew,[11] one of our delegates who went off for Paris this morning. . . .

Send a note to Hutton's to know how much extra he will charge me if I go home by the mail and leave his carriage here at his coachmakers. Let me have an answer to this question, darling, by the return of the post because, sweetest, I am weary of London and glory and long for the sweet society of my wife and children. . . . I am weary of being absent from you and I feel the Swiss *malade du pays*, as they call it. . . . I shall have another interview, I hope, with Plunket before dinner.

I am *returning* to do good in various ways to Ireland. Pray to God, darling, to prosper the good work.

SOURCE : Fitz-Simon Papers

1 His son.

2 On 10 February 1825 a select committee was appointed to inquire into the state of Ireland with special reference to disturbances there (*Lords Journal,* LVII, 29-30).

3 Arthur (Wellesley) (1769-1852), created duke of Wellington, 1814; son of first earl of Mornington. Chief secretary for Ireland, 1807-09; prime minister, January 1828-November 1830 and November-December 1834.

4 John Bowring (1792-1872), poet, linguist and pamphlet-writer. First editor of the *Westminster Review*; M.P. for the Clyde burghs, 1835-37; Bolton, 1841-47. Knighted, 1854. See *DNB*.

5 James Silk Buckingham (1786-1855), newspaper editor, author and traveller; established the *Calcutta Journal*. M.P. for Sheffield, 1832-37. See *DNB*.

6 Dr. William Bengo Collyer (1782-1854), minister of the Congregational church and religious writer. See *DNB*.

7 Dr. Robert Morrison (1782-1834), Protestant missionary to China. Established Anglo-Chinese College at Malacca for missionary training, 1818. See *DNB*.

8 Samuel Parkes (1761-1825), manufacturing chemist and scientific writer. See *DNB*.

9 Charles Brownlow, M.P.

10 George R. Dawson, M.P.

11 Unidentified.

1185

To his wife, Merrion Square, Dublin

London, [Monday] 14 March 1825

My darling love,

I seize with rapidity one *moment* to indulge my heart by writing to you, my sweetest Mary, and to transmit to you the overflowings of the tenderness of my fond heart. Since I wrote on Saturday we have been engaged in the dry details of the bills.[1] The Bishops[2] are here. The machine is working well in all its parts and carrying us on daily to Emancipation. It is indeed cheering to think on the prospects of carrying this great measure in a manner which will leave our religion untouched whilst it not only increases our liberties but at this moment will actually inundate Ireland with English capital. I have, sweetest, done much to attain this desirable object and, believe me, I expect nothing in return but ingratitude, but I am, sweetest, not the less happy.

Now, love, send off Maurice to Mr. McNevin. His name is Daniel McNevin,[3] a Galway Attorney. He lives in one of the Gardiner Streets. You knew his lady in France. Let Maurice bid him write to me as soon as notice of trial is served in the Kirwan cause and if he does that he may be quite certain of having me at Galway. . . . The bishops are here and to them the question of a provision for the clergy is of course referred. It would bring about £250,000 a year of English money into Ireland. The stipends are said to be intended at £1500 a year for an Archbishop, £1000 a year for a Bishop and about £200 a year for each parish priest, with indeed three rates of salary for the Catholic Clergy [about one word illegible] third order. Darling there is not to be the least interference of the Crown with any kind of appointment in our church. The truth is there never was anything conducted on a more fair and rational footing with perfect attention to all our feelings and opinions. . . .

SOURCE : Fitz-Simon Papers

1 The Emancipation Bill and the suggested provision for the clergy.

2 Five Catholic prelates from Ireland were examined by the select committee of the Commons: Patrick Curtis of Armagh, 22 March; Oliver Kelly of Tuam, 22 and 23 March; Daniel Murray of Dublin, 22 March and 17 May; James W. Doyle of Kildare and Leighlin, 16 and 18 March; James Magaurin of Ardagh, 25 March. Those examined by the select committee of the Lords were Curtis, 24 March; Kelly, 26 April; Murray, 24 March; Doyle, 21 March and 21 April.

3 Daniel McNevin (born c. 1786), 8 Middle Gardiner Street, Dublin; only son of Thomas McNevin, Gort, Co. Galway, and Elizabeth Walsh.

1186

To Edward Dwyer[1]

London, 14 March 1825

(Confidential)

My dear Sir,

I have been so busily employed this day on Catholic affairs as to be totally unable to write to or for the Association. I have however, prepared four resolutions which Mr. O'Gorman[2] will send by this post as suggestions for the Association, but it will be better, I think, to adjourn till Friday in order to give the gentlemen in Dublin, who take a part in the proceedings, time to deliberate on their resolutions—and to give me time—which I have not this day—to state my reason for its being necessary to vest the funds in a single individual. That, however, is my decided opinion. If Lord Killeen declines the task, the Association must fix on somebody else; but *in an individual* it must be vested. With this and some few differences of a similar nature, there will be no difficulty in working the Catholic cause—if it shall be necessary hereafter to work it further. But I have great happiness in saying that I do not think it will—nay, I am perfectly convinced that Emancipation *must* take place this session. In fact we are now working the *manual* labour of it. The drafts of the Bills are nearly ready—that for mere Emancipation is out of my hands.

This letter *must not* be printed. You will, however, from it procure the Association more full details as to the termination of their labour than have been hitherto stated. I mean as to the mode of expressing our submission to this new law without injuring the cause.

The bishops are here, and to them is referred all questions as to the acceptance of a provision,[3] and the details of such provision if accepted, which without Emancipation could not possibly be.

Everything is most cheering. Several of us will go tomorrow to the Duke of York's Levée. Take care that this letter is not printed. But tell everybody that Emancipation is *certain and speedy*.

[P.S.] My next letter will arrive on Thursday. I think you should have a meeting of the Committee ready for the arrival of that post, before the last meeting of the Association is opened. You should make provision for paying Mr. O'Gorman for his time here. His expenses he calculates at about £70. Mr. Sheil should also be paid his expenses, and for his time. I, of course, will never accept one shilling. Again, *let not this letter be printed*. Let no man even speak of paying me either my expenses or anything else to me.

SOURCE : FitzPatrick, *Corr.*, I, 108-9

1 Edward Dwyer (1767-1837), permanent secretary to the Catholic Association, 1825-29. From 1829 until his death O'Connell paid

Dwyer £300 per annum privately out of his own pocket (*Pilot*, 20 Oct. 1837).

2 Nicholas Purcell O'Gorman.

3 One of the ' wings '. See letter 1180, note 2.

1187

From Henry Brougham, Northern Circuit, Lancaster, 14 March 1825

Expresses apprehension concerning the proposed Emancipation Bill. [The paper is so damaged by decay that the letter is now almost illegible.] The only meaningful passage is the following: 'But I fear they [the Catholics] and I hate absolute power in different degrees. They are very forgiving and would fain be on friendly terms with power. I am suspicious and distrustful, as is my duty, of all power, all executive power especially.'

SOURCE : Fitz-Simon Papers

1188

To his wife, Merrion Square

London, 15 March 1825

My own sweetest love,

I have now the happiness to tell you that all is going on well, right well. The Cabinet ministers are at work, and within a week I expect resolutions of *both* houses in favour of Emancipation. These resolutions are to precede the bill. . . .

Darling, I must conclude. Having written the foregoing before I went out—I was at the Duke of York's levée and was received with the greatest kindness. He even joked with me on the advantage my profession gave me in my long examination before both houses. . . .

SOURCE : Fitz-Simon Papers

1189

To Edward Dwyer

London, 15 March 1825

My dear Dwyer,

For the information of the Committee of the Catholic Association—but not to be printed, I give the following opinion.

1st. All the purposes for which the Catholic Rent was collected remain perfectly legal notwithstanding the recent Bill for the Suppression of the Association. Indeed it would be *impossible* to render those purposes illegal without creating great confusion. They remain untouched.

2ndly. Although the purposes of the Catholic Rent remain quite legal, yet these purposes cannot now be carried into effect by any society, Committee or body of persons of a more permanent character than for the space of fourteen days. There must not now be any connection between any two bodies of persons thus acting either by communication when the plan is different or continuation in point of time from one period of fourteen days to another.

3rdly. The purpose of the Catholic Rent as *already* collected may however be carried into effect by any one person acting fairly and *bona fide*. But then such person, although he may get as a gift the present Catholic Rent for the present purposes, cannot be rendered responsible to any body of persons—and two individuals constitute a body of persons.

4thly. It follows therefore that the only legal disposal of the Catholic Rent that can now be made is by vesting it in some *one* individual of such integrity and honour as to be a sufficient assurance of the faithful and delicate execution of the confidential character which such a donation naturally requires. It is perfectly plain that if Lord Killeen will accept this donation we shall have such an individual as we could desire.

5thly. It will be distinctly understood that in my opinion it is utterly impossible to appoint any *guardians* of the fund or, in short, more persons than one. You cannot possibly *combine* a second person with that one. It would be in all cases desirable that there should be several combined for public purposes to manage the money, but that would now be an unlawful combination—and we must not in any way violate the law.

6thly. The collection of the Catholic Rent should immediately cease in all quarters. It is to be hoped that our present prospects preclude all fear of its being necessary to resort again to any such measure; but should such necessity arise, means can be found to meet the occasion, and that without violating the law.

Everything is going on as well as possible—better cannot be. The plan of our bill has been changed by *one* of the Cabinet Ministers. We thought to have a bill read this week. It is now deemed more expedient to pledge *both the Lords* and the Commons to the measure in the first instance. Accordingly resolutions will again be submitted to the Commons and carried there probably by more than one hundred majority—perhaps 150—and then submitted to the Lords, when there will either be no division or a majority with probably of about twenty, perhaps more. The *bills* will then be brought in and no doubt exists of their being carried. Mr. Lawless had indeed published a furious tirade in the *Herald* this morning calculated to do extreme mischief here and to raise a flame in Ireland.[1] I look upon his conduct as very wrong, and in saying this I use milder language than the occasion justifies. He does not in fact belong to the deputation. I freely forgive him the base motives he attributes to me such as the selling the people for a silk gown. I would undertake to demonstrate that my journey here will be a loss altogether of £2,000 to me, and *this* is my recompense.

P.S. Just come from the Duke of York's levée. We were received with the greatest courtesy, I would indeed call it kindness if condescension were not the fittest name from the Royal personage. I am quite pleased.

SOURCE : FitzPatrick, *Corr.*, I, 109-11

1 Lawless's letter, dated 13 March, is published in the *Freeman's Journal* of 18 March. He attacks O'Connell on the grounds that he has accepted the disenfranchisement of the forty-shilling freeholders and a provision for the clergy in a manner likely to lead to their corruption by the government.

1190

To his wife, Merrion Square

London, 16 March 1825

My own, own Love,

. . . Send to Mr. McNevin[1] and bid him write to me *on Friday night* if he wishes me to be in Galway at this ensuing assizes. Darling, we are indeed cheered here by all that happens notwithstanding the ripple in the current created by John Lawless. . . . Darling, they forget what a triumphant thing Emancipation would be. They do not recollect the advantages of getting rid of the triumph of Orange insolence.

SOURCE : Fitz-Simon Papers

1 Daniel McNevin, attorney.

1191

To his wife, Merrion Square

London, 17 March 1825

My own darling Heart,

. . . I did intend to buy Ellen a watch here, but I find I can get one for her as cheap in Dublin as in this city but the chain and seals are more handsome here and accordingly I will take them with me and add the watch when I arrive in Dublin. I *will* arrange everything, you may rely on it, with Col. Fitz-simon.[1] Depend on that, my own darling. With respect to the Catholic cause everything goes on well, extremely well. We have completely subdued the force of our enemy and gained a victory over their inclination to oppose us, but strange to say, darling, the present delays and dangers spring from our friends. They are, to tell you the truth, jealous of our allowing our question to be carried by a portion of the ministry. It is surprising to see what a miserable spirit of wretched jealousy they have put in motion. The two last days have been consumed in endeavouring to conciliate our former friends. Heaven help us into what strange shapes is our cause drawn. That miserable maniac Lawless has served them as a pretext for disunion. But, darling, do not be one bit uneasy—*the game is won*—it is only the manner of playing it that makes any difference. How I smile at the folly which surrounds me. Darling, they think themselves great men, but the foolish pride of your husband would readily make him enter into a contest with them. I have not the least fear of being *looked down on* in Parliament. This is miserable vanity—but, darling, it means that I have a poor opinion of them and a greater one than I ought of myself. Tell each of my children of my fondest love. I never was so hurried as I am here. Dr. Doyle was examined yesterday and he has made a most powerful impression in our favour. Again, darling, tell each of my children of their fond father's love.

SOURCE: Fitz-Simon Papers

1 Lt. Col. James Henry Fitz-Simon.

1192

To his wife

London, 18 March 1825

My darling heart,

I told you several letters ago that I dined with the Langdales. Kit Fagan,[1] my old College companion, is here. He is a colonel in the company's service. . . .

I wish, darling, I could afford to be a member of parliament but I cannot and therefore have no regrets on *that* account. Yesterday I sported a flaming shamrock and dined at the City of London tavern at the grand dinner.[2] You will see an account of it in the papers. The best report of it will be found in the old Times, and that paper contains an account of the violent conduct of John Lawless which, in fact, put an end to the meeting. I was extremely well received both by peers and people. It is impossible to be better received than I was. I have been this day at a meeting about the Poor Laws at which I was forced to make a speech on the Irish Catholic Clergy and poor people. It is a novelty in London to hear them praised. With respect to *our cause* all is going on admirably. The bills are prepared. Plunket remains to move them—that is, 'the Clauses', as they are called. Everybody now admits that we must succeed. That point is gained in public opinion decidedly. The tone of opposition has quite subsided. It is strange darling what a revo[lu]tion we have made. I am quite settled to leave this on Monday and have *therefore* broke up a dinner party which was actually arranged to be given us on that day. Fitz-simon has been *commanded* by Ellen[3] to sit for a bracelet miniature and therefore I cannot find him to go to his uncle[4] to make our final arrangements, but they shall be made tomorrow, depend on that. . . . I can . . . start after Mass on Sunday *which* will take me easily on Monday morning to Galway.

. . . As yet everything that has occurred has been matter of triumph and unmixed exultation without one single circumstance to mitigate the gradual progress of our triumph. Darling, tell each of my children of my most sincere affections. Tell them how I long to press them to my heart. I go back to you, thank God, in triumph and with victory.

SOURCE : Fitz-Simon Papers

1 Christopher Fagan, son of John Fagan of Kiltallah, Co. Kerry. Colonel of an infantry regiment in East India Company.

2 The annual dinner of the Benevolent Society of St. Patrick, Lord Londonderry, its president, presiding. The *Morning Chronicle* of 18 March says, 'During the dinner the party at the head table were much amused by a bottle of genuine (illegal) poteen, neat as imported from the Emerald Isle; being handed to the Chancellor of the Exchequer who, forgetting the good of the Revenue in the good of his palate, put a portion of the naughty liqueur in his glass and drank it with becoming devotion.'

3 Christopher Fitz-Simon and O'Connell's eldest daughter, Ellen.

4 Lt. Col. James H. Fitz-Simon.

1193

To James Kiernan,[1] 18 March 1825

Apologizes for not being able to meet him on Monday (21 March) since all his friends must leave town on that day.

SOURCE : O'Connell MSS, UCD

1 Lawyer, London.

1194

From his son Maurice

Merrion Square, Friday, 18 March 1825

My dearest father,

We met today for the last time.[1] A glorious day for Ireland. I send you a copy of a resolution which passed unanimously.

You will perceive by it the feelings of the Association towards you. Colonel Butler will write tomorrow. It is as follows: 'Resolved that Daniel O'Connell esq. continues to enjoy the *undivided* and *undiminished* confidence of the Catholic Association for his splendid and disinterested exertions on behalf of the Catholics of Ireland on all occasions. Pierce Butler.'

SOURCE : O'Connell Papers, NLI 13645

1 At this meeting on 18 March 1825, Hon. Pierce Butler in the chair, the Catholic Association voted their own dissolution (*FJ*, 19 Mar. 1825).

1195

To his wife, Merrion Square, 19 March 1825, from London

'I have time only to tell you that all is going on admirably. Every difficulty as it arises is smoothed away.'

SOURCE : Fitz-Simon Papers

1196

From Count O'Connell to Brooke's [*recte* Cooke's?] *Hotel, Albemarle Street, London*

Paris, 20 March 1825

My dear Daniel,

Your letter surprised me very agreeably as I could not have expected it after you had been so long in London without writing me a line. I sincerely congratulate you on the cheering result you anticipate for the important cause you have advocated these many years with so much and such commendable zeal, perseverance and ability. May your labours be crowned with full success, and may I have, ere I depart, the great comfort to see my native country happy and united.

I am sorry to perceive some discrepance [*sic*] in opinion amongst the deputation. I have read a letter[1] published by one of the gentlemen (Mr. Lawless), with whom I confess I differ wholly in opinion although I am willing to admit his candour and honest intentions.

I am informed that Ellen is soon to be led to the hymeneal

altar by a young gentleman of great personal worth, of an ancient and respectable family and easy fortune (Mr. Fitz-Simon).[2] Nothing could afford me greater pleasure. . . .

I cannot close this letter without give [*sic*] vent to my grief. The loss of a most dear and most amiable only brother[3] has left an indelible impression of sorrow on my heart and mind. I now remain a solitary wreck of an entire generation. I thank you, my dear Daniel, for the expressions of respect and regard for me you utter in your letter. My only recommendation to you is to have a parental solicitude for your own family and to consider that your minor children have a sacred claim on you. Your proportion of the large sum of ready money left by your uncle will be, I hope, more than sufficient to wipe off your debts. If so, your income with the perquisites accruing from your profession (£6,000) will leave you a clear income of nearly £10,000, a moiety of which you can save with ease for the benefit of your family. Need I observe to a fond *parent,* to one so deeply impressed, so devoted to the conscientious discharge of his moral and religious duties, that you would be answerable before God and man for a neglect of an obligation so sacred.

. . . I have to thank you for procuring me the acquaintance of Mr. Bellew.[4] He seems to be well deserving of the flattering idea you gave me of his character. . . . James has given me no details of what my dear brother died possessed of.[5] . . .

SOURCE : Fitz-Simon Papers

1 See letter 1189, note 1.
2 Christopher Fitz-Simon.
3 His only surviving brother, Hunting-Cap.
4 Unidentified.
5 £52,000 in cash, securities, mortgages and other assets and a landed estate yielding a net rent of perhaps £7,000 (this estimate is partly a statement of, and partly a deduction from, information in Maurice R. O'Connell, 'Daniel O'Connell: Income, Expenditure and Despair', *Irish Historical Studies,* XVII, no. 66 [Sept. 1970]).

1197

To his wife, Merrion Square, 21 March 1825, from London

Says he is setting out for Ireland this evening.

SOURCE : Fitz-Simon Papers

1198

From Thomas Fitzgerald, Cork, 29 March 1825, to Merrion Square

Mainly concerning bills of exchange. 'Mr. O'Keeffe[1] was highly pleased when I read to him that passage relative to the clergy. Believe to a man that they are rejoiced at the [provision] entered for them.'

SOURCE : O'Connell Papers, NLI 13647

1 Rev. Thomas O'Keeffe, dean of Cork.

1199

From his wife, Dublin,—April 1825

'We are, God be thanked, in perfect health. How I wish Derrynane may agree with me! Beside the delight of being with you I think I should be able to do a great deal of good for the poor people about Derrynane.'

SOURCE : *Irish Monthly*, X (1882), 778

1200

From William Corbet[1]

Patriot Office, 2 April 1825

Dear Sir,

I enclose you the last *Patriot*[2] and regret it was not sent before. I am glad my suspicions, which you will see, as to the evidence not having been fairly given, are sustained by your letter in the [Dublin *Morning*] *Register* this day.[3] I have not yet received a copy of the report. Strange it is how inattentive Lord Wellesley's friends are to the press, notwithstanding the unceasing activity of his enemies! I feel very sensibly your kind and friendly dispositions towards me. . . . You may rely on the most implicit secrecy as to any communications you may please to send me. If marked *private* and addressed to me, they might be sent through the penny post with an anonymous signature.

SOURCE : O'Connell Papers, NLI 13647

1 William Corbet, law and mercantile printer, 3 Upper Ormond Quay,

Dublin. Editor of the *Hibernian Telegraph,* 1795-1810. Proprietor of the *Patriot,* 1810-28.

2 Of 31 March 1825. This contained extracts of the evidence given by O'Connell and others before the select committee of the House of Lords in March. An editorial stated that these extracts, republished from the *Dublin Evening Mail,* were erroneous.

3 This letter was written by O'Connell from Merrion Square and dated 31 March 1825.

1201

From his brother James to Merrion Square

Lakeville [later Lakeview], 9 April 1825

My Dear Dan,

. . . With respect to the personal property of my dearest uncle, John and I will make no division of it until we three meet. . . . I have received interest money from Lord Kenmare and Mr. Cronin[1] and will do so from the other persons, *if I get it.* Until we meet which will, please God, be at farthest at the next Tralee assizes, the property is then very easily divided. Indeed, I thank God we never had any difference of opinion about money matters, nor is it possible we should on the present occasion.

I have succeeded in getting many of the persons you owe money to [to] reduce the interest to 5%. Mr. Collis[2] has done so from the 20 of last month (on Major Bottet's debt of £1,200) so has William Fagan of Cork and all the Iveragh people you owe money to with the exception of Roger O'Sullivan's widow.[3] Mr. Nolan,[4] the priest, refused to take less than 6% and I paid him £542 and, of course, took up our bond and will get the judgement he *had against me satisfied.* He entered no judgement against you. I would strongly recommend to you to leave the House of Derrynane as it is for the present. As a Bathing Lodge it is quite good enough. When you come to Kerry you could then see what was necessary to be done. Perhaps an application to Lord Cork, stating that you intended to build *a residence* there, may induce his Lordship to give you a renewal.

I regret to find that you think it likely you must again go to London on this Catholic question but perhaps circumstanced as you are, you cannot avoid it. God knows, you have sacrificed enough to that question.

I lately received a letter from the General,[5] written the 21 of March. He desired me remit him the 100 guineas left him by my uncle Maurice which I of course did. He also desires me remit him *regularly* the £300 a year left him by my uncle. The £500 the General remitted last February for the use of your son John has been ever since in Coutt's Bank. . . .

SOURCE : O'Connell MSS, UCD

1 Probably Daniel Cronin of The Park, Killarney.
2 Probably John Collis, Kinsale, Co. Cork.
3 Unidentified.
4 Unidentified.
5 His uncle, Count O'Connell.

1202

To his wife, Merrion Square, 15 April 1825, from Liverpool

Announcing his arrival in Liverpool from Dublin and his departure for London that afternoon.

SOURCE : Fitz-Simon Papers

1203

To his wife, Merrion Square

St. Petersburg Hotel, Dover Street, London,
18 April 1825

My darling Heart,

. . . We could not find room at Cooke's where we were before and so *with difficulty* got into this hotel. . . . I found the bishops here, Dr. Doyle somewhat recovered but as yet not quite well. We are in a great lottery with the Catholic cause. Do you know that our principal peril consists in the danger least the Whigs should desert us? The truth is they have a direct interest in preventing the ministry from emancipating us. If they were true to us we should certainly be emancipated, but *in spite* of them we will be so. They cannot vote against us. The utmost they can do is to stay away and I am told Mr. Lambton and Mr. Michael Angelo Taylor,[1] two leading opposition members, mean to stay away. We shall tomorrow night have a majority of upwards of thirty. This night the English Catholic petition is to be presented.[2] We go down to the House to be present at its presentation. Lord Nugent, who presents it, is no great orator. He it is who resembles John Howley so much. I know you will like him for *that*. I have as yet no more political news for you but I expect to have a good deal for tomorrow. At least I will then be able to form a better view of our ultimate prospect of success. I have at present no reason to doubt our triumph. . . .

[Bric] was very much disappointed at not being a member of the deputation. I suppose Finn[3] will be wild with me on the same account although I am quite blameless.

SOURCE : Fitz-Simon Papers

1 Michael Angelo Taylor, White Hall, Co. Middlesex, M.P. for Durham city, 1820-31.

2 Lord Nugent postponed the presentation of the petition (of the Roman Catholics of Great Britain in favour of Emancipation) from 18 to 19 April since the Emancipation Bill was debated on the latter date (Commons debate 18, 19 April 1825; *MC,* 19, 20 April 1825).

3 William F. Finn.

1204

To his wife

St. Petersburg Hotel, Dover Street [London],
19 April 1825

My darling Heart,

. . . It is said that the King is not well enough to hold a levee tomorrow and if he be not it must be doubtful whether he will be able to hold one in a week. The truth is that the only act of government in his power is the signing the list for execution on the Recorder's report. He literally does nothing else that can be called *business*. This certainly is against us, but what is more unfavourable is the coldness and apathy of our friends the Whigs. It is curious to see how they demonstrate the truth of what they have been so often accused of, namely, of looking for their own party purposes instead of supporting our claims on the merits, but perhaps I wrong them. We shall see how the fact stands by the debate and division on this day's motion. The second reading of the Catholic bill comes on this night and we now calculate on a majority of about 40. If we have that majority all will be well. Less than that would much depress the public expectation and yet I am not in the same spirits I used to be nor does there appear to be so much to cheer and animate as there was in the hey-day of our first advance. However one or two *lucky* speeches this day would shift the balance in our favour considerably. My letter tomorrow will probably be decisive both of the measure and of the length of my stay in London. I cannot leave this for another week, but I hope I will before the 3rd of May be on my way back to Ireland. This however must depend on circumstances over which at present I have no control but, darling, I need not say that I am a good deal fretted at being away from my family and my business but some good has been done and more may yet be in store. Plunket is arrived and is making, I dare say, great preparations for this night's battle. I was a good while tête-à-tête with Sir Francis Burdett and he will, I think, make a great exhibition. I think him much better prepared this time than the last. There have been many petitions against us but not one from a public meeting. Those in our favour are not numerous. I wish the scoundrels would give me an opportunity of speaking at a public meeting but that, darling, to a certain extent is vanity. Maurice is fulfilling his duty as secretary. We have set him *up* with a secretary's book and all the implements of his trade and occupation. . . . Give me an exact account of my Kate's[1] leg and let me know if my Betsey[2] has been at her Easter duty; poor darling, her scruples annoy her much. Tell her that her father loves her most tenderly. I have some more letters to write and to call at one or two places before three o'clock *this day* when we muster to go down to the house. I feel very feverish about *this* division but the will of God be done. It may be for the better to postpone the ultimate success of the measure.

SOURCE : Fitz-Simon Papers

1 His daughter.

2 His daughter.

1205

To his wife, Merrion Square, Dublin

St. Petersburg Hotel, Dover Street
[London], 20 April 1825

My darling Love,

I am in spirits again this day although I did not get out of bed until eleven o'clock. I was not asleep before two this morning. The debate[1] was a favourable one certainly for us. Brownlow has amply vindicated everything I said of him.[2] He began the debate with a strong and an eloquent speech. He is a warm-hearted fellow and I shall like him the longest day I live. Mr. Bankes,[3] the next speaker, was not listened to by the house. He is father to the young man[4] who made himself ridiculous against me on a former debate.[5] Dawson made a virulent speech against us, fresh from Mr. Peel's office. When Goulburn came to speak about half after twelve the house became impatient, nobody listened to him and the house adjourned till tomorrow. North made a speech which reads well in the newspapers and was in itself rather a good one, but it made no impression on the house and in fact was a total failure. He is gone as a public speaker in the house, both parties equally disregard him. In short, the debate was altogether favourable to us. It will recommence on Thursday and I daresay there will be another adjournment. *So* far *so* well. I hope and believe all will be right. . . .

Darling, I am this day obliged to write but little, surrounded as I am with the deputation, visitors etc. . . . I *could* not tell you how much, how tenderly, how ardently I love you my *own, own* darling heart. Do console yourself with knowing that no woman ever was so much loved as you are and that *years* have only increased the tenderness and force of that affection.

SOURCE : Fitz-Simon Papers

1 The debate on 19 April on the second reading of Burdett's Emancipation Bill.

2 In the debate Charles Brownlow announced his conversion to the support of Emancipation (*MC*, 20 April 1825).

3 Henry Bankes, M.P.

4 William John Bankes (died 1855), traveller in the East and M.P. for Cambridge University, 1822-26. See *DNB*.

5 In the debate on 1 March on Burdett's motion (see letter 1172, note 8), which he opposed, Bankes quoted O'Connell's statement on church rates and tithes in parts of Ireland where no Protestant clergy or laity existed. This quotation led to laughter and sarcastic applause in the House (*Hansard*, N.S., XII, 799-801). Hansard erroneously gives the date of this debate as 28 February.

1206

To his wife, Merrion Square

St. Petersburg Hotel, Dover Street [London],
21 April 1825

My darling heart,

. . . We go down to the House this day as early as three o'clock in order *certainly* to be in the House during the debate.[1] Darling heart, affairs are this day looking right well. I think now that in spite of our hollow friends we shall still be emancipated. It is curious to observe the manner in which public opinion veers about in this country. It is sufficiently strange but there are circumstances telling in our favour here which cannot be deceitful. . . .

SOURCE : Fitz-Simon Papers

1 The continuation of the debate on the second reading of Burdett's Emancipation Bill.

1207

To his wife, Merrion Square

London, 22 April 1825

My darling Heart,

I am again in spirits this day. I am in great spirits. The fullest House that ever sat—there never was such an attendance of members and yet we carried the question by a majority twice as great as at the first reading. You may recollect we had at first only 13, we now had 27,[1] thus we improve. Today all is bustle and *vivid* interest. Mr. Brownlow and I came together from the House after three o'clock this morning and I was not out of bed until near eleven. Everything is in great agitation and one or two days must now decide the question. That decision, believe me, will be favourable. The debate last night was all greatly useful to Emancipation. Goulburn [? spoke] miserably. He is a wretched creature. He was followed by Lord Binning[2] in an admirable speech. There was a Wallace,[3] an old rascal who spoke against us, Canning made an admirable speech for us, one of the best I ever heard anywhere, and Peel made a wretched discourse against us. The fact is, there floats amongst the individuals in the House a great portion of real substantial bigotry. It really is bigotry which stands between us and Emancipation but we are quite sure of going through the House of Commons and we must as rapidly as possible take our measures for assailing the House of Lords. Darling, we have now really a very hard card to play. If we concede the freeholds, we shall get over many enemies but we shall perhaps lose some who at least call themselves our friends. *Thus* are we circumstanced for the present.

. . . I hate being in London on *many, many* accounts.

Maurice is quite well. He, I think, was near getting us put out of the House of Commons by flinging himself over bannisters and down a flight of stairs to show his agility. Luckily it was not noticed. . . .

SOURCE : Fitz-Simon Papers

1 The adjourned debate on Burdett's Emancipation Bill took place on 21 April and the second reading was passed by 268 to 241 (*Commons Journal,* LXXX, 327).

2 Thomas (Hamilton) (1780-1858), styled Lord Binning, 1795-1828. Succeeded as ninth earl of Haddington, 1828; M.P. almost continuously, 1802-27. Created 1827 Baron Melros. Lord-lieutenant of Ireland, December 1834-April 1835.

3 Thomas Wallace (1768-1844), son of James Wallace, Asholme, Knaresdale, Northumberland. M.P. for various constituencies, 1802-18; Weymouth, 1818-28. Created Baron Wallace of Knaresdale, 1828.

1208

From William Cobbett to St. Petersburg Hotel [*London*]

Fleet Street [London],
Saturday, 23 [April] 1825

My dear Sir,

I called at your hotel today in order to thank you for the great kindness which you and your son had the goodness to show to William[1] in Dublin and also to beg you to come and see us at Kensington as soon as you can; to which let me add a prayer that you will not suffer yourself to be disheartened by the proofs that you will soon receive of the baseness and perfidy of politicians. . . .

SOURCE : *Irish Monthly,* X (1882), 631

1 Cobbett's son.

1209

To his wife, Merrion Square

London, 25 April 1825

My darling Heart,

. . . I went out yesterday after Mass and spent an hour with old Cobbett. I found him writing some of the history of the Reformation. I dined at Lord Stourton's with the bishops[1] and Lord Fingall and went in the evening to the Catholic party at Mrs. Blount's.[2] There were all the Catholic ladies of distinction there—Cliffords, Shrewsburys, Petres, Howards, etc. Old Lady Petre[3] and her daughter whom we saw at Southampton inquired very particularly for you. Do you know that the daughter is very pretty? There are three other great fat girls, her sisters. The younger Lady Petre[4] is a very nice woman. She was a Miss Howard. This morning was spent in the city canvassing for *votes,* that is, for a public meeting in favour of the Catholics. The rest are gone to the House of Commons but I shall not go. The debate is to be on the freeholders bill. I heard this day favourable news about the House of Lords so that there are many reasons to expect that we may succeed there also. At least things are looking better. I am of opinion myself that the bill will *actually* pass this sessions. *Recollect I tell you so. . . .*

SOURCE : Fitz-Simon Papers

1 Probably some or all of the five Irish bishops who had come to London in order to be examined by the select committees.

2 Probably wife of Edward Blount, secretary of the English Catholic Board.

3 Mary Bridget (1767-1843), first daughter of Henry Howard of Glossop, Derbyshire. Married 1786 tenth Baron Petre.

4 Emma Agnes (1803-61), second daughter of Henry Howard of Corby Castle, Cumberland. Married 1823, as his second wife, eleventh Baron Petre.

1210

To his wife, Merrion Square

Dover Street [London], 26 April 1825

My own Love,

I can write only on this scrap of paper. I have been very

busy all day, and lost a great deal of time with the Duke of Sussex though it was not time thrown away at all. . . . We are to go tomorrow in great style to the *levée*. I will write you one line in the morning and you probably will miss a day as I will scarcely be able on Thursday to write to you from Birmingham.

SOURCE : Fitz-Simon Papers

1211

To his wife, Merrion Square

Dover Street, 27 April 1825

My own darling love,

I am this moment come in from the *levée*. It was greatly crowded so that my hand is unsteady as I write. The King is looking in very good health, and I have the pleasure to tell you that he is likely to shut the worthy Duke of York out of any chance of a speedy reign. We were at least as well received as usual. The King looked cheerful and even gay as we were presented to him. Your son Maurice, you will easily believe, looked very well in his court dress. He kissed the King's hand immediately after me. The King is fatter but looks, I think, more healthy than he did when in Ireland. Everything conspires to make me hope that the ferocious speech[1] of the Duke of York will do us good. Lord Selsey[2] got himself introduced to me at the *levée* and told me he was determined to vote for us in future instead of being against us as he had hitherto been. Admiral Blackwood[3] told me he believed his brother Lord Dufferin[4] would vote for us. He has been a great Orangeman, and a single vote in the Lords is now of great value. In short, the crisis has arrived. God send us a good deliverance and may his will be done in everything.

I certainly will leave Birmingham on Friday having made no less than two appointments with Ladies for Saturday. One of them seems rather curious. I do not understand it at present. It may be either very foolish or very useful. . . .

[P.S.] Do not let *any thing* I write appear in any paper.

SOURCE : Fitz-Simon Papers

1 In the Lords on 25 April the duke of York presented a petition against Emancipation and spoke strongly against the measure, ex-

pressing as his personal opinion the view that the king could not assent to it without violating his coronation oath (*Hansard,* N.S., XIII, 138-42).

2 Henry John (Peachey), third Baron Selsey (1787-1838).

3 Sir Henry Blackwood (1770-1832), fourth son of Sir John Blackwood, baronet, of Ballyleidy, Co. Down, and Dorcas, Baroness Dufferin and Clandeboye. Rear-admiral, 1814; vice-admiral, 1825. Created baronet, 1814. Had a distinguished naval career. See *DNB*.

4 James Stevenson (Blackwood), second Baron Dufferin and Clandeboye (1755-1836), first surviving son of Sir John Blackwood, second baronet, and Dorcas, Baroness Dufferin and Clandeboye. M.P. for Killyleagh, 1788-1800; Helston, 1807-12; Aldeburgh, 1812-18.

1212

To his wife, Merrion Square

Birmingham, 28 April 1825

My darling love,

I left London yesterday about five and travelled 44 miles. . . . I was in bed before eleven and up at four this morning. I came in here before twelve, having travelled about 66 English miles. I am now waiting for their Catholic meeting or for some account of it. I have breakfasted and dressed since my arrival but as yet have heard nothing of *my friends* although I am told my coming down has been placarded through the town. . . .

Darling, I have reason to hope that the outrageous conduct[1] of the Duke of York will be of use, perhaps be the means of securing our emancipation these sessions. . . .

I now think I raised your curiosity about the ladies I am to meet on Saturday but it is about law business and besides you *could not* be very jealous, could you, darling, especially when the world's worth would not tempt me to give you cause.

SOURCE : Fitz-Simon Papers

1 See letter 1211, note 1.

1213

From Rev. Joseph Stokes[1] to Merrion Square

Charleston, S.C., 29 April 1825

My dear Sir,

I cannot suffer the present letters to pass over to Ireland

without taking leave to express to you my warmest gratitude for enabling me to assist in the valuable labours of our Bishop.[2] If I can render any services to religion, if I ever contribute to the salvation of others you shall have the merit and most sincerely do I wish it. . . . I always bear in mind the words with which your liberal donation of £20 was accompanied ' to remember you at the holy sacrifice '. . . .

SOURCE : O'Connell MSS, UCD

1 A priest from Ireland serving in the diocese of Charleston (died 16 July 1854).

2 John England.

1214

To his wife

Dover Street [London], 30 April 1825

My darling Love,

. . . I was going to write while ago when I was tempted to go to an Anti-Slavery meeting. The Duke of Gloucester[1] was in the chair. When I was perceived I was *hustled* up to his side and compelled to speak for an hour.[2] . . .

Darling, the meeting[3] at Birmingham was excellent. I delight in all I saw there. I left this about five on Wednesday and after I had written my letter to you from Birmingham I went to the Catholic meeting and spoke for an hour and three quarters, was of course cheered and made from time to time some good points. We had afterwards a grand dinner and several speeches. Bric made an excellent one at the dinner. . . . I spoke highly of Bolívar and was much cheered. The Duke of Gloucester was most attentive and kind to me; in fact, they set me down here as a first rate orator and you, *without any partiality, love*!!!, will agree with them. . . .

I paid my visit this day to one of the ladies and found it, as I expected, after much parade but a foolish errand so that you have been *jealous* for nothing. My own own love, you are my heart's fondest treasure and my only, my tenderest love.

SOURCE : Fitz-Simon Papers

1 William Frederick, duke of Gloucester (1776-1834), nephew and son-in-law of George III.

2 At the Freemasons' Hall on 30 April 1825. The attendance included Brougham, Thomas Spring Rice and Thomas Fowell Buxton. In his

speech to the meeting O'Connell said: 'The blacks, having become free, would in time become members of society, would fill offices of importance and finally work out their independence' (*MC*, 2 May 1825).

3 At the annual general meeting of the Midland Catholic Association which was held at the Royal Hotel, Birmingham, on 28 April, Edward Blount, secretary to the British Catholic Association, in the chair (*FJ*, 6 May 1825).

1215

To his wife, Merrion Square

Dover Street [London], 1 [and 2] May 1825

My darling Love,

This morning about seven your second son[1] arrived in the Dover coach. He is looking perfectly well and appears as gay and as good as ever. I am happy also to be able to tell you that the French surgeon declares him quite convalescent and has no doubt of his being able to return into the Cavalry. . . . We have arrived at a most critical period in our affairs and if we are not now successful it is not known when we shall. Our prospects are indeed daily brightening. Certainly the Lords are now completely at the disposal of Lord Liverpool.

2 May

Darling, we dined yesterday at Lord Fitzwilliam's. Lord Grey, etc., were there to the number of about thirty. O'Gorman[2] went with me there, but he and I have quarrelled, I believe for ever. Only think that when we stood up to leave the room after dinner O'Gorman worked his way to the upper end of the table where Lord Fitzwilliam stood and addressed Lord Grey on the subject of the 40s freehold in a way to *sustain* that peer in his opposition probably to the *entire* of our claims. I was in a rare passion and think perhaps that more mischief was done than really occurred. However, at this moment it was a very indiscreet measure and when we came home I expressed myself so strongly to him on the subject that I suppose we shall not soon speak to each other. This I deem quite a prudent course without entertaining any kind of animosity to the poor man. On the contrary, I would and probably will be able to do him some service. I have got up a requisition in the city for *an aggregate*. It is in a course of being signed and I believe I shall have an opportunity to make *a display*. Darling, I send you today the *Morning Herald* and the *British Press* to show you some speeches of mine. The *Morning Chronicle* appears to treat the entire with an air of contempt. . . . The committee on the Catholic bill is postponed till Friday in consequence of the illness of Sir Francis Burdett who has a violent attack of the gout. *This* enables me to go to a charity dinner at which the Duke of Sussex presides and at which I am *to plead in favour of the Charity*. Darling heart, I am tired of London and deeply anxious to be at home with you. I need not tell you that my quarrel with O'Gorman can have *no* consequences. The boys and he continue on perfectly good terms. *You know* that I would not deceive you, sweetest, and I solemnly assure you that I do not. I would not tell a wilful lie to anybody, much less to you, sweetest. . . . Depend on it that the Duke of York's speech is doing us great good. I am of opinion that it will contribute to emancipate us *this* session.

SOURCE : Fitz-Simon Papers

1 Morgan.

2 Nicholas Purcell O'Gorman.

1216

To his wife, Merrion Square

Dover Street [London], 3 May 1825

My darling Heart's Love,

. . . The committee is postponed and, of course, so is the discussion in the Lords. As yet the subject is in the hands of Lord Liverpool and one word from him certainly carries it. It is as yet *unknown* how he will decide but there are various grounds for hope and none at all to despair. The declaration of the Duke of York has *certainly* done us good and is daily working in our favour. The public sentiment *certainly* is with us. There was a great dinner[1] yesterday at the Freemason's tavern. You will see a poor sketch of it in the *Morning Chronicle* and a most miserable report of one of my speeches and none of another and a *good* speech the second was. I sat next the Duke of Norfolk who was himself at the right hand of the Duke of Sussex. Both were civil to me. There were a number of ladies present and, darling, I *flatter* myself that

I am a favourite but you need not be *jealous*. Darling, the two ladies who made *appointments* with me are the one a Mrs. Byrne[2] whose great national business with me turned out to be the endeavour to get leave for an United Irishman of 1798 to return to reside in his native country. The other lady was a Miss Masterson[2] who was an acquaintance of Ally's at Florence. She has had a Sir William Gerard,[3] an English Catholic baronet, who proposed to marry her and is now sorry for it. I believe she will bring an action against him. I am glad I am rid of both ladies. . . . Morgan has . . . written to my Uncle to say that . . . he will return by Paris to his regiment. I endeavoured to persuade him to adopt a different course but he seems quite determined. He likes the Austrian service very much. In short, his mind is quite made up to going back after a couple of months at home. What think you darling of his plan? It now remains for you to decide.

SOURCE : Fitz-Simon Papers

1 The anniversary dinner of St. Patrick's Charity Schools and Asylum for Female Children, London, which was held at the Freemason's Tavern, the duke of Sussex in the chair (*FJ*, 6 May 1825).

2 Unidentified.

3 Sir William Gerard, eleventh baronet (1773-1826).

1217

To his wife, Merrion Square

Dover Street, 4 May 1825

My own darling Love,

. . . You are the solace and sweetness of my existence and my heart feels widowed and solitary at being so long separated from you, whilst in absence when you do condescend to write to me in terms of love you cannot imagine what *a drink of honey* these tender expressions are to me. Darling, mine to you spring warm from my heart, and I would feel miserable amidst the splendour of the world if I were to live thus separated from my sweetest darling companion. I know my Mary has some gratitude to her husband for his fondness, but I have come to a time of life when it is not [? possible] that I should have a woman's love.

Darling, I dined yesterday at Lady Petre['s][1]. . . . The

Duke of Norfolk dined with us as did the Earl[2] and Countess of Surrey. I do not think her handsome but she is a very nice woman. The son of Lord Grosvenor, whose title is Belgrave,[3] and his Lady were of the party. I however left the belles and beauties early and came home to dream of my wife and children. No man has such a darling wife. No man has such darling children as I have. Our boys dined with Fitzsimon at a tavern and went to the play. My Morgan wins on me every day and becomes hourly more inexpressibly dear to my heart. Oh, how can I bear to part with my noble boy! But he is fixed on going back and I know not how to retain him. . . . I was also paid a great compliment[4] by Denman in the House of Commons. He is really a fine fellow. . . .

We have it in agitation to wait on Lord Liverpool who now holds our fate in his hands. For this purpose we have consulted Sir Francis Burdett and Lord Donoughmore. The latter is strongly for the measure. The former doubts but at present the matter is, I may say, under consultation with Lord Grey and the leaders of the opposition. The determination will be known tomorrow or the day after. Sir Francis is the same manly, *delightful,* honest man on this as on every other occasion. Our interviews lasted with him and with Lord Donoughmore about an hour. Lords Fingall, Gormanston[5] and Killeen, Sir Thomas Burke[6] and I were *the delegation* to these persons but Mr. O'Gorman[7] made up his mind to go and, without being at all appointed, he accordingly attended. Indeed his conduct was by this much the worse that he had been named to go but not being seconded or any vote put upon his going he was not of *our number.* I am quite convinced that I have done wrong in giving this man so much countenance but I will not, darling, in future put him forward in any way. He had no business here at all. Let that however pass. My boys and he continue to speak and to be on as good terms as usual. I do not of course entertain any resentment to him. I need not tell you that it is not a sentiment suited to my mind, but I feel how precarious it is to have a man without either tact or talent engaged at the critical moments of the cause. . . .

SOURCE : Fitz-Simon Papers

1 Widow of tenth Baron Petre.

2 Henry Charles (Howard) (1791-1856), styled earl of Surrey, 1815-42, when he succeeded as thirteenth duke of Norfolk. M.P. for Hor-

sham, 1829-32; West Sussex, 1832-41. Married c. 1814 Charlotte Sophia, first daughter of duke of Sutherland.

3 Richard (Grosvenor) (1795-1869), styled Viscount Belgrave, 1802-31; styled earl of Grosvenor, 1831-45; 1845 second marquess of Westminster. M.P. for Chester, 1818-30; Cheshire, 1830-32; South Cheshire, 1832-35. See *DNB*. Married 1819 Elizabeth Mary, youngest daughter of first duke of Sutherland.

4 On 3 May Thomas Denman presented a petition to the Commons from Nottingham corporation in favour of Emancipation. The petition, he said, mentioned the injustice of withholding from O'Connell the professional honour of a silk gown. He drew an analogy between O'Connell and Henry Brougham who had been discriminated against likewise but on political grounds (*Patriot,* 7 May 1825).

5 Jenico (Preston), twelfth Viscount Gormanston (1775-1860). Married Margaret, first daughter of second Viscount Southwell.

6 Probably an error for Sir John Burke, second baronet, Marble Hill, Co. Galway, son of Sir Thomas Burke, first baronet.

7 Nicholas Purcell O'Gorman.

1218

To his wife

Dover Street, 5 May 1825

Darling Heart's Love,

. . . Blake[1] is very ill today and I missed seeing Plunket, *so* I do not know one word more than I did when I wrote last. Believe me that there is no reason to despair. The cabinet is extremely divided. Lord Eldon and Peel are endeavouring to throw out Canning but the latter is supported by Lord Liverpool. If this controversy shall end in favour of Canning it may give us Emancipation at once so that our fate is in the scale and although I did not see Plunket I am told that he entertains strong hopes of success. I will see him, I hope, tomorrow. You must not speak to any one of Blake's illness as it may come to his wife's ears. There is no use in giving her unnecessary alarm. Darling, you will see in the newspapers a very short sketch of the dinner[2] at the London tavern for a Catholic charity at which I presided. I made several speeches, at least one dozen of them but there is a *lousy* report of the entire. . . . These dinners are not deemed sufficiently important to attract public attention. . . . The truth is, darling, that I am become so weary of London and of everything belonging to it that I feel heartless when I write of anything else but of my chance of departure or my love for you because, darling, I do love you most tenderly. The progress of the bill in the House of Commons has been unusually slow. It was this day fortnight that it got the second reading and the committee on it will not sit till Friday. It cannot be in the House of Lords before the middle of next week and then another week must elapse before the great and *final* battle. I say *final* because if we win that day we are certain of ultimate and complete success this sessions. Certainly our chances of that success are much increased by the undoubted fact that the public opinion is greatly in our favour. Did I tell you that the English Catholics are about to print the speech[3] I made at Birmingham and to circulate it throughout the country? This is done at the instance or at least by the advice of Mr. Thos. Grenville,[4] the brother of Lord Grenville, and is no small compliment to me. Darling, the Corporation of Nottingham have paid me a greater compliment[5] than even the Irish Catholics. They have actually complained to Parliament that I did not get a silk gown!!! I suppose you saw *that* in the newspapers. I dine this day in company I dare say with the Welds as it is with *the father-in-law*[6] of the present Lord Petre. Did I tell you that I *admire* not a little the present Lady Petre? She is really a fine, *honest* looking person but, sweetest, there is a little smart cocknosed woman who is ten thousand times more cheering to my eyes *although* I have yet to scold her, of which put me in mind.

SOURCE : Fitz-Simon Papers

1 Anthony Richard Blake.

2 The anniversary dinner of the Rotherhithe Catholic Charity which was held on 4 May at the London Tavern, Bishopsgate Street, London, O'Connell presiding (*DEP*, 10 May 1825).

3 See letter 1214, note 3.

4 Thomas Grenville (1755-1846), M.P. for Buckinghamshire, 1780-84, 1807-1813.

5 See letter 1217, note 4.

6 Henry Howard (1757 1842), Corby Castle, Carlisle, Cumberland. His second daughter, Emma Agnes, married 1823 eleventh Baron Petre.

1219

To his wife, Merrion Square

Dover Street [London], 6 May 1825

My darling Love,

The *fates* are against us this day. It seems *at present* that Canning's defeat is expected and that the hostile part of the Cabinet will prevail. This does at present appear to be the order of the day. Darling, this at length puts me out of spirits and if it lasts, we must be defeated in the Lords. Blessed be God for everything and may we not thank him that even by the confession of our enemies the fault is not ours. Lord Liverpool *has* it seems expressed an opinion perfectly hostile. Well, well, let them abide any evil consequences that may ensue. We are not to blame. . . .

[P.S.] I am just going to the House of Commons. The freehold bill[1] is, I am told, to be rendered so bad that no person can sustain it. It may be some comfort that Goulburn is *not* to go back and that Plunket is to be [Lord] Chancellor.[2]

SOURCE : Fitz-Simon Papers

1 See letter 1180, note 2.

2 O'Connell was mistaken; Goulburn remained chief secretary until 1827 and Plunket did not become lord chancellor until 1830.

1220

To his wife

Dover Street [London], 7 May 1825

My own and only love,

At present our prospects are clouded. The bill[1] has taken a very triumphant course certainly through the House of Commons but it can be saved as *at present advised* in the Lords only by a miracle or the exertion of popular sentiment. I am therefore determined to try a meeting in the city and in Westminster. There has been one[2] at Manchester attended by the happiest results. There was a petition got up under the auspices of *the swaddlers*[3] and hawked about in the most impudent manner. Fortunately this put the liberals on their metal and they ventured to call a public meeting. The scoundrel swaddlers attended. I will call them nothing in future but swaddlers but they were totally defeated. This will necessarily give courage to meetings at other places, and we may yet *force* upon Lord Liverpool the adoption of the measure. I spent a considerable time this day with Plunket. His hopes of the Lords for the present fail him. That vile villain, the Duke of York, *they say* made no impression but the House of Lords is after all so sorry and sad a gang that, sweetest, we have little to hope from them for honesty or liberality while the heir apparent or presumptive chooses to take a stand for folly, bigotry and knavery, and then indeed, darling, they say the Royal Duke is quite at home. His conduct with Mrs. Clarke, etc.,[4] is as familiar as day and his tradesmen are, they say, unpaid, his debts even of honour undischarged, and with honesty and morality on a par with those of the vile women who infest the midnight streets. This royal rascal has scruples of conscience forsooth!!! You see what a rare passion I am in with him, darling, but as that you know, love, is a mood in which except *towards you* I do not long continue, I dismiss him with my hearty contempt, only wishing I may live to see their proud and vile peers want us, darling, more than we want them. Mary, I doat of you and that phrase, which is true to the very letter, at once relieves my bile and makes me quiet again. . . . The Scully cause[5] may come on next Thursday. I wish most heartily that it may. It would be a great *relief* to me to be able to speak to it. . . . Nothing could be better than our progress through the Committee of the Commons last night and on Tuesday will be the third reading.[6] I saw Sir John Newport and he reckons on a majority of forty-six at least on that occasion. They all say we must succeed next year but in my opinion it is *now* or never. I cannot endure the idea of any postponement. It is cruel to everybody. The debate in the Lords will take place on next Wednesday week. Without Lord Liverpool we could not succeed. With him we would drive every opposition out of the field. Darling, *we may* have him yet.

. . . You have now two sons at home. You will, however, find it impossible to keep Morgan there but he appears to enjoy the service and therefore, love, we must allow him. . . .

SOURCE: Fitz-Simon Papers

1 The Catholic Emancipation Bill.

2 A public meeting in support of Emancipation which was held in the

Manor Courtroom in High Street, Manchester, the borough-reeve in the chair. The *Dublin Evening Post* of 12 May 1825 has a long account of the meeting at which a large minority unsuccessfully opposed the pro-Emancipation resolutions.

3 An Irish term of disdain for Methodists.

4 Mary Anne Clarke (1776-1852), mistress of the duke of York.

5 *Denys and James Scully* v. *Jeremiah Scully and Others*. The case concerned the will of James Scully of Kilfeacle, Co. Tipperary, banker and landowner who died in 1816. The appellants, James's two eldest sons, appealed the judgement of the Irish court of chancery to the House of Lords, O'Connell acting as one of their counsel (Fagan, *O'Connell*, I, 432-7).

6 Of the Emancipation Bill.

1221

From his wife

Dublin, 7 May 1825

My own darling love,

. . . Tell me, love, what reason have you to suppose you are not the idol of my heart? Oh Dan, it is impossible for me to give you the smallest notion how beloved you are by me. Why should you speak of your age or allude to it? Surely, my own heart, I am for a woman much older. If I had not real love for you, would not my pride make me love you? By real love I mean loving you for yourself alone. Do not, my own heart, vex me by ever writing or speaking in this manner again. . . .

SOURCE : *Irish Monthly*, X (1882), 630-1

1222

To his wife

Dover Street [London], 9 May 1825

My own heart's love,

. . . I who love you with a romance and an enthusiasm which are supposed to belong to earlier stages of life and to unrequited love but which to my mind has double charms from the pure and holy ties of wedded affection which link us to each other. . . .

I have been at a Bible meeting where I was hissed by some and now I can only say, darling, that the state of ignorance in which they remain in England upon everything Irish is most ludicrous.

You do not say that you read my Birmingham speech.[1] I sent you the *Morning Herald* which contained *that* as well as another paper which contained my anti-slavery speech.[2] . . .

The Catholic bill will be through the Commons tomorrow; on Wednesday week it will get *through* the Lords one way or the other. I then go by Manchester and Liverpool to Ireland. . . . How bitterly do I regret being so long away from my family and my profession but, darling, it shall be the last time. I cannot afford to come again. We are this day endeavouring to get up public meetings and I trust we shall have at least two in London and in Westminster within the next week.

SOURCE : Fitz-Simon Papers

1 See letter 1214, note 3.

2 See letter 1214, note 2.

1223

To W. C. Plunket

9 May 1825

Private and Confidential

My dear Sir,

I cannot resist communicating to you these *two facts*. You will, perhaps, smile at the importance I attach to your knowing them; but, at all events, no human being shall ever learn from me that I communicated them to you.

1. I have good reason to be convinced that the entire *body* of the opposition would readily join Mr. Canning, the Grenvilles and Lord Liverpool to the exclusion of Lord Eldon, Peel and their followers. If anything could arise from your knowing this fact, I would probably be able to reduce it into a tangible shape, while I would, and do, consent to be disavowed, as wholly unauthorized by you and your friends, if it be at all desirable at any time to disavow me. I am ready to act with the full understanding that I am to be the sole sufferer if any arrangement attempted on this fact should fail.

Throw this letter in the fire when you read it if you choose, and forget that it was written if you think it foolish or useless. I myself feel its awkwardness. . . .

The second *fact* is one not existing but capable of being realized. It is proposed that, in the event of the Catholic Relief Bill being thrown out in the Lords, every Catholic in England and in Ireland should call for gold at all the banks and thus, to the extent of their properties, add to the embarrassment now created by the increased rate of exchange. I need not tell you that I do not approve of this project and yet I should not be surprised if it became hereafter *necessary* to carry it into effect. The Catholics are now combined. The Government has *now* the offer of the aid of that combination to assist every work of mutual conciliation and it may *now* fling to pieces that combination itself, simply by taking away the causes which keep us together and force us to combine. May I add, what insanity not to seize this most propitious moment! But I have written quite enough to annoy you with its length.

I repeat that, while you are at perfect liberty to use—if any use can be made of these facts—you may, of course, be certain of never hearing again of them unless you desire it.

I hope my anxiety to quiet Ireland and to strengthen England will be to you an excuse for this venture.

SOURCE : David Plunket, *Lord Plunket,* II, 205-6

1224

To his wife, Merrion Square

Dover Street [London], Tuesday,
10 May 1825

My own heart's love,

. . . I was detained in the House until after one. The debate on the freeholders bill was very stupid. Young Grattan has behaved on this bill exceedingly ill.[1] I gave him a strong hint to that effect when I saw him last night after the debate. In his speech he said '*I do not think this bill will cure the remedy*'!!! Only think, darling, of such blockheads being the persons who govern and make laws for us. The ruffian Duke of York has published his speech[2] in full in the newspapers of this day. You will see it in a day or two. I will give him a hand-dragging one day or another at some public meeting before I leave England. What an execrable rascal. . . .

SOURCE : Fitz-Simon Papers

1 In the Commons debate on the Forty-Shilling Disfranchisement Bill on 9 May James Grattan opposed it, using the obviously two-edged argument that if Irish Catholic forty-shilling freeholders were unfit to vote they were also unfit to be emancipated (*Hansard,* N.S., XIII, 453-4).

2 His speech of 25 April 1825. See letter 1211, note 1.

1225

To his wife, Merrion Square

Dover Street, 12 [*recte* 11] May 1825,
Wednesday

My heart's darling love,

. . . Maurice[1] had a letter this day from John Primrose. *He,* Primrose, says that the house at Derrynane will not be ready for your reception before the middle of June. . . . You can give Primrose in your letter any further directions about Derrynane house you may deem necessary.

Darling, we had last night a majority of only 21.[2] Lambton and several Whigs, with also several of those who were of opinion that the clergy should get a provision, went away without voting. The bill will this day be read a first time in the Lords. There are now two reports in circulation, one that the King is dangerously ill and I have some reason to believe that it is *so,* the other that Lord Liverpool is for a limited emancipation, that is, everything but Parliament. The latter report is now universally believed. It is also rendered much more probable because of what fell last night from Mr. Peel. In short, it seems at present a conceded fact. It would give us sheriffs and judges and of course all offices in Corporation as well as silk gowns, etc., etc. A day or two will tell us much more. In the meantime, darling, give my fondest love to our children. I was *not* in bed this morning till three o'clock. However my late sittings are *now,* thank God, at an end. Blake,[3] I am glad to tell you, is much better. He will sit up today for some hours. Darling, I am going to the House of Lords for a short time.

SOURCE : Fitz-Simon Papers

1 His son.

2 The third reading of the Emancipation Bill was passed in the Commons on 10 May by 248 to 227.

3 Anthony R. Blake.

1226

To his wife, Merrion Square

Dover Street [London], 12 May 1825

My darling Love,

I got while ago your letter of Monday. I am glad you are all so cheerful and happy in my absence. I know that you, sweetest, sometimes sigh for your *old man* who doats of you with the tenderest, the truest fondness. Indeed I do, my own own Mary, the love of my youth, the sweet partner of my maturer years and the darling mother of my children. . . .

Darling, I have heard nothing about the King today, so that he *must* be better. There are plenty of persons to spread bad reports. I have nothing *political* to tell you today save that there are still hopes of emancipation, excluding only the Chancellorship and the Privy Council. This would give us both houses of parliament and indeed would be complete emancipation because the Privy Council is open only to ministers or their immediate assistants, and if ever a Catholic arrived at that situation they would soon repeal that prohibition, but nothing short of parliament can content us or ought. I was settling a Church rate bill[1] this day with Sir John Newport which would do much good if we can get it passed. It will prevent *a load* of jobbing in Church rates. This shows of what inestimable advantage it would be to have an active, intelligent Catholic in Parliament. In matters of detail he could do an immense deal of good. I introduced a clause[2] in the act to prevent their compelling Catholics any longer being churchwardens. *That* will be a great relief because Catholic Churchwardens are frequently made liable for Church rates which they did not actually receive. I am thus working for *the cause*, darling, content with your love and my own consciousness of right and careless of any ingratitude which I may meet with. *But after all,* darling, the poor people are not ungrateful. Amongst them there is a lively sense of kindness which I as yet never found deficient. *Yet after all* what is popularity? Let a man deserve it really and he either gets it or can afford well to do without it. So much for that dissertation. I have just accepted the Manchester invitation for Monday the 23rd, Whitsun Monday, and yet I may be obliged to return to London for the Scully[3] cause for Thursday the 26th. . . .

SOURCE : Fitz-Simon Papers

1 In the Commons on 13 May Sir John Newport introduced a bill to alter the law as to church rates in Ireland. It received the royal assent on 6 July 1825 as 6 Geo. IV c. 130. The measure does not appear to have attracted much attention either inside or outside parliament.

2 This clause was proposed by Thomas Spring Rice on 6 June (*DEP*, 11 June 1825) and formed part of the measure as enacted.

3 See letter 1220, note 5.

1227

To Henry Brougham

Thursday, 12 May 1825

(Confidential)

My dear Sir,

I know that Dr. Doyle *intends* to request that you will be so good as to read a letter from him to you denying explicitly any contradiction between the publications of J.K.L. and his evidence before the committees.[1] He wishes to have the letter read this day in the House of Commons so that it may appear tomorrow in the newspapers.[2] If you have any objection to do so, let me know by one line and I will stand between you and the request.

Would you allow me for myself to say that no person has promised or could promise to keep Ireland quiet in ' the coming event ' of the rejection by the Duke of York's party of *the bill* in the Lords. You seemed to think that some such promise was made.

I cannot conclude even such a note as this without expressing to *you* our deep and lasting gratitude and saying even to yourself that our admiration of your powers which I thought could not be increased is beyond the means of expressing it.

SOURCE : Brougham MSS, University College, London.

1 The evidence which Bishop Doyle gave before the select committee of the Lords on 21 March and 21 April and the select committee of the Commons on 16 and 25 March 1825.

2 Brougham did not read the letter in the Commons but Sir John Newport did so on 13 May (*DEP*, 17 May 1825). Dated 12 May, addressed to Brougham and written from Blake's Hotel, Jermyn Street, London, the letter is published in the *Dublin Evening Post* of 19 May 1825.

1228

To his wife

Dover Street [London], 13 May 1825, Friday

My darling Love,

I am so much out of spirits that I cannot write much but still less can I refuse myself the pleasure of writing to you to tell you that you are my *comfort* and my *sweetness*. Indeed, Mary, you are both. I now wish I was at home with you and my children. The miserable ministry is divided. The Duke of York is active, persevering and malignant. The health of the King is very precarious although it does not appear this day that he is as ill as was represented yesterday. But at best his health cannot be relied on for one week. The only comfort is that the Duke of York is also as bad a life as can well be imagined. Plunket spent the day yesterday with Canning at Lord Liverpool's but although I saw him first—Plunket—but could not learn from him anything on the subject. I therefore take for granted that the ministry have come to no kind of conclusion save that of leaving the bill in the Lords to *its fate*, in other words, to the tender mercies of the Duke of York's faction, one which English ignorance of Catholicity and Ireland has armed with much power in this country. The only consolation is that we certainly have made great way in the public opinion and that the ribald trash that used to be employed against us can no longer serve the purpose. A day or two will tell much more, but I must say that now every hour seems to lessen our prospects. Lord Liverpool appears too much of an old woman to take any active or decided part, and thus we are to be left to the mercy of the Eldons and Peels but, darling, it cannot, it *shall* not last. We must pour upon them unremittingly. Every possible means of agitation must be resorted to.

Darling, I have written more politics than I intended. I am for the present weary of them. All hope is not gone but much of it has certainly evaporated. *Who knows?* is a foolish question, but it still may wisely be asked. . . .

Our question will take two days in the Lords and there will be a Catholic meeting here on Saturday week, that is, Saturday the 21st. I will leave town after Mass the next day so as to reach some Catholic town *that* night and hear Mass there and so go on on the following day to Manchester. . . .

SOURCE : Fitz-Simon Papers

1229

To his wife, Merrion Square

London, 14 May 1825, Saturday

Darling,

. . . The only good news I have to give this day is that Goulburn is *not* to return to Ireland but is to be succeeded there by Wilmot Horton,[1] brother-in-law to Lord Kenmare. This will be a change every way for the better. In the first place he is a decided friend to the Catholics. In the next, he is a friend generally to Irish interests which Goulburn is not, and thirdly he is a clever man and Goulburn is an arrant blockhead. This change and Plunket being made Chancellor will have a powerful effect on the domestic policy of Ireland. When the rascally Corporation feel that those who participate in Orange principles are deprived of the best prospects of promotion they will become at once surprisingly liberal, the rascals!!!

It is strange but yet our fate still remains undecided. Until Monday I will not be able to speak with *final* certainty and even this day at five I am to hear more upon the subject and something which may be favourable. . . .

I have thrown away my time and much money and my thanks will not after all be the greater for all these sacrifices. But that, sweetest, we must not mind. Do you hear anything of Comerford[2] and his picture of me? . . . I should have had the first artists in London pressing to do my portrait if he had not made me promise, and yet there is not the slightest symptom of his engraving ever coming out. . . . Darling, I wish I had time to get you a handsome miniature but what is the use in wishing. . . .

SOURCE : Fitz-Simon Papers

1 Robert John Wilmot Horton (1784-1841), M.P. Newcastle-under-Lyne, 1818-30. Under-secretary for war and colonies, 1821-28. Assumed name of Horton, 1823. Knighted, 1831. Succeeded his father as third baronet, 1834. In fact, Horton was not appointed, Goulburn staying on as chief secretary until 1827. Plunket did not become lord chancellor until 1830.

2 John Comerford (c. 1770-1832), an Irish portrait-painter of ability. He executed a miniature of O'Connell about 1800 and a drawing in 1824 which was engraved. See W. G. Strickland, *Dictionary of Irish Artists*, 2 vols. (Dublin and London 1913).

1230

To his wife, Merrion Square

Dover Street [London], 16 May 1825,
Monday

My own sweetest Love,

. . . Why do you fret yourself, love, about Coppinger[1] and his prophesies? He really does not wish for Emancipation and will be sadly disappointed if it shall be carried. At present, darling, he is likely to have a triumph, and yet even now there are expectations thrown out of a *short bill* this sessions, that is, a bill giving all but parliament. They little think how vain that all would be because we never can have anything like fair play until we get into parliament. We never will be able until then to confront and ridicule the ignorant and impudent assertions of our absurd and malicious enemies. Parliament we must have and without it we cannot be content or tranquil. We have no chance of the vote of either Lords Roden,[2] Enniskillen[3] or Courtown,[4] not the least. The Duke of York has given heart and consistency to that party and the miserable dogs have not intellect or manhood enough to induce them to think or act for themselves. I intend to be with you before the close of next week. our project is at present changed. The dinner to Sir Francis Burdett from the Westminster Electors is to take place on Monday next, this day week. We must remain for that, and then on Wednesday we are to be at a great public dinner at Manchester and another on Thursday at Liverpool. . . .

We dined yesterday with Dr. Collins[5] at Southall Park eleven miles from London. Maurice and I went there in a chaise and returned *in the same*. Lord Hutchinson and a very pleasant party met us. We remained until eleven but these English miles scarcely count. We dine today at Mr. Kelly's[6] at Acton. He is the person who got old Pentony's fortune, £100,000.

On Saturday there is to be a Catholic meeting to begin the war over again. The Ministry are and have been miserably divided and that which is decided on one day is totally abandoned the next. I have great pleasure in telling you that Dr. Magee,[7] the Protestant Archbishop of Dublin, has totally broken down on his examination[8] and is the object of ridicule and scorn. Lord Lansdowne said to a friend of mine that his bitterest enemy could not wish him more degraded than he is at present. He abused the Committee on Friday last, said they asked him indecent and insulting questions and actually scolded several individual Lords by name. He was then called to order and was under the necessity of making an apology. His next *flight* was a long dissertation about his calling the Catholic ' a church without a religion ' and the Presbyterian ' a religion without a church '. He got so violent and so disgustingly inflammatory on this subject that at length he was turned out of the Committee room, and then a debate took place respecting the expunging a great part of his evidence, which was at last agreed to be expunged ' in mercy to him and least the publication of it should tend to disturb the public peace '. Such were the grounds Lord Liverpool took. You may imagine what a sensation the total disgrace of the unfortunate man has made. To be sure it is not a little strange that Parliament should have gone on with a committee, the effect of which is to put in the clearest light the vast superiority of Catholicity and even of Catholic divines and the miserable inconsistencies and disgraceful equivocations of the Protestant clergy. Besides, it has set almost everybody upon inquiring into the real nature of our doctrines and that, sweetest, with the help of God, is all we want. I hope I am not either superstitious or profane when in all this I venture to think I recognize the all good as well as all wise hand of the great God, blessed and loved be his holy name. Darling, perhaps the hour of mercy to his long benighted nation is at hand. Certainly everything tends to that object by means of the exertions of the Protestants themselves. . . .

SOURCE : Fitz-Simon Papers

1 Stephen Coppinger.

2 Robert (Jocelyn), third earl of Roden (1788-1870), M.P. for Co. Louth, 1806-07, 1810-20. Created 1821 Baron Clanbrassil (U.K.).

3 John Willoughby (Cole), second earl of Enniskillen (1768-1840), M.P. for Co. Fermanagh, 1790-1800, 1801-03. Created 1815 Baron Grinstead (U.K.). Married 1805 Charlotte, sister of first marquess of Anglesey.

4 James George (Stopford), third earl of Courtown (1765-1835), governor of Co. Wexford, 1813-31. Married 1791 Mary, first daughter of third duke of Buccleuch.

5 Unidentified.

6 George Bourke O'Kelly (1760-1843), Acton House, Acton, Middlesex. Married 1799 Mary, second daughter of Peter Pentheny, M.D., Tara, Co. Meath.

7 William Magee (1766-1831), son of John Magee, Enniskillen, Co.

Fermanagh. Protestant bishop of Raphoe, 1819-22; archbishop of Dublin, 1822-31.

8 Before the Lords select committee on the state of Ireland (see letter 1184, note 2).

1231

To his wife, Merrion Square

[London,] 18 May 1825

My darling love,

I could not write yesterday. This day I have nothing to say or sing but defeat.[1] Blessed be God. We must begin again. The English Catholics are as furious as we are. I was eight hours standing in the thickest crowd imaginable for the spectators in the Lords have no place to sit. I now write at the Parliament House where I am waiting for the cause of *Scully* v. *Scully*. . . . But we must never despair, we are daily getting stronger in point of Catholic numbers in England, and the longer these discussions continue the better it will be for our religion. Ireland in the meantime is condemned to more tyranny and distraction. . . .

[P.S.] I did not go to bed till *six* this morning.

SOURCE : Fitz-Simon Papers

1 The Emancipation Bill had been defeated in the Lords on the previous day.

1232

To his wife

Dover Street [London, 19 May 1825]

My darling Love,

You must have received the hasty note I wrote you yesterday from the House of Lords. I argued the [Scully] case this day for two hours and will give it an hour or two the next sitting day, namely Thursday. . . . I believe I argued the Scully cause pretty well but so long in detail that I have not time to write to you, sweetest. I will be able, however, to write a long letter tomorrow as it will be my first idle day since preparing a speech for Saturday. The Chancellor[1] was very attentive to me, very much so indeed, and I have the greatest hopes of setting aside or altering the decree. Indeed I do not think the former decree can stand. My own Love, we are all *in a great rage* about that scoundrel Lord Liverpool and that greater rascal, if possible, the Duke of York, but our friends are rallying about us and we are *now* greater favourites with the opposition than we were some days ago. We will attack the rascals in every quarter that the law will allow, and they shall be disappointed in their expectation of putting down the Catholics of either country. It is vain for them to expect it. I do not know what they mean to do with Plunket. Darling, a thousand loves to our children. . . .

SOURCE : Fitz-Simon Papers

1 Lord Eldon.

1233

To his wife

Dover Street [London], 20 May 1825

My darling Heart's Love,

. . . By *this* hour you are acquainted with our total defeat. Never certainly was anything more complete and *for the present* we are without hope, but it is only for the present because, sweetest, it is impossible to keep down the Irish millions and the Catholic talent and intelligence. Besides the Catholic faith must gain ground wherever it is dispassionately known. There are great doubts now arising upon the propriety of having a Catholic meeting held which is advertised tomorrow. There is so much of timidity about these English Catholics there is no managing them at all. But we shall see. Did I tell you that Jack Lawless and I are reconciled? He met Maurice[1] at a tavern the other night and in speaking of me he burst into tears and wept a long time. So you know, darling, I must forgive him and I have done so accordingly. I have also made peace with O'Gorman[2] for I am fond of peace. I am now detained here by various causes, first, there is a report that Canning and Lord Liverpool have quarrelled and that one or other *must* go out. I am sure Canning would now get great support from the opposition. Secondly, I have to wait for another day in *Scully* v. *Scully* to give it another brushing. It is believed now that we shall succeed in the appeal. They are satisfied with my being able to do my business as well as any of them. It is curious enough that a Catholic should be the first Irish barrister to be heard by the English House of Lords. If we do, as I think we *must*, succeed, I will get the credit of it all.[3] . . . If there be a meeting tomorrow you shall hear from me in the form of a violent speech. I have no notion of mincing the matter with Lord Liverpool. He is a public enemy and must be hunted down like a wild cat. He had a character in this country for honesty but that is pretty much at an end by this time and I hope to make it more so tomorrow. My own dearest darling, I do doat of you with the most tender fondness. . . .

SOURCE : Fitz-Simon Papers

1 O'Connell's son.

2 Nicholas P. O'Gorman. See letter 1215.

3 See letter 1220, note 5.

1234

To his wife, Merrion Square

Dover Street [London], Saturday, 21 May 1825

My darling Love,

I am just come in from the aggregate.[1] I spoke two hours and a half. I made an *elegant* speech, was applauded to the skies but have time only to ask why I did not get a letter from you this day and to tell you that I love your children and you most tenderly.

SOURCE : Fitz-Simon Papers

1 A general meeting of the British Catholic Association at the Crown and Anchor Tavern, Strand, London, the duke of Norfolk in the chair.

1235

To his wife

Dover Street [London], 23 May 1825

My darling heart,

I send by this post the *Times* of this day and the *Morning Herald,* both contain much better reports of my speech[1] than the *Morning Chronicle*. Indeed that paper has gone back much in point of merit and, if you choose, send Connor[2] to the post office and he will get the *Times* substituted in future for the *Chronicle,* that is, if you choose. You may at all events make the experiment and return to the *Chronicle* the moment you dislike the *Times* but, darling, do just as you please in that and in everything else, sweetest love. Send Connor to Staunton[3] to say that the worst report of my speech is in the *Chronicle,* the second best in the *Times* and the best of all in the *Morning Herald*. I wish this may be communicated to him speedily because I observe that he always gives the worst possible versions of my speeches. Darling, the meeting was a brilliant one, upwards of three thousand persons attended it. I have nothing consolatory to tell you about Catholic affairs. There is no comfort in calling rascals and scoundrels and yet these are the only words suited to the persons who are our enemies. They are such certainly. There is great talk of there being a junction between Mr. Canning and the opposition to turn out Lord Liverpool, Eldon and Peel and to keep in the friends of the Grenvilles and of Canning. *That* would do but it is, I believe, quite imaginary or at best a delusive hope held out. We have nothing for it but to keep up the fire of agitation as much as we possibly can.

There is to be an aggregate meeting in Dublin as I learn by a letter from Bric. I hope it will not be before Thursday, the 2d of June. If it stands over for that day, I undertake to be at it. . . . Send to Bric to say that I give *this undertaking* and let him speak to Sheil on the subject. . . . I see at present that the cause has certainly gained in the public mind and that everything depends on our keeping up the agitation. With the blessing of God it shall be kept up. I am to go this day to the Burdett dinner at the Crown and Anchor. Some of our *worthy* friends have been advising me not to go there but I beg leave to be decidedly of a different opinion and go there I will. It is strange what a disposition our friends have to throw Catholics into the background. Darling, send Morgan to the Dublin library to announce as if by accident that I will be at the aggregate meeting if held on the 2d of June. . . .

SOURCE : Fitz-Simon Papers

1 See letter 1234.

2 His clerk.

3 Michael Staunton, editor of the *Morning Register*.

1236

To his wife

Dover Street [London], 24 May 1825

My darling Heart's Love,

. . . You will see in the *Times* . . . a better report of what I said at Burdett's dinner[1] than can be found elsewhere. The *Morning Chronicle* reports my speeches infamously. I am quite sick of it. The crowd was immense at the Burdett dinner, about 500 persons sat down to dinner. James Mahon and Maurice were there. I did not speak till late in the evening and was received as well as I would be by one of our own little aggregates. In fact I was cheered throughout and thus the apprehensions of those who wished me not to go there were altogether vain. On the contrary, this dinner proved that the electors of this city are decidedly favourable to the Catholics and indeed unfavourable to the line of conduct adopted by Mr. Lambton. The person who principally hissed Lambton was much applauded when he gave his reasons for doing so. I was not sorry that Jack Lawless' friend[2] came in for some reprobation. Burdett was very powerful in his speech. I was quite pleased with the force and manliness of it. It was a speech calculated to do great good among the English. There was much good sense in it mixed with great zeal. All was conducted quite to my satisfaction. . . .

SOURCE : Fitz-Simon Papers

1 The eighteenth anniversary dinner to celebrate the ' Purity of Election and Triumph of Westminster ' at the Crown and Anchor Tavern, London, on 23 May, Sir Francis Burdett presiding.

2 Presumably John George Lambton, the most radical of the aristocratic Whigs.

1237

To his wife, Merrion Square

Dover Street [London], 25 May 1825

My dearest Love,

. . . Darling, send Morgan to Mr. Sheil and to Bric to tell each of them that I will be in Dublin for any meeting to be held on Thursday the second of June but let him also inform them that Sir Edward Bellew, who has become excessively violent, has proposed that all the Catholic peers and baronets should attend the next aggregate meeting in Dublin at any inconvenience to themselves. This proposal is to be debated tomorrow and will I am certain be adopted. . . . Let him tell Sheil I think it would have a striking effect to have all the peers and baronets assembled so that they may publish to the world a solemn declaration of our wrongs. Let him further inform Sheil that Lord Milton, son to Earl Fitzwilliam, is gone to Ireland. Ought he not to get a public dinner? It would be perhaps a rallying point for Protestants as well as Catholics to come together and now join in a hearty declaration of their sentiments. Oh, if some noble spirit would take up the repeal of the Union! *That, that* would be the cry. Darling, you perceive that I begin to be cheered again with the chance of a better agitation than ever. In the meantime I am however distracted between Liverpool and Manchester. I do not think it probable that I shall be able to go to either place. What am I to do? I cannot desert the Scully cause and it is quite uncertain if it will be on before Monday. . . .

SOURCE : Fitz-Simon Papers

1238

To his wife, Merrion Square

Dover Street [London], 26 May 1825

My darling Love,

. . . I cannot go to Liverpool or Manchester at all. I must attend to the cause of *Scully* v. *Scully* on Monday, . . . I *have sat* for the bracelet, darling, and it is finished and is in my opinion a very strong likeness. . . . It is, darling, very like, younger and better looking but very, very like. You shall have both bracelets set as you like them to be. Now, darling, as to politics. We will certainly have a great aggregate meeting. All the Lords will be there or at least most of them.

. . . Lord Manners will certainly leave Ireland. Plunket will certainly be shortly Chancellor.

SOURCE : Fitz-Simon Papers

1239

To his wife, Merrion Square

Dover Street [London], 27 May 1825

My darling Love,

. . . I think he [Daniel, Jr.] will soon be fit for Clongowes but there he never shall go without your full and entire aye and your cheerful consent. So rest easy on that score, darling. Plunket goes off today and goes in excellent spirits. He *will* put Lord Manners out, that is some comfort at all events. I do not at present know that Goulburn is to remain. I believe it is undetermined as yet what is to become of him. But I have the pleasure to tell you that the liberal part of the Cabinet are very anxious that we should *agitate* as much as possible. We must immediately form 'the New Catholic Association'. I have it all arranged. They shall not get one hour's respite from agitation, I promise you. The English Catholics are *wild* for our being as wicked as possible. We will have a uniform—blue frock and white pantaloons in summer—blue pantaloons in winter—a blue velvet cape on a [one word missing] coat. Depend on it, sweetest, I never was *up* to agitation till now. I will tell you a secret respecting our rulers which I cannot write even to you. Get Sheil to set up a great dinner for Lord Milton. Send Morgan from me to Sheil for that purpose. Send to stop the newspapers.

SOURCE : Fitz-Simon Papers

1240

To his wife, Merrion Square

Dover Street [London], 28 May 1825

My own darling Mary,

. . . I have actually paid for the places for James[1] and me in the mail of Monday. Scully's cause[2] does not come on until late that day but the House of Lords never sits in causes beyond the hour of four so that at the worst I am certain of leaving town in the mail. The journey at this time of the year is nothing because the nights are so short that one does not perceive the weary, unpleasant feel which a long night in a mail-coach does not fail to give. Do you know, darling, that I shall be greatly disappointed indeed if you are not before me at Howth? Send to Jerry McCarthy to let him know I shall want as speedily after my arrival as possible the uniform of 'The New Catholic Association'. It will be a blue frock-coat with blue velvet collar, the king's colour, buff waistcoat and white pantaloons. I think it will soon come to be universally worn in both countries as it will be deemed a pledge of hostility to Lord Liverpool who certainly is, at this moment, *most* unpopular with all that is liberal in the country. The greater part of the supporters of this government are anxious for our agitating as much as possible. . . . Tell [Fitz-Simon] . . . that he must be married in the Association uniform. The Duke of Norfolk was here yesterday and said he would himself wear it. There will be two gilt buttons with the Irish Crown and Harp, the two upper buttons, the rest of the colour of the cloth. . . . I called on Lord Cork but got little encouragement from him. I am however to make a written proposal to him and to get a written answer. I also called on Crumpe Bland[3] and was most kindly received by him. I think I may get the life of a son or two in the lease I hold under him. Comerford, the painter, is here about the engraving. It will certainly be out in a few days. The first sketch of the print did not satisfy Comerford and it was on that account he came here. I confess I think it very fine. However it is now certain that he will very soon have it published. I believe I will give you another miniature during the winter by Comerford.

[P.S.] Send Morgan with the enclosed to be inserted in the *next* [*Morning*] *Register*. *No* hint that it comes from me, not the least.

SOURCE : Fitz-Simon Papers

1 His man-servant.

2 *Scully* v. *Scully*.

3 Nathaniel Crumpe Bland, Randallo Park, Surrey, a member of a Kerry landowning family.

1241

To John Primrose, Jr., Hillgrove

Merrion Square, 14 June 1825

My dear John,

I hope my family will be at Derrynane about this day month. I am greatly pleased with your account of what you are doing there. Let everything be snug and warm. Mrs. O'C[onnell] will send down some parlour chairs and tables. . . . If the place agrees with her it will have much of our company. I should delight to spend my Christmas there in old Iveragh festivity. Give us as many bedrooms as you can and, above all things, an excellent barrack room. There *was* also one most *necessary* accommodation wanting. In truth it was a cruel grievance there. Let it be built out of sight of the windows—back either of the fowl house or of that of the other range of offices. It would be also a great convenience if another and a small necessary were built in a lonely spot of the garden. . . .

My English journey has drained me excessively of cash. In fact it is a pure loss of upwards of £3,000 to me. . . . The late fairs have been very good. Have you made any sales of my stock or have the tenants sold any? I want money very, very much and from £500 to twice that sum would be very acceptable. The price of small cattle has been so good that I think you ought or at least may be in funds. . . .

SOURCE : Kenneigh Papers

1242

To John Primrose, Junior

Merrion Square, 29 June 1825

My dear John,

. . . The early fairs have been good. I am sure it would have been wise to have *made* the tenants attend to them for the sale of their small cattle. As to my own I leave them to your discretion. You will however keep up the stock by frequent purchases from the tenants, taking care to allow them excellent prices out of their rents.

I will consult with James[1] on the subject of removing the town[2] or, rather, of building it at Carhen. I believe he is quite right. The steam company will certainly take place. Our Act of Parliament[3] is passed.

Attend, my dear John, to everything at Derrynane and give John O'Connell[4] every encouragement possible. I am now receiving money fast. If I had not gone to England I should be really rich.

[Half a page cut out, apparently in order to have O'Connell's signature.]

Send off immediately an express to Kit Bland[5] to beg that he will not go into any composition for the tithes of Kilcrohan[6] until I go to the country in September. Let me have his answer. Write also to John Segerson of Cove to put it off till my arrival.

SOURCE : O'Connell MSS, UCD

1 His brother.

2 What later became the town of Cahirciveen, about one mile to the west of Carhen.

3 6 Geo. IV (local) c. 167. This act, which received the royal assent on 22 June 1825, provided for the establishment of a joint stock company to be named 'The American and Colonial Steam Navigation Company'. It would establish navigation between Valentia Harbour, Co. Kerry, and places abroad. Among the stockholders of the proposed company named in the act were O'Connell, Lord Kenmare, the Knight of Kerry and David and Pierce Mahony.

4 John Charles O'Connell.

5 Francis Christopher Bland (died 16 Sept. 1838), son of Rev. James Bland, Derryquin Castle, Co. Kerry.

6 The official name of the parish of Cahirdaniel in which Derrynane is situated.

1243

To his wife, Merrion Square

Wexford, 20 [and 21] July 1825

My darling Love,

. . .

21st July

. . . Darling, nothing could equal my triumphant entry *by water* into Wexford.[1] The dinner was splendid, everything went off most admirably. I should attempt a description but that we had newspaper reporters in abundance and you will see all the details. I am to be voted a *piece of plate* at the aggregate meeting. It was intended to make *it* a couple of soup tureens but I see I can easily have the money applied to a pair of salvers as *that* is what you wish. Darling, the clock is only striking nine and yet I hear the judges trumpet going to court. I therefore must conclude. . . .

SOURCE : Fitz-Simon Papers

1 In the afternoon of 20 July O'Connell embarked at Ferrycarrig and sailed the two miles down the river Slaney to Wexford in a procession of some fifty boats. On landing he was received by a deputation led by Sir Thomas Esmonde and was the guest of honour at a public banquet in the ' poor school adjoining the Roman Catholic Chapel ' (*FJ*, 25 July 1825).

1244

From James Henry Fitz-Simon, 18 Bury St., London, 24 July 1825, to Merrion Square

Expressing his pleasure at the recent marriage of his nephew Christopher Fitz-Simon to O'Connell's daughter Ellen.

SOURCE : O'Connell Papers, NLI 13646

1245

From Rev. Peter Kenney, S.J., Clongowes Wood College, Clane, 26 July 1825

Inviting O'Connell to attend Academy Day and to stay overnight.

SOURCE : O'Connell Papers, NLI 13647

1246

To his wife, Merrion Square

Belfast, 30 July 1825, Saturday

My own Heart's Love,

. . . I have been defeated in the record after a two days' trial[1] but that, sweetest, is no fault of mine. I worked hard and perhaps well. . . . I never was in better health or spirits than I am at present. The town of Carrickfergus is just nine miles from this town although, as I said, the post makes a difference of 24 hours. I thought they managed those things better in the North. The drive to Carrickfergus is along the seashore and nothing can exceed it in loveliness. . . . Darling, the trial was a most curious and interesting one, and we were defeated by evidence of a description which we could not foresee. I spoke to the case for full two hours and a half and certainly could not for my part make a better speech, all in vain. My sweetest love, I shall be with you certainly in such time on Wednesday as to get out of town as far as Kilbeggan,[2] that is a distance of thirty miles. I have written to Judge Vandeleur to fix Friday for the other trial[3] and if I can get the one[4] at Downpatrick over on Monday it will be to me a great object gained.

SOURCE : Fitz-Simon Papers

1 A case in which John Francis Hamilton O'Hara claimed that his father, Francis Hamilton O'Hara, Crebilly, Ballymena, Co. Antrim, was legally married to his mother, a Catholic, before his father went through a form of marriage with Miss Jackson, a Protestant (a niece of John, first Viscount O'Neill). O'Connell tried to establish the legality of the alleged first marriage, contracted under Scottish law, but failed (*Northern Whig,* supplement, 4 Aug. 1825).

2 Co. Westmeath. Mary travelled with her husband to Galway (*FJ, DEP,* 8 Aug. 1825).

3 *Kirwan* v. *Kirwan* in Galway town.

4 A family case involving alleged fraud which was nonsuited at the request of the plaintiff, John Blackwood, Bangor, Co. Down, the defendant being Fleming P. O'Reilly, attorney, 6 Middle Gardiner Street, Dublin. O'Connell acted for the defendant (*Northern Whig,* supplement, 11 Aug. 1825).

1247

From the Knight of Kerry to Dublin, c/o T. D. La Touche, Castle St.

London, 10 August 1825

My Dear O'Connell,

I enclose you nineteen shares.[1] The ten percent is of course English money. Ireland and Kerry in particular has done little for us. I trust we shall eventually place our shares in good hands. The market is pretty well tired of companies but it is odd that those which *catch* them most are the [? mere] frauds of the day—the large amount of our deposits is a difficulty in our way which the real value of the undertaking will eventually get over.

SOURCE : O'Connell Papers, NLI 13647

1 In the American and Colonial Steam Navigation Company (see letter 1242, note 3).

1248

From Richard Lalor Sheil to Post Office, Cork

Clonmel, 11 August 1825

My dear O'Connell,

Your letter of the fourth instant did not reach me until this day. . . . The mention made by Cobbett[1] of my name has occasioned me a good deal of annoyance. He does me, however, the justice to state that in the conversation which took place on the 10th of March last, so far from intimating any unfavourable sentiment, I expressed my satisfaction at what I considered as quite certain—your promotion in the event of Emancipation. I do not exactly recollect what passed between me and Cobbett. Whatever I said was altered in the heedlessness, I should perhaps call it the giddiness, of an after-dinner dialogue. It is but candid upon my part to tell you at once that I certainly *collected* from Blake[2] and from conversations with yourself that the liberal part of the Administration intended to give you a patent of precedency in case Emancipation should pass. . . . It was generally supposed that Lord Wellesley was anxious to do you this out of justice (for so, everybody considered it) but that it had been opposed by Lord Manners. I inferred (and it was no more than inference) that Plunket had signified his favourable disposition at a moment when he himself looked forward with confidence to the success of the measure. This conjecture I communicated to Cobbett and probably in a shape which he not unnaturally construed into the statement of fact.

As to *terms,* I never insinuated anything of the kind. I recollect your having mentioned at Albemarle St. that you expected no *favour* from government and that you anticipated from Emancipation no personal benefit to yourself beyond the concession of a professional right for that your opinions on parliamentary reform would operate as a permanent obstacle to your advancement. The great national results of Emancipation appeared to me to engross your mind and to its consequences as far as you were individually concerned you attached little importance.

I trust that the citation of my name as an authority by Cobbett has left no disagreeable impression upon your mind. . . .

The feeling of the public in your regard is even more ardent than ever. It is so at least wherever I had an opportunity of observing it.

SOURCE : O'Connell MSS, UCD

1 In a letter dated 19 July 1825 Cobbett addressed the Catholics of Ireland in his *Political Register*. He attacked O'Connell as responsible for the failure to procure Emancipation, and ascribed O'Connell's motive in accepting the 'wings' to a desire for a patent of precedence. He named Sheil as the source of the information that O'Connell was being granted the patent. Cobbett's letter was published in the Dublin *Morning Register* of 26 July 1825.

2 Anthony R. Blake.

1249

From his wife to Carhen, Derrynane

6 September 1825

[No salutation]

. . . *Pray* what was the necessity to order six dozen of bottled cider and six of bottled ale, love, just at this time? I perceive I must exert *my authority* and *try* to keep you in *proper* order.

. . . Every day I get more pleased with Derrynane. I never was better and with the blessing of God I shall next season pay it an early visit. I always liked Iveragh but now I like it extremely. A *home* endears the most solitary place to those who have everything in this world to make them happy. . . . We had Mass here this morning. Mr. Teahan came to offer his services. . . .

Your girls and little boys unite in fond love to you. Fitz-Simon desires his affectionate regards. I won't send my love to Morgan as he cares not for it. . . .

Farewell, my own love. May God protect you. I hope you have had at least two good hunts. . . .

[P.S.] Take care of my letter.

SOURCE : O'Connell Papers, NLI 13651

1250

From his brother James, Lakeville [later Lakeview], *Killarney, 3 October 1825, to Derrynane*

'I am glad to hear your family were to remain there [Derrynane] until next May.'

SOURCE : O'Connell MSS, UCD

1251

To Thomas Wyse[1]

Derrynane, 14 October 1825

Dear Sir,

I have most unfortunately mislaid the letters you did me the honour to write me on the subject of registering my freehold in Waterford and the Catholic Rent. I am, therefore, unable to answer your letters with the proper direction. It will not, I am sorry to say, be in my power to attend in Waterford before November. I must be at the Provincial meeting on the 24th of this month at Limerick.

With respect to the sum collected of Catholic Rent it was by a vote transferred to Lord Killeen.[2] He is the proper person, therefore, to be applied to with respect to any disposal of that money. It is time for me to avoid involving myself out of my sphere in that disgusting obloquy which in Catholic affairs has always attended those who have struggled for this unfortunate country.[3] I beg, therefore, respectfully to decline giving any opinion on this subject.

SOURCE : FitzPatrick, *Corr.*, I, 112

1 Thomas Wyse (1791-1862), eldest son of Thomas Wyse of the Manor of St. John, Co. Waterford. M.P. for Co. Tipperary, 1830-32; Waterford city, 1835-47; lord of the treasury, 1839-41; secretary to the board of control (India), 1846-49. Married 1821 Laetitia (Letizia), daughter of Lucien Bonaparte and niece of Napoleon. Knighted, 1857. See *DNB*.

2 At the meeting of 18 March 1825 when the Catholic Association resolved on its own dissolution, it was decided to vest its funds in Lord Killeen (Dublin *Morning Register*, 21 Mar. 1825).

3 A reference to the many attacks on him during the summer and autumn of 1825 because of his acceptance of the 'wings' (see letters 1180, note 2, and 1248, note 1) in London during the spring.

1252

To his wife, Derrynane

Listowel [Co. Kerry], 22 October 1825

My darling Heart's Love,

. . . My brother James was in Tralee before me and he is coming on with me to the aggregate meeting in Limerick. . . . Darling, now for business. There are ten oxen of mine to be sold. I gave directions to have them sent to Cahirciveen fair. Do you order that they shall not be sold under £10 a piece. . . . Let me hear that *the works* are going on briskly. . . . The road out of Iveragh is in a very bad state. I must get it repaired before you travel over it. . . . Darling, get John Primrose to send Mic Casure[1] a gun and powder and shot and he will supply you with wild fowl.

SOURCE : Fitz-Simon Papers

1 Michael O'Sullivan, Eightercua, Waterville, Co. Kerry. His family had the soubriquet 'Casure' (Gaelic for 'hammer'). He was a brother of Patrick O'Sullivan.

1253

To his wife, Derrynane

Limerick, 25 October 1825, Tuesday

My darling love,

. . . I did not tell you that 'the mob' drew me into and about Tralee. . . . By the by there is an excellent inn at Listowel, that is, the former inn is made perfectly warm and comfortable. . . . The provincial meeting[1] has gone off admirably. We had no less than six protestant speakers—Lords Lismore,[2] Cloncurry and Dunally,[3] Spring Rice, Counsellor Lloyd[4] and Capt. Stowell.[5] Lloyd is a candidate for the County of Limerick and will, it is generally believed, throw out the son of the Chief Baron[6] and everybody is glad of it. I gave him considerable support yesterday. It is terrific to think how the Chief Baron made the Court of Exchequer subservient to his county electioneering purposes. I got a flaming address from the *trades* of Limerick.[7] They made a great procession in the streets to the Chapel and accompanied me back again. I spoke for something less than an hour and was as well received as it is possible for anybody to be. The crowd was immense. We had gentlemen in numbers from all the counties in the province. Waterford mustered strong, so did Cork. . . . The dinner[8] was splendid in every respect. I am, darling, in perfect health and in great *fresh* spirits. I find so much kindness and affection from the Catholics everywhere, especially the people. I need not bid you write to me every post. It would be *cruel* not to write. Give me details of our children. Again tell Morgan I rely on his promise not to leave Derrynane until he is well. He wanted to go to Carhen at a time when the journey would certainly have ruined him, and probably for life. . . .

SOURCE : Fitz-Simon Papers

1 The Munster provincial meeting of the Catholics was held on 24 October in St. Michael's chapel, Limerick, Hon. William Browne (brother of Lord Kenmare) in the chair (*DEP,* 27, 29 Oct. 1825).

2 Cornelius (O'Callaghan), second Baron Lismore (1775-1857), created 1806 Viscount Lismore, created 1838 Baron Lismore (U.K.). Married 1808 Eleanor, sister of first marquess of Ormonde and youngest daughter of seventeenth earl of Ormonde. She was divorced by act of parliament, 1826.

3 Henry Sadleir (Prittie), second baron Dunalley (I) (1775-1854), M.P. for Okehampton, 1819-24. Married firstly 1802 Maria, daughter of Dominick Trant of Dunkettle, Co. Cork, by Eleanor, sister of John, first earl of Clare. Married secondly 1826 Emily Maude, eighteenth child of first Viscount Hawarden.

4 Thomas Lloyd, K.C. (c. 1770-1830), Beechmount, Rathkeale, Co. Limerick; M.P. for Co. Limerick, 1826-30. Married 1792 Katherine, daughter of Eyre Evans, Miltown Castle, Charleville, Co. Cork.

5 Capt. James Ludlow Stawell, South Cork Militia, 1810.

6 Standish Darby O'Grady (1792-1848), son of Chief Baron Standish O'Grady (created Viscount Guillamore, 1831); M.P. for Co. Limerick, 1820-26, February-May 1830 and 1830-34. Married 1828 Gertrude Jane, first daughter of the Hon. Berkeley Paget. Succeeded as second Viscount Guillamore, 1840.

7 A copy of their address is in the *Dublin Evening Post* of 27 October 1825.

8 A public dinner in the Assembly-room, Charlotte's Quay, followed the meeting, Thomas Wyse presiding (*DEP,* 29 Oct. 1825).

1254

To his wife, Derrynane

Merrion Square, 27 October 1825

My darling Love,

. . . The coach from Limerick carries six inside, and Dan O'Connell of Kilgorey and I were two, so you may imagine how I was *stuffed* but I got an outside passenger to change with me at Nenagh and from that place up I travelled in a soft small rain but very comfortably for I had my large cloak and umbrella that kept off the wet effectually.

You would fall in love with Boyle,[1] the editor of the *Cork Freeholder*[2] if you saw his description of your eldest son. He says, 'Dan went to Kerry accompanied by his eldest son, *a whelp we understand of extraordinary impertinence.*' You see, love, what glory your eldest son is acquiring. I laughed very heartily at the thankfulness you would feel to my friend Boyle.

. . . Tell Maurice I expect he will tell you if Morgan attempts to leave Derrynane even for one hour until his sore is *quite healed,* I say quite healed because one hour's ride may throw him back for six weeks and he is near being well if he will suffer his cure to go on. . . .

I have settled with John Roche[3] about the hooker. I will easily get a most capital one of about 25 tons for 200 guineas. Darling, she will easily come to Dublin, and will bring everything we can want, besides supplying us with fish. Give me full details of my works. I am anxious the buildings should proceed.

SOURCE : Fitz-Simon Papers

1 John Boyle (died 1832), journalist; owned and edited *Boyle's Magazine,* 1807; the *Freeholder,* c. 1820-30.

2 Not extant.

3 Unidentified.

1255

To his wife, Derrynane

Merrion Square, 29 October 1825

My darling Heart,

. . . The only thing talked of is the marriage of the Lord Wellesley with Mrs. Patterson[1] who is the widow of the brother of the lady who married Jerome Bonaparte. She gives him £40,000 and keeps as much more for herself. The marriage cannot take place this day as she is ill with a sore throat. She is a Catholic and a strict one. She dined some days ago with Saurin and somebody introduced Catholic politics. Saurin at once damned Pope and Popery to the lowest pit of Hell. She said nothing at the time, but before dinner was quite over she took occasion to mention her being a Catholic just as a matter of course. You may judge of Saurin's confusion. He said nothing but next day she got from him a long apology which of course she disregarded. If you come up before she leaves this you *must* go to the Castle, but they say that this marriage will hasten the removal of Lord Wellesley and that we shall have another Lord-Lieutenant by Christmas. At all events, darling, whoever is Lord-Lieutenant, I will be with you to dinner on Christmas day if some accident to my health does not intervene. I am now in great spirits and will go to the Association with more than ordinary pleasure. Darling, I never began a winter's campaign with better health or more animation. You would laugh to see me over my solitary meal—*stirabout*, milk and two eggs, not very fresh but good. . . .

SOURCE : Fitz-Simon Papers

1 Marianne (died 1853), widow of Robert Patterson and daughter of Richard Caton, Baltimore, Maryland, U.S.A.; granddaughter of Charles Carroll, Carrolton; married 29 October 1825 the lord-lieutenant, Marquis Wellesley.

1256

To John Primrose, Jr., Hillgrove

Merrion Square, 29 October 1825

My dear John,

. . . 1st. Give me the state of the building. Carry with you that I am extremely desirous of going on with it as rapidly as possible. The comforts which my family would receive from remaining at Derrynane must arise from a good house. To me it is of the greatest value that they should stay there.

2nd. What have you done with the digging of my potatoes? Do not let John O'Connell[1] neglect *that*. If you do not yourself go to Derrynane and remain there till the potatoes are all housed, they will be lost to me.

3rd. Is there anything necessary *at present* for next year's crop? . . .

4th. You will sell my bullocks at Killarney fair at the latest whatever they bring unless in the interval a sudden fall takes place. . . .

6th. Send me an exact list of the tenants who owe the May rent on the first of November. I am very much obliged to you for having sent round another caution. I perceive I shall have many lands to let. They may depend upon it that I will get new tenants. The *fall* I made in the rent roll ought to have induced them to come in cheerfully. But the fact is that they do not believe me. . . .

SOURCE : O'Connell MSS, UCD

1 John Charles O'Connell.

1257

From his wife to Merrion Square

Derrynane, Saturday, 29 [and 30]
October 1825

My dearest Love,

The only news I have as yet heard from the fair is unfavourable to us. The bullocks were not sold and milch cows sold high. Of the latter, I directed Primrose purchase one for me as the cow we were to have got lost her milk and her calf, the natural consequence of having come before her time. This new cow, with another in expectation, will I hope be quite enough as after this week the workmen will be dropping off. . . .

Before dinner, love, we expect an addition to our society. At all events we shall have Mr. O'Flaherty.[1] What a delightful thing it would be if we could get a good road between this and Waterville. Don't forget to exert yourself about it. Now that our Vice-Queen[2] is a Catholic, perhaps your application to government would be listened to with a favourable ear. How fond of rank and title the lady must be. I hope she may have influence sufficient over the old Marquis[3] to induce him to become a Papist even in secret. . . . Our present post[4] is attentive and very expeditious but there is not one of them ' that don't dread meeting a *ghost* on the mountain '.

Sunday morning after breakfast [30 October]

. . . The building is getting on rapidly. The rock is quite gone and the slaters are to be on *the* wing, slating it tomorrow. We have had an addition to our tradespeople last night, two men with your uncle's[5] monument to have put up. They could not have come at a more inconvenient time and, of *course*, they are billeted here. They will take a full week and six men to attend them. . . .

Kate is always regretting our stay here. Dublin is so gay and so many of her friends there. I have as yet escaped cold and am, thank God, quite well and have a good deal to occupy me. . . . I despise Boyle too much to be annoyed at what he says of Maurice.[6] We got no *Patriot* last night. I read your speech at the Limerick meeting[7] and like it greatly.

SOURCE : O'Connell Papers, NLI 13651

1 Rev. Edward [O'] Flaherty.

2 Lady Wellesley.

3 Marquis Wellesley.

4 The letter carrier.

5 Hunting-Cap.

6 See letter 1254.

7 See letter 1253, note 1.

1258

To his wife, Derrynane

Merrion Square, 1 November 1825

My own darling Heart,

. . . Darling, your handwriting is quite a charm to my eye and to read your letters is the very honey of my heart. I speak literally the truth when I say so because I know no other language that could convey to you an idea of how delightful your letters are to me.

Let me first scold you, sweetest. It is your own fault that you have a cold in your head. Nobody need have a cold at Derrynane unless *they* earn it for themselves. So let me hear that you are quite well and do not attempt to get another cold if you value my affection or fear my high and haughty displeasure.

Sweetest, I have no news to tell you. The papers tell you all. You will see by the next [*Dublin Evening*] *Post* a long and tame answer of mine to Mr. Marmion of the County of

Louth.[1] I have gone through the charges distinctly and at length. I wish you may like my letter but I fear not because seriously, darling, it is not saucy enough for you. You are besides more angry with my assailants than I can afford to be. However, darling, I think you will not be displeased with what I have written. There has been some *stir* occasioned by the Lord-Lieutenant's marriage. They had it inserted in the papers that the marriage would not take place on Saturday merely to prevent the crowd from gathering but they were married. Dr. Murray was attended by two other priests. *She* always goes to Mass publicly and is quite a regular Catholic. Her sister, Miss Caton[2]—it was originally Keating—is with her. Another sister[3] married an aide-de-camp of Lord Wellington's. This marriage has, you may imagine, given some mortification to the *Orangists*. I wish the Marquis may be left here another year or two. It would be pleasant to observe the discountenance which a Catholic vice-queen would necessarily throw upon the *ribaldry* of the oppressing faction. You perceive, sweetest, that we are beginning to agitate again. Tomorrow we will hold a little aggregate and if that shall succeed we will hold one every Wednesday. The New Association will meet on Saturday so that I hope the effect of the anti-association bill[4] will be to give us two meetings in the week in the place of one.

Darling, you do not say anything of the works that ought to go on in the housekeeper's part of the house, I mean the buildings that were roofed before I left home. I wish these were slated and the inside work proceeded on as rapidly as it is possible. That part of the house will add greatly to your comforts. . . .

I have paid so much money for interest that I am quite sick of being in debt and if I had but one or two years of strict economy I would be entirely out of debt and be able to pay Kate's fortune *on demand*. These are the sources of my *parsimony*. Only *help* me, darling, to get out of debt and then you will, as you always did, command every shilling I have in the world. I suppose Maurice will be off before you receive this letter. I hope he will leave no debts of his own in Iveragh but indeed, indeed heart, I tremble for him. You see he attends to nothing useful. I trust my unfortunate Morgan will by his sore experience learn a little wisdom.

. . . How does my sweet Betsey get on? My darling, darling Kate, I do doat of her. How are you all off for milk and butter?

SOURCE : Fitz-Simon Papers

1 The Catholics of Co. Louth met in the Catholic chapel of Dundalk on 17 October, Sir Edward Bellew in the chair and Anthony Marmion as secretary to the meeting. When Nicholas Markey proposed a vote of thanks to O'Connell, Marmion proposed an amendment to it for the purpose of censuring O'Connell for having supported the ' wings '. In the course of debate he accused O'Connell of having acted on ' corrupt and personal motives '. The amendment was rejected and the vote of thanks was passed (*DEP*, 20 Oct. 1825). O'Connell's letter to the Catholics of Co. Louth, in reply to Marmion, written from Merrion Square and dated 31 October 1825, appeared in the *Dublin Evening Post* of 3 November 1825.

2 Sister of Marianne, Marchioness Wellesley, and daughter of Richard Caton, Baltimore, Maryland.

3 Unidentified.

4 The act for the suppression of the Catholic Association (see letter 1173, note 4).

1259

To Denys Scully[1]

Merrion Square, 2 November 1825

My dear Scully,

I enclose you our account. . . . My wish is to close it. I propose by a cash payment of £206.3.11½ to reduce it to £375 and for that sum to give you five notes payable with interest on the 10th of every month after this, . . . till the five are discharged, getting up of course my mortgage and other securities. . . .

SOURCE : Scully Papers

1 With the above letter was a financial statement of account enclosed by O'Connell which shows that on 1 February 1825 O'Connell owed Scully £850 and by 2 November 1825 had reduced this sum to £375.6.0. Financial entries in Denys Scully's hand, which are not very legible, suggest that O'Connell's debt was liquidated by a final payment on 10 November 1825.

1260

From John K. Dunbar, Clanbrassil Place, Dublin, 2 November 1825, to Merrion Square

The writer describes himself as a liberal Protestant and reports a case of two Catholic women thought to be dying in the

Richmond Bridewell, who had received the last rites of their church and then were abused by the deputy governor, Wilson,[1] who asked them *'if they supposed anyone on earth could forgive them their sins in this world'* and said other such things.

SOURCE : O'Connell Papers, NLI 13647

1 Archibald Wilson, deputy governor and steward, Richmond Bridewell, South Circular Road, Dublin.

1261

From his daughter Kate to Merrion Square

Derrynane, 12 November 1825

My darling father,

Mod tells me you wish for a letter from me and she tells me also that for my own interest I ought to write as you will get too fond of Mrs. Fitz-Simon and forget you have got a daughter down in the wilds of Iveragh who dotes upon her darling father. . . . We have quite a large party at present. . . . It makes the time pass quickly to have the house full. . . . The new building is getting on very fast. All the window frames are up in the parlour. . . . Did he [Maurice] give you a great account of his laying the first stone of the chapel at 'Carreg O'Connell '[1] (is that the way you write it)? I understand they had a most *imposing ceremony*. . . .

SOURCE : Kenneigh Papers

1 Unidentified. The statement has a note of flippancy so that it may refer merely to some family joke.

1262

From his wife to Merrion Square

Derrynane, 14 [15 and 16] November [1825]

My dearest love,

. . . The bullocks were not sold at the Killarney fair, only £8.10.0 offered for them. On Thursday they are to be at the fair of Castlemaine where I hope they will be well disposed of. . . . Tell me did he [James O'Connell, brother of O'Connell] pay for his seat in the carriage and four to Limerick or did he pay for your servant's seat in the coach? Either, I think, he is bound to do.

Tuesday, the 15th.

Thank God we are in the middle of this month. I got your letter, love, last evening. Why do you mind Harry Morris[1] or T. O'Mara? The latter in my *opinion* can't tell truth. Surely your uncle[2] knows as much of the Austrian Ambassador's intentions towards Morgan as Mr. Morris can! Don't you think he would at once write to prevent Morgan from going to join if he was considered out of the service! . . . Morgan is the life and soul of gaiety. May God preserve him to us and mark him with grace. You need not fear, love, that I shall do away any of your plans respecting the new building. . . . I perceive Mr. Lawless is still attacking you.[3] Bishop England's letter may as well be kept back.[4] I am glad you are all so well. . . .

Wednesday [16 November] . . .

SOURCE : O'Connell Papers, NLI 13651

1 Unidentified.

2 Count O'Connell.

3 On the subject of the ' wings '.

4 John England, bishop of Charleston, wrote five public letters to O'Connell on Emancipation and the ' wings ' which were published in the *United States Catholic Miscellany* for 1825. They were written from Charleston and dated 8, 15, 22 and 30 July and 12 August. Later, they were published in the pro-O'Connell (Dublin) *Morning Register* on 2, 22 and 30 November and 10, 16, 24 and 26 December. The letter referred to by Mary O'Connell was obviously the second one which condemned any disfranchisement of the forty-shilling freeholders and which was published in the *Morning Register* of 22 November. The five letters are published in Sebastian Messmer, ed., *The Works of . . . John England, First Bishop of Charleston,* 7 vols. (Cleveland, Ohio, 1908), VI, 13-93.

1263

From his wife to Merrion Square

Derrynane, 19 [and 20] November [1825]

My own love,

Sunday, the 20th.

Darling, I got your letter last night but not a word about the bullocks. I have therefore taken upon me to direct their being sold for £8.10.0. Will you scold me for this? I wish Primrose had taken the £9 that was offered on the spot for them this day three weeks. I told you, love, not to mind O'Mara's talk. I well know the General[1] was more in the confidence of Baron Vincent concerning our dear Morgan than Harry Morris could be. . . .

SOURCE : O'Connell Papers, NLI 13651

1 O'Connell's uncle, Count O'Connell.

1263a

To Lord Darnley

Merrion Square, 20 November 1825

My Lord,

I fear you will deem me inexcusable in addressing you on the subject of the election of a representative peer but the unfortunate Catholics of Ireland are so deeply interested in the result of that election that I am induced to do so. If Lord Farnham shall be elected[1] the flame of party spirit which has been and is dying away fast will acquire fresh vigour, and the insolence of triumph on the one hand, the bitterness of defeat on the other may and probable [*sic*] will lead to deplorable consequences especially in the North of Ireland where a reconciliation has already commenced but may be blasted for ever if Lord Farnham shall be successful.

SOURCE : Duke University Library

1 O'Connell failed to prevent Farnham's election as a representative peer.

1264

To John Primrose, Junior, Hillgrove

Merrion Square, 22 November 1825

My dear John,

. . . You *must* receive the tenpennies[1] as long as the poor people have them. Say you will receive them only in payment of rent and get in as much as possible in that way. It is only sending a messenger with a *horse load* to Cork at the worst but do not allow them to remain in the poor people's hands. Take them at the full value but conceal your intention of continuing to take them after Christmas. However, I repeat, I would rather lose than allow the poor people to suffer. . . .

SOURCE : O'Connell MSS, UCD

1 On 6 January 1826 the Irish currency was assimilated to the British (6 Geo. IV c. 79). This meant the withdrawal of Irish notes and coin from circulation. The ten penny piece was peculiar to Ireland.

1264a

From his wife to Merrion Square

Derrynane, 22 November [1825]

My own Love,

My heart was too sore yesterday even to write a line to you. My darling Morgan left me about half past seven in full health and spirits for Carhen where he stops until tomorrow in every sense of the word. Yesterday was a miserable gloomy day, dreadfully severe and wet from ten o'clock in the morning. The night was tremendous and stormy nor is this day much better. The people of the country say that for four years there has not been so severe a winter as the present one. This house with all our precautions is miserably cold, wind blowing from every direction, but I believe it is the case in every other house in such weather. You would be satisfied if you could see the care I take of myself. I breakfast in my room since I had the cold. From the time I go to the drawing room until dinner, I do not quit it for a moment. I have got [a] large wooden clothes horse as a screen between me and the drawing room door. I am, thank God, perfectly recovered from the cold I had and have nothing new to complain of but the absence of my husband, and since your letter, darling, last night was so blotted I could scarcely read it, I believe you fold up your letters before they are dry. I hate, Love, to lose a word of your letters.

John O'Connell is of opinion that the carrying on of the building at present is very expensive, the weather so bad. The people are often half the day idle. At all events there is a great deal to be done before it is ready for roofing. They have not lime only sufficient for this work. No account of the timber, and it is only this day that ropes came from Cahir[civeen] for the scaffolding. They have been obliged to substitute something else this time back. The building near the parlour is going on. It will be finished without stopping. Primrose has not been here since yesterday week. He is, I think, in Killarney, report says about some unpleasant words that passed between him and Whitwell Butler at old Primrose's *election.*[1] Why, Darling, did you influence or *allow* your tenantry to be influenced either for Primrose or Mahony. I thought you were a candidate for the *freedom* of *Election.*

Richard Mahony stopped here last night on his way today to Kenmare. Doctor Barry also stopped last night. He came to visit a tenant of yours who, I fear, is dying of an infection of the bowels. The monument[2] is completed at length. I am told it is very handsome. I think, heart, your brothers and you ought to erect another monument to the memory of your father and mother or at least a good tomb stone.[3]

It is bad news, Love, to have the prices falling. How unfortunate we did not sell *our* bullocks for the £9 offered [? but] Primrose was afraid of you. I am delighted you have given up the hooker. John O'Connell says you can build one here for half the [? price] that Davy German[4] has just completed a very handsome hooker.

Our visitors at present consist of Ellen and Tommy Connor[5] and Tom O'C[onnell]. Tommy is a great acquisition to Danny. He is a fine, most intelligent boy. I think he fair promises for a good attorney. Edward McSwiney and his sister Ellen[6] are to be here about Sunday or Monday next. Kate will then have *some one* to ride with her. . . . Wednesday. I am sorry to tell you, Love, the bullocks returned last night. There was only £7 offered for them. John Primrose was at the fair. If this day was not so dreadfully wet I suppose he would come here. It is only this day I could get John O'C[onnell] to commence killing the pigs. The building takes all his time and all that is [one word illegible] for the house just at this time. What would you think of stopping it until after we leave this? This day [about one word illegible] at the housekeeper's garret there is not one of the men at work. Tell Ellen with my love I shall save my bacon according to her recipe. Now, Love, don't be fretting about me for I am perfectly well. So are your children who unite in fondest love to you.

SOURCE : Office of Public Works, Dublin

1 Probably the election of a commissioner by the special parish vestry held for the composition of tithes under the act of 4 Geo.

IV c. 99. All persons holding land subject to tithe on which they paid more than twenty shillings a year in county rates were eligible to be members of such vestries.

2 Hunting-Cap's tomb.

3 O'Connell's parents are buried in an unpretentious tomb in Cahirciveen old cemetery. The tomb has no inscription. For this information I am indebted to Sister M. de Lourdes, Presentation Convent, Cahirciveen, and Mr. Eugene Ring, Cahirciveen.

4 Of Scart, Castlecove, Co. Kerry.

5 (c. 1799-1866). Eldest son of James and Betsy Connor and nephew of Mary O'Connell.

6 Cousins, children of Myles and Bridget McSwiney.

1264b

From his wife to Merrion Square

Derrynane, 26 [and 27] November 1825

My Dearest Love,

John Primrose came here yesterday. He tells me he had a letter from you regretting he did not use his own *discretion* and dispose of the bullocks for what he considered a good price. Now, Love, I don't want to defend Primrose but from your letter to him it would appear that I was the cause of the bullocks not being sold. Do you recollect your letter from Listowel to me contained *strict* injunctions to Primrose not to sell the cattle under £10 each? *This* message I gave and certainly recommended an observance of it as I am aware how much you like to have your *orders* strictly obeyed. There is still a chance of the bullocks being sold for £8:10:. Now, Love, that I have *scolded* you I will bid adieu to the subject of bullocks, cows and pigs for the future in my letters. Let these matters be between you and your agent.[1] Take care you make no remark to him on the report I mentioned to you was in circulation respecting him and Whitwell Butler. What I tell you is not to be mentioned as coming from me. Primrose will write *this* post and give you a detail of every thing you wish to hear from this on business.

I wish, my heart, I had influence sufficient to prevail upon you not to build a third storey. You have no notion how bleak this place is in winter and I think the new building is very much exposed to the weather. There is scarcely a chimney in this house that does not smoke. Will they not be worse when there are other chimneys higher than they are? The new parlour and drawing room will give you two large additional bed chambers. These with the six we have in this house, the garret rooms and the housekeeper's and butler's apartments will give us quite room enough. We must expect our family will be lessening instead of *increasing*. Your daughters will be married and none of them[1] are inclined to make Derrynane their residence. At all events, heart, don't determine on the third storey until you come down. You will, I trust, be with us on the 20th. *We* reckon on leaving this the 2d of January, going to Tralee the 4th and stopping there until the 7th. I must have at least *two* days to stay in Tralee independent of the day we arrive there. Oh, Darling, we have horrid weather. Yesterday was *fine* but this day is dreadfully *wet. I am a complete* prisoner. Should I stay here another winter I must have some kind of covered machine to go out to take the air when the weather is favourable. Sunday, the 27th. Darling, I got your letter last night and I slept the better for it. Rest assured the air of Derrynane was not the cause of my illness. The [? attack] on my chest did not last above an hour. I went to bed at four o'clock on Saturday and remained there until the same hour the Monday after. I was but three days confined to my room but *that* was caused by the badness of the weather. If the air of this place disagreed with me my chest would never be free. I am now, thank God, quite well. This winter is [one word illegible] severe. Could I exercise in the open air it would be of great service to me. Next winter I *must* have some kind of covered carriage to travel about the *strand*. Your girls and Danny are very well. Kate has no objection to Derrynane in summer but a winter, she says, is *horrible*.

Enclosed you have half notes for a £100. Primrose encloses you the other halves. Pray when you write of me to any person why don't you call me Mrs. O'Connell? In your letter to Primrose you *style* me Mary. You should recollect I am the *Protector's* Wife and like to keep up my consequence. There is a scolding for you. Dear Morgan, I hope, is with you. I have supplied him with what he wanted in linen and other necessaries. Kiss him for me. . . .

SOURCE : Office of Public Works, Dublin

1 John Primrose, Jr.

1265

From Rev. Jerh. O'Donovan, C.C.,[1] *to Merrion Square*

Maynooth [Co. Kildare], 27 November 1825

My dear Mr. O'Connell,

. . . Amongst the gentlemen who are of opinion that we are bound, at the sacrifice of unanimity, to record our execration of the wings and refuse to accept emancipation on terms on which it never was and never will be offered, I find that Mr. D. O'Reilly[2] holds a conspicuous place. Although our bishops would have accepted emancipation with them and Mr. O'Connell and Mr. Sheil approved of them, and are now willing to recall that approval for sake of unanimity, yet such is Mr. O'Reilly's horror of them that he is fired with indignation at the very mention of them and seems to glory in his *assumed* consistency and congratulate himself that '*he is not like unto them a sinner.*' . . . This same Mr. D. O'Reilly has recorded his unqualified approbation of the wings in a letter addressed by him to Mr. Reilly, P.P.,[3] of Mitchelstown. . . . Should you have occasion to refer to the document, I should recommend, if possible, to have it from Mr. Reilly or at least an acknowledgment to that effect. . . . As I do not wish to have *my name* brought before the public I must request that you consider this letter, as to *that particular*, confidential. . . . Unqualified emancipation is quite enough to satisfy the most scrupulous and if Mr. O'Reilly refuses to accede to that term of union, without a formal condemnation of the wings and of course an implied censure of their *quondam* advocates, it is but fair that he should participate in the justice of his own sentence and hold his place amongst them. . . .

SOURCE : O'Connell Papers, NLI 13647

1 Probably the same as Jeremiah Donovan. See letter 1273.

2 Dowell O'Reilly, B.L. (1795-1855), fourth son of Matthew O'Reilly, Knock Abbey, Co. Louth; called to the bar about 1824; attorney-general of Jamaica, 1831-55.

3 *Recte* John Keily, (died 1833) P.P., Mitchelstown, Co. Cork, from 1814.

1266

From his wife to Merrion Square

Derrynane, 28 [and 29, 30] November [1825]

My own Love,

This is perhaps one of the most awful days that could possibly be—stormy, wet and boisterous. If I was not assured the house is perfectly secure I should be miserable. The sea is one sheet of foam with tremendous breakers. Notwithstanding all *this,* would you believe that your youngest son took a *ride before* breakfast, came into me dripping with wet and covered with sand? . . . In point of spirits and animation he is a second edition of my poor Morgan. . . . I fear John O'Connell's *expectations* of *more timber* from wrecks will be fulfilled. God help those that are at sea in such weather as the present.

Tuesday [29 November]

. . . Did you give directions to have no benches made in the new wine cellars for casks or hogsheads? Pray, where is beer, cider and wine in wood to be kept? Would it not be right to have all these things in the house and to turn the old wine cellar into a laundry or dairy? *Both* are much wanting of a good kind. . . . Kate . . . is in very good spirits and generally dances every evening with her cousins. She has a sufficient number for the French country dance. . . . I must now, love, talk to you *seriously* about your attentions to Mrs. Somers[1] in my absence. *It* is *well* I have my Nell to give me a *hint* on the subject. You know I often told you I *suspected Mrs. Somers* and *you* were carrying on the *war quietly*. I am sincerely sorry to hear her husband is in such a bad state of health.

Wednesday, 30 November

A fine frosty morning and every appearance of a good day of which Kate and the young people are preparing to take advantage. . . . I hope White's school[2] is getting on well. Except to him, it would be hard to prevail upon me to send Danny at so early an age to a public school.

. . . John O'Connell will go on with the building so as to finish the second story. He will not have timber for more and *this* I do not regret, hoping when you see *it* you will comply with my wish of not extending the building to a third story. As soon as timber is had the wine cellar will be roofed. . . . I am told James[3] remarks that I will never *again* be *caught* at Derrynane. I don't know what authority he has for *this*. I never made use of the expression. On the contrary I could tell him I would not give him Derrynane for Lakeview and, please God, I will come to Derrynane every summer that I have health to come there for I am very partial to it. I hear John[4] has purchased an estate from Colonel Blackwood[5] for his son Maurice. I hope, love, you will get a *few* pounds by the purchase. The General was greatly delighted with John's Morgan.[6] He remarked to me that Morgan bid fair to be your representative. God forbid *he* ever should while my Maurice and my Johnny are in existence. Morgan O'Connell has a great deal of show and confidence which our sons have not. May God protect them all and you over them. . . .

SOURCE : O'Connell Papers, NLI 13651

1 Probably the wife of Alexander Somers, 1 Upper Mount Street, Dublin, a near neighbour of O'Connell (see letter 987).
2 Of Grafton Street, Dublin. See letter 365, note 1.
3 O'Connell's brother.
4 O'Connell's brother.
5 Unidentified.
6 Morgan John O'Connell (1811-75), eldest son of O'Connell's brother John, Grenagh, Co. Kerry; M.P. for Co. Kerry, 1835-52. Married 1865 Mary Anne, daughter of Charles Bianconi. See *Boase*.

1267

From his wife to Merrion Square

Derrynane, 1 [and 2] December 1825

My own Love,

. . . I scarcely remember a worse season than the present and I fear we shall have a continuance of it. Ought you not, love, write to Primrose about the broken bridges and bad road between this and Carhen? He told me yesterday I should not be able to have the carriage come further for me than Ellen's did for her when she was leaving this. She can tell you the *spot*. It will be terrible except the day be very fine, for me who am at present such a prisoner to be obliged to ride a mile beyond Butler's[1] or more before I can get to the carriage. Surely if there were men got to repair the way it would make the road passable. . . .

Friday the 2d.

I am glad to hear our dear Maurice is arrived in Dublin and I trust by this dear Morgan is with you. Tell him, with my love, I got his letter from Tralee, that the number of shirts he got from the nuns is quite correct. He has now a dozen of most excellent shirts which is a very good supply for any man. I am delighted, love, that you have entirely abandoned *the idea* of *asking us* to stop here for the next month. There is no sacrifice I would not make for you but, love, it would be unjust and cruel towards my Kate to take her to Dublin when all the gaiety was over. She is now at that age to enjoy life. You married Ellen at nineteen and *why* should you not marry Kate at least as early? I am [? sorry] you were not able to reserve *her* fortune for I feel quite sure you will be soon called upon. If *we* are, darling, obliged to give a dinner and a ball to great folks, let us not ask as many *folks* of the other description as we have been in the habit of asking. Derrynane at this season of the year is a dreary place for young people. . . . Please God, I shall get a fine day to cross the mountain. I hope such a day as the present (a dry mild day for the season) and when once I am over the mountains I shan't mind the rest of the way. . . . This day month Kate and I have settled for our departure from Derrynane. I really think if Kate was told she was to stop here longer than she was first told, she would get into a decline. I would not even hint to her that you had any notion of asking her to stay, aware how miserable she would be until she was actually on the road to Carhen. . . . Now, darling, give all these directions to James[2] in the same way and with the same *strictness* with which I obey and carry into execution all your commands. . . . It is, heart, a great trial to me to be thus separated from you but what would I not do to have you out of debt and my children independent. May God bless you and them and spare you all to me. . . .

SOURCE : O'Connell Papers, NLI 13651

1 James Butler's house in Waterville, Co. Kerry.

2 O'Connell's man-servant.

1268

From his wife to Merrion Square

Derrynane, 3 [and 4] December 1825

My own dearest Love,

. . . Maurice did not lose much time since he quitted this country last. He is just as anxious to come to Iveragh as ever his father *was* at his age. Have you *still,* darling, the *same love* for Iveragh and anxiety to be at Derrynane? It is you, own love, that will be welcome to this house, not only to me and to your children but to every individual in it, high and low. . . . The windows of the drawing-room will be all in today and as soon as the second story is completed the work will be stopped until after Christmas. . . .

Sunday the 4th.

Darling, your Kate and I have been doing good this morning as *well* as you. Betsey was too *scrupulous* to go without being three or four times at confession. She will, I trust, go on Christmas Day at the latest. . . . My health, darling, is quite good. Don't fret about my journey to Dublin. Travelling always agrees with me when I do not expose myself to the night air. My dear Morgan . . . ought to lose as little time as possible or he will miss seeing Baron de Vincent at Paris. *He* is ordered off to Austria. . . . Were I in your place I would not go a step to the *Carlow* meeting and, what is more, I would give up Catholic politics and leave the nasty ungrateful set to sink into insignificance. Of course Finn[1] must be at all times opposed to you, and *Master* Sheil, I think, is wheeling round again. Leave them all *there* and you in a short time make a fortune without sacrificing your time and your health. Would to God Mr. L'Estrange could be prevailed upon to give up politics. I really think many oppose you from their dislike to Mr. L'Estrange. The *Patriot* is now attacking him[2] and I really think with some justice. I thank you, heart, for giving up the intention of having a third story to the new house. . . . I *am* to kill more pigs on Tuesday next. . . . One of our cows *calved* last week, not before she was *wanting*. We have been rather badly off as to milk and salt butter. . . . There were five firkins of butter sold for you last week in Cork . . . for which was got £13.5.0 after paying *all* expenses except the carriage. They have already taken at Scariff[3] forty dozen of rabbits and they hope they will get as many more. . . . I am quite at a loss who I shall leave in charge of this house, I mean what female. . . . I was thinking that perhaps poor Maurice's widow[4] would be a good person to leave in charge of Derrynane. A female that would have our interest at heart is what we want. She understands country business and manufacturing flax. It would be an object to her to be here and her little children with her. . . . I have not spoken to Mary O'Connell on the subject and I feel now delicate in mentioning her to you as I have that feeling about me (it is pride I believe) not to have any of my family living at your expence when I brought you no *fortune*. In this *instance* I think that instead of an expence Mary O'Connell would be quite the reverse at Derrynane. . . . Betsey[5] will not come out until she is seventeen and that won't be until 1827. She loves her father greatly. Miscreant[6] is well and merry and more *beautiful* than ever. I was trying to prevail upon him to confess to Mr. Flaherty[7] but he told me he would not confess to *anybody* but Mr. L'Estrange. . . .

SOURCE : O'Connell Papers, NLI 13651

1 O'Connell's brother-in-law William F. Finn, who condemned the 'wings' at the Catholic aggregate meeting in Carlow on 28 November though he was careful to state that he was not attempting to censure O'Connell (*MR*, 30 Nov. 1825). At the Leinster provincial meeting of the Catholics at Carlow on 15 December Finn spoke in similar terms (*MR*, 17 Dec. 1825).

2 On 1 December the *Patriot* attacked Fr. L'Estrange's proposal to provide a cheap edition of a history of the Penal Laws (very probably Henry Parnell's *A History of the Penal Laws against the Irish Catholics* . . . [London 1808]) as unnecessary and ill-advised.

3 An island, inherited by O'Connell from Hunting-Cap, about four miles off the coast near Derrynane.

4 Mary O'Connell (died 13 May 1862), daughter of James Mountain Mahony and widow of Maurice O'Connell, brother of O'Connell's wife.

5 Their youngest daughter.

6 Their youngest son, Daniel.

7 Rev. Edward [O']Flaherty.

1269

To his wife, Derrynane

Merrion Square, Tuesday, 13 December 1825

My darling Heart,

Baron Smith sits at *nisi prius* and has left me but one moment to write to you.

. . . I go down tomorrow evening after the court rises to Naas or further if I can.[1] There is a most violent party raised against me. What a world we live in! The object probably is to drive me off the stage of Catholic politics but, darling, while I may be useful I will struggle with the enemies of Catholic Ireland. It would be a great triumph to them if they could drive me off. Obloquy and reproach have been the certain salary of those who in every age or country have honestly struggled for the welfare of their native land. It is all for the better. Be it so, I say, twenty times. . . .

SOURCE : Fitz-Simon Papers

1 On his way to attend the Leinster provincial Catholic meeting at Carlow on 15 December.

1270

From his wife

Derrynane, 16 December 1825

[Copy of part of the letter. The copy is erroneously dated 1823.]

My own love,

You may judge how anxious I am to hear the result of your *trial* yesterday at the Carlow meeting.[1] How cruelly and ungratefully the Catholics are acting by you. Is it not enough to make you retire with disgust from their service? It seems in vain to serve Ireland. While disunion and petty jealousy influence the educated portion of the people what can be expected? They will succeed, I fear, in setting to rest for ever the question of Emancipation. They deserve to be slaves and such they ought to be left. It only surprises me, heart, that you should persevere. Is it not enough to drive one to distraction to think of all you have lost in the Catholic cause in a pecuniary and in every other possible way and to have you treated like a betrayer of the rights and privileges of your country? I could almost cry when I reflect for a moment on the many sacrifices you made to be of service to your Catholic countrymen and the return you met with. It is foul ingratitude and base duplicity.

SOURCE : O'Connell Papers, NLI 13651

1 The Leinster provincial Catholic meeting at Carlow on 15 December.

1271

To his wife, Derrynane

Merrion Square, 17 December 1825

My own, own Love,

I love you exceedingly. I love you the more for being able to write to you in the highest spirits. At Carlow, darling, at Carlow where we were to have been defeated[1] and put down for ever, at Carlow with William Finn's three weeks of organization,[2] at Carlow *we were triumphant*. We beat the Wingers[3] out of the field. O'Gorman was most heartily hissed and all but pelted to pieces. I never, darling, will forsake the people. The good sense, the good feeling of *my* poor people, may the great God bless them. They would not listen to the Wingers and their fantasies. It would do your heart good if you were to know how harshly the Wingers used me in the first instance, to see their total defeat by the people. They really thought they had nothing to do but to declaim that they were the friends of the people and that I was their enemy, but you never saw or heard of anything like the popular kindness to me and their contempt for the enemy. In short, darling, I never in my life was so delighted with any meeting.

The salver[4] which the Wexford *men* presented to me is beautiful in the extreme. It is quite round and wider than our plated salver, elegantly embossed with the arms in the centre. . . .

SOURCE : Fitz-Simon Papers

1 The Leinster provincial Catholic meeting on 15 December.

2 That is, activities hostile to O'Connell. See letter 1268, note 1.

3 Those critical of O'Connell for having accepted the 'wings'.

4 Presented to O'Connell at Carlow on the morning of 15 December by a deputation on behalf of 'the Roman Catholics of the County of Wexford'. The address is published in the *Morning Register* of 17 December 1825. The salver is now on exhibition at Derrynane.

1272

To John Primrose, Junior, Hillgrove

Saturday, 17 December 1825

Private

[No salutation]

I write one line, my dear John, to say that it is possible that I may be in Carhen in time on Thursday to go on to Derrynane. I would not wish Mary should know that possibility lest she should be impatient or uneasy at my not arriving there. . . . A thousand thanks for selling the bullocks.

SOURCE : O'Connell MSS, UCD

1273

To Rev. Dr. Jeremiah Donovan[1]

Merrion Square, 18 December 1825

My respected Friend,

You will attribute to the proper cause—extreme hurry—my not answering letters. If I had time, yours would certainly be one of the first.

I know you are intimate with Dr. Doyle, and in a kind of despair I write to you in strict confidence about him. His mind is full of something towards me that indeed I do not understand. In truth, he is so high in my opinion, I respect and admire his talents and qualifications so much, I know and feel his incalculable value, I estimate the magnitude of his utility so justly, that I can scarcely conceal the anguish his hostility to me produces. I am, of course, convinced that such hostility arises from conscientious conviction in his mind. I have said or done something that he judges to be wrong, and his conduct to me is certainly regulated by that conviction. The attack of Mr. Kinsella;[2] the omitting to anticipate the provincial meeting at Carlow;[3] the speech at the College Dinner;[4] the interference the next day under the supposition that I had accused the prelates of inconsistency; the total absence of a recognition of an error in fact on that subject, even after I had explained;[5] the personal salute which I was obliged literally to extort from him—all these circumstances convince me that I have said or done something to make Dr. Doyle displeased with me. Could you, my respected friend, find out what it was? Believe me most sincerely that I would not ask you to find it out if I were not resolved to repair it when discovered. It is, indeed, painful to me that a man whom I so unfeignedly respect and reverence should entertain towards me sentiments of an adverse nature. Perhaps it is ambition which makes me desire his co-operation instead of his opposition. But if it be, I deceive myself. I think that it is a sincere desire to serve Catholicity and Ireland which regulates my anxiety to have his countenance and protection. Do not, I beg of you, let him know I have written to you on this subject. I write merely to throw off a burden from my heart and feelings, and with the simple wish of procuring such information as may enable me to avoid in future that which has created present displeasure to him.

I have written unconnectedly, but that is because I feel more on this subject than I can express.

SOURCE : FitzPatrick, *Corr.*, I, 113-14

1 Jeremiah Donovan (died 1846), a native of Macroom, Co. Cork; professor of classics in Carlow College, 1816-20; professor of rhetoric in St. Patrick's College, Maynooth, 1820-29. Author of *Translation of the Catechism of the Council of Trent* (1829) and *Rome, Ancient and Modern* (1842-44).

2 Rev. Professor William Kinsella (1796-1845), Carlow College; born Ballinunnery, Ballon Parish, Co. Carlow; bishop of Ossory from 1829. At a meeting of the Catholics of St. Audoen's parish in Bridge Street chapel, Dublin, on 9 July O'Connell had defended his conduct in London with the assertion that it had the 'entire concurrence and sanction' of Bishop Doyle and Archbishop Murray (*FJ*, 11 July; *MR, DEP*, 12 July 1825). On 14 July Rev. Professor William Kinsella of Carlow College wrote a public letter denying that Bishop Doyle had given any sanction to O'Connell's acceptance of the 'wings' (*FJ*, 20 July 1825). In a public reply to Dr. Kinsella, O'Connell claimed he had been misreported and that his assertion as to the concurrence of the two prelates related only to the measure of clerical provision (*MR*, 26 July 1825).

3 In this statement the word 'omitting' may well be an error for a word of the opposite meaning such as 'attempt'. The day before the Leinster provincial meeting some fifty persons from the different

counties held a preliminary meeting at Carlow College at which an attempt—apparently successful—was made to prepare resolutions for the provincial meeting condemning the 'wings'. These resolutions were, by implication, a censure of O'Connell who did not arrive in Carlow until the following morning (*Patriot*, 15 Dec.; *MR*, 16 Dec. 1825).

4 On the evening before the Leinster provincial meeting the president of Carlow College entertained the persons who arrived for the meeting to a formal dinner at which Bishop Doyle made a speech in which he vigorously condemned the 'wings', especially the measure for clerical provision which he described as a 'paltry bribe' (*MR*, 16 Dec. 1825).

5 O'Connell's speech at the Leinster provincial meeting is so inadequately reported by the newspapers that no comment can be made on how he dealt in that speech with the alleged hostility of Bishop Doyle.

1274

To John Primrose, Jr., Hillgrove

Merrion Square, 7 January 1826

My dear John,

You will be glad to hear that we all arrived here on Wednesday last quite well and merry.

1st. You will also be glad to hear that I have got a promise from Lord Cork[1] of a renewal of Derrynane. The terms are high—£300 per annum that is a rise of £175 over my present rent. The new lives are Maurice's and Danny's.[2] I do not think you will disapprove of my taking it at *that* rent. It gives another generation of the family a tenure of the place and gives a *zest* to the expenditures making there.

2d. You will therefore see that we should make the most of the land. I wish to increase the demesne by taking in the flat ground next the meadow and between it and the hill beginning at the tide and running by the ditch which is next to the little meadow on the flat at the off side from Derrynane house. That ditch will be my boundary until it crosses where the old path to the high road passes it, and then I would make something of a sweep towards the high road and as soon as you get to the high road continue my boundary by it to the bridge over the stream at Ballymacan. Encroach as little on Derrynane Beg as possible. I propose to take *out of this* Jim Mahony's holding so as, if possible, not to dispossess anybody else, and the reason

I select him is because he necessarily must become *a pensioner* of mine. In truth he is so already, as the best definition of a pensioner is a man who gets money without earning it. Tell him as I take away his land I will give him £6 a year in addition to his present salary. I will also allow for *the tillage* on the enlarged part of the demesne. . . .

4th. If you could visit Derrynane and turn John O'Connell's attention as much as possible from idle to useful work. The beach seems his hobby. I would wish to have a solid bounds ditch made between me and Derrynanebeg. One that would defy the *casual* entry of the tenants' cattle. I also would wish to have *an immense* deal of tillage, and the labourers seemed to me to be employed in digging out sand when it was sure to be filled in the ensuing day. . . .

SOURCE : O'Connell MSS, UCD

1 O'Connell's head landlord for Derrynane and the land in its vicinity.

2 His eldest and youngest sons.

1275

From Archibald Hamilton Rowan

Leinster Street [Dublin], 9 January 1826

My dear Sir,

When I offered my insignificant name and my trifling subscription to the Catholic Rent, it was because its objects were not only legal and praiseworthy in my opinion but were of the highest importance to the community at large.

In the same spirit, and in compliance with the law which, in dissolving that Association has pointed out another mode[1] for collecting the voice of the people, on a measure which concerns the property, the safety and also the happiness of Irishmen of every religious persuasion, I take the liberty of troubling you with my name and subscription.

[Noted on letter:] January 16, A. H. Rowan to be inserted in the minutes—C.F.

SOURCE : Dublin Diocesan Archives

1 The mode was the *temporary* revival of what was in a sense the old association. The act designed to suppress the Catholic Association (see letter 1173, note 4) declared all such organisations illegal but only if they existed for more than fourteen days. Accordingly,

on 16 January a 'Catholic Association for 1826' was established for a period of fourteen days and dissolved on 29 January (*DEP*, 17, 31 Jan. 1826). The *Dublin Evening Post* considered that this fourteen-day association succeeded in uniting the Catholics after the dissensions caused by the 'wings' (*DEP*, 31 Jan. 1826). This temporary organisation must not be confused with the New Catholic Association which was virtually a continuation of the old (suppressed) association. The New Catholic Association was founded by an aggregate Catholic meeting in Clarendon Street Chapel, Dublin, on 13 July 1825. Its expressed aims were 'public and private charity, and such other purposes as are not prohibited by the said statute of the 6th Geo. IV. chap. 4' (*DEP*, 14 July 1825).

1276

To Charles D. O. Jephson[1]

Merrion Square, Dublin, 12 January 1826

Sir,

The Catholics of Ireland have determined to offer a public dinner—as a mark of respect and gratitude—to the Noblemen who signed the resolutions adopted at Buckingham House and to the other distinguished friends of civil and religious liberty in Ireland.

It is my duty, and I feel it a pleasing one, to solicit—which I very respectfully do—your presence as the guest of the Catholics of Ireland at that dinner on the 2d of February in this city.

Besides the expression of our gratitude it is our anxious wish to make this an occasion of increasing mutual affection and reciprocal kindness between all classes of his Majesty's subjects. We are convinced of your sincere desire to cooperate with us in this most useful and truly loyal design.

I have the honour to be, Sir,

Your very obedient servant

Daniel O'Connell

SOURCE : Jephson Papers

1 This was a circular letter of invitation to the dinner on 2 February (see letter 1278, notes 2 and 3). The letter is in O'Connell's handwriting duplicated, the name of the addressee being added.

1277

From his brother James

Lakeville [Lakeview, Killarney],
13 January 1826

My Dear Dan,

As neither John[1] nor I go to Dublin I will not any longer postpone expressing to you our surprise at that part of your letter that related to the General's[2] £700. Let me first remind you of the facts. In December 1821 the General's property in our hands, including the sum he paid to redeem Hickson's[3] annuity [and] the arrears due on that annuity, amounted to £12,400. The General's plan, when he disposed of what money he had in the Funds in January 1817, was to allow the sum it produced, £9,900, to accumulate until it amounted to £20,000 which was to be then divided share and share alike between our younger sons. To carry this plan into effect you promised to pay the interest on the £3,600 lent you to redeem Hickson's annuity and to pay the principal by £500 a year, but from the time Hickson's annuity was redeemed in January 1817 until December 1821 you paid but one sum of £100 on account of principal and interest. I repeatedly called on you . . . for money but never got one shilling more than the above sum of one hundred pounds. You put me off from gale to gale during the entire of this time. The General thought everything was proceeding according to the very wise plan he laid down. . . . When I perceived that you neither would nor could perform your part of the contract with respect to Hickson's annuity, I was determined not to deceive the General any longer. . . . I told you I would recommend to the General to give each of us three his share of this money to manage in the best way he could for our children, to which the General at once consented. He conveyed to you Hickson's annuity which, as I stated before, amounted to more than your third and the remainder he gave to my brother John and me.

. . . You most earnestly requested we [John and James] would neither call for principal nor interest until after my Uncle Maurice's death when you would of course cheerfully pay the entire to which arrangement we consented and on the 27th of August last *we met here* to divide my Uncle Maurice's personal property and on that occasion you, as you were bound to do both by law and justice, paid us all principal and interest due on that mortgage. You never made the slightest complaint of being charged interest. *We wound up* all money transactions between us from the beginning of the world to that day and, as John and I were convinced, parted in those affectionate terms we ever did. You met us repeatedly since and never gave us reason to suppose you felt annoyed with any part of our conduct, and now, in four months after, *you coolly sit down and write me a letter charging John and me with an act, if not unjust, of the greatest unkindness towards you. Such an act, as you say, would have killed you if you had not turned your mind from it.* Good God, Sir, I ask you [remainder of letter missing]

SOURCE : O'Connell MSS, UCD

1 His brother.
2 His uncle, Count O'Connell.
3 John C. Hickson.

1278

From the Duke of Buckingham and Chandos[1]

Stowe [Buckinghamshire], 15 January 1826

Sir,

I am favoured with your letter of the 10th inst. acquainting me that the Catholics of Ireland do me the honour to invite me, with the other peers who signed the resolutions[2] at my house in the month of June last, to a public dinner[3] in Dublin on the 2d of February.

I regret extremely that my parliamentary duties, which commence on that day, will necessarily prevent me from accepting their flattering invitation.

I trust however that the Catholics of Ireland will believe how deeply impressed I am by the honour which they have done me in noticing my feeble efforts in their cause. Considering it, as I do, to be the cause of political wisdom as well as of constitutional freedom, involving in its fate not only the peace of Ireland but the welfare of the Reformed Church, the Throne and the People of the United Empire, I shall never fail to give it my warmest support in Parliament, whenever the parliamentary friends of the measure and especially those so highly valued in Ireland who have proved to the Catholics how worthy they are of their confidence shall deem the discussion discreet and salutary.

To the Catholics of both countries I presume with all respect but also with the deepest anxiety for their success to recommend moderation in order to secure unanimity amongst themselves and disarm their adversaries. And a determination, by a continual system of loyalty towards the Crown and obedience to the Laws, to prove themselves resolved and worthy to obtain by legal means a participation in the blessings of a constitution which their ancestors assisted in establishing and which consequently they had a right to hope their posterity would be permitted to enjoy in common with their fellow subjects.

SOURCE : Dublin Diocesan Archives

1 Richard (Temple-Nugent-Brydges-Chandos-Grenville), first duke of Buckingham and Chandos (1776-1839).

2 On 27 June 1825, following the rejection by the Lords of Burdett's Catholic relief bill (see letter 1231, note 1), several peers met at Buckingham House, London, where they drew up a series of resolutions advocating Emancipation. By 29 June sixty-five peers in all, describing themselves as 'Protestant Peers possessing property in Ireland', had given their assent to the resolutions (Edward Augustus Kendall, *Letters to a Friend on the State of Ireland* . . . [London 1826], pp. xiv-xvi).

3 On 2 February 1826 the Catholic Association gave a dinner to the 'friends of civil and religious liberty' which was described as 'by far the most sumptuous public dinner we ever witnessed. . . . All the Catholic Noblemen, Baronets and Gentlemen now in Ireland were present' (*DEP*, 4 Feb. 1826). O'Connell had arranged at a Catholic meeting in Dublin on 23 November 1825 to issue invitations to the sixty-five Protestant peers who had assented to the resolutions at Buckingham House, such Irish M.P.s as supported Emancipation, 'those amongst the Irish Protestant Gentry who have distinguished themselves for liberality', the Anglican bishops of Norwich and Rochester, and Rev. Sidney Smith, Rev. William Shepherd and John Wilks (*MR*, 24 Nov. 1825).

There are extant in the Dublin Diocesan Archives 132 replies to the invitation of which 11 are published (letters 1280-9 and this letter, 1278). The remaining 121, being largely of a conventional nature, are listed below (name of writer, address and date of letter).

Peers accepting the invitation

Lord Cloncurry, Lyons Castle, Celbridge, Co. Kildare, 20 Jan. 1826
Lord Dunsany, Dunsany Castle, Co. Meath, 26 Jan. 1826
Lord Portarlington, Emo Park, near Maryborough, Queen's Co., 15 Jan. 1826
Lord Riversdale, Lisnegar, Rathcormac, Co. Cork, 25 Jan. 1826

Commoners accepting the invitation

Richard Barrett, James's Gate, Dublin, 26 Jan. 1826
William Wrixon Becher, M.P., Ballygiblin, Mallow, Co. Cork, 20 Jan. 1826
Lord Bective, M.P., Headfort, Kells, Co. Meath, 18 Jan. 1826
Richard Newton Bennett, Dublin, 23 Jan. 1826
John Boswell, 28 Blessington St., Dublin, 30 Jan. 1826
Sir Simon Bradstreet, Bart., 22 Jan. 1826
Pierce Butler, Ballyconra, Ballyragget, Co. Kilkenny, 22 Jan. 1826
James Crosbie, M.P., Ballyheigue Castle, Co. Kerry, 19 Jan. 1826
Eccles Cuthbert, St. Stephen's Green, Dublin, 23 Jan. 1826
John Finlay, 31 North Cumberland St., Dublin, 20 Jan. 1826
W. Fletcher, Merrion Square West, Dublin, 25 Jan. 1826
William Preston Leech, Parade, Kilkenny, 29 Jan. 1826
Frederick Lidwill, Morrison's Hotel, Dawson St., Dublin, 1 Feb. 1826
Thomas McKenny, Fitzwilliam St., Dublin, 19 Jan. 1826
Rev. R. Martin, Dunboyne Glebe, Co. Meath, 21 Jan. 1826
T. C. Morgan, Kildare St., Dublin, 21 Jan. 1826
P. H. Patrick, Aston's Quay, Dublin, 20 Jan. 1826
J. R. Price, Westfield Farm, Mountrath, Queen's Co., 23 Jan. 1826
John Purser, James's Gate, Dublin, 26 Jan. 1826
Baron Robeck, 4 Lower Mount St., Dublin, 21 Jan. 1826
George Roe, Fitzwilliam St., Dublin, 22 Jan. 1826
Sir Marcus Somerville, Bart., M.P., Somerville, Co. Meath, 25 Jan. 1826
Robert Henry Southwell, Castle Hamilton, Killeshandra, Co. Cavan, 21 Jan. 1826
Isaac Stewart, 12 Bachelor's Walk, Dublin, 24 Jan. 1826
Col. Richard Wogan Talbot, M.P., Malahide Castle, Co. Dublin, 20 Jan. 1826
Henry White, M.P., Gardiner's Row, Dublin, 17 Jan. 1826
Anthony Willis, 17 Upper Gardiner St., Dublin, 23 Jan. 1826
John Willis, Trinity St., Dublin, 21 Jan. 1826

Peers not accepting the invitation

Lord Albemarle, Ussington, Lincs., 29 Jan. 1826
Lord Bessborough, Malton, Yorks., 18 Jan. 1826
Lord Caledon, Castleblayney, Co. Monaghan, 19 Jan. 1826
Lord Clanmorris, Newbrook, Co. Mayo, 24 Jan. 1826
Lord Cremorne, Dawson Grove, Co. Monaghan, 30 Jan. 1826
Lord Darnley, Cobham Hall, Kent, 16 Jan. 1826
Duke of Devonshire, Chatsworth, Derbyshire, 28 Jan. 1826
Lord Donoughmore, Palmerstown House, Co. Dublin, 2 Feb. 1826
Lord Dunalley, London, 23 Jan. 1826
Lord Dundas, Marsk Hall, Yorks., 24 Jan. 1826

Lord Essex, Cassiobury Park, Herts., 17 Jan. 1826
Lord Fortescue, Castle Hill, Devon, 22 Jan. 1826
Lord Gosford, Worlingham Hall, Suffolk, 24 Jan. 1826
Lord Howth, Howth Castle, Co. Dublin, 30 Jan. 1826
Lord Kingston, Mitchelstown, Co. Cork, 16 Jan. 1826
Marquis of Lansdowne, Bowood, Wilts., 19 Jan. 1826
Marquis of Londonderry, Wynyard Park, Durham, 19 Jan. 1826
Lord Meath, St. Stephen's Green, Dublin, 16 Jan. 1826
Lord Northland, Paris, 25 Jan. 1826
Lord Nugent, Lillies, Bucks., 27 Jan. 1826
Marquis of Ormonde, Kilkenny Castle, Kilkenny, 20 Jan. 1826
Marquis of Sligo, Westport, Co. Mayo, 27 Jan. 1826

Commoners not accepting the invitation

Christopher Antisell, Gloucester St., Dublin, 22 Jan. 1826
William Bagwell, M.P., Marlfield House, Clonmel, Co. Tipperary, 18 Jan. 1826
R. D. Beamish, 32 South Frederick St., Dublin, 31 Jan. 1826.
William Beamish, Beaumont, Cork, 23 Jan. 1826
Thomas Bernard, M.P., Castle Bernard, King's Co., 20 Jan. 1826
Rev. Mr. Bird, Rectory, High Hoyland, Wakefield, Yorks., 28 Jan. 1826
Dominick Browne, M.P., Bognor, Sussex, 29 Jan. 1826
James Browne, M.P., Claremont, Co. Mayo, 24 Jan. 1826
Charles Brownlow, M.P., 19 Queen Square, Bath, 22 Jan. 1826
Sir Francis Burdett, Bart., M.P., Bath, Somerset, 28 Jan. 1826
Peter Burrowes, 57 Lower Leeson St., Dublin, late January 1826
Robert Shapland Carew, M.P., Castle Boro, Co. Wexford, 26 Jan. 1826
Henry Caulfield, M.P., Hockley, Armagh, 22 Jan. 1826
Peter Chaigneau, Fitzwilliam St., Dublin, 23 Jan. 1826
Sir Arthur Chichester, Bart., M.P., Belfast, 29 Jan. 1826
A. Colles, M.D., St. Stephen's Green, Dublin, 23 Jan. 1826
Charles Coote, Bellamont Forest, Co. Cavan, 26 Jan. 1826
William S. Curry, Lismore Castle, Co. Waterford, 21 Jan. 1826
Rev. ——— Douglas, 31 Jan. 1826
George Ensor, Ardress, Loughall, Co. Armagh, 17 Jan. 1826
Andrew Finucane [? Thomas's Hotel], Kildare Place, Dublin, 30 Jan. 1826
Richard Fitzgibbon, M.P., 3 Park Crescent, Portland Place, London, 25 Jan. 1826
Viscount Forbes, Castleforbes, Co. Longford, 25 Jan. 1826
Matthew Forde, M.P., Seaforde, Co. Down, 20 Jan. 1826
Rev. Henry Griffin, Trinity College, Dublin, 20 Jan. 1826
Robert Harty, Merrion Square East, 23 Jan. 1826
Peter Van Homrigh, M.P., Listoke, Drogheda, Co. Louth, 26 Jan. 1826

John Hyde, M.P., Sidmouth, Devon, 24 Jan. 1826
James Jameson, Mont Rose, Co. Dublin, 21 Jan. 1826
The Knight of Kerry, M.P., 3 Devonshire Terrace, London, 26 Jan. 1826
Lord Kingsborough, M.P., Mitchelstown, Co. Cork, 19 Jan. 1826
James S. Lambert, Craughwell, Co. Galway, 22 Jan. 1826
Edward Lawson, William St., Dublin, 1 Feb. 1826
Nicholas Philpot Leader, 51 Leeson St., Dublin, 21 Jan. 1826
Charles H. Leslie, Patrick St., Cork, 25 Jan. 1826
John Leslie, Courtmacsherry, Co. Cork, 25 Jan. 1826
John Lloyd, Merrion Square, Dublin, 20 Jan. 1826
Thomas Lloyd, Beechmount, Rathkeale, Co. Limerick, 22 Jan. 1826
William Nugent Macnamara, Doolin House, Co. Clare, 29 Jan. 1826
Maurice Mahon, 7 Upper Mount St., Dublin, 29 Jan. 1826
Lt. Gen. Stephen Mahon, M.P., Connaught Terrace, London, 23 Jan. 1826
Richard Malone, Baronston, Ballinacargy, Co. Westmeath, 22 Jan. 1826
Sir Henry Meredith, Rutland Square North, Dublin, 31 Jan. 1826
Rev. Hon. Frederick Mullins, Beaufort House, Killarney, 18 Jan. 1826
Sir John Newport, Bart., M.P., Clifford St., London, 29 Jan. 1826
Standish O'Grady, M.P., St. Stephen's Green, Dublin, 29 Jan. 1826
John Plunket, 21 Jan. 1826
Richard Power, M.P., Clashmore, Co. Waterford, 21 Jan. 1826
Thomas Spring Rice, M.P., Hunsdon House, Chichester, Sussex, 23 Jan. 1826
Robert Roe, Crampton Quay, Dublin, 26 Jan. 1826
Rev. Richard Ruxton, LL.D., 8 Merrion Square East, Dublin, 1 Feb. 1826
Francis Sadleir, Trinity College, Dublin, 20 Jan. 1826
Arthur St. George, Tyrone House, Co. Galway, 23 Jan. 1826
Sir Robert Shaw, Bart., M.P., Bushy Park, Dublin, 28 Jan. 1826
Lt. Col. Merrick Shawe, 25 Jan. 1826
Rev. William Shepherd, Gateacre, Lancs., 29 Jan. 1826
John Singleton, Quinville, Quin, Co. Clare, 29 Jan. 1826
W. M. Smyth, M.P., Cheltenham, Glocs., 21 Jan. 1826
Joseph Spencer, Dominick St., Dublin, 20 Jan. 1826
Hon. Charles Vesey, Merrion Square, Dublin, 30 Jan. 1826
Charles William Wall, Trinity College, Dublin, 21 Jan. 1826
M. Wallace, 21 Jan. 1826
Richard Wellesley, M.P., Brighton, Sussex, 29 Jan. 1826
Samuel White, M.P., Killakee, Rathfarnham, Co. Dublin, 21 Jan. 1826
John Pratt Winter, Agher, Summerhill, Co. Meath, 29 Jan. 1826
Charles Wray, Shanganagh, Bray, Co. Wicklow, 26 Jan. 1826

1279

To Archibald Hamilton Rowan

Merrion Square, 16 January 1826

(Copy)

My Dear Sir,

I have the pleasure to enclose your admission ticket to the Association[1] which meets this day. We are proud at being enabled to enroll your respected name amongst our members. And we are grateful for the patriotic and christian sentiments which give increased value to your subscription.

[Noted on copy of letter:] January 16, to be inserted in the minutes—C.F.

SOURCE : Dublin Diocesan Archives

1 The 'Catholic Association for 1826' (see letter 1275, note 1).

1280

From Sir Edward O'Brien, Bart., M.P.

Dromoland [Newmarket on Fergus, Co. Clare],
18 January 1826

My dear Sir,

As I propose attending the opening of the session of Parliament I regret it will not be in my power to accept the kind invitation[1] you have forwarded to me from the Catholic Body.

My sentiments in regard to your claims have been recorded by an uniform and zealous support both in and out of Parliament for the *last thirty years* and every day's experience has more fully confirmed my opinion, that to place all his Majesty's loyal subjects on the same footing would be no less an act of policy than of justice.

SOURCE : Dublin Diocesan Archives

1 To the Catholic dinner (see letter 1278, note 3).

1281

From Lord Westmeath

London, 21 January 1826

My dear Sir,

I have to acknowledge your flattering invitation to the dinner fixed for the 2nd of Febry, and lament exceedingly that private business of material importance to myself confines me to London and will prevent my having it in my power to avail myself of the honour intended me; but as I am unwilling to send an empty excuse on such an occasion, when I would gladly have been present, and have never had an opportunity of openly expressing my sentiments on the great question respecting my Roman Catholic countrymen, I beg to take this opportunity of assuring the Body . . . that no one can regret more than I do the fate of the Bills[1] [*recte* bill] brought in last session of Parliament for their relief, and I lament it the more as there has since been apparently a great change of temper in the Body itself respecting the two accessory measures called *Wings*,[2] on the anticipated success of which many of the best friends of the cause on both sides of the water had calculated an accession of and strength for the prosperity of the grand measure of general Emancipation.

. . . I equally deplore that there should have been any share of disapprobation thrown on any of the members of the talented and zealous deputation[3] who came to this country for the management of the cause entrusted to their care, whose moderate demeanour and conciliating conduct whilst here had certainly brought the measure nearer to a successful termination than had ever before been contemplated. . . . The best hope for the Roman Catholics exists in the generosity and in the sympathies of the people of this great country, who must be convinced before they will concede, but whose sentiments of latter years have been progressively, nay rapidly inclining to the relaxation and repeal of those Laws. . . . Tens of thousands of brave souls with the *political sin* of Roman Catholicism on their backs have bled and given their last breath in the field and at sea *abroad* for the honour of Great Britain in her national quarrels. This is the proud record of the loyalty of the dead, and I should scorn to insult the living *at home* by presuming to doubt it. . . .

SOURCE : Dublin Diocesan Archives

1 Sir Francis Burdett's Catholic relief bill of 1825 (see letter 1183, note 9).

2 See letter 1180, note 2.

3 In the 'Catholic Association for 1826' Jack Lawless asserted that some of the members of the Catholic deputation of 1825 had agreed to a barter with ministers. He called for a resolution which would 'have them stamped with the reprobation of the country' (*DEP*, 17 Jan. 1826).

1282

From Sir William Cusac Smith

21 January 1826

My dear Sir,

I feel honoured and am highly gratified by the invitation which I have just received. I accept with pride and gratitude a portion of the title which your letter kindly gives me. I *do* belong to the class of 'friends of civil and religious liberty' though I cannot claim to be what that letter[1] calls me, a 'distinguished' member of that liberal class. Your candour will, I am persuaded, induce you to agree with me that this class includes more than those who are favourable to the pretensions of my Roman Catholic fellow subjects. You will assent to my suggestion that in the ranks of those who are in opposition to their claims 'friends of civil and religious liberty' are to be found . . . and I in my turn may lament that on a question so momentous and on which so much of the political welfare, the harmony and social happiness of our country must depend, wise and estimable persons, who all of them have the same object in their view, should differ so widely as to the means by which this common end is to be attained. . . .

The annals of my parliamentary career of course are, like myself, obscure but such as condescend to search them will not find me in the list of those who were adverse to the claims of my countrymen of your religion; while I trust (for their honour as well as for my own) that it also will appear that I only espoused them because they seemed to me compatible with the permanency of British connection, with the safety of our church and stability of our constitution. . . . [If I were to review my opinions on the subject of Catholic Emancipation] it is not clear that the result might not be my serving as a steady private in those ranks which Mr. Canning, Mr. Plunket and other distinguished statesmen lead; at least it is not unlikely that I might take those views which have long been countenanced by the Bishop of Norwich,[2] my now venerable and always amiable and very early friend.

[The writer then explains at great length that he, as a judge, cannot attend a political meeting, however praiseworthy it may be, and therefore cannot attend the dinner.]

SOURCE : Dublin Diocesan Archives

1 The circular letter of invitation to the public dinner on 2 February (see letter 1278, note 3).

2 Henry Bathurst.

1283

From the duke of Leinster

Dublin, 22 January 1826

Sir,

Having been absent from home the last week it was not until late yesterday evening on my return that I received the invitation of the Catholics of Ireland to dine with them on the 2d of Feb.[1] . . .

It is with extreme regret I decline the honour they propose, but I beg you will assure them that they have not a warmer friend to their cause.

SOURCE : Dublin Diocesan Archives

1 See letter 1278, note 3.

1284

From George Lidwill

Dromard [Roscrea, Co. Tipperary],
22 January 1826

Sir,

In reply to your letter of the 22d instant which only reached this place this day (and which has the postmark of the 20th notwithstanding the date) I beg leave to state that I will feel great pride and pleasure in availing myself of the honour conferred upon me by the Catholics of Ireland by their invitation to a Public Dinner[1] . . . provided I shall get sufficiently well of an inflammation on my eyes that renders it extremely painful to me at this moment to answer your letter.

. . . It would be most satisfactory to myself to be present at that grand and gratifying spectacle, if only to witness that happy spirit of union which now subsists among the Catholics of Ireland, the want of which has often been most injurious to their objects. . . .

I have at all times thought that every law which by its operation placed the Catholic on a position inferior to his Protestant and other Dissenting fellow subjects should be repealed without qualification or compromise. . . . But when so many are against any concession, when even amongst those friends who are willing to extend relief on the great and essential points, yet but few are willing to repeal all those statutes without other provisions and guards. Under these circumstances I would hold myself . . . acting under the delusion of very mischievous error if I was to set up a basis founded upon my own opinion as the only rule to guide the conduct of others. . . . When I view this fertile country a prey to poverty and anarchy growing out of those dissensions, I know no sacrifice too great, except some departure from a fundamental principle of Liberty, if by making it so great a blessing could be attained thereby; for it is as absurd as it is untrue to say the Catholics enjoy liberty of either kind, excluded as they are from offices and from Honours, and indebted to the wise and impartial government of Lord Wellesley *alone,* for even the benefits of the existing laws in their favour; as, until his Administration, these laws were converted into instruments of persecution instead of protection to the Catholics by many of his predecessors in the government of the country, and they have no security that they will not experience the same treatment from some of his successors.

Though I differ decidedly with many most respectable members of the Catholic Association respecting the operation of both the measures[2] which were intended to accompany the Catholic Relief bill[3] which was lost in the Lords in the last session of Parliament, more especially that relating to the election franchise of the forty shilling freeholder[4] which, in its present state, I hold to be an aristocratic and not a popular measure and one in'urious to Catholics more than to Protestants, which I have little doubt at the proper time and place I will make evident; may I also differ with many in that body respecting the utility of the Tithe Composition Act,[5] and which I advocated not because it was the best that could be devised upon the principle of commutation but because it was the only one that would be granted and, even as it was, far preferable to the old tithing system. . . . I only mention so much now that, at any county meeting composed of freeholders of all classes and creeds where I shall be present, I may be at full liberty to advocate these measures without the impeachment of having changed my opinions. And as I conceive such meetings the only place fitting to discuss the propriety of submitting those measures to the consideration of parliament, I cannot help thinking it an act of injustice to send them to any tribunal for the expression of public opinion prejudged by an *ex parte* censure from Catholics alone.

SOURCE : Dublin Diocesan Archives

1 See letter 1278, note 3.
2 The 'wings' (see letter 1180, note 2).
3 Sir Francis Burdett's Catholic relief bill of 1825 (see letter 1183, note 9).
4 In Ireland prior to 1829 persons occupying freehold property to the value of forty shillings per annum were entitled to vote. One of the 'wings' (see letter 1180, note 2) had embodied a proposal for raising the Irish electoral qualification so as to disqualify this class of voter.
5 See letter 1006, note 9.

1285

From C. D. O. Jephson

The Castle, Mallow, Co. Cork, 23 January 1826

Dear Sir,

I have only this evening received a letter from you, dated the 12th January, inviting me to the Dinner[1] to be given by the Catholics of Ireland, on the 2d Feby. prox., together with one from Mr. Dwyer stating that a previous letter had been sent, which *I never received,* and thus no answer from me had arrived.

It will, I assure [you], give me the sincerest gratification to be present at this Dinner, and, however short the notice has been, I will use every exertion to arrive in Dublin in time for it.

SOURCE : Dublin Diocesan Archives

1 See letter 1278, note 3.

1286

From Alexander Robert Stewart, M.P.[1]

Ards [Co. Donegal], 29 January [1826]

Sir,

[In a long letter he declines the invitation.[2] He has always supported Emancipation but does not approve of employing means to that end other than 'a temperate appeal to the wisdom of the legislature. . . . Angry threats or impassioned language can only create enemies . . . but will never either soften prejudices . . . or hurry the British Parliament into precipitate or ill-digested legislation'. He supported the act[3] for the suppression of the Catholic Association and has been dismayed to see the spirit of that act violated by the reorganization of that body[4] in a different shape. If he attended the dinner he might feel obliged to introduce a discordant note by stating his opinions.]

SOURCE : Dublin Diocesan Archives

1 Alexander Robert Stewart (1795-1850), Ards, Co. Donegal; nephew of the celebrated Lord Castlereagh. M.P. for Co. Londonderry, 1818-30.

2 To the Catholic dinner (see letter 1278, note 3).

3 See letter 1173, note 4.

4 See letter 1275, note 1.

1287

From Joseph Huband, B.L.[1]

Charlemont Mall [Dublin], 31 January 1826

My dear Sir,

[He accepts the invitation to the Catholic dinner.[2] He had hoped, but did not have sufficient time, to make some observations on the present state of the Emancipation cause 'particularly on what are called the *Wings*[3] of which, and more especially the freehold one', he has always been an advocate 'partly on account of the knowledge of that subject I derived from my professional attendance on any contested elections'.]

SOURCE : Dublin Diocesan Archives

1 Joseph Huband (c. 1750-1835), son of Edward Huband, Dublin. Called to the Irish bar, 1773. Commissioner of bankrupts, 1780-1806.

2 See letter 1278, note 3.

3 See letter 1180, note 2.

1288

From Lord Fitzwilliam to the Secretary of the Catholic Association[1]

London, 31 January 1826

Sir,

I must begin by apologizing for having neglected acknowledging your letter of invitation to a dinner,[2] which occurrences since my arrival in town brings to my recollection, but I must add to my shame by being obliged to admit that I do not know the Gentleman whose name is affixed to the letter: He will, I trust, pardon me if I address this to the Secretary of the Catholic Association.

But to the subject, generally speaking I can address my answer—it seemed to request for information if I continued in the same way of thinking on Catholic Emancipation that I had manifested last year. To this I can most conscientiously affirm that I do—and I will add still further that I remain in the same opinion that I entertained in 1795 when, in consequence of the support I gave to the question then mooted in the Irish Parliament, I was removed from the situation I then filled as His Majesty's Representative in Ireland.

I beg the favour of your communicating these sentiments to the Catholic Association.

SOURCE : Dublin Diocesan Archives

1 This letter is published partly because it was really intended for O'Connell and partly because of its own special importance.

2 See letter 1278, note 3.

1289

From Samuel Ward, LL.D.[1]

107 Dorset St. [Dublin], 1 February 1826

My dear Sir,

[Declines the invitation to the Catholic dinner in a long letter.]

. . . Is it not, therefore, of vital moment to prove that the tenets of Catholicity are not repugnant to the existing order of things—not only that they are not repugnant, but that in the full and complete concession of their claims a greater stability would be obtained.

Having at length by argument and conciliatory demeanor in aid of unerring truth chased the film of prejudice from the mental optic, emancipation, founded as it is in justice, humanity and political expedience, must necessarily and speedily ensue. . . .

Nor can these advantages even in their utmost latitude, be unproductive to Great Britain; for the strength and prosperity of an empire arises from the harmony of all its parts and the fair development of their resources.

[He describes himself as] sincerely solicitous for the final adjustment of the Catholic claims, unfettered by any ungenerous enactment. . . .

SOURCE : Dublin Diocesan Archives

1 Attorney.

1290

From Jeremiah McCarthy, 62 Dawson St., Dublin, 4 February 1826

Asks O'Connell's advice on how to deal with Patrick Finn[1] of Carlow who has behaved very insultingly to him, calling him '*a robber, a notorious bloody robber and rascal*' and 'in a menacing manner shook his umbrella at me and said if I was a gentleman he would know how to deal with me'.

SOURCE : O'Connell Papers, NLI 13646

1 Patrick Finn, son of rich Carlow merchant who owned Finn's *Leinster Journal,* Kilkenny, and brother of W. F. Finn, O'Connell's brother-in-law.

1291

From Count O'Connell to Merrion Square

Paris [postmarked 10 February 1826]

My dear Daniel,

Your son Morgan arrived here the 26th of December and departed for Vienna on the 16th ult. He informed me you had established for him on a house in that city a credit for £80 yearly which I deem amply adequate to meet all his reasonable exigencies. I strongly recommended prudence and economy. He made fair promises. I wish he may keep his word. He seems to be more inclined the other way.

I lament to think, my dear Daniel, that the large sum left you by my dear brother[1] and the money you received from me (£20,000)[2] have proved inadequate to expunge the enormous mass of your debts. You were always so reserved with me on that subject that I refrained from asking any questions. I am of course incompetent to form an accurate estimate of your financial situation. One thing, however, enforces itself on my mind, namely, that the progress of years will disable you from pursuing your professional labours and that the fate, nay, the very existence of your large family hangs on your life. I am therefore impelled by the feelings of nature and affection to make and to urge the following proposal which, by securing an independence to your three younger sons, will have the effect of setting your mind at rest as far as regards them and of enabling you to apply your savings from your large income to the extinguishment of any remaining debts and establishing your two unmarried daughters.

I have therefore to propose to you to insure your life for *ten thousand* pounds sterling, the interest of which at £4.16.6 will amount to £482.10.0. If you agree to this, my proposal, I shall assist you towards the discharge of the said premium of insurance to the amount of the annuity, £150, you are bound to pay me. Thus you will have to retrench from your income only about £332.10.0 which you can afford without any material sacrifice or privation, but . . . you must allow me to make my conditions *sine qua non* and, as they have for their end object the interest of your three sons, I can't imagine you will object to them. The conditions are as follows: [The conditions are substantially that James, O'Connell's brother, will exercise control over the transaction and will ensure that on O'Connell's death the £10,000 will be distributed equally between his three younger sons, Morgan, John and Daniel.] . . .

I rejoice to find you came forward so handsomely to sacrifice your private opinion to the general interest of your cause and country.[3] You have thus triumphed over the enemies of your talents and reputation and acquired an additional title to the esteem and lasting gratitude of all honest Irish Catholics. . . .

[P.S.] I shall expect a prompt and explicit answer to the contents of this letter. If you adopt my idea, lose no time to carry it into effect. . . .

SOURCE : Fitz-Simon Papers

1 Hunting-Cap.

2 That is, a *total* of £20,000 from Hunting-Cap and Count O'Connell.

3 A reference to O'Connell's agreeing to abandon the 'wings' (see letter 1180, note 2) as a basis for Emancipation.

1292

From Lord Amiens[1] to Merrion Square

13 February 1825 [postmarked 1826]

To Danl. O'Connell Esq.,

. . . private pique should not influence a public man. Hazard no opinions or assertions. Reflect well. The writer imputes in a great measure your indiscretion in speech to the multiplicity of affairs you are engaged in. It is quite observable too that the acting members of the Association do not appear to come to the Meeting Room as if about to enter on public business, Christopher Fitz-Simon Esq. excepted.

The writer with grief has to add that it is the collected opinion of many of the most respectable of the Roman Catholics that by indiscretions (certainly unintentional) you have gravely contributed to retard the progress of R.C. Emancipation. This is public opinion also from good authority.

SOURCE : O'Connell Papers, NLI 13647

1 Mason Gerard (Stratford) (1784-1849), styled Viscount Amiens, 1823-33; succeeded as fifth earl of Aldborough, 1833.

1293

To John Primrose, Junior, Hillgrove

Merrion Square, 18 February 1826

Private

My dear John,

I ought to have near £1,800 as my last gale, having paid myself the College rents and Lord Cork, and I would really feel as rich as any man in Europe if I had that sum. Dumas[1] called on me at an hour's notice for £300 which I paid him; out of £1,000 I owed him when I came up I now owe him but £500. I do not know the moment he may bounce on me for that sum as he is a strange rascal. I wish you could make me a large remittance. Endeavour to do something handsome for me. I would readily allow the tenants a shilling or two in the pound for prompt payment. Urge everybody as much as possible but do not actually injure anybody. You cannot think how a sum of £1,000 would not place me above all care. . . . The times are bad but will certainly be worse. There is no use in tying over but I do not wish to have any serious driving and certainly no selling. . . .

[P.S.] I am to get Maurice's, *John's* and Dan's lives of Derrynane.

SOURCE : O'Connell MSS, UCD

1 Thomas Collins Dumas.

1294

From Peter Loughnan[1] to Merrion Square

Crohill Lodge [postmarked Kilkenny]
21 February 1826

Private

Sir,

I have this day received an *anonymous* letter from Dublin stating that I am to be *exhibited in a Farce on the stage*. If you will use your influence to prevent this you will have my blessing for ever. I now solemnly assert that I had no motive in writing the different letters I did to Mr. Dwyer[2] or in wishing to have my tithe letter[3] published but a sincere with to add my humble efforts to assist in exposing oppression and serving my fellow countrymen. . . .

SOURCE : O'Connell Papers, NLI 13647

1 Peter Loughnan, probably son of James Loughnan, Crohill Lodge, Kilkenny. Sometime member of the Catholic Association.

2 Edward Dwyer.

3 Unidentified.

1295

From his son Morgan to Merrion Square

Güns [Hungary], 22 February 1826

My dear Father,

[Morgan writes that he has just purchased a good horse for £36 British which means that he must ask his father for £20 in addition to the £80 already given. Morgan assures his father that the extra £20 is urgently needed. A horse was not needed in Italy where he was garrisoned in towns but in Hungary 'where we are stationed in villages where one officer is separated an hour's ride from the other and in whose neighbourhood families live to whose house he is invited, how can he go there without a horse?'] . . .

SOURCE : O'Connell Papers, NLI 13645

1296

From Peter Loughnan, Crohill Lodge, Kilkenny, 3 March 1826, to Merrion Square

A more urgent letter than that of 21 February but to the same effect.

SOURCE : O'Connell Papers, NLI 13647

1297

To W. C. Plunket, Attorney-General

Merrion Square, 7 March 1826

Confidential

My dear Sir,

I regret that I feel it a duty to inform *you* that the accounts from the country by those who are well acquainted with the people are terrific. The Ribbon connection[1] has assumed a new form. There is now no oath nor any very distinct assertion of object. It is spreading fast through Leinster—in the southern counties almost as much as the northern. It has got extensively into Connaught and it is beginning to accumulate in Munster. The present system has its origin in the north; the counties of

Cavan and Fermanagh are the places of its commencement in this shape. The Orangemen—or lower orders of the Protestants in Cavan—have armed themselves with daggers of about fourteen inches in length in the blade or, what is nearly as bad, the lower orders of Catholics have been made to believe that they are so armed, and in consequence of such report the Ribbonmen are getting similar arms. There is this peculiar to the present system, that it is sought not to involve the married men or fathers of the society—but *all* the unmarried peasants are expected to be in it and some are received as young as nineteen. One priest assured me that no less than seven youths in his parish, of regular habits, left his confessional rather than renounce the system or abstain from supporting it—the oldest of the seven was not eighteen years of age.

While I deem it my duty to communicate these facts, I have no remedy to suggest save the increase of the King's troops in Ireland. The exhibition of such a force may alone do good. The yeomanry are worse than useless; they irritate and provoke and are very little to be depended on for any active exertions. Even the police have, in spite of apparently a good deal of attention to keep them free from party spirit, a good deal of inclination to display Orange feelings and to insult when they should merely assist to subdue illegal violence. The King's troops are, in my judgement, the best calculated in every respect to meet emergencies of this description.

The Ribbonmen in the present system are believed to be cautioned against useless outrages or exhibitions of their strength. They are to deal in buying and selling, etc., only with Catholics or Protestants of known liberality. You are probably aware that there is a good deal of mere reaction in this part of the system.

I have done my duty in communicating these facts to you. The diminution of the currency in both countries will certainly create still greater distress among our landholders and of course increase the tendency to Whiteboyism[2] of every species. I am, I perceive, quite an alarmist but it is only because those who give me this information cannot be deceived and are themselves greatly horrified.

SOURCE : David Plunket, *Lord Plunket,* II, 230-1

1 A form of agrarian secret society.

2 That is, the existence of agrarian secret societies.

1298
To his wife

Tralee, 18 March 1826

My own sweetest Love,

If I were to remain in Tralee, you would certainly make a rake of me, and I will tell you *how*. The post does not come in until past ten at night, and then you would keep me up until after the letters were given out. I came here yesterday from Limerick. We had Mass at my lodgings and were able to leave it by six in the morning. I got to Rathkeale; an immense multitude collected who took the horses from my carriage and with a piper, fife and fiddle and flag, carried me about a mile out of the town. They took me to the avenue leading to the house of Mr. Roche[1]—Howley's father-in-law. It must have annoyed some of the Orange bigots of the neighbourhood not a little. I got here before six in the evening. It was one of the pleasantest days for travelling I ever experienced in my life, and the view of Tralee Bay with the declining sun making the sea quite a flood of gold, and the majestic mountains in various masses skirting the opposite side with vapours assuming the consistency of white clouds covering a portion of the hills here and there but leaving the base and summit in every spot plainly visible. It was a scene for a painter, and made me half poetic and entirely patriotic. I do love the beauteous land of my birth. . . . There is a good deal of criminal business which I hate, and of course a good crop of civil bill appeals which, although too small for other assizes, are taken into the net. I write a long letter by this post to Maurice.[2] I hope he will attend to it *at once*. Let me know when he does that I may write another letter to him; but if one letter were to overtake another uncopied, he would soon neglect all. He should read each letter a couple of times attentively and then copy it into a book. Give my more than tender love to our children. My Kate liked the ball,[3] I hope. Did Lady Wellesley say anything to them? Or was it like a levée, a curtsey and away? Darling, tell my Maurice I beg of him to attend to his legal studies.

SOURCE : FitzPatrick, *Corr.*, I, 117-18

1 Stephen Roche (died 1856), eldest son of Stephen Roche, Limerick, and Sarah O'Brien, Moyvanine, Co. Limerick. One of the four banking brothers—Stephen and James in Cork, Thomas and William in

Limerick. The Cork bank suspended payment in 1820. Stephen Roche's daughter, Sarah, married 1826 John Howley (1789-1866).

2 His son.

3 At Dublin Castle.

1299

To his wife

Tralee, 18 March 1826

My own Love,

. . . All our buildings [at Derrynane] are going on gaily. John O'Connell[1] is planting the world and all. I hope I will be able to prevail on my daughters to come down very, very early next summer. It would be a great object to me to get rid of £1,000 of my debts during the two next terms. If I were able to do *that* out of my profession, I would soon be altogether free. How I long for *that* day, darling. Nothing, however, but some substantial remaining at Derrynane, without anything like an establishment in Dublin, will do it.

SOURCE : FitzPatrick, *Corr.*, I, 118-19

1 John Charles O'Connell.

1300

To his wife

Tralee, 21 March 1826, Tuesday

My darling Love,

I merely hope that your pains have left you for I perceive with sorrow that you do not say that they have. Do, my darling, tell me precisely how you are and if possible give consolatory news. Darling, the assizes are nearly over. The man and woman[1] have been convicted for the murder of her former husband. The evidence was by no means satisfactory, but they were, I believe, really guilty. The woman is large with child and cannot be executed until after she is brought to bed. What a horrible state for the wretched being to be in! . . . These judges do an immense deal of business in seven working days. I will have but two days at Derrynane. I go there merely to take care that the place shall be ready at an early period in summer for your reception. I am not a little impatient to have all my building then quite finished and at an end. . . . I delight to indulge myself in writing of my children. Darling, talk to them of their father in terms of the fondest kindness. Tell them I rave of their sweetness and goodness, and fold to your heart the fond consciousness of being the most loved woman in the world.

SOURCE : FitzPatrick, *Corr.*, I, 119

1 Thomas Lovett and Johanna, his wife, were tried at Tralee assizes for the murder of the latter's former husband, Thomas Creane, at Gallerus, Co. Kerry, in 1820. (*DEP*, 4 April 1826).

1301

To his wife

Tralee, 22 March 1826

My darling Love,

. . . I gave your scolding message to *Miss Connor.*[1] I am to get credit for eleven shillings British or, as the common people here call it, *Protestant money*, from Betsey.[2] I spoke *a little* this day to Betsey about religion but got no great encouragement. I did not select the proper mode. I dined at Rick's[3] this day, when we had an excellent dinner of various fish; but fish, darling, is a rascally article. I have the most cordial and popish hatred of fish of every kind. . . .

The unfortunate woman[4] lay in last night after her sentence was pronounced, and will therefore be executed in a few days. The execution would have been long postponed if her horror and affright had not made her miscarry. What an unhappy wretch! May the great God be merciful to her. I have no kind of Kerry news to send you. The county is as dull as dullness can possibly be. They attempted to get up a ball on Monday but it was put down by universal consent. Darling, your disappointment at not having your visit returned shows how idle it would be to attach any importance to courtly smiles. I am quite sure you do not; but it is the more unaccountable because Serjeant Goold assured me that the Lord-Lieutenant declared he would invite us both to one of his state dinners. What a grand little woman you will be then, my sweet, darling heart! . . .

SOURCE: NLI, MSS 5759

1 Ellen Connor.
2 Wife of Rickard O'Connell.
3 Rickard O'Connell.
4 See letter 1300.

1302

From Edward Bowles Symes[1] *to Dublin*

Brynhafod, Llandilo, Carmarthenshire,
25 March 1826

Dear Sir,

. . . On February 25 there appeared in the *Cambrian* newspaper, printed at Swansea, an address to the Freeman of Glamorganshire, signed Gwladwr,[2] to which I replied in that now enclosed, signed *Oxoniensis*.[3] I am of opinion that there is no other mode of disseminating information of this kind with any probability of success. In Wales it is even more hopeless than in England. A very great majority of the newspapers are decidedly opposed to the Catholic cause and will not insert any article in its vindication excepting in the way of advertisement. . . . This however is a mode of proceeding too expensive for an individual to embark in. . . . [He goes on to suggest that the Catholic Institution[4] should adopt this procedure instead of publishing books and pamphlets which are almost impossible to get into circulation.] . . .

P.S. . . .

SOURCE : O'Connell MSS, UCD

1 Unidentified.
2 This letter described the danger of allowing political rights to Catholics and referred to the recent papal bull 'granting to all Catholics in Great Britain and Ireland a year of Jubilee, in the belief that the period for extermination of Protestants is at hand . . .' (*Cambrian*, 25 Feb. 1826).
3 This letter accused 'Gwladwr' of being totally ignorant of the Catholic religion, 'Oxoniensis' (Symes) claiming to have lived in Dublin (*Cambrian*, 11 Mar. 1826).
4 Unidentified.

1303

To his wife

Cork, 3 April 1826

My own sweet Love,

. . . I have, however, had the happiness to close with Hedges[1] for the young O'Sullivans,[2] and now that family is safe and independent. *That is* some comfort to your husband, God's holy name be praised and glorified. . . . I should rather travel on Thursday as I hate travelling on a *fish* day, and besides I am not a little impatient to be at home. I found, darling, that whiskey is extremely cheap at present. It is as low as 5s. 9d. a gallon. I have availed myself of this cheapness to send a tierce of it containing 43 gallons to Derrynane not to be opened until after your arrival there. It will be the better for lying by much longer, and I hope to continue to give it age. If I can get down from Dublin another cask of excellent spirits, we will *manage* them, love, in great style. At all events, we will not have occasion to be sending for them in small quantities. The business I have now to detain me here *first* are six briefs; these I hope to get over tomorrow. *Secondly* the Coulagh lease from Hedges which will be altogether arranged tomorrow. *Thirdly,* the O'Mullane[3] debts which I ought to be able to settle tomorrow. . . .

SOURCE: NLI, MSS 15540

1 Robert Hedges Eyre, Macroom Castle, Co. Cork, head landlord of Coulagh, Berehaven, home of the O'Sullivans.

2 The children of Morty O'Sullivan, Coulagh, Berehaven, who died in 1825.

3 Those of his first cousin James O'Mullane.

1304

From F. Blake Foster[1] to Merrion Square

Ashfield [Gort, Co. Galway] 20 April 1826

My dear Friend,

I enclose you a letter[2] I published in our Co[unty] paper [*Connaught Journal* of 17 April] *against James* Daly. I send it you because I know your opinion of that worthy gentleman's *honest* politics.

You will serve R. Martin,[3] if you cause that letter to appear also in the *Evening Post* and [*Morning*] *Register*.[4] . . . Tell MacNevin[5] that *his friend* James Daly's vile conduct is fully set forth *by me* in the Galway paper. Nothing will annoy MacNevin more, as he almost worships James Daly.

I have a most important *cause*[6] in which *you are* my chief counsel, that of Martin J. Blake.[7] I am in the *greatest* difficulties, caused by the vast expense of law, these 5 or 6 years in defence of my property in the appeal from poor Lord Manners' weak decree.[8] This chancellor[9] is the greatest curse to Ireland that we ever had.

I am in such difficulties that I can't go to public places. If I shall succeed against M. J. Blake my difficulties will cease, I rely on your *all-powerful* exertions. The case will be heard this term and my entire reliance is on you. . . .

SOURCE : O'Connell Papers, NLI 13647

1 Landowner.

2 A long letter dated 13 April 1826 and signed 'Vindex'. It contains a sweeping attack on the political conduct of James Daly, which, the letter alleges, renders him unworthy of Catholic support in the coming election for Co. Galway. Among other accusations Daly is charged with being in league with the Bible Society. The writer calls on the Catholics to support James S. Lambert, Richard Martin, who is a member of the new Catholic Association, and A. F. St. George (*Connaught Journal*, 17 April 1826). In the election of 1826, Daly retained his Co. Galway seat.

3 Richard Martin (1754-1834), Ballinahinch, Co. Galway; M.P. for Co. Galway, 1801-26. Duellist. Known as 'Humanity Dick' because of his interest in the welfare of animals. He was the eldest son of Robert Martin, Dangan, Co. Galway, and Brigid, third daughter of eleventh Baron Trimleston. See *DNB*.

4 Neither the *Dublin Evening Post* nor *Morning Register* appears to have published Foster's letter.

5 Daniel McNevin.

6 Unidentified.

7 Martin Joseph Blake (1790-1861), elder son of Walter Blake, Ballyglunin Park, Athenry, Co. Galway. M.P. for Galway town, 1833-57.

8 Unidentified.

9 Lord Manners.

1305

From Edward Dwyer

[probably 20 April 1826]

Private

My dear Sir,

I must entreat your excuse for reminding you of the amount of the tickets,[1] as I am tormented daily by persons to whom debts are due by the Association. I regretted your absence[2] yesterday as the largest assemblage we have had for some time were much disappointed.

SOURCE : O'Connell MSS, UCD

1 Presumably for the Catholic dinner held 2 February 1826.

2 From the Catholic meeting in Dublin on 19 April 1826, in favour of unqualified and unconditional Emancipation (*DEP*, 20 April 1826). O'Connell was one of the signatories to the requisition for the meeting (*DEP*, 18 April 1826) but did not attend. On 22 April 1826 he apologised to the new Catholic Association for his absence which, he said, was due to professional business (*DEP*, 25 April 1826).

1306

From Myles McSwiney, Cork, 15 May 1826, to Merrion Square

Sending his rent for Carhen demesne and also payment of a private debt.

SOURCE : O'Connell Papers, NLI 13646

1307

From James Callaghan[1] to Merrion Square

[postmarked Kilkenny, 19 May 1826]

Sir,

. . . We have at length succeeded in getting up an independent newspaper[2] on a truly Catholic principle which is the principle of universal civil and religious liberty. Since its establishment I have been frequently called on for the letters of 'Lycurgus'[3] and to each call I was constrained to give an evasive answer, with the exception of the Hon. Col. Butler and Counsellor Finn. Where these letters are, is a mystery. The counsellor fears that from the great press of public business they have been mislaid. I do confess that I am now beginning to participate in the like apprehension. May I respectfully entreat that you would spare one moment in searching for them but, if they are lost, . . . I could not wish them a better fate than to die in your possession.

P.S. One of the letters, in detailing the sanguinary precursors of the Union, states this hidden and most egregious fact (the original and officially authentic document of which is *in my possession* and which to the future historian of Ireland should be of some consequence), namely, that in Kilkenny and in that year (1798) when the war dogs was [*sic*] let loose on a misguided people no less a number suffered capitally, that is, by the gibbett, in the short space of a few months by courts martial *than 37,* besides, between two and three thousands of the population otherwise *disposed* of, that is, by whipping, transporting, etc., an awful mirror for the nocturnal legislator to look on or into. . . .

SOURCE : O'Connell Papers, NLI 13647

1 A journeyman saddler.

2 Perhaps the *Kilkenny Independent.* Its surviving files date from October 1826 to June 1828 and show it to have been strongly Catholic in its views.

3 A pseudonym for an unidentified writer. Lycurgus was the legendary Spartan statesman.

1308

From Henry Villiers Stuart[1] *to Merrion Square*

Dromana, Cappoquin, 9 June 1826

Dear Sir,

I am reminded by the issue of the writs that the time now fast approaches when we may look forward to your presence amongst us in the County of Waterford. . . . Should you have . . . a few days' leisure ere the actual commencement of the election[2] which is appointed by the Sheriff for the Thursday after next, you will do me the honour of passing them at Dromana. Such an arrangement would afford to you an insight into the political circumstances of our County and which could not be obtained so well by any other means, whilst it would prove a source of the most unmingled gratification to dear Sir,

Your very faithful servant,

Henry Villiers Stuart

SOURCE: O'Connell MSS, UCD

1 Henry Villiers Stuart (1803-74), Dromana, Co. Waterford; son of Lord Henry Stuart, a son of the first marquis of Bute; M.P. for Co. Waterford, 1826-30; Banbury, 1830-31. Created 1839 Baron Stuart de Decies of Dromana.

2 The famous Waterford election of 1826.

1309

To John Primrose, Jr., Hillgrove

Merrion Square, 10 June 1826

My dear John,

Your last letter has driven me to despair with respect to Derrynane. I suppose it will not be habitable this summer. When I reflect that two months have already elapsed and almost nothing done I am quite in an agony of regret. My family ought to be there *now*. . . . I must look out for some place to put my family in for the summer instead of having them cheaply at Derrynane. . . .

SOURCE : O'Connell MSS, UCD

1310

From Rev. P. Scully, P.P., Barrendary, Dunganstown, Co. Wexford, 10 June 1826, to Merrion Square

Sends O'Connell a long list of quotations from the church fathers in support of Transubstantiation in controversion of the denial of it by a Protestant clergyman, Rev. Mr. Daly.[1]

SOURCE : O'Connell Papers, NLI 13647

1 Robert Daly (1783-1872), second son of Denis Daly, M.P., Dunsandle, Co. Galway. Rector of Powerscourt, 1809-43. Dean of St. Patrick's, Dublin, 1842-43. Bishop of Cashel, Emly, Waterford and Lismore, 1843-72. The controversy was published in a pamphlet (Dublin 1826), *Letters of Rev. Robert Daly to Daniel O'Connell with the reply of Mr. O'Connell*. Daly's letters were dated 11 and 27 May 1826 and O'Connell's reply 22 May 1826.

1311

To John Primrose, Jr., Hillgrove

Merrion Square, 14 June 1826

My dear John,

. . . I read with the deepest surprise your statement that you had given John O'Connell[1] the directions I wrote in Cork and left *him* to carry them into effect. For my part I would not have given him the finishing of a pig sty unless I wished it never to be finished. I surely intended and hoped to have your attention to these things but I see I am left on the strand with the tide out. . . . I implore of you to write the moment you see Derrynane after you get this and tell me when it is you imagine my family may go to reside there. . . . I am, however, so feverish about my bitter disappointment respecting Derrynane House that I can not relish any other subject. If my family were there now I should feel so happy. . . .

SOURCE : O'Connell MSS, UCD

1 John Charles O'Connell.

1312

To his wife

Dromana [Co. Waterford], 19 June 1826

My own sweet Love,

Here I am at this lovely spot.[1] I believe it is that which Lady Morgan makes the scene of many of the incidents in *Florence McCarthy*.[2] It is really a beautiful situation. As to yesterday, *first,* I wrote to you from Waterford and enclosed you a cheque for £35; next, sweetest, we heard an early mass at Waterford and then started for Dungarvan. We breakfasted at Kilmacthomas, a town belonging to the Beresfords but the people belong to us. They came out to meet us with green boughs and such shouting you can have no idea of. I harangued them from the window of the inn, and we had a good deal of laughing at the bloody Beresfords. Judge what the popular feeling must be when in this, a Beresford town, every man their tenant, we had such a reception. A few miles farther on we found a chapel with the congregation assembled before mass. The Priest made me come out and I addressed his flock, being my second speech. The freeholders here were the tenants of a Mr. Palliser,[3] who is on the adverse interest, but almost all of them will vote for us. We then proceeded to Dungarvan on the coast. There are here about four hundred voters *belonging* to the Duke of Devonshire. His agents have acted a most treacherous part by us, and our Committee at Waterford were afraid openly to attack these voters lest the Duke should complain of our violating what he calls his neutrality. But I deemed that all sheer nonsense, and to work we went. We had a most tremendous meeting here; we harangued the people from a platform erected by the walls of a new chapel. I never could form a notion of the great effect of popular declamation before yesterday. The clergy of the town most zealously assisted us. We have, I believe, completely triumphed, and I at present am convinced we shall poll to the last man of these voters. We then had a public dinner and great speeching. We broke up about nine, and Wyse and I came here with Mr. Stuart in his carriage. We arrived about half after ten, and are going this day to Lismore on another mission.

I cannot tell you what a sweet spot this is. The tide rises to a considerable distance away and gives this noble river a most majestic appearance. Darling, I must give up poetic ideas and tell you in plain prose that I do doat on you and your children.

SOURCE : *Irish Monthly,* XII (1884), 216

1 Dromana, Cappoquin, Co. Waterford. Residence of Villiers Stuart, successful pro-Catholic candidate in the Waterford election.

2 *Florence McCarthy : An Irish Tale,* by Sydney Owenson, Lady Morgan (1818).

3 Wray Palliser (1789-1862), Kilcomragh Lodge, near Kilmacthomas, Co. Waterford. Son of John Palliser, Derrylusken, Co. Tipperary. Lt. Col. in Waterford Militia, 1810-62.

1313

To John Primrose, Jr., Hillgrove

Dromana, Co. Waterford, 19 June 1826

My dear John,

I got your long letter yesterday. It has quite convinced me that I was wrong in being so much disappointed. I now write only to thank you for having done so much and to say that I will not have any cut stone at all nor any expense that can be avoided. Grates and fenders we must have. I will send down from Dublin '*the Cobbet Stove*' for the large parlour. Do nothing with the roof of the old castle till next year. . . .

[P.S.] This is the greatest contest[1] ever known. We *will* win.

SOURCE : O'Connell MSS, UCD

1 The Waterford election.

1314

To his wife, Merrion Square

Waterford, 21 June 1826

My darling heart,

I found yesterday on my arrival from Dromana two letters from you. . . . Darling, I wrote to Primrose approving of all his plans except that I bid him order grates and fenders everywhere save in the large parlour. Do you also write to him for I forgot the dog kennel. He may place that where he says at Dunbreen. Though you appear so anxious to be off for Kerry before my arrival in Dublin, I hope I will disappoint you. . . . The election of Stuart *now* appears to me *quite certain*. I took my former opinions from timid persons here. My present is founded on actual experience. The priests have gained over a sufficient number of the *adverse* voters to ensure us a decided majority. We have already in town a sufficient number of the enemies' forces to decide the victory. When I wrote last on Monday I was at Dromana. We started soon after for Cappoquin and Lismore through the loveliest scenes in nature. I was with Stuart in his own chaise with four horses but we had no great occasion [for them] for they were taken off before we got to Cappoquin and we were drawn by freeholders three miles into Lismore. I never had a notion of popular enthusiasm till I saw that scene. My name was often and often mixed with his. There were thousands covering the precipitous banks of the Blackwater at Lismore. The chapel is extremely spacious. It was crowded to suffocation. We made several harangues and your husband was as usual much cheered but, what was better, the freeholders crowded in and put down their names in groups and they are all now arriving in shoals. The Duke of Devonshire was to have been *neutral* but I believe I have helped to put an end to the absurd notion of neutrality.

Now darling, you wished to take some of the present furniture to Derrynane. Do so, darling, take as much of it as you choose. I refused you this before. Now I am sorry I refused you anything. . . .

SOURCE: NLI, MSS 5759

1315

To his wife

Waterford, 22 June 1826

Darling,

You *could* not deceive me, darling, and you never, never wilfully did so. The moment I read the passage in your letter which said that Kate would write to me the next day, I felt that you were conscious of an approaching heavy fit of illness —and oh! how bitterly have my fears been realized. You are, darling, very ill, otherwise there would be one fond line from that hand which delighted my youthful love, and does indeed, darling, cheer the beginning autumn of my life. . . .

Darling, if I were in spirits I would tell you with an air of triumph that the return of Stuart is now nearly certain. Indeed I think quite certain.

SOURCE: FitzPatrick, *Corr.*, I, 124-5

1316

From Nicholas Markey[1] *to Waterford*

Dundalk, 22 June 1826

My dear Friend,

I have just time to let you know that 'the fight is begun and victory certain.' Louth,[2] after slumbering 55 years, is again awake and determined to be free.

Counsellor Sheil's speech astonished *all parties* but when he announced himself a *freeholder* of the County, I cannot describe to you the effect it produced.

The entry of Mr. Dawson[3] into town was splendid; not less than 5,000 persons accompanied him.

You may judge of the state of our *opponents* when 20 sovereigns was offered last night in my neighbourhood for a single vote although not a man has polled yet.

Public spirit is at such a pitch, *no money* will tempt them.

You'll excuse my troubling you at present. I know you'll be gratified to hear the news.

SOURCE : O'Connell Papers, NLI 13647

1 Nicholas Markey (c. 1772-1866), Welchestown, Co. Louth.

2 In 1826 a pro-Catholic candidate, Alexander Dawson, successfully contested Louth against the sitting members, who were both opponents of Emancipation.

3 Alexander Dawson (1771-1831), Riverstown, Co. Louth. Called to the bar, 1793. M.P. for Co. Louth, 1826-31.

1317

To his wife

Waterford, 23 June 1826

[No salutation]

I write only to say, darling love, that I will not have one moment of happiness till I see a letter in your own handwriting; and yet do not—do not, sweetest, run any risk by attempting to write before you are perfectly able to do so. I cannot avoid telling you that we are winning fast on this day's poll,[1] and on this day alone we shall have, I hope, a majority of from sixty to one hundred. I cannot write more; I am out of spirits.

SOURCE : FitzPatrick, *Corr.*, I, 125-6

1 In the Waterford election.

1318

To his wife

Waterford, 25 June 1826, Sunday

My own sweet darling Mary,

Need I tell you that I was delighted to get a letter all in your own handwriting?—but I was *a little* uneasy at its being so long lest you should thereby have incommoded yourself; and yet, sweet Mary, I *do* like to get a long letter from you. Now, saucy little woman, let me scold you for getting this attack. I will lay a pound to a penny that I know how you got it. The hot weather made you dress lighter and so, in this climate, it not being capable of being done with impunity, you caught cold. Do not deny it, sweetest, like a little *fibbing* old woman as you are. For my part, I continue to wear my winter dress except my cloak, and even that I put on after nine in the evening if I go out. But I never, thank God, enjoyed better health. There is all the *buoyancy* of youthful spirits about me now that you are well, and all the *racy* triumphs at the success of agitation which an agitator by profession can alone enjoy. Indeed, darling, as you are better I am happy. The Beresfords are determined to die hard. They will continue the poll to-morrow and probably Tuesday, but I think they must be exhausted by Tuesday at the latest. The moment the election is over I will fly to you.

SOURCE : FitzPatrick, *Corr.*, I, 126

1319

To his wife

Waterford, Monday, 26 June 1826

[No salutation]

. . . I have every reason to be in spirits. We are beating those bigoted and tyrannical wretches,[1] they are now practising every species of delay and spinning out the time. The fact is there is no artifice whatsoever but is resorted to in order to gain time. At this rate we will not be out of this before Saturday or *at least* Thursday. Nothing can be more vexatious to a person so *impatient* as I am to be with you and my darlings—but we are beating the *scoundrels* in such style that it is quite a comfort to me in this delay to gain such a victory over them. It is really ludicrous the length they go to in delaying us—so much so that I am delaying *you* by this tedious account of the delays of others. I am writing in a crowded court where I came at nine o'clock and will have to remain until at least seven o'clock this evening, and then we are to have speaking to the people, so that this, like many others, will be indeed a busy day. . . .

SOURCE : FitzPatrick, *Corr.*, I, 126-7

1 The Beresfords.

1320

To his wife

Waterford, 27 June 1826

My own darling Heart,

How well I knew it was the change of dress that brought on the attack. My constitution is, thank God, excellent, but it is preserved by the care I take not to yield to the temptation of giving myself present relief by making my clothing lighter. But let me not think of scolding you *for fear* I should pay for it. Darling, John[1] sent me an express from Killarney to announce the dreadful massacre[2] committed in Tralee by the orders, John says, of Major Mullins[3] and George Rowan.[4] He is very anxious with me to go off to Tralee, but I cannot leave this until it will be too late for the Tralee Election.

Mullins and Rowan caused the police to fire in the streets of Tralee and shot five men dead and wounded eight. John was looking on and says there was nothing like an adequate cause for firing. It is, however, likely that this circumstance alone may put an end to the contest. I believe you will be glad to hear that I have bought myself a noble, stout, grey horse. They say in my family that the grey mare is the better horse—but this grey horse is a noble one. . . . It would now be impossible for Beresford[5] to succeed, and yet I must remain here as long as they can poll a single man.

SOURCE : FitzPatrick, *Corr.*, I, 127-8

1 His brother.

2 This occurrence took place in the course of the Kerry election of 1826. On 24 June the sheriff was alleged to have declared that the show of hands taken from the electors assembled in Tralee favoured one of the candidates, Col. James Crosbie, but Crosbie's opponent, William Hare, nevertheless demanded a poll (petition of James Crosbie, *Commons Journal,* LXXXII, 81). On Sunday, 25 June, the day before polling was due to begin, some stones were thrown by a crowd, whereupon police and troops fired on them, killing five persons and wounding about a dozen others. The orders to fire were said to have been given by the high sheriff, John Hickson, and two magistrates, Major Mullins and George Rowan (*DEP,* 27 June, 1 July 1826).

3 Edward Mullins, J.P. (1777-1841), fifth son of first Baron Ventry and brother of William Townsend, second Baron Ventry. Major in 28th Regiment (Foot), 1813-14; half-pay, 1814.

4 George Rowan, J.P., Ralanny, Tralee.
5 Lord George Thomas Beresford (1781-1839), third son of first marquess of Waterford. Defeated candidate in the famous election in Co. Waterford, 1826. M.P. for Co. Waterford, 1830-31.

1321

To his wife

Waterford, 28 June 1826

My own Love,

. . . You may, however, imagine how anxious I am to learn again from Kerry. The newspapers, I see, contain no kind of notice of the Kerry murders.[1] Here, where passion and party spirit run highest—here, where the feeling of triumph over faction is at its height, we have not the slightest species of disturbance. We have kept the people perfectly tranquil. You cannot conceive what an impression I amongst others made on the people to keep them perfectly quiet. Nothing can provoke them to any, even the slightest, breach of the peace. There were many regiments brought into the county and several additional bodies of police, and it must be most pleasing to form such a contrast with other counties. Darling, I hate *the place* whence I write. It is in the open court where I am obliged to cover every line which I write to prevent *accidental* over reading.

½ after two. The poll is almost over on Beresford's side. *We* are polling on in almost all the booths so that we will this evening have a most enormous majority. All we have to take care of is some paltry trick on the part of these vile Beresfords. I hope to be able to leave this tomorrow, but even *that* is so uncertain that I beg of you to answer this letter although I hope I will be with you before that answer can reach me. We had a duel this morning between two of our attorneys; they fired two shots each without any mischief. Our attorney was a Mr. O'Brien Dillon[2]—theirs a Mr. Charles Maunsell.[3]

SOURCE : FitzPatrick, *Corr.*, I, 128-9

1 See letter 1320, note 2.
2 O'Brien Dillon, attorney, 42 Gloucester Street, Dublin. Second son of Garrett Dillon, Nenagh, Co. Tipperary, apothecary, and Mary Smith.
3 Charles Maunsell, attorney, 46 Aungier Street, Dublin. Fourth son of John, Ballybrood, Co. Limerick, and Catherine Widenham.

1321a

To his wife, Merrion Square[1]

Waterford, 29 June 1826

[No salutation]

I got, darling love, your letter covering Morgan's. My sweet fellow is for the present disappointed. I am sorry for it particularly as it seems to prey on his spirits but his natural gaiety will soon revive and he will not, I am sure, suffer in his health from any disappointment. But whoever writes to him must beg of him in my name not to quit his present regiment without an absolute *promise* of promotion in some other regiment. It is *so* probable that he will get the next vacancy. At all events he would be placed at the foot of the cadets in any new regiment or to meet the jealousy of the other cadets in his new regiment. Let this, darling, be done as speedily as possible.

This election *must* be over this day and all the suspended votes will be disposed of during this night or early tomorrow so that I will be certainly able to start on tomorrow. *Do not answer this*. You are not sorry to see that sentence. Nor am I to be able to write it.

Darling, I understand from you that our horses will leave Dublin on Wednesday next, the 5th. They will therefore be in Limerick by the ensuing Saturday. I will take care to have my horse there before the men. Give the coachman a pound British as his perquisite on the purchase of this horse. It is better to spare the horse the journey to Dublin. I will have my friend Mr. Sheehan to have a saddle and bridle made for the horse before the other horses arrive there. Thus there will be no delay in Limerick. I would enter into more details but that I intend to have the happiness of discussing *these* questions with you in person. Indeed, indeed, darling, I am most impatient to be with you, and you may be quite certain that I will not remain here one hour or one half hour after my share of the business is over. Indeed I believe I need not say so to you, my own darling Mary.

The election is—this moment—closed.

I will be off in the morning.

SOURCE: Office of Public Works, Dublin

1 This letter is franked and addressed by the newly elected M.P., Henry Villiers Stuart, on 29 June.

1322

To a kinsman

Merrion Square, 4 July 1826

My dear Friend,

Mary's illness and the shocking state of arrear into which the Waterford election threw my professional business necessarily brought me to Dublin, and the County election here deplorably wanted my assistance. All, however, is now right.[1] I wrote yesterday to John[2] to give my advice about the election. Col. Crosbie *must* insist on his being returned, as he had the show of hands the first day and as Hare[3] it is who calls for a poll. That poll is plainly illegal.[4] The sheriff[5] ought certainly to be hanged; but if he escape the gallows—which God forbid! —he will be imprisoned for months in Newgate. There were five Catholic peasants justly hanged for the horrid murder of one Protestant[6] at the cross of Shinah. It was quite just that it should be so. Shall it be said that five Catholics shall be basely slaughtered in the streets of Tralee without retribution or atonement? I think it impossible. The sheriff who ordered the firing and the officers, soldiers and policemen who fired are all guilty, according to the coroner's inquest, of wilful murder, and we all would participate in their guilt if we permitted the assassins to escape with impunity. This is a solemn and sacred duty to which, for one, I devote my best energies '*to bring murderers to justice*'. I will not, however, attend an illegal poll. This election must be set aside.[7]

SOURCE : FitzPatrick, *Corr.*, I, 129-30

1 In Dublin County, though there occurred 'no grand revolt of the freeholders', the liberal candidates, Talbot and White, were successful (Reynolds, *Emancipation Crisis,* p. 98).

2 His brother.

3 William Hare (1801-56), grandson and heir of first Earl of Listowel. Styled Viscount Ennismore, 1827-37. M.P. for Co. Kerry, 1826-30; St. Albans, 1841-46. Succeeded to the earldom, 1837.

4 In accordance with a legal opinion sent him from Waterford by O'Connell, Col. James Crosbie declined on the third day of polling to contest the election further by this means (*DEP,* 4 July 1826). He protested against what he alleged was illegal conduct on the High Sheriff's part in postponing polling unnecessarily until 3 July when most of the electors favourable to him had left Tralee (*DEP,* 4 July 1826; petition of James Crosbie, *Commons Journal,* LXXXII, 81-2).

5 John Hickson, J.P. (born 1782), The Grove, Dingle, Co. Kerry; eldest son of Robert Hickson. High Sheriff, 1826.

6 Unidentified.

7 A petition against Hare's return (see letter 1320, note 2) was lodged by Crosbie on 5 December 1826 (*Commons Journal,* LXXXII, 81-2). Hare, however, succeeded in retaining the representation of the county.

1323

From Rev. John Sheehan,[1] *Waterford, 9 July 1826*

Introduces Mr. Edward Hayes,[2] a painter, for whom he seeks O'Connell's patronage.

SOURCE : O'Connell Papers, NLI 13647

1 Rev. John Sheehan, P.P., St. Patrick's, Waterford, 1828-54. Died 20 February 1854.

2 Edward Hayes (1797-1864), a native of Co. Tipperary. Practised as a miniature-painter in Clonmel, Waterford and Kilkenny; moved to Dublin, 1831. Member R.H.A., 1861-64. See Strickland, *Dictionary of Irish Artists.*

1324

From Peter Martin[1]

Saint Michael Hill [Dublin], 11 July 1826

Dear Sir,

As my lands do not qualify me to vote for Members of Parliament it will be some pleasure to me to add my mite to the general fund[2] for supporting these honest freeholders who have voted for their country and against their cowardly and coldblooded landlords. . . .

SOURCE : Dublin Diocesan Archives

1 Peter Martin, 1 St. Michael's Hill, Winetavern Street, Dublin. Carpenter and undertaker.

2 With the suppression of the old association in 1825, the Catholic rent lapsed (Reynolds, *Emancipation Crisis,* p. 59). Following the Waterford election O'Connell launched the new Catholic rent for the purpose of protecting the rebellious freeholders from eviction (Reynolds, *Emancipation Crisis,* p. 27; see also letters 1325, note 2, 1340).

1325

To Edward Dwyer

Limerick, 13 July 1826

My dear friend,

I send in a parcel to Mr. Jeremiah McCarthy, 62 Dawson Street, two letters *for the cause* which you will be so good as to answer. Continue to have a New Association[1] meeting on Saturday and let whatever new rent[2] is received be *read out* as of old instead of being advertised. You will find in the letters £2, the one speaks for itself, the other put down from ' Master John O'Connell, Clongowes Wood College '. I think ' the rent ' will be got up again. If anybody begins everybody will follow. I should be glad that Mr. Peter Martin's letter was published. . . . Write to as many persons as you know urging them to continue the collection of ' the rent '.

I will take care to have you appointed to the office of Secretary to ' the Liberators '.[3]

SOURCE : Dublin Diocesan Archives

1 New Catholic Association (see letter 1275, note 2).

2 The new Catholic rent was launched by O'Connell in July 1826 (*DEP,* 8 July 1826: O'Connell to the Catholics of Ireland, 10 July 1826; *DEP,* 11 July 1826).

3 The ' Order of Liberators ', an organization formally launched by O'Connell in September 1826 (see letter 1337, note 2). The order was in imitation of a society founded by Simon Bolívar in South America. Membership of the order was to be obtained through the performance of acts of distinctive service to Ireland. Members were to be ranked according to service as knights companion, knights of the grand cross and liberators. The organization was intended mainly to promote electoral activities, protect the freeholders and put down secret societies. It proved, however, a failure, partly perhaps because of the too vivid uniform which O'Connell insisted its members should wear (Reynolds, *Emancipation Crisis,* pp. 100-1; Oliver Snoddy, ' The Order of Liberators ', *North Munster Antiquarian Journal* [1966], pp. 82-4).

1326

To Edward Dwyer

Limerick, 14 July 1826

My dear friend,

I enclose you £1 being the contribution of 'Counsellor O'Loghlin '[1] to the 'New Catholic Rent for all useful purposes not prohibited by law and in particular for national education '[2]. Let it appear amongst the contributions acknowledged tomorrow '*be the same more or less*'. This letter, of course, is not to be read at the meeting[3] nor are any letters of mine to you unless the subject particularly calls for it of which in that case I will give you *a hint*. I regret that I did not last Saturday make a return of Dr. Keenan's[4] five pounds and my sixteen to set the thing agoing but continue to have a return tomorrow read and so published.

SOURCE : Dublin Diocesan Archives

1 Michael O'Loghlen (1789-1842), third son of Colman O'Loghlen, Port, Co. Clare. Called to the bar, 1811; solicitor-general, October 1834-January 1835 and again April-September 1835; attorney-general, August 1835-November 1836; master of the rolls, 1837-42. M.P. for Dungarvan, 1835-37. Created baronet, 1838. See *DNB*.

2 This was the form in which the new Catholic rent was advertised in the press.

3 Of the New Catholic Association.

4 Unidentified.

1327

To Edward Dwyer

Limerick, 17 July 1826

My dear friend,

. . . Will you be so good as to get the following advertisement inserted in *the usual* papers: . . . [Announcing the holding of a Catholic meeting at Waterford on 16 August.]

Let this advertisement appear *at once*.[1] There is nothing like working the cause. You must contrive to be in Waterford at this Grand Meeting. It will be truly grand. The Rent[2] is beginning to take everywhere. I hope it will be as extensive as the former and more durable. Our aggregate here takes place tomorrow. There will be a resolution to put the Rent in collection. . . . Put the £2 to the *New Rent* thus:

'Mrs. O'Connell additional subscription £2. 0. 0'

SOURCE : Dublin Diocesan Archives

1 In fact the meeting did not take place until 29 August 1826.

2 The new Catholic rent.

1328

From Lord Cloncurry

26 July 1826

My dear O'Connell,

I enclose my freehold rent[1] as a mark of my anxious desire to promote the freedom of election.

Though fond of my rights as a landlord I never presumed to dictate to a tenant on that subject. On the contrary, I would extend that sacred and necessary privilege, make it of frequent recurrence and by ballot render unfair influence impossible. I see by the newspapers that I have refused to be one of the Order of Liberators before I was invited to be so—a piece of foppery of which my friends know me to be incapable. . . .

SOURCE : FitzPatrick, *Cloncurry*, p. 362

1 New Catholic rent.

1329

To his wife

Cork, 29 July 1826

My own Love,

I feel lonely at not hearing from you. Do, darling, write to me as soon as you receive this letter.

All the City records are tried except one. We begin with the county records on Monday, and I think three days will be quite sufficient for that purpose; so that, love, I hope and trust I will be with you by this day week. You perceive that I can thus spend a week with you in Tralee before the Waterford meeting[1] and then, my Heart, I will at once be back with you for the rest of the Vacation. . . .

We have had a busy day. I spoke to evidence with some

effect in one cause—the only heavy one that was tried. It was a poor man against a rich one. I was on the right side. . . .

SOURCE : FitzPatrick, *Corr.*, I, 130

1 See letter 1334, notes 2 and 3.

1329a

To William Conyngham Plunket

Cork, 29 July 1826

Private and confidential

My dear Sir,

I deem it a duty to inform you *personally* of the state of my native county with respect to the civil bill jurisdiction. Mr. Rice, the assistant barrister (a man generally and deservedly beloved by all his acquaintance and by no person more than by me) has been chairman of that county (Kerry) for near thirty years, certainly much more than twenty, has fallen into ill health and his mental powers are so weakened that he has become a mere nuisance. I say this with unaffected regret and I say it solely from my conviction that it is a duty to give you this species of information to act upon if you please or to neglect if you do not choose to act upon it. I am desirous that it should not be *unnecessarily* made known that I gave you this information and unless you communicate it yourself to others it never shall be known that I have written thus to you.

There were about eighty appeals from Mr. Rice's decisions to the judge at the late assizes. This is an enormous over-proportion and could not have occurred if Mr. Rice still continued in possession of his once powerful as well as delightful talents. He is entitled to the retiring pension and if it were deemed right to increase that pension to him and to give him as much emolument from the government as he now derives from his situation, it would *under such circumstances* be most desirable to have his chair filled by some other person.

We would expect that in that case a *liberal* should be sent amongst us although the recent elevation of Mr. Blacker[1] who is *hard bitten* at the Orange side, leaves the liberal part of the bar in great despair. Perhaps it is not [? wise] to promote those who would willingly aid the enemies of Lord Wellesley['s] government but—pardon me for treating of a subject with which I have nothing to do nor any concern save what arises from my anxiety for that part of the Irish government to which you belong.

SOURCE: NLI, MSS 17070

1 Maxwell Blacker (born c. 1774), son of St. John Blacker, clergyman of Co. Donegal; called to the bar 1795; appointed chairman of Dublin quarter sessions 1826.

1330

To his wife

Cork, 31 July 1826

[No salutation]

I had the happiness to find your letter of yesterday before me. How I hate to be away from you—how I detest being separated from my own darling Mary. . . . Do you know why I am cheerful this day? Almost every client of mine got verdicts. We had two *sporting* cases[1] against that *nasty* Lord Mountcashel.[2] I could not have written to you yesterday. We went down to Cove in a noble steamboat. There were about three hundred persons on board; no rocking or unpleasant motion. There was a charity sermon at Cove—a very excellent one—in support of a fever hospital. We then dined with a very cheerful and pleasant party at the Bishop's[3] and came up again in as crowded a company in the steamboat. We got to the quay at near ten o'clock but had not water enough to land for about an hour. Much as you dislike *Navigation* you would, I think, be pleased with the Cove steamboat when the water is delightfully smooth and the scenery most beautiful. Good night, sweetest darling. . . .

SOURCE : FitzPatrick, *Corr.*, I, 130-1

1 Unidentified.

2 Stephen (Moore), third Earl Mountcashell (1792-1883).

3 Dr. William Coppinger, bishop of Cloyne.

1331

To his wife, Derrynane

Cork, 2 August 1826

My darling Love,

Judge Torrens fortunately is sitting this day but he is taken up with civil bills. He, however, is so far getting on that I disposed of five briefs in his court this day. I hate, darling, these delays and it is this which makes me dream of having you here. It is foolish to think of it and yet you *could* come to Killarney to Kitty's,[1] and Kate and you and Betsey and Edward Connor *could* take the entire inside of the Lady of the Lake coach the next day and so be here with me at little expense; but it is a dream. . . .

I have been just this moment counsel for a man who has been convicted for the murder of his wife.[2] I am not quite satisfied with the verdict, and yet I conjecture that he did kill her; if so, *even you* will admit that he deserves his fate. Darling, it vexes me to think that I should be kept here by this *unreasonable accident* of Judge Torrens' illness. . . . I will send horses from Killarney to be at Killorglin the night before you leave Tralee. We will take as little luggage with the carriage itself as possible. . . . I intend to ride my own horse all the way, or at least as far as he will carry me comfortable, at least from Killorglin. The lighter the carriage goes on that road the better, and I think that horse will take me in great style. . . .

SOURCE: NLI, MSS 5759

1 His sister Kitty Moynihan, Rathbeg, Rathmore, Co. Kerry.

2 The case of James Collins who on 2 August 1826 was tried and sentenced to death in Cork for the murder of his wife, Ellen, at Leamlara, Midleton. O'Connell was counsel for Collins (*CMC*, 2 Aug. 1826).

1332

To his wife, Derrynane, 7 August 1826, from Cork

Will soon depart for Tralee.

SOURCE: NLI, MSS 422

1333

From Edward Dwyer to Tralee, redirected to Cahirciveen

Corn Exchange Hotel, Dublin, 14 August 1826

My dear Sir,

I beg leave to state my having fully complied with your

instructions and to ask whether I shall offer your name to the . . . requisition[1] for the purpose of addressing Earl Fitzwilliam. I expect to have the signatures of Lords Gormanston and Killeen this evening. In that case I shall take the liberty of adding yours.

I have heard lately from different sources of information that the greatest surprise is expected and felt at the withholding such assistance to the persecuted 40/- freeholders as we have in our power to give.[2] They say, 'Why not devote a portion of that fund collected from the poor, for their relief now in the day of their distress?' I must candidly give my opinion that there is much of justice in the expectation for, without such aid, numbers of poor creatures, particularly in Monaghan where persecution rages to a great degree, must be ruined and sent to beggary. . . . [Dwyer suggests an aggregate meeting be called for the purpose of laying before them] the state of the suffering poor, and [he would] propose that a loan of three or four thousand pounds should be granted to the Finance Committee of the 'New Catholic Rent' out of the £13,000 of the old Association fund in order to enable them to support the suffering patriots. I am confident that if what I suggest was put into practice, our funds would be considerably added to and the persecution would very soon cease. In Waterford, where I understand a large sum was collected, there is no persecution going on. They sent us £50[3] after receiving the letter[4] you sent to Mr. Kenny. Dowel O'Reilly has just been with me to say that the money collected in Cavan will be sent in. . . .

I regret very much that it does not suit your convenience to be with us just now. Your presence would give an interest to our meetings which they have not. However, we usually have a greater number than our best days at Coyne's.[5]

If you think proper to write to me with your opinion on the above-mentioned loan, I shall have the pleasure of reading it at the Saturday meeting. . . .

SOURCE : O'Connell MSS, UCD

1 A requisition for a meeting to be held on 21 August 1826 for the purpose of inviting Lord Fitzwilliam to the grand provincial dinner in Waterford (*DEP*, 15 Aug. 1826). An address to Fitzwilliam was drawn up at the meeting, which actually took place on 22 August 1826 under the chairmanship of Lord Killeen (*DEP*, 24 Aug. 1826).

2 See letter 1340, note 3.

3 There had earlier been some disagreement in Waterford as to

whether the money collected there for the protection of the freeholders should be kept in the hands of the Waterford Protection Association or sent to the New Catholic Association in Dublin (*DEP,* 29 Aug. 1826).

4 Unidentified.

5 A bookshop at 4 Capel Street owned by Richard Coyne. Early meetings of the Catholic Association were held in a room over this shop.

1334

To his wife

Waterford, Monday, 28 August 1826

My darling Heart,

My life has literally been a journey since I saw you. On Wednesday to Carhen, Thursday to Lakeview. James[1] *shyed* at spending eight or ten pounds and would not come here. We had a preparatory meeting yesterday at which I was obliged to draw all the resolutions.[2] We met this day at ten and, in fact, I had to arrange everything of the details of the business. We had, indeed, a grand meeting[3] today. The Church is beautiful. William Roche[4] of Limerick was in the chair. Wyse moved and spoke to the first resolution. He made a very good speech. Coppinger moved the second resolution with a good *sing-song* speech. The third resolution was moved by John O'Brien[5] of Limerick in a *neat speech*. But why should I detain you with details which you will see in the newspapers? I spoke for an hour and a half, and they say I made a *brilliant* speech. I suppose I did not because, in fact, I do think I made a good one, and nobody is half so bad a judge of his speech as the speaker himself. But I never was more cheered, neither did I ever *move* an assembly so much. I am sorry Maurice did not come. Our grand dinner takes place tomorrow and Lord Fitzwilliam, the great and good, dines at it. It will be very splendid.

SOURCE : FitzPatrick, *Corr.,* I, 132-3

1 His brother who lived at Lakeview, Killarney.

2 Some twenty resolutions in all were passed by the Waterford provincial meeting. One of these declared in regard to the forty-shilling freeholders, '. . . we solemnly pledge ourselves, not only never to accede to any proposal to limit that Franchise, but also to oppose any attempt to introduce any such limitation; and . . . to use all legal

means in our power to protect the Freeholders from any vindictive proceedings on the part of their landlords' (*DEP,* 7 Sept. 1826).

3 The grand provincial Catholic meeting for Munster, held in Waterford cathedral on 29 and 30 August 1826. No person of rank, and only one M.P., Robert Shapland Carew, appear to have participated in this meeting (*DEP,* 31 Aug., 2 Sept. 1826).

4 William Roche, son of Stephen Roche and one of the four banking brothers (Stephen and James in Cork—Thomas and William in Limerick). Partner in the banking firm, Thomas and William Roche (the 'Limerick Bank'). M.P. for Limerick city, 1832-41.

5 John O'Brien (1794-1855), Thomas Street, Limerick, and Elmvale, Co. Clare. M.P. for Limerick city, 1841-52. Father of Lord O'Brien of Kilfenora.

1335

From Christopher Fitz-Simon to care of Roger Hayes Esq., Waterford

Ballinamona House, Arklow, 28 August 1826

My Dear Sir,

. . . I am more than drained by my fitting up and furnishing this place. By the way it has come to above the double of what I had expected. . . .

I never saw my beloved Ellen in better, I may say in so good, health. She likes this place much, and only wishes for some of our Derrynane friends to be nearer to her to complete her happiness. She expects Miss Gaghran[1] on a visit to her shortly. . . .

Ellen . . . at this moment is busy counting the number of names to the Munster Requisition.[2] . . .

SOURCE : O'Connell Papers, NLI 13646

1 Former governess to O'Connell's daughters.

2 The requisition for the Waterford provincial meeting. It contains no names of M.P.'s or titled persons (*DEP,* 22 Aug. 1826).

1336

To Edward Dwyer

Waterford, 31 August 1826

My dear friend,

I beg leave to enclose £1 being my Sept. gale of the new Catholic rent for all public purposes not prohibited by law.

I avail myself of this opportunity to enter my respectful but firm protest against the allocation of any part of the old rent[1] to any other purposes than those[2] for which it was collected. After the decisive opinion[3] evinced at the Provincial meeting here against such allocation, I am sure that the very patriotic and rational gentlemen who may differ[4] with us in sentiment will not persevere in acting on that sentiment. The 40s freeholders have been praised by many who will not now come forward to relieve them. What do praises and votes of thanks signify to the family who are starving for having acted honestly? A pound note is a better tribute than a good set phrase.

The new Catholic rent like the old requires only persons to collect it. It is not the sending in of large donations that I desire so much to see as the extension of the collection to various parishes. Multiply the number of contributors and then the penny a month will be most abundantly sufficient.

The old rent fund has more than enough of demands on it. It is not lying idle or *fructifying* as some gentlemen seem to think. The interest is applied to the purposes 'as far as it goes' for which that rent was originally collected, and the principal remains a sacred fund to be applied in the same manner when an emergency shall require. Drawing from that fund, even if it were competent to do so, would only relax the efforts of the *real* friends of the 40s freeholders. Besides, the money drawn could not be replaced without violating the Algerine Act[5] and making the new rent illegal.

SOURCE : Dublin Diocesan Archives

1 The rent collected by the Catholic Association of 1823-25 of which a substantial sum remained (see letter 1333).

2 See letter 1340.

3 See letter 1340, note 3.

4 See letter 1340.

5 The act for the suppression of the Catholic Association (see letter 1173, note 4).

1337

To his wife

Cork, 2 September 1826

My darling Mary,

. . . We had, you know, a great dinner.[1] I made a famous speech; everything was superb. On Wednesday I quietly installed my Liberators.[2] They will make a noise yet. You would laugh to hear the multitude of wiseacres I had advising me on that subject. My brother John was one of those who think that I do not know what I am about in politics. How much I mind their sapient advice! The Liberators will *do* yet. Darling, we had on Wednesday night a Catholic Charity ball. It was the first the Catholics ever gave in Waterford. Stephen Coppinger *must* needs dance in a quadrille with Madame Wyse.[3] You never saw anything so ludicrous—his sepulchral aspect and funereal step were most powerfully contrasted with her elegant *Italian* dancing, almost too airy indeed for a sober company without being at all indelicate. I was greatly amused at it. They had great fun at supper when they made him make several speeches and give her health three times in various shapes. The next day, Thursday, was *my dinner*.[4] Nothing could be better. We had a most numerous, respectable and honest meeting, an immense deal of good speaking, &c. Yesterday at nine in the morning I left Waterford in the mail or, rather, on it. I was received with great cheering in all the towns. At Tallaght there were bonfires blazing, and when I came to Orange Youghal—for it is very Orange—the people had a chair and flags, and I was regularly chaired through the town. Such shouting and then hooting at the *adverse faction* I never heard. It was very ludicrous and very amusing. I did not get in here till ten at night. I have been working at my trade all day long. I never was in my life better. Oh, that I had but such a sentence under your sweet hand! I believe I did not sign my last letter at all, but you could guess who it came from. I mean on Monday to go to Tralee, on Thursday back to Killarney and on Friday at the latest to sweet Derrynane.

SOURCE : FitzPatrick, *Corr.*, I, 133-4

1 The grand provincial dinner held to round off the Waterford meeting. The attendance included Lords Fitzwilliam and Ebrington, and Sir John Newport, M.P. (*DEP*, 5 Sept. 1826).

2 The Order of Liberators (see letter 1325, note 3, and note 4 below).

3 Laetitia (Letizia) (1801-71), daughter of Lucien Bonaparte and niece of Napoleon. Married 1821 Thomas Wyse from whom she separated 1828.

4 A dinner to O'Connell by his Waterford admirers. O'Connell appeared at this dinner in the regalia (see letter 1325, note 3) of the Order of Liberators, but according to the *Dublin Evening Post*, ' no other gentleman, who sat at any of the tables, appeared to belong to this Order ' (*DEP*, 7 Sept. 1826).

1338

From Henry Howard[1]

Corby Castle, Carlisle, 8 September 1826

Dear Sir,

I wish the joy of the success of your elections[2] in Ireland and think that here they have been far more favourable than expected and certainly the cry of no Popery has completely failed. The health of the Duke of York[3] taking away a *point d'appui* of calculating politicians, is also a strengthener to our cause. Brougham, whom I have this day seen, thinks that as they will ring the changes on Lord J. Beresford's speech and accusations,[4] that it would be well if Dr. Murray or Dr. Curtis or any bishop who happens to have to speak on any occasion, would declare that any threat of excommunication or withholding the rites of the Church on the part of any priest would be entirely inconsistent with our religion and most culpable, and that if ever such conduct had been used it was irreligious and most incorrect and reprehensible, and if any of our revered bishops do make such a speech that it should be sent to all the principal papers for insertion. . . .

[P.S.] . . . *Brougham* does not think that Sir Jn. Copley will accept either the Rolls or the vice chancellorship. Mr. Leach[5] gets the Rolls. . . .

SOURCE : O'Connell Papers, NLI 13647

1 Henry Howard (1757-1842), Corby Castle, Carlisle, Cumberland. Prominent in the struggle for parliamentary reform and Catholic Emancipation. Author of many works including *Memorials of the Howard Family*. See *DNB*.

2 In the elections of 1826 pro-Catholic candidates were returned in counties Waterford, Louth, Dublin, Westmeath, Monaghan and Armagh and in Cork city.

3 In July 1826 York developed dropsy and died in January 1827.

4 *Recte* Lord G. Beresford. At a dinner in his honour in Cavan Lord George Beresford declared that his defeat in the Waterford election was due to the fact that, 'The Freeholders were torn from their Landlords' sides by Priestly authority, by the refusal of Church rites, by actual excommunication' (*DEP*, 7 Sept. 1826).

5 Sir John Leach, Kt. (1760-1834), vice-chancellor of England, 1818; master of the rolls and deputy speaker of the House of Lords, 1827-34. Knighted, 1818. See *DNB*.

1339

To Christopher Fitz-Simon, Ballinamona House, Arklow

Derrynane, 13 September 1826

My dear Kit,

I received your letter in Waterford and would long since have sent you the money you wrote for but, unfortunately for that object, I have bought the O'Mullane property[1] which drains me of ready cash and my buildings here have run away with the rents. I pay £3,200 British to O'Mullane[2] or, rather, to his creditors and get no return during his life, but it will be valuable to my children. . . . You would not know Derrynane it is so changed for the better even in the short space since you were here. I think and hope my own Nell will like it when she comes here next summer with little Mary Fitz-Simon who must have a cock nose and on whom I do verily *believe* her grandpapa will actually doat. . . .

[P.S.] I implore of you to set on foot the new Catholic rent, ever so little will help and small contributions are the best because their tendency is to multiply themselves.

SOURCE : Fitz-Simon Papers

1 The property of his mother's family at Brittas, Mallow, Co. Cork.
2 Edward O'Mullane.

1340

To Edward Dwyer

Derrynane, 13 September 1826

My dear friend,

I enclose you £16 for the new Catholic rent for all public purposes not prohibited by Law. . . .

I frankly confess that I am very much disposed to apprehend the result of the proceedings of the late aggregate meeting.[1] What I fear is that it will damp the ardour of the collectors of the new Catholic rent. I may perhaps be mistaken but I very much apprehend that if it be over-magnified that there is a large fund already accumulated out of which the 40s freeholders may be compensated, many of those who would otherwise exert themselves to collect the new Catholic rent may relax their efforts.

I have a painful duty to discharge when I repeat that the old rent cannot be advanced as a loan to the new. I do not, of course, presume to stand between the vote of the late aggregate meeting and the treasurers of the old rent, but I am bound distinctly to declare that none of the new rent *can* or *shall* go to replace such parts of the old as the treasurers may advance in consequence of the resolution of the late meeting, for this reason, that if such reimbursement were not distinctly disclaimed, it might be urged as a legal objection to the new rent that it was collected for purposes which, however useful and wise in themselves, have been rendered illegal by the Algerine Act.[2] I speak thus strongly because we *must* not be involved in any legal difficulties. There are *none* in the present treasurers' converting as much of the old rent as may be required for the indemnification of the 40s freeholders to that purpose. The treasurers are quite safe in converting the old rent to that purpose, but they would not be safe in receiving any part of the new rent to replace the monies so converted. If they receive the new rent to replace the old they will be liable to an indictment. The old rent therefore must be a gift to the freeholders, not a loan, I mean there must be no loan of the old rent though there can be a gift of it. I wish my original plan had been put forward by me to the public, that of *individuals* guaranteeing the treasurers for advancing the old rent. I was there and am still ready personally to enter into a guarantee for £500 or a £1000 for that purpose whilst the new rent was accumulating to indemnify the freeholders. But in truth I never was so disposed to despair as I am upon this subject. Every energy should be used to collect the new rent, and so essential a difference[3] as that between the provincial meeting and the aggregate ought, I think, to have been avoided, but it is vain to look to the past for any other purpose than to obviate any ill effects of it. Those effects can be obviated by strenuous exertions in every quarter to collect the new rent. There is nothing encourages our friends so much as the readiness to contribute in money exhibited universally. There is nothing that affrights our enemies so much as the combination of feeling which a general contribution to the rent evinces. Depend on it that if the new rent succeeds to the extent that it ought, we will either be emancipated or a new and further Algerine Act must be passed to suspend but not to suppress, 'for that is impossible', our exertions. . . .

SOURCE : Dublin Diocesan Archives

1 At this meeting in Dublin on 7 September 1826, the question of whether those forty-shilling freeholders who at this time were being evicted should be relieved from what remained of the old Catholic rent or from the new Catholic rent which was only now being collected was discussed. It was decided that in the event of the new rent not being sufficient part of the old rent should be used (*DEP*, 9 Sept. 1826).

2 The act for the suppression of the Catholic Association (see letter 1173, note 4).

3 At a meeting of the new Catholic Association on 2 September 1826 a letter was read from Fr. John Sheehan, secretary of the Waterford provincial meeting, informing the association that that meeting had resolved unanimously against touching any part of the old rent (*DEP*, 5 Sept. 1826). O'Connell had declared at the Waterford meeting that the old rent 'ought to be preserved for the purposes for which it was intended. They all knew its ultimate destination; the very moment that Catholic Emancipation is granted, it would be handed over to their respected prelates, for the purpose of promoting education' (*DEP*, 2 Sept. 1826). O'Connell stressed that the freeholders must be protected by the new rent. Arrangements for setting this in motion were made and £400 collected for this purpose in Waterford (*DEP*, 2 Sept. 1826, see also letter 1334, note 2).

1341

To Edward Dwyer

Derrynane, 17 September 1826

My dear friend,

I enclose you a letter I received from my most valued friend Mr. Kelly of Acton. This is the gentleman who so nobly contributed £100 to the old rent and now sends for himself and family £30 for the new rent. He has inherited a large fortune in Ireland and with his family do honour to their wealth no less by their public spirit than by their amiable private virtues. I beg you will in my name propose him and his four sons to be members of the New Catholic Association.

I hope before the next day of meeting to send you the first collection of the Catholic rent from a remote and poor parish in this county.

SOURCE : Dublin Diocesan Archives

1342

To John Primrose, Jr.

Derrynane, 18 September 1826

My dear John,

I beg of you to repair to Berehaven and to take upon yourself the entire management of the O'Sullivan property.[1] Whatever you do under my title from Hedges Eyre I will fully ratify. Mrs. O'Sullivan will arrange respecting the arrears due at her husband's death.

SOURCE : O'Connell MSS, UCD

1 That of Morty O'Sullivan (died 1 June 1825), Coulagh, Berehaven, Co. Cork, a popular magistrate and a noted smuggler. Cousin of O'Connell. Son of John O'Sullivan (died 1796) and nephew of Captain Daniel O'Sullivan, Coulagh. Married first Mary, daughter of Roger O'Sullivan, Garnish, Glengariffe, Co. Cork (she died 1822), and secondly, 11 April 1823, Ellen O'Sullivan.

1343

From his brother James to Derrynane

Lakeville [Killarney], 23 September 1826

My Dear Dan,

I take it for granted you have long since received my letter from Tralee in which I mentioned my not being able to procure the loan of £1,000 for you. . . .

. . . His [Count O'Connell's] plan of your insuring a sum of £10,000 on your life for the benefit of your younger sons I do not approve of. There would be an annual premium of £500 and you, I thank God, are as likely to live many years as any person of your age in Ireland. I do not think the General will agree to your getting the property of your sons in my hands to pay for Brittas.[1] It cost you no doubt £2,500 Irish currency but will not produce *one guinea* during the life of Edward O'Mullane who is but six years older than I am, and then but £200 a year and no further use until *all the O'Mullanes are dead,* so that I would have little trouble. . . .

SOURCE : O'Connell MSS, UCD

1 See letter 1339.

1344

From Edward Dwyer to Derrynane

Corn Exchange Hotel, Dublin,
25 September 1826

My dear Sir,

Mr. Conway[1] has just shown me part of a letter from you requiring that I should send you the residence or address of the Irish R.C. Bishops which I have now the pleasure to annex. You will observe from the report[2] in the [*Morning*] *Register* that the rent is getting on in good style. Sir John Burke[3] has sent me his subscription of ten pounds this morning. I am now and have been some days employed in sending letters to Parish Priests requesting their exertions to forward the collection of the rent, calling the meetings, forwarding of Petitions, the census,[4] etc. . . . From the manner in which the Dublin parishes are arousing from their stupor, I expect the best results. I am quite certain the Catholic *Old Fund* will not be touched. . . .
[A list of names and addresses of Irish Catholic bishops is enclosed with this letter.]

SOURCE : O'Connell MSS, UCD

1 Frederick W. Conway.
2 *Morning Register,* 21 September 1826.
3 Sir John Burke, second baronet, Marble Hill, Co. Galway.
4 Sheil had devised a scheme for a census of the Catholic population which was adopted by the new Catholic Association. Although never completed, the figures it provided made excellent Catholic propaganda (Reynolds, *Emancipation Crisis,* pp. 24, 54, 70-1).

1345

To Edward Dwyer

Derrynane, 27 September 1826

My dear friend,

. . . I have commenced the collection of 'the New Catholic Rent for all public purposes not prohibited by law' in this remote and poor parish. We are upwards of 200 miles from the metropolis but if every parish intervening would imitate our humble example the 40s freeholders would be amply indemnified and we should have a fund sufficient to deter any future tyrant from attempting to force his Catholic tenants to vote for an Orange candidate. I think it right to transmit to you our first collection however small, being only £12. It cannot be too often repeated that our national exchequer—for so I may well call it—can be safely and certainly filled only by the multiplication of small sums. Of this money one pound is the donation of our worthy rector, the Rev. Mr. Teahan [P.P.]. I beg of you to propose him to become a member of the New Catholic Association. Of this money £5 are my subscription in this parish. My fellow labourers for Emancipation may justly reproach me with being unwilling that any part of the Old Rent should be applied to the indemnity of the 40s freeholders but no person can truly reproach me with any unwillingness to apply (as far as my limited means allow) my own money for that purpose. On the contrary, I deem it a sacred duty to avail myself of every possible occasion to throw in my mite to this really patriotic fund and also to exert myself in every way I can to promise its increase.

We are, I am most happy to say, agreed upon one point, namely, that the Old Rent should not be touched save in the case of absolute necessity.[1] I deny that any such necessity can exist unless it be created by the apathy or tardiness of those who ought not only to set the example of contributing themselves but of stimulating others to contribute. The new rent wants only collectors. If collectors *will* but act the fund will soon swell to more than a sufficient amplitude. Nothing in Catholic affairs for a long time gave me more pleasure than to see the respectable requisition in the parish of St. Michael's and St. John's, amongst other purposes, to put the New Rent in collection. A few examples of that description would do more good than if any agitator of us was preaching for a month. If the rest of Dublin follows, the collection will spread throughout the entire country. You should use every possible exertion to procure collectors in each parish in Ireland.

Can it be forgotten that if we get one shilling a year each from the one-eighth of the Catholics of Ireland (for they are eight millions) 'we shall have £50,000, that is if one million of persons contribute one farthing a week each we shall have £50,000. Let this never be forgotten'.

West Division, Parish of Kilcrohan, Co. Kerry
per Daniel O'Connell £12. 0. 0

SOURCE : Dublin Diocesan Archives

1 See letter 1340, note 3.

1346

To Edward Dwyer

Derrynane, 4 October 1826

My dear friend,

I have been able to do little for the New Catholic Rent during the last week. However I have not been quite idle of which the proofs will hereafter appear.

I now beg to enclose you £2 which you will credit as follows :

A protestant gentleman in aid of the New Catholic Rent for the parish of Kilcrohan, County of Kerry	£1. 0. 0
Daniel O'Connell his October gale of the New Catholic Rent for all public purposes not prohibited by law	£1. 0. 0
	£2. 0. 0

SOURCE : Dublin Diocesan Archives

1347

From his son John to Merrion Square

Saturday, 21 October [1826]

My dear Father,

[John asks that he be allowed to enter the navy, which he has a strong inclination for, rather than enter the legal profession which is his father's wish. But he will obediently do whatever his father desires.] . . .

[P.S.] If you do give me joy by consenting, settle about it at once for I am getting *older* and might in another 7 months or year be too *old* for it. However, as you choose.

SOURCE : O'Connell Papers, NLI 13645

1348

From Rev. M. Walsh, C.C.,[1] *to Tralee*

Ardfert [Co. Kerry], 22 October 1826

Dear Sir,

Enclosed is an outline of what Mrs. Crosbie[2] has resorted to in this village for the seduction and annoyance of its inhabitants. At every step she has been resisted, and successfully, for her establishment is now reduced to a few families and those at all times not remarkable for good character. When I heard she seduced the mistress and her scholars I waited on her at the school to know the painful reality. I introduced myself as the Catholic curate of the parish and said I wished to know would it be a Bible school. On hearing me say the priests would oppose it she was greatly excited. . . . Agitation pervaded her frame and soon she exhibited the Bile Splendid! Darkness, ignorance, error and superstition were poured out in impetuous current on the ears of those present, and I was given to understand in no ambiguous terms that our present bishop[3] (who opposed her) was a shoeboy. . . . Every new stratagem is called by her benevolent and she is frequently ringing the changes on liberality, education and moral improvement. . . . The first day McCrea[4] came to preach here the people hooted him in the street when he came out of his meeting-house and confounded him with . . . perplexing questions as to his mission and authority to preach. One of his party affected fear from the crowd, but a young man named Connor made an answer that should not be forgotten. There is no danger, said he, 'We are loyal to our King and are ready to fight for him if necessary. We respect his law and will not break it, but we hold our religion dearer than all and disclaim every idea of violence in supporting it.' This is the way in which an Ardfert farmer defeated the dexterity of a Biblical in trying to give a character of turbulence and riot to a peaceable people. The newspaper which accompanies this letter contains McCrea's last fanatical performance. . . .

SOURCE : O'Connell Papers, NLI 13647

1 Died 19 September 1866, C.C. Ardfert, 1825-29; P.P. Sneem, 1829-66. The 'Fr. O'Flynn' of Alfred P. Graves' song.

2 Probably Jane, wife of Rev. John Talbot-Crosbie, Ardfert, Co. Kerry.

3 Cornelius Egan (1780-1856), son of Daniel Egan, Lismickfinan,

Killorglin, Co. Kerry. Principal of Diocesan Seminary, Killarney, and professor of theology there, 1806-11; parish priest, Tralee, 1811-24; coadjutor bishop of Kerry, 1824; bishop of Kerry, 1824-56. See *Boase*.

4 Rev. John B. McCrea, Protestant minister of the Independent church, and author during the 1830's of many anti-Catholic tracts.

1349

From Rev. John Sheehan to Merrion Square

Waterford, 3 November 1826

My dear Friend,

I have been urged by the members of the Protecting Committee[1] to write to you and to call your particular attention to the call we have last made upon the N[ew] C[atholic] Association for money.[2] The want of it produces the most fatal results amongst our persecuted people. The gentry and the aristocracy here have resolved to wage war *usque ad internecionem* against the Forty-Shilling Freeholders who overturned their power at the last election. The Marquis of Waterford's Trustees have adopted a most harassing system towards them. Our agent, O'B Dillon, will detail to you at length the nature of the persecution when he goes up to term. The contest lies then between the Association and the enemies of our liberties. Will you, my dear friend, use your influence to have a remittance made to us? If we had a sufficiency of money at the present moment, we would put them down with ease.

. . . I am . . . writing to you again. . . . One of the principal objects of my letter was to get from you a petition founded upon the resolutions adopted at the provincial meeting.[3] If it be not too late, let me even now have the petition I require that I may procure the signatures of the people of this County. I have been directed by the Bishop[4] to convene the clergy of the dioceses of Lismore and Waterford to petition for Emancipation.[5] We meet on this day week in this city. . . .

SOURCE : O'Connell Papers, NLI 13647

1 Probably an organ of the Waterford Protection Association, set up for the purpose of relieving the forty-shilling freeholders in that neighbourhood (see letter 1333, note 3).

2 A letter from Waterford calling for the remission of £400 for the relief of the freeholders in the neighbourhood was read at a meeting

of the New Catholic Association on 2 September 1826 (*DEP*, 5 Sept. 1826). Waterford had just remitted £236 to the association (*DEP*, 5 Sept. 1826).

3 It was resolved at the Munster provincial meeting that a committee should prepare the draft of a petition to parliament for 'total, unqualified, and unconditional Emancipation' (*DEP*, 7 Sept. 1826).

4 Patrick Kelly (died 1829), bishop of Richmond, Virginia, U.S.A., 1820. Bishop of Waterford and Lismore, 1822-29.

5 Resolutions appealing to the Catholic prelates and clergy of Munster to forward petitions to parliament in favour of Emancipation had been passed at the Munster provincial meeting (*DEP*, 7 Sept. 1826).

1350

From Franc Sadleir,[1] *Trinity College, Dublin, 1 December 1826, to Merrion Square*

Concerning land tenancy business.

SOURCE : O'Connell Papers, NLI 13647

1 Franc Sadleir, D.D., S.F.T.C.D. (1774-1851), bursar and librarian, Trinity College, Dublin. Provost of Trinity College, Dublin, 1837-51. Strongly supported Catholic Emancipation. See *DNB, Boase.*

1351

To Rev. W. L'Estrange, O.D.C.

Merrion Square, 15 December 1826

Very Rev. Sir,

As chairman of the Committee for making arrangements for the aggregate meeting of the Catholics of Ireland to be held on the 19th inst., I am directed to apply in the most respectful manner to you and the other reverend gentlemen of your House for the use of your chapel[1] on that occasion.

The Catholics are so often and so deeply indebted to your very reverend fraternity that they respectfully anticipate a kind compliance with their wishes.

SOURCE: NLI, MSS 5759

1 The Carmelite chapel, Clarendon Street, Dublin.

1352

To John Primrose, Jr., Hillgrove

[postmarked 20 December 1826]

[First part of letter missing.]

. . . Let me also know how matters are going on at Derrynane. I have bought a clock to go down by the first steamboat to Cork. On receipt of your answer I will write to you again. I do not leave town this vacation.

P.S. I hope you will avail yourself of the first possible opportunity to complete the house at Derrynane. All that is absolutely necessary is the passage to the kitchen and room over it, and raising the old house. It seems to me that the timber should be sawed and ready to roof at once and that at the latest the passage should be *put in hands* before January closes. I wish very much to have it habitable for my family by the first of June. We have I hope stones enough raised. Any further works at Derrynane save planting I would do at my leisure. Go to Derrynane occasionally and take special care that John O'Connell[1] is not running me to foolish expense by half finished vagaries. I am anxious about the entrance road, and if you can *job* it cheaply it would be well to do so. You say nothing of the preparations for next year's crop. You know how anxious I am to have that abundant, especially *all kinds* of tillage. The garden will easily be taken care of. . . . If the war[2] goes on it will produce great changes. At present everything looks very warlike.

SOURCE : O'Connell MSS, UCD

1 John Charles O'Connell.

2 A reference to the sailing of a British expeditionary force to Portugal for the purpose of repelling a threatened Spanish invasion. The expedition entered the mouth of the Tagus on 1 January 1827 (*Annual Register*, 1826, pp. 342-3).

1353

To John Primrose, Jr.

Derrynane, 26 December 1826

My dear John,

. . . The tithe composition[1] is not paid by the tenant *at all* and the outgoing tenant, even if he were to pay it and in the cases where he is made to pay it, is liable only to the May gale. The composition is not payable out of the crop or by reason of the crop but is payable out of the entire land, agistment[2] and all, that is, it is equivalent or rather more potential than the landlord's rent. The fact is that the composition is payable by the landlord, not by the tenant.[3] That is the law. The practice is otherwise but that practice must still bend to the legal principle which discharges the crop of the tithe and converts the payment into rent. It follows that the outgoing tenant pays no more to the Parson than to the landlord, that is, the May gale and no proportion of the November.

SOURCE : O'Connell MSS, UCD

1 See letter 1006, note 9.

2 Pasture or its produce, with special reference (at least in Ireland) to dry stock rather than dairy cattle.

3 In all leases granted in compounded parishes, the landlord was allowed to add the amount of the new composition to the rent (Angus Macintyre, *The Liberator: Daniel O'Connell and the Irish Party,* 1830-1847 [London 1965], p. 171, n).

1354

To the Knight of Kerry

Merrion Square, 31 December 1826

Copy

My dear Sir,

I feel ashamed that you should deem it necessary to make any excuse to me for giving me advice. I did hope you knew me better; and now I assure you that there is no political man from whom I should be more happy to receive counsel or more grateful to for taking the trouble of giving it. I trust I shall hear from you as often as you have anything you deem useful to suggest. After this preface, which is very sincere, I think I am at liberty to discuss freely the contents of your letter and to tell you that, with all deference to your judgement, I have the misfortune to differ entirely with you. Perhaps it is that I am grown weary of being temperate, moderate and conciliatory to no one useful purpose and without having obtained any one single advantage. These qualities seem now to me to be worse than useless. They promise impunity to our enemies and give no promise of active support to our friends. After all, the Established Church, with her millions of acres and pounds, is our great foe and she may be frightened; but one may as well endeavour to coax a pound of flesh from a hungry wolf as to conciliate the Church.

From our numbers, our combination and the continued expression of our discontent something *may* be attained, especially if we ourselves keep within the law and succeed in procuring the people to avoid illegal excesses. If that could be achieved there would be no great difficulty in getting the Catholics in every parish in Ireland to meet for the purpose of petition on one and the same day; and where they were so organized by community of sentiment as to meet *thus* all on the same day three or four times and to separate peaceably, there would appear such a union of physical force with moral sentiment that Mr. Peel would be insane if he continued his opposition. We *never, never, never* got anything by conciliation. Could it be possible to be more conciliatory than we were on the deputation?[1] Yet have we not, in fact, been flung back by our disposition to accede? No, I do solemnly assure you that I have the strongest and *most quiet* conviction that *temperateness, moderation* and *conciliation* are suited only to perpetuate our degradation but that, if we want to succeed, we must call things by their proper names—speak out boldly, let it be called intemperately, and rouse in Ireland a spirit of *action* which will bring all our people to show in a legal manner their detestation of that truly *English* and quite *un-Irish* policy which, for the sake of a few worthless statesmen, and many *supernumerary* parsons, would continue the worst possible system of government in Ireland.

We mean to *enforce* a discussion[2] as early as possible before 20th February at the latest. Do you think Lord Eldon likely *to pick up* the Duke of Clarence?[3]

SOURCE : Lansdowne Papers

1 The Emancipation deputation to London of 1825.

2 Of the Catholic claims in parliament.

3 Prince William Henry, duke of Clarence (1765-1837), third son of George III. Ascended the throne as William IV 26 June 1830.

1355

From his son Morgan to Merrion Square

Güns [Hungary], 1 January 1827

My dear Father,

. . . I have the additional pleasure of informing you that I have been appointed lieutenant in the regiment[1] a couple of days since. . . . A vacancy having occurred, our colonel recommended me to go up to Vienna and pay my respects to Vincent[2] who is now there for a short time, and the result was that he instantly went himself to the Council of War and, in an hour after I had presented the Colonel's letter, I was strutting about Vienna as a bold lieutenant. With respect to the equipment money which I require as officer I hope you will soon send it [to] me, indeed the sooner the better as I want it immediately. The General,[3] I believe, told you once that £100 would be sufficient and, indeed, it would but . . . I would be better off if with £150 than £100 but, however, if you don't wish to give it [to] me, I hope you won't be vexed at my asking it nor don't think the demand is occasioned by any extravagance on my part. . . . I assure you I am not at all in debt, behave myself very well and you may depend on it that the request is not at all unreasonable. . . .

SOURCE : O'Connell Papers, NLI 13645

1 The 6th Leger Cavalry.

2 Karl Freiherr von Vincent.

3 Count O'Connell.

1356

To Bishop Doyle, Carlow

Merrion Square, 2 January 1827

My lord,

It is my duty respectfully and earnestly to entreat the attention of your Lordship to two subjects which I deem of paramount importance to the Catholics of Ireland.

The first relates to the Education Census which has been for some time in progress under the auspices of 'the New Catholic Association', the second to the establishment of the 'New Catholic Rent for all public purposes not prohibited by law'.

I most respectfully submit to your Lordship the propriety of affording your kind countenance to both these important, *and I conceive,* highly useful measures. Should I have the misfortune to differ with your Lordship on these subjects, I implore you at all events to pardon the anxiety which makes me solicit, as I now do most earnestly, your very valuable and most esteemed support. Believe me, my Lord, that I make this request from an honest conviction of the paramount utility of these measures to our religion and country.

The 'New Catholic Association' are extremely desirous to procure one or two clergymen in your Lordship's diocese who would condescend to assist them to obtain speedy and accurate returns for the Education Census in each parish. But they would not think of requesting of any of your Lordship's clergy to give them this assistance unless they were perfectly convinced that such a measure would not meet your disapprobation.

I beg leave at the other side to annex a list of the parishes in your Lordship's diocese of which we have obtained already the census. I beg leave to inform your Lordship that the persecution of the 40s. freeholders has recommenced, and that we are much pressed for relief by persons who suffer persecution for not sending their children to proselytizing schools or who themselves refuse to be perverted. We [? are very] anxious to relieve all these persons and, believe me, that if the Catholic Rent *on the new plan*[1] were universal, it would afford abundant funds for these purposes.

[overleaf]

Imperfect from	Rev. Danl. Nolan	Paulstown etc.
do.	— Corn. Dowling	Mayo
do.	— John Dunne	Union of Portarlington
	— Thady Dunne	Rosenallis etc.
No tithes mentd.	Very Rev. Dr. Duane	Mt. Mellick etc.
	Rev. John Kelly	Clonmore etc.

SOURCE : Kildare and Leighlin Diocesan Archives

1 The 'new plan' seems to have been merely an intensification of the methods of collection already in being.

1357

To John Primrose, Jr.

Merrion Square, 5 January 1827

My dear John,

I do not want to persecute that unfortunate Sam McCarthy[1] and if you can manage to have the informations disposed of without John Connell's forfeiting his recognizance I am quite satisfied you should forgive him this time, but get as many *promises* as you can that he will not behave so ill in future. If you can get his wife to promise, forgive him at once.

You delight me with the prospect you give of my rent roll keeping up in these times. If the tenants are *now* able to pay, there would be no fear of them if prices rose—as sooner or later they must.

I beg again to repeat my earnest entreaty to have the house at Derrynane completed as speedily as possible. I hope to have my family there in May. If the house be fit for them I certainly will have them in Kerry as soon after Lent as possible. It is foolish to take down the carriage horses. If I get a decent price for this pair I will sell them about Easter which is the dearest timc for draft horses in Dublin and then I may buy another pair when the family come up after Christmas. [Remainder of letter missing.]

SOURCE : O'Connell MSS, UCD

1 Of Bahoss, Co. Kerry.

1358

To the Knight of Kerry

Merrion Square, 15 January 1827

My dear Sir,

I received your second letter and again implore of you to believe that I shall always feel grateful for any suggestion you may favour me with. Nay, I ask you to have the kindness to give me any information or advice that may tend to the settlement of the Great Question—in other words, the settlement of Ireland—in which you have just the same interest that I have and are, I am sure, just as anxious to see carried.

I hope you were satisfied with what we did, or rather what we said of the Duke of York.[1] There has not been the least impropriety—nothing of triumph or exultation. If anything a little too much of flattery, but that, perhaps, was naturally to be expected whilst compassion for human suffering predominated in its influence over the overflowing kindness of Irish feelings. We are a strange people, perhaps the most sensitive in the world to the kindly and affectionate motives of the heart, but we can be fierce too. And, apropos of that, when I wrote[2] so fiercely on the subject of the necessity of our being *intemperate,* I had in view the continuance of the Eldon and Peel dynasty; but if the rumours afloat—and not discredited here in quarters where there *ought* to be information—if those rumours be true and that the Marquis of Lansdowne be about to share power, *believe me* it will, with friends of his description in the Cabinet, be no difficult matter to bring the tone and temper of our proceedings into a key which would banish discord and produce the truest harmony. I have myself the greatest confidence in the integrity and intelligence of the Marquis of Lansdowne. He is a practical man from whom everything solid and useful may be expected. He is, besides, a man of steady principle and will not join anyone who will not join with him in some of the vital measures for securing the *Peace* and *Strength* of the Country. I mean domestic peace and strength of foreign as well as domestic purposes. Should he come into office, I should strongly hope that your political connections and opportunities will enable you, with honour and consistency, to join him. I am sure that the most independent part of your constituents would be highly pleased with such a junction if sanctioned by your own judgement. In fact I think I may venture to say that the Marquis of Lansdowne would bring with him into office all the support which the Catholics of Ireland and liberal Protestants could give to any administration, and I am convinced that such support would, if aided by ministerial countenance, be of the utmost strength in Ireland. Such an administration would tranquillize the country in one Hour. One would ask with astonishment, 'What has become of the Orange party?' just as at the Restoration it was asked, 'Where are they who dethroned the King?'

SOURCE : FitzPatrick, *Corr.,* I, 137-8

1 At a Catholic meeting in Dublin on 10 January 1827, following the death of the duke of York, some uncomplimentary observations were made about him. O'Connell, however, declared, 'We war not with

the dying or the grave. Our enmities are buried there. They expired with the individual who . . . caused them' (*DEP*, 11 Jan. 1827).

2 See letter 1354.

1359

To Richard Newton Bennett

Merrion Square, 15 January 1827

My dear Bennett,

Give the enclosed *yourself* to Lord Althorp. If you find that he thinks I ought to have sooner answered his letter, convince him of my most sincere respect and of the attention I paid to his suggestion. It was to support[1] Lord Duncannon[2] in Kilkenny Co.

I beg of you, my dear friend, in the next place to discover for me privately and discreetly how the wind blows in a certain quarter.[3] Commit nobody but, however, you may if necessary commit *me*. You can pledge yourself to the strong attachment of the Catholics to the connection and to the family if they shall but get fair play. All they want is a clear stage and no favour and they are disposed to be the most attached people in the world. In plain English the Duke[4] can command Ireland heart, hand and soul if he pleases, and with Ireland he may defy the world. We are stronger than may be imagined. Why, even in London if Pat took it into his head he would go near to beat ' the Guards ' but for efficient strength at home it is but folly not to appreciate us justly. The manner the Catholics received the King[5] ought to convince the royal family that we want but *permission* to serve them. If you can give me any suggestion of what course would be most pleasing in that quarter, rely on it that it will be most respectfully attended to. I can confide in your tact and good sense. I know no human being in whom I would more implicitly rely and I write this letter in a way that shows you I do so. Be discreet and if possible learn *the wishes* of that party without committing any of them. They *shall* be obeyed. All I want is '*the map of the land*'. I want only the compass, I think I can steer by it. . . .

SOURCE: NLI, MSS 837

1 In the general election of 1826 Duncannon successfully contested Co. Kilkenny despite O'Connell's opposition.

2 John William (Ponsonby) (1781-1847), styled Lord Duncannon until 1844; Bessborough, Co. Kilkenny. M.P. for various English con-

stituencies, 1805-34, except Co. Kilkenny, 1826-32; created Baron Duncannon (U.K.), 1834; home secretary, 19 July-15 December 1834. Succeeded as fourth earl of Bessborough in 1844. Lord-lieutenant of Ireland, 11 July 1846-16 May 1847.

3 A reference to the duke of Clarence (later William IV), now the heir presumptive to the throne since the duke of York's death on 5 January.

4 The duke of Clarence.

5 A reference to George IV's visit to Ireland in 1821.

1360

From Eneas MacDonnell

15 Duke St., Adelphi, London, 19 January 1827

Private

Dear O'Connell,

I have this morning read with very sincere pleasure your speech *on the opening of the session.*[1] . . .

You are right in your conjectures as to Wellington's appointment[2]. . . . I have good reason to expect that you will see it gazetted on next Tuesday. I now request your attention to my advice that petitions be immediately presented to the *Lords* and Commons on the subjects . . . in the enclosed. I think that Lord Grosvenor[3] would be a good presenter in the Lords and Lord Althorp in the Commons, as the latter is always supported by friends. Pray read the enclosed through, and a firm but not violent or personal introductory speech on your part, referring to the foreign stations of your own family and others would, be assured, produce a beneficial discussion particularly if you are at all acquainted with the origin and histories of the Irish Brigades.[4]. . . I attended yesterday a meeting of the English Catholic Committee, the Duke of Norfolk in the chair. There are generally good feelings prevalent but be assured that there are intriguers at work. . . . I have it from very peculiar authority that certain negotiations are proceeding and that Lord Lansdowne is looked to as a great object. A ministerial convulsion is *certainly* expected by some persons who have official opportunities of obtaining information. I believe that Canning was defeated in the Cabinet on the question of Wellington's appointment. [MacDonnell suggests that if the present efforts at Emancipation fail, the Association should set up a statistical committee to inquire into 'the state of the different counties, the different church rates, land tithes, etc., *and the general conduct of the Protestant bishops and parsons* in Ireland in *all* matters. Mark now that all the examinations hitherto have placed us, the injured party, on the defensive. This plan would place the injuring party on the defensive and, believe me, would startle them and their friends more than any other proposition.' He also suggests that the Association should publicize the Catholic position so that foreign states would know how badly they had been treated.]

I understand that Canning has sent to the English legations at all the Catholic states inquiries to ascertain how the Protestants are treated there. He is such a false one that one cannot know whether this is done with good or evil intent. . . .

SOURCE : O'Connell MSS, UCD

1 The opening meeting on 16 January of the fourteen-day Catholic Association for 1827. Referring to England's current difficulties abroad, O'Connell declared, 'This is the time for a statesman to preserve England by rallying her strength at home. Let England become really powerful by conciliating Ireland.' His speech was marked by outspoken attacks on Peel, Liverpool and Eldon (*DEP*, 18 Jan. 1827).

2 Wellington was appointed commander-in-chief of the army following the death of the duke of York. Referring to his appointment O'Connell declared him a person upon whom 'the people of Ireland look with . . . execration. . . . Did he not build his fortunes on the efforts of Irish valour? . . . Was not his first vote, after he had obtained that Dukedom won by Catholic blood, given against the freedom of the Catholics of Ireland? ' (*DEP*, 18 Jan. 1827).

3 Robert (Grosvenor), second Earl Grosvenor (1767-1845). Created marquess of Westminster, 1831.

4 In continental armies during the eighteenth century.

1361

From Jeremiah McCarthy, 62 Dawson Street, Dublin, 9 February 1827, to Merrion Square

States that, in response to O'Connell's request, he has agreed to settle his action against Finn[1] out of court.

SOURCE : O'Connell Papers, NLI 13646

1 Patrick Finn.

1362

To the Knight of Kerry

22 February 1827

My dear Sir,

We are here in great affright at the idea of the Duke of Wellington being made Prime Minister.[1] If so, all the horrors of actual massacre threaten us. That villain has neither heart nor head. It is impossible to describe the execration with which his name is received amongst us. Could you suggest any act of the Catholic body which might facilitate the views of the Opposition at this moment? And, in particular, could we do anything to forward or support the Marquis of Lansdowne? To him much of our hopes, almost all, are turned. We could have Catholic county meetings, addresses to the King, petitions to parliament or anything else that public bodies may do, if you deemed it useful. But perhaps our interference may have a contrary effect. Still I do not like a timid policy. I beg your opinion speedily.

SOURCE : FitzPatrick, *Corr.*, I, 140

1 Lord Liverpool suffered a stroke on 15 February 1827. Peel wished to have Wellington become prime minister. Upon Canning's assuming that office, six members of the cabinet, including Wellington, resigned.

1363

From William Hare, M.P.

London, 22 [or 28] February 1827

Sir,

In reply to the letter which you have done me the honour of addressing to me, I beg leave to say that far from thinking that its contents were dictated by any unkind or offensive feelings, I am thankful for any suggestions that my constituents have the goodness to offer me. . . .

. . . I look upon Catholic Emancipation as an all-important step. I regard it as a measure that would form the bond of union, tranquillity and welfare in a country that has been too long distracted by well-grounded discontent. It is therefore my intention to pursue the course I have adopted with steadiness and zeal, unabated by any trivial circumstances and unaccompanied by injudicious or compromising conduct.

SOURCE : O'Connell Papers, NLI 13647

1364

To Eneas MacDonnell, 15 Duke Street, Adelphi, London

Merrion Square, 23 February 1827

My dear MacDonnell,

I saw your last letter and can pledge myself that you may act upon my instructions, that is, you may commit yourself with perfect safety to the extent I will now point out.

First, that the Catholics of this country are most anxious to see an administration purely composed out of the present opposition members.

Secondly, that next to an administration entirely composed of *now* oppositionists it would be very desirable to us to have an administration with the Marquis of Lansdowne at its head although composed in part of the present men.

Thirdly, that if the administration is to be formed of the existing material then Mr. Canning must have the decided preference over the Peels, Eldons, Wellingtons, etc.

If you possibly can act on this information, do so. If it be practicable see such men as Daly and Martin of Galway, both members of your own county, Vesey Fitzgerald, Hare of Kerry, Lloyd of Limerick, the Tipperary members, King's County members, etc. And by etc. I mean other ministerial members, and tell them that as agent to the Catholics of Ireland you feel it your duty to apprise them that the Catholics will deem every man *an actual enemy* who does not support Canning against Peel, Eldon and Liverpool. You can go farther and pledge yourself that the men who at this crisis decline to support the Catholic against the no-popery part of the cabinet will meet with decided opposition at every ensuing election. In short it strikes me that you should now take a decided part with *all* our Irish members—[one word illegible] to rally them all if you can for a new cabinet, failing that to a partially new cabinet, failing that to a decidedly Canning administration. James Daly and Vesey Fitzgerald are both Peelers. If you can get *at* these gentlemen, assure them that we will organize an immediate opposition to them in their own counties unless they take a decided part with Mr. Canning in any ministerial struggle now going forward. *You may pledge yourself* to have these sentiments re-echoed by public meetings and carried into practical effect.

With respect to the discussion of our claims we are decidedly of opinion that it should not *under any circumstances* be postponed. Circumstances should bend before great national interests. The rights of the Irish people should never be compromised by reason of party inconveniences. I implore you *to insist* on the discussion taking place on the appointed day. Believe me they are not our sincere friends who will allow themselves to be embarrassed by the present position of affairs. A discussion is always useful *to us,* and at this moment it is peculiarly necessary to press forward. That man would gain no fame as a general who hesitated whether he should *charge the* enemy at the moment they were in any confusion. Do not let your firm and excellent judgement be swayed by your respect for *friends. Press forward, urge, insist* on a discussion. When they tell you what *will be* if you postpone, reply with the old adage, *What will be, shall be.* Use my name if it be of the least value either here or in England as the author of this advice. Terrify *our* ministerial friends into an abandonment of Peel, etc., and *insist on* an immediate discussion.

SOURCE : Fitz-Simon Papers

1365

From Maurice FitzGerald, Knight of Kerry

London, 24 February 1827

My dear O'Connell,

As you express a strong wish to hear from me speedily I will not delay answering you though I write from my bed to which I have been confined for these two days by a severe cold. All *great* men must be ill, it seems.

My head is so bothered that I cannot adequately answer the very serious question you put to me, but to the best of my judgement I shall endeavour to do so by Monday's post.

In the meantime I would merely observe that considering it quite impossible that a no-popery Cabinet can be thought of by anyone, and feeling convinced that neither Peel nor the Duke of Wellington would lend themselves to such a project, I think you need not be alarmed as to the *colour* of the new Minister. Either Canning will endeavour to place someone of their own body who agrees with him in that situation or he will demand some powerful accession to the Cabinet. I have been 24 hours without any political news beyond the papers which at such a crisis is a great blank but I hope to get out this evening.

So complicated is the case that it requires consideration how far any extraneous interference may embarrass or promote the desirable issue of this most important arrangement. It is of no small importance that Canning *saw* the King, I believe twice, before leaving Brighton.

It seems that Lord Liverpool had a previous paralytic attack in December. He has now suffered also with [?] apoplexy. . . .

SOURCE : O'Connell MSS, UCD

1366

To John Primrose, Jr., Hillgrove

Merrion Square, 27 February 1827

My dear John,

I was glad to find you had the house covered in and hope that the passage to the kitchen and barrack room is also slated. I am very anxious to have everything completed as speedily as possible—I need not repeat *that*. The water channel to the bath *was* very badly constructed. I hope it carries the stream through the bath. Do you recollect the alteration in the back bedroom and the room under it—back of the old drawing-room? The bedroom required the stopping up of the western window and the room under it the stopping up the western door, opening a window near that door and either stopping or converting into a window the southern door. The only other alteration in the interior was the enlarging the door of the chapel as much as may be consistent with perfect safety to the wall.

That unfortunate Barry[1] must be taken care of. Give him every assistance in medicine, etc., and allow him besides live as a working man while he is kept from work by his wound.

. . . Maurice[2] and I go to Ennis on Wednesday next, the assizes there commencing on Thursday. I go round the entire circuit with Maurice to initiate him completely. . . . Give me full details of Derrynane. Is all the interior work completed save of the new garret rooms? Where are the new garret stairs? The old [one word illegible] room and the old parlour are before now, I hope, restored to their former size. . . .

SOURCE : O'Connell MSS, UCD

1 Unidentified.

2 His son.

1367

From Eneas MacDonnell

London, 27 February 1827

PRIVATE

My dear O'Connell,

. . . I had interviews with Sir F. B. [Francis Burdett] and several others and stated the views of the Cath[olic]s in Ireland. . . .

I think we should not express any sentiment as to the new cabinet[1] till we know something more than is at present known; and least of all should we meddle with Canning, who is a very slippery gentleman and might throw us overboard, as would suit his convenience. I shall, however, keep your sentiments in view, and if any fair opportunity should arise, I will avail myself of it: at the same time that I fear no opportunity will come sufficiently strong to overcome my general disinclination to enter into any communications with such folk. It struck me that it might be well to write an official note to Mr. Canning expressing the expectations of the Catholics in his friendship, at this crisis. . . .

I am in correspondence with the Bishop of Norwich and his son,[2] the archdeacon. They have got a petition signed already by 83 ministers on our behalf. . . .

I hope you will not persevere in your motion[3] as to Plunket, not in love of him, but because I fear that it might be prejudicial to have the laity in direct opposition to the Bishops,[4] whether by accident or otherwise on any point.

SOURCE : O'Connell MSS, UCD

1 That about to be formed under Canning's premiership.

2 Henry Bathurst (died 1844), eldest son of Henry Bathurst, bishop of Norwich. Archdeacon of Norwich from 1814.

3 At a Catholic meeting in Dublin under the chairmanship of Anthony Browne on 21 February 1827, O'Connell accused William Conyngham Plunket, the Irish attorney-general, of being secretly an enemy of Emancipation (*DEP*, 22 Feb. 1827). He does not appear to have moved any formal resolution against Plunket.

4 Plunket had been entrusted by the Irish Catholic bishops with the presentation of their petition in favour of Emancipation (*DEP*, 3 Mar. 1827).

1368

From Bishop Doyle (J.K.L.),—March 1827[1]

Excerpt

'May I request of you to read over the fifth and sixth chapters of the Book of Exodus before you complain that our arguments are left unanswered, that our prayers are slighted, that our sufferings are unpitied and that our efforts to extricate ourselves only serve to rivet faster our chains. To add that I pity and despise the men who substitute clamour for argument and who accuse those who cannot defend themselves, is unnecessary; you can estimate my feelings on the subject by your own. But our cause is in the hand of God and God is just.'

SOURCE : FitzPatrick, *Dr. Doyle*, II, 6

1 This letter was probably written shortly after the defeat of Sir Francis Burdett's motion in favour of Catholic Emancipation (see letter 1370).

1369

From Denys Scully to Merrion Square

Dawson Street [Dublin], 4 March 1827

Dear O'Connell,

I enclose you the 2 bills for £2,100 and £900 . . . They will *certainly* be paid on the days when they become due and you will not have the trouble of applying for a renewal of either of them. Get the bill of £2,100 discounted for me at any rate. I am very much obliged to you for the accommodation to me on the present occasion and will be very glad to do the like again for you whenever it may be necessary.

SOURCE : Fitz-Simon Papers

1369a

From the Knight of Kerry

London, 7 April [*Recte* March] 1827

My dear O'Connell,

Before this reaches you the fate of Burdett's motion[1] will be public. I was not sanguine as to numbers and yet by no means prepared for the impression which this result has made on my mind. Canning's language[2] was like that of a man who was determined to resign. His office is the issue. We shall see whether his actions correspond. No further course has yet been resolved on but we meet tomorrow. I have given notice for the 1st of May of a motion[3] which may bring out the whole of their pledges which were used to facilitate the Union. In the meantime the less *that* point is talked of the better.

I am so very ill that my attendance was difficult, and speaking out of the question. I had intended to state the Juggernaut case but was obliged to hand over the papers to Plunket.

[P.S.] I remain of opinion that neither Peel nor the Duke of Wellington could think of a 'no-popery' ministry, but how much better are we with [one] as effectually bars any measure of Relief?

SOURCE : O'Connell MSS, UCD

1 On 5 March Sir Francis Burdett made a motion in the Commons in favour of Catholic Emancipation. After a two-day debate it was defeated by 276 to 272.

2 George Canning spoke vigorously in support of Burdett's motion.

3 A motion recommending that the Commons 'shall take such course as may be best calculated to realize the policy in which the Union of Great Britain and Ireland was recommended to the Legislatures of both countries'. The Knight of Kerry withdrew this motion on 7 May 1827 (*DEP,* 10 May 1827; *Hansard,* XVII [1826-27], 576-7).

1370

To Edward Dwyer

Ennis, Friday [9 March 1827]

My dear Friend,

I have just read your letter announcing the Orange triumph and the last sad defeat[1] of Ireland. Another crime has been added to those which England has inflicted on this wretched land; another instance of genuine Reformation bigotry has disgraced the British nation. But a just and good God is looking on and in his own good time will be his own avenger. I agree with those who totally refuse to despair. We must rally for a new exertion. To address the King cannot be an unwise or disrespectful measure, although it is not one from which I expect much. His Majesty owes a deep debt of gratitude to Ireland. He asserted his rights over the British oligarchy when he was prince. We, the Catholics, threw down our resentments and flung away our legitimate prejudices to do him honour and make him a king indeed,[2] when in England the popular voice was raised against him and his person was scarcely safe from violence. Yet during his reign no benefits have hitherto flowed to the Catholic cause. Well, let us hope that the period is not remote when his Majesty will give us cause to rejoice at our fidelity. Some good must come from an address. It is in itself constitutional and legal. But we must not rest our efforts there. We must renew our petitions to the Houses of Parliament. We must have another debate immediately after Easter: we must never let the question rest. The more we exhibit our determination to pursue perseveringly constitutional courses and the more frequently we exhibit the bigotry of the boasted British nation to the contempt of all the enlightened people of the civilized world, the better. Strong measures should now be resorted to—as strong as are consistent with legal and constitutional limits. A petition for the Repeal of the Union should be immediately prepared. There are but few patriots among the Irish Protestants, but the few there are would join us in that; or if not, let us petition alone for the repeal of a measure which has increased every evil Ireland before endured and taken away every prospect of a mitigation of the causes of the poverty and wretchedness of the country.

SOURCE : FitzPatrick, *Corr.*, I, 138-9

1 On 5 March Sir Francis Burdett introduced in the Commons a motion in favour of Catholic Emancipation. After a debate lasting two days his motion was defeated 276 to 272.

2 Probably a reference to the visit to Ireland of the king in 1821.

1371

From Thomas Fitzgerald, Cork, 10 March 1827, to Ennis

Concerning bills of exchange. Has obtained lodgings for O'Connell in Cork.

SOURCE : O'Connell Papers, NLI 13647

1372

To his wife, Merrion Square

[postmarked Ennis 11 March 1827]

My darling Love,

. . . Forgive me for being *so angry*. The defeat[1] of the Catholics contributed not a little to my *malignity*.

We have had a grand and glorious meeting[2] here this day. We agreed to various petitions and to many wicked resolutions. They will appear on Wednesday. We will have another meeting here on Tuesday.[3] I promise you I will keep the ball up. . . .

I loved you when you were young and the prettiest little girl that ever picked a clean spot for a sweet little foot to tread on amidst the mud of a dirty pavement.

We, your son and I, are just going out to O'Gorman's[4] to dine. The weather is very mild and he is perfectly well and so is your husband, love, only old and bold but not cold. . . .

SOURCE : Fitz-Simon Papers

1 See letter 1370, note 1.

2 A meeting of the Catholics of Co. Clare held in Ennis chapel on 11 March 1827 under the chairmanship of James O'Gorman Mahon. Among the resolutions passed was one which attributed the recent defeat of the Catholic claims in parliament to ' the narrow-minded and selfish policy of the most worthless portion of the present Administration '. It was declared that any Irish M.P. who should support that administration ' is unworthy of the confidence of the

Catholics of Ireland, and must be actuated by mean and mercenary motives'. Preparations were made to draw up petitions for unqualified Emancipation, Repeal and parliamentary reform, and to commence the electoral organization of Clare in readiness to return pro-Catholic candidates at the next election (*DEP*, 17 Mar. 1827).

3 The adjourned meeting of Clare Catholics was held on 15 March 1827 when the drafts of the petitions to parliament were agreed on (*DEP*, 17 Mar. 1827).

4 Possibly James O'Gorman, Ennis, a brother of Nicholas Purcell O'Gorman.

1373

To Edward Dwyer, 12 March 1827, from Ennis

States that Scott[1] will send up the resolution of the last meeting in Ennis (Sunday) for insertion in the press.

SOURCE : Dublin Diocesan Archives

1 Richard Scott, attorney, Ennis, Co. Clare, and Dublin. Election agent to O'Connell at the famous Clare election of 1828.

1374

To Edward Dwyer

[Limerick] 21 March 1827

My dear friend,

I enclose you £16 Catholic rent of which you will be so good as to have the particulars inserted in the next Saturday's list. . . .

I got both your letters. I am very much afflicted at the proceedings in Dublin. There is a want of spirit and of energy, a crouching beneath defeat which both surprise and afflict me. The resolutions[1] of the separate meeting were puling and weeping but suggesting nothing. There was no manly *rebound*.

By the by there was a very foolish discussion about my letter.[2] Whenever you chance to have a letter of mine not expressly *committed* for the meeting, do not read it if any one member objects. I am sorry you read the last although I cannot have any blame to you for doing so.

The paper[3] given you by Mr. James Dwyer[4] is a very unwise one. The project of a permanent committee to control separate meetings would be at once illegal and in the next plan highly unwise as introducing secret management into Catholic affairs. I wonder who it is that they would appoint, a species of conservative senate to be *deputies* over the Catholics at large. . . .

I am often blamed for not having managed Catholic affairs so as to have attained Emancipation long since. Alas, how little do the fault-finders know the species of *material* with which I have to deal, the kind of persons who eternally clog every movement and who would prefer breaking my head to smashing the pates of 500 Orangemen. James Dwyer always takes the wrong side. I do not think I ever saw him right. He is sure to be at the side of *power* and *authority*.[5] . . .

I am agitating famously. Clare will be immediately in full play and you may I think expect, I think, a good deal of rent from it. We had a very numerous meeting[6] this day here and a proper spirit of indignation was manifest. The repeal of the Union seems the general sentiment. I will also leave Kerry quite organized for collection of Catholic rent, registry of freeholds, etc. Sheil appears to be doing nothing. No county stirring but those I put in motion. Well, well, I may [remainder of letter missing].

SOURCE : Dublin Diocesan Archives

1 At a Catholic meeting in Dublin on 12 March under the chairmanship of Sir Thomas Esmonde, 'awful forebodings for the future' were expressed in consequence of the recent defeat of the Catholic claims in the Commons, but the people of Ireland were recommended to adopt a spirit of 'peace, perseverance, and Christian piety—to place their dependence upon God and the justice of their cause—calmly to look forward to the course of events . . . still clinging to the hope that the legislature will . . . reconsider the . . . late vote, before the Catholics of Ireland are driven to . . . despair' (*DEP*, 15 Mar. 1827).

2 At the above meeting, the chairman, Sir Thomas Esmonde, attempted to prevent Edward Dwyer from reading O'Connell's letter of 9 March 1827. Esmonde objected to the letter because it was 'couched with a warmth . . . produced by the late disastrous intelligence [i.e., the defeat in the Commons of Burdett's Emancipation motion] and entered upon topics not now under discussion, such as a Repeal of the Union'. Dwyer read the letter upon Lawless's threatening to do so in his stead. It was received 'with great applause' (*DEP*, 13 Mar. 1827).

3 Not extant.

4 James Dwyer (born 18 Mar. 1793), fourth son of Jeremiah Dwyer,

Dublin. Called to the bar, 1827. Secretary of the Hibernian Bank from its foundation in 1824 until 1827. Appointed queen's counsel, 13 January 1846.

5 At the meeting above, James Dwyer cautioned the Catholics against excesses which would tend to alienate their friends in parliament (*DEP*, 13 Mar. 1827).

6 A meeting held in the Augustinian church in George's Street, Limerick, under the chairmanship of William Roche (*DEP*, 31 Mar. 1827, quoting *LEP*).

1375

To his wife, Merrion Square

Limerick, 22 March 1827

Darling Mary,

. . . We had a great meeting[1] yesterday. Maurice spoke distinctly and well but I believe there was no reporter present, at least I saw none.[2] I never was more dissatisfied with myself. We however passed some strong resolutions and there was a great deal of strong talk from the *natives of the bay*. But after all I prefer Clare to this place for public spirit and energy. I am sorry to perceive that Sheil and Fitz-Simon are not agitating the country at all. It seems to me to be the height of folly to allow the enemy any respite and as far as I can I will keep the cause in motion.

Darling, these conversions[3] are exceedingly foolish things. They are buying wretches in every direction who are a disgrace to them and no loss to the church they desert. It will have, in my judgement, a considerable reaction on the minds of the dispassionate, and by a letter I got from England since I came here I have reason to think it has already commenced that effect to a considerable extent. . . .

SOURCE : Fitz-Simon Papers

1 See letter 1374, note 6.

2 Maurice O'Connell proposed a vote of thanks to Sheil (*DEP*, 31 Mar. 1827, quoting *LEP*). O'Connell's own speech is not recorded.

3 Various Protestant bodies were currently claiming converts from Catholicism in several parts of the country, particularly in Cavan (*DEP*, 15, 20, 29 Mar. 1827).

1376

To Edward Dwyer

Cork, 5 April 1827

My dear friend,

I enclose you £2 New Catholic Rent for all public purposes not prohibited by law. One pound of this money is the subscription of Richard Mahony of Portmagee in the County of Kerry, Esq., an active, intelligent and most useful magistrate. The other pound is my own gale for the month of April. I wish I could prevail on every man who wishes well to the welfare and happiness of Ireland to recollect that the continuance and permanence of the Catholic Rent can be secured only by giving the example of unabated perseverance in the payment of small sums month after month. In fact the people who are both zealous and honest are everywhere ready to pay. If there could be found individuals of the more wealthy class to take the trouble of acting as collectors.

There is nothing our enemies dread so much as the extension and permanence of the Catholic Rent. Any falling off in its amount gives our enemies the greatest satisfaction.

I also enclose you a list of names to be affixed to the requisition[1] for the aggregate meeting, being decidedly of opinion that we should find means to have a full discussion on the general merits of our question or on some particular details of it every week while the Parliament sits. We should give the Eldons, Peels and other bigots no species of rest or relaxation until they are compelled or induced to do us justice. We are at the right side of the question and therefore discussion even with an unfavourable result is in itself necessarily advantageous. The bigots are in the wrong and therefore discussion must necessarily expose them to ridicule and contempt. The English people are to be sure greatly degenerated and are daily declining in those qualities which elevated them amongst nations but their pride still remains and is perhaps increased by the absence of the noble qualities on which it ought to be founded. Now the wretched exhibition of sophistry and bigotry which is made by the reported discourses (as they appear in the newspapers) of their leading statesmen is so calculated to wound English pride and to debase the English character in the eyes of the civilized world that I would for that reason alone, if I had no other, insist on the repetition of discussion. The English may be shamed into liberality or if not they should be made to earn the contempt and execration of the world.

[P.S.] Would you ask Mr. O'Dwyer[2] to postpone his [one word illegible] motion[3] for one week?

SOURCE : Dublin Diocesan Archives

1 A requisition for a meeting of the Catholics of Ireland to be held in Dublin on 20 April 1827 to consider the propriety of petitioning parliament in favour of Emancipation. Among the signatories were the Catholic primate, Archbishop Curtis, Lords Fingall, Kenmare, ffrench, Killeen, Gormanston and Southwell and Sirs Thomas Esmonde, Patrick Bellew and John Burke (*DEP*, 7 April 1827).

2 Andrew Carew O'Dwyer (1800-77), son of Joseph O'Dwyer, merchant, Cork and Waterford. Called to the bar, 1830; M.P. for Drogheda, 1832-34, re-elected 1835 but unseated on petition June 1835. Appointed filacer of the exchequer, 1837, with a subsequent pension of £3,000 p.a.

3 Probably a motion proposed by Andrew Carew O'Dwyer in the new Catholic Association on 31 March 1827 on the burning of the Catholic chapel at Tartarraghan, Co. Armagh, allegedly by Orangemen (*DEP*, 5 April 1827). On 6 April 1827 O'Dwyer agreed to postpone his motion in favour of voting the parishioners money for the rebuilding of their chapel from the funds of the association, Jack Lawless contending that this money was needed for the relief of forty-shilling freeholders (*DEP*, 10 April 1827). After a further postponement by O'Connell (*DEP*, 17 April 1827) O'Dwyer's motion that the finance committee take into consideration the granting of £50 for the rebuilding of the chapel was passed on 21 April 1827 (*DEP*, 24 April 1827).

1377

This letter is now numbered 1369a.

1378

From the Knight of Kerry

London, 14 April 1827

Confidential

My dear O'Connell,

I am not aware of any negotiation with the Opposition and therefore what I say is not mixed with any personal consideration. But on public grounds and with a view to Catholic interests it suggests itself to me that a course of the greatest forbearance at this moment would promote your cause and weaken and disappoint the enemy. The arrangements as far as they are understood are all in favour of a liberal policy and the opposers of Emancipation are resigning *in shoals*. The Duke of Clarence is appointed High Admiral. The whole principle of the nominations seems sound and such a government is likely to command our support in such circumstances. What would you think of *adjourning* your Association with the double object of evincing confidence and disarming the prejudices which will be attempted to be inspired into the public feeling here, as against a ministry '*too Catholic*'. Unwilling as you know me to be to advise in counsel, the case appears to me so pregnant with great results and you have so little real information from hence that I cannot reconcile it to myself to withhold my mite. I believe what I recommend would have very important consequences. The King is acting with great decision.

P.S. I should add that there are strong *rumours* of negotiation and I believe them. Lord Duncannon, Newport, Rice and all the best opinions I have consulted entirely concur in my views. The situation of the new ministry[1] will be critical and their opponents (Tory) very powerful *in Parliament*. Do not let them wield no-popery against it if possible.

SOURCE : O'Connell MSS, UCD

1 That of Canning, who became prime minister on 10 April 1827.

1379

From the Knight of Kerry

London, Monday, 16 April 1827

Confidential

My dear O'Connell,

Since I wrote on Saturday things have not taken so decided a course as to allow any positive inference as to the policy which Canning may be *able* to pursue. Copley is Chancellor. The riddance of Eldon is a positive good.[1] The other appointments are of a nature which might be considered merely provisional in case any more enlarged scale of Administration be practicable for, as it stands, it is too narrow, but whatever way the communication [was] made to opposition, it was not deemed sufficiently satisfactory on the subject of Ireland and it is off. It may however be well for you to suspend any expression of opinion until the real character of the new ministers may be sufficiently pronounced. Should anything more decided occur, I shall give you notice.

P.S. I write a line to say that since I sealed my letter I have received serious assurance that the aspect of things is improving.

And you will be glad to hear that the committee of Dublin Election[2] has decided 12 to one against the bribery charge which may be considered conclusive in favour of White.

SOURCE : O'Connell MSS, UCD

1 On 12 April 1827 Eldon resigned from the lord chancellorship in protest against Canning's appointment as prime minister. He was succeeded as chancellor by Lord Lyndhurst.

2 On 1 May 1827 the committee appointed to consider the petition of George A. Hamilton and others against the return of Richard W. Talbot and Col. Henry White for Dublin County in the election of 1826, reported those members duly elected (*Commons Journal*, LXXXII, 417).

1380

From the Knight of Kerry

London, 19 April 1827

Confidential

My dear O'Connell,

Although I have not any peculiar sources of information as I perceive that in conversation and in print the delay in forming a ministry gives rise to sinister conjectures, I think it right to say that I draw no unfavourable conclusion from such delay. It is notorious that Canning has great difficulties to encounter, that he has to manage the King as well as the public feeling, both adverse to any sudden change of policy, and that those difficulties will be in proportion to any good which he may meditate.

The wrath of the Tory faction augurs well but it will require great prudence not to throw the King back upon them. He is, for the present, very angry with them but will require at least in particular Departments (as the Home) decided Protestants. Nothing has hitherto been arranged beyond the Admiralty, Chancery and the Ordnance, and in the meantime I am sure that the quieter matters are kept the better. Whatever be the turn up, we shall have credit for moderation and forbearance, and I have fully ascertained the truth of what I suggested to you at the outset of this crisis.

I think the course you took in the discussion[1] at the Association as reported in the *Register* which reached me yesterday perfectly judicious and at this moment very valuable.

SOURCE : O'Connell MSS, UCD

1 In the New Catholic Association on 14 April 1827, O'Connell pledged Irish Catholic support for Canning in the event of his forming a liberal ministry (*DEP,* 17 April 1827).

1381

From Eneas MacDonnell to Merrion Square

London, 23 April 1827

Private

Dear O'Connell,

Be assured it was a most grievous error to have stopped your proceedings[1] for a moment in deference to the party manoeuvrings here, and I greatly fear that you will have reason to think so very soon after this note will have reached you. In the *Morning Chronicle* of this day, mark the conduct of the Opposition, now anxious for office, throwing us overboard notwithstanding their repeated taunts against Plunket, Canning and others for holding place in a cabinet which agreed to exclude our question, and notwithstanding their declarations of the danger of postponing our question for a day. . . . Go on, even now, and determination will mitigate the evil, an evil, be assured of it, that never would have occurred, if you had not evinced vacillation in your Dublin proceedings.

What you have now to guard against is running to the opposite extreme of violent reproach against the Whigs, though Heaven knows 'tis hard to avoid it. Give no credit to their professions. They are all fraudulent cajoleries; at least we have a right to treat them as such. . . .

The questions in controversy now, 'tis said, are who of the Opposition goes in with Lansdowne.[2] Canning, 'tis said, wishes some Whig to be Chancellor of the Exchequer but this is an office not likely to be a sinecure and shunned by all. The Whigs could only get two places in the Cabinet while the Tories will have three. In fact, the former appear to have acted most meanly towards them*selves* and most basely towards us. . . .

I saw Plunket and Blake[3] about one o'clock going to Canning's house. *You* are the maddest man on the earth if you place the slightest confidence in either of them. I shall keep my letter to Dwyer open as long as I can. . . . I must conclude but on parting must declare my conviction that unless you take high station for our question at this crisis, you will have flung it back a very long distance. . . .

[P.S.] I imagine you will feel little difficulty in guessing why Sir John Burke advised you to leave the petition[4] in the hands of Lansdowne and subject to his Lordship's management. You see and know something [*sic*] of what is going on. You are grossly misled, believe me. Remember 1825.[5]

SOURCE : O'Connell MSS, UCD

1 At a Catholic meeting in Dublin on 18 April 1827 O'Connell carried a resolution favouring the postponement of an aggregate meeting to 1 May. He feared that at this meeting 'discussions might take place that might be disagreeable to some of their sincere friends' and urged that the Catholics wait to test the character of the new administration (*DEP,* 19 April 1827).

2 Lansdowne was mainly instrumental in April 1827 in effecting a coalition between a section of the Whigs and the followers of Canning. He entered Canning's cabinet at first as a member without office, but in July 1827 he became home secretary.

3 W. C. Plunket and Anthony R. Blake.

4 In favour of Catholic Emancipation.

5 A reference to the failure to gain Emancipation in 1825.

1382

From the Knight of Kerry

London, 23 April 1827

Confidential

My dear O'Connell,

Plunket has given up the Rolls in consequence of the objection he understands to exist in the English Bar to his appointment. He takes the Peerage.[1]

I believe it is now more likely that Lord Lansdowne may accede to the propositions made to him—I believe very much against his individual feelings and a sacrifice to what he considers the interest of Ireland. It is indispensable that some effectual bar should be raised against the return to power of the desperate faction that has so long weighed down these countries. But the difficulties at the outset are great and numerous. We must hope that they will gradually give way but I believe and you can easily understand that it requires great management. All the official arrangements are merely *provisional* except those I before pointed out.

I see some of the language at your meeting[2] would calculate on an entirely favourable ministry—*the thing is totally impossible*. Do you think the King is to have no voice on that subject? He cannot disguise what his feelings have been. We must hope that he will gradually come round.

SOURCE : O'Connell MSS, UCD

1 Plunket was never actually appointed as master of the rolls in England. He succeeded Lord Norbury as chief justice of the common pleas (Ireland) and was raised to the peerage as Baron Plunket. See *DNB*.

2 The Catholic meeting of 18 April 1827 (see letter 1381, note 1). At this meeting O'Connell declared, 'If a cabinet not unfavourable to their claims was formed, as they had every reason to expect, it would be their duty to adopt a conciliatory tone' (*DEP*, 19 April 1827).

1383

To John Primrose, Jr., Hillgrove

Merrion Square, 24 April 1827

My dear John,

[Re rents and bills] . . .

Let me know how matters go on at Derrynane. Have my sheep been again rubbed? Let them be rubbed and rubbed and rubbed again while any appearance of disease remains. If they cannot be cured I had better have them drowned because I would not consent to propagate the disorder by selling them.

I am exceedingly anxious to have *all my tenants* give their butter this year to Tom Fitzgerald. Send round to every house with that message and state the allowance and let it be rigidly made to them. You could not oblige me more than by enforcing this regulation. When I give my tenants the indulgence I do it is not too much to expect that they will gratify me in this respect. . . .

There is no certainty yet of our fate but my hopes are strong that something must be done for Ireland.

SOURCE : O'Connell MSS, UCD

1384

From Henry Brougham to Merrion Square

Hill St. [London], Saturday [28 April 1827?]

My dear Sir,

After congratulating you on the successful termination of the later negotiations which you and yours (I mean your country) have a deep interest in, and towards which I have contributed my endeavours[1] with a zeal proportioned to what I feel for the cause of sound opinions and civil and religious liberty, allow me to suggest to you what an infinite service you will render [? to the] new administration, how [about two words missing] you will strengthen its [about two words missing] good purposes, without giving it any power at all for evil by bringing, at least for the present, the Association to a close. If our proceedings shall disappoint you, you have still the remedy in your hands and your power would then be greater in proportion as [about two lines missing].

If you wish any communication on this most momentous head to reach Lord Lansdowne and the Govt. here with safety and with your own private comments and opinions, you may write to me forthwith. . . .

SOURCE : O'Connell Papers, NLI 13647

1 Brougham was instrumental in winning the support of a number of moderate Whigs for Canning's ministry (see *DNB,* s.v. ' Brougham, Henry Peter ').

1385

From Philip O'Hanlon,[1] *9* [postmarked May] *1827, to Merrion Square*

The writer complains that the local committee, due to a faction, kept back from forwarding to Dwyer, the secretary of the Catholic Association, parish money collected until they should know the fate of the old association on its suppression,[2] and wish to put the money to the repair of the chapel. O'Hanlon asks O'Connell for advice on what to do.

SOURCE : O'Connell Papers, NLI 13647

1 Probably Dr. Philip O'Hanlon, Rathkeale, Co. Limerick.

2 See letter 1173, note 4.

1386

From the Knight of Kerry

London, 15 May 1827

Confidential

My dear O'Connell,

I need hardly tell you how much I rejoice at the course[1] which you have taken and which materially baffles the enemy. I begin to hope that they will be *let down* more easily than the most sanguine could have calculated.

I hope the arrangements[2] will be announced in two days. The delays have arisen from an earnest wish to secure as far as possible a consistent course towards Ireland without hazarding the main purpose of precluding the return of the Tories.

The difficulties have been great and the personal sacrifices of the leading oppositionists most disinterested. The Catholics have certainly done *their* duty.

SOURCE : O'Connell MSS, UCD

1 It was agreed at the Catholic aggregate meeting in Dublin on 1 May to postpone the sending of a petition to parliament (*DEP*, 3 May 1827). On 5 May the New Catholic Association resolved to adjourn for six weeks in order 'to evince the anxiety of the Catholics of Ireland to conciliate their enemies, and to exhibit their confidence in their friends' (*DEP*, 12 May 1827).

2 In connection with the formation of Canning's ministry.

1387

To the Knight of Kerry

Merrion Square, 16 [and 18] May 1827

Confidential

My dear Sir,

I again heartily thank you for your attention to me *during the crisis,*[1] and I wish now that you should be in full possession of the feelings and opinions of the Catholics in the present position of affairs.

First, we are very bitterly sorrowful at the part Earl Grey has taken.[2] We do not know how to reconcile that line of conduct with his undoubted anxiety to pacify Ireland.

Secondly, we are all impatience to see the Marquis of Lansdowne and his friends join [and] actually form part of the administration. We do not believe in the reality of a change of men while the Marquis and his friends are supporters only of, and not participators in, the Government.[3]

Thirdly, you may pledge yourself that the Catholic claims can be managed for the proper season if we get in this Cabinet a change of men. If, for example, Gregory[4] be removed from the Castle—his removal is *indispensable*—the Corporation, controlled as it easily can be in the offices of the police, *all held at will,* and if the Law offices be well filled. It will not do to have Joy[5] Attorney-General or either of the Orange serjeants promoted. Indeed, indeed they ought to be dismissed at once. Lefroy is an exceedingly poor creature in point of intellect and Blackburne[6] is excessively overrated. If they were dismissed it would give infinite satisfaction. Really it is not honest to have such a man as Lefroy in office when he has to exercise judicial functions.

I repeat that, if men were changed, it would not be difficult to postpone to the proper season the Emancipation Bill because the exauguration of the system is so peculiarly attributable to the bad passions of those who have administered it; but it would be really infinitely less obnoxious if mitigated by good and liberal men.

18 May

I wrote the foregoing pages before I got your letter of the 15th, and I rejoice to think that the period is approaching when the *Provisional Government* will terminate. Believe me that you cannot possibly be of more service this moment to this Country and to the new Ministry than by representing to them the absolute necessity, as well as the extreme facility, of changing the men who have abused power and, above all, patronized abuse in Ireland. The Orange faction is already powerless from the mere apprehension of losing government support; but if the partisans of that foe are continued in power their insolence will be redoubled, and the consequent disappointment of the Catholics will cause a reaction the ultimate result of which cannot but be excessively mischievous. I know this Corporation well, and I would pledge my existence that, with a change of men and a fair prospect of measures, in a reasonable time the Government might send out of Ireland every regiment of the line, horse and foot, and maintain perfect tranquillity with the police; but, of course, with a police animated by and conducted on the new system. But really the Government of Peel and Lord Manners would be more popular and fully as sedative as the new, provided the Trenches[7] continue to rule the Custom House, the Gregorys to *manage* the Castle, the Darleys and Kings to sway the Corporation and the Joys, Lefroys and Blackburnes to top the Profession of the Law and *promise* the people a succession of partisan judges. Besides, everyone in Ireland knows that the persons to whom I thus allude have nothing to give the Government in return. It will be a pure gratuity to continue them in office. They have nothing of talent or influence of [*sic*] high character to give them importance. They are as infants in the political world and may be flung aside by a manly and straightforward Ministry with as much facility as a group of children.

I write thus anxiously because, in the first place, it is just impossible I should have any personal motive, and next I have contributed so much to make the Cabinet throw the reins into the hands of our friends that I feel a species of secondary responsibility for the conduct of the Government. Everybody exclaims, Why is not Plunket Chancellor? Why are the Corporation allowed to nominate bigots for Sheriffs, etc.? I must conclude.

SOURCE : FitzPatrick, *Corr.*, I, 140-2

1 In connection with the formation of Canning's ministry.

2 Unlike most of his fellow Whigs, Grey refused to co-operate with Canning. He sharply criticized his conciliatory attitude to the Catholics and his conduct of foreign affairs (see *DNB,* s.v. 'Grey, Charles, second Earl Grey').

3 Lansdowne did ultimately participate in the government (see letter 1381, note 2).

4 William Gregory (1766-1840), youngest son of Robert Gregory, M.P. Educated Harrow and Trinity College, Cambridge. M.P. for Portarlington, 1798-1800; under-secretary for Ireland, 1812-31. A prominent opponent of Catholic Emancipation. See *DNB*.

5 Henry Joy (1763-1838), youngest son of Henry Joy, Belfast (proprietor of *Belfast Newsletter*); solicitor-general, 1822-27; attorney-general, 1827-31. Chief baron of exchequer, 1831-38.

6 Francis Blackburne (1782-1867), attorney-general for Ireland, 1831-35, 1841-42; master of the rolls, 1842-46; chief justice of queen's bench, 1846-52; lord chancellor of Ireland, 1852. See *DNB*.

7 Hon. William Le Poer Trench (1771-1846), third son of first earl of Clancarty. Member of the board of customs (Ireland).

1388

From his brother James to Merrion Square

Lakeview, 19 May 1827

My dear Dan,

. . . I know nothing of unfortunate Myles McSwiney's affairs. His son left this last March to go to Cork. . . .

The deed that you executed in September 1823 in consequence of my joining you in bonds for £1,500 *I never saw*. It was left in John Drew Atkins' office and on your giving me funds to discharge this debt in September 1825 when John, you and I divided the personal property of my Uncle Maurice, I desired Atkins give you up this deed. I at the same *time cancelled your Bond for £1,500* which you also sent me as an additional security. . . .

As to the £1,500 now in my hands, the property of your younger sons, I have put by a bond of Lord Kenmare's for that amount and will, please God, place the interest as I receive it, either in the Funds or lend it on landed security for 10 years for their use, agreeable to the instructions of the kind donor, their grand-uncle, General O'Connell, when it is to be distributed in equal shares between your three younger sons. . . . On no account could I consent to give you this money nor indeed, my dear fellow, could I do so without a breach of a most solemn promise I made our uncle. It was by the accumulation of interest on various *sums remitted me by the General since 1823, that the entire amounted* in March last to £1,500. . . . Your children will also be entitled to another sum of £500 on the death of Walter Baldwin. This also they owe to the bounty of their grand-uncle. This £500 I received when I was last in Dublin.

I do assure you, my dear Dan, I bitterly regret to perceive that your pecuniary embarrassments are so great, nor have I at present the means of affording you any assistance. The different purchases I have made have completely drained me of the personal property I got from my uncles. . . .

I was glad to find by the newspapers that the price of butter is high and the late fairs much improved.

SOURCE : O'Connell MSS, UCD

1389

To the Knight of Kerry

Merrion Square, 28 May 1827

My dear Sir,

I received your *quieting* letter[1] and, of course, gave it the most unaffected consideration. But you will recollect that the question does not rest with me. *I* can easily be *quieted,* but there are the people at large; there is the Irish nation kept in the miserable state of hope deferred, with the extinguisher of Royal Speeches[2] held over us, and without one single movement in Ireland favourable to an alteration in the system, save only the appointment of Mr. Doherty. That certainly gave great satisfaction, but then there is the drawback of Joy, an open and avowed Orangeman, who becomes Attorney-General. Can you blame us for impatience? You know perfectly well that this country has been governed for the last twenty years by the triumvirate of Lord Manners, Saurin and Gregory, and they still continue to govern. They brought Ireland to the very verge of a sanguinary struggle. If the system were pursued without a hope of alteration for one year more there never yet was so bitter or so bloody a contest in this country, often as it has been stained with blood. And the first step to bring us back to peaceable courses would be to deprive those of power who were the prime movers of discontent and the most prominent causes of irritation. Indeed, I am quite convinced that but for the influence which was obtained over the people, they would have sooner rushed into violence and to their own destruction. The country remains in a feverish state, and it requires to be soothed by a change of system which cannot possibly take place without a change of men. The herd of Orangemen would not believe that Gregory could be perfectly impartial between them and the Papists. As to Lord Manners, he is certainly without disguise, and even the shallowness of his understanding makes him the more dangerous because of the open countenance he gives to every species of 'illiberality'. Again, there is not one of the friends of Ireland—I mean of the patriotic Irish members—in office. The English have got in, the Scotch Whigs have also obtained stations but neither Newport nor Rice nor *you*, allow me to add, have been, it would seem, thought of. Lord Plunket appears to be totally forgotten. Ireland most wanted the change, and in Ireland there appears to be none. Why, then, will you blame me for being impatient, especially as the promotion of Joy announces that enmity to the Catholics is no bar whilst the oblivion of Lord Plunket demonstrates that friendship to our claims is a fatal barrier?

There is another reason which makes me exceedingly anxious to have the Ministry act with decision in Ireland. It is this. They have it in their power to make nine-tenths of the people of Ireland join in petitioning for Emancipation next session. Let liberal Protestants be but once preferred and, as every other impulse tends that way, you would have a magical change almost instantly. Why? I could myself, with very little aid from Mr. Lamb,[3] put the Corporation of Dublin into a total change of system—three or four of the Police offices and at the Paving Board taken from notorious delinquents and given to honest and independent men, a Baronetcy to Alderman McKenny and a Knighthood or two would make this Corporation as liberal as ever they were the reverse, and the force of their example would, *with its causes*, soon spread through the other towns. But I weary you.

SOURCE : FitzPatrick, *Corr.*, I, 143-5

1 See letter 1386.

2 A reference, apparently, to Lord Grey, who early in 1811 had refused to sanction the draft of a speech drawn up by the Prince Regent in reply to the address of parliament (see *DNB*, s.v. 'Grey, Charles, second Earl Grey').

3 William Lamb (1779-1848), succeeded as second Viscount Melbourne, 1828; M.P. almost continuously, 1806-28; chief secretary for Ireland, April 1827-June 1828; home secretary, 1830-34; prime minister, July-November 1834, 1835-41. See *DNB*.

1390

From the Knight of Kerry

London, 2 June 1827

Confidential

My dear O'Connell,

I am not at all surprised at your impatience, still less at that of the Irish public because they know less, and you will give me credit for my share of indignation, and I know but one motive for controlling these expressions which would naturally spring from the heart in such a case and that is the extreme danger of our thereby re-seating the deposed Tories. I believe Canning and I am sure his colleagues are disposed to name liberal men to any department as vacancies occur, but I fear that in each instance they have a severe struggle from the strong feeling either of alarm or objection which prevails in the King's mind. And with all my feelings of regret and disappointment for the public cause I ask myself are they to throw up office because they can effect no more. Trifling as was the object comparatively of a solicitor-general, the appointment of Doherty was difficult.

I place the strongest reliance on the good sense as well as purity of Lord Lansdowne and cannot but feel that [he] sees a great public motive to justify to him the irksomeness of office under such circumstances. How long it may be before ministers feel themselves in a situation to take a bolder course it is not easy to conjecture, but I cannot reconcile it to common spirit or sense that they should go in without some reasonable prospect of that kind in *their* view though it may not be in ours. When therefore I give you *from the spot* the best counsel I can furnish, it is not because it is *palatable* to myself, however wholesome. I am fully aware of the difficulty and responsibility of your situation, but can you relax your efforts to keep all quiet for the present without incurring a risk, the effects of which we might have to deplore for our lives? I believe that if the ministry can stem the present difficulties, especially during the session, that a very beneficial tendency may be given to the public mind by the natural influence of the prevailing policy in the Government and that from them some satisfaction [?] may be derived. You will see that the anti-ministerial spirit in the Lords has lost the Corn [?] Bill[1] which had satisfied the landed interest in the Commons.

[P.S.] My letters from *Dublin* speak of Joy as to succeed Norbury.

I shall press and have pressed the policy we agree on in the strongest manner in my power.

SOURCE : O'Connell MSS, UCD

1 A ministerial bill entitled, 'An Act for granting certain Duties of Customs on Corn'. On the Lords going into committee on this bill on 1 June 1827, the duke of Wellington carried an amendment to it (*Hansard*, N.S., XVII, 1086-98). It was thought that the Commons could not accept this amendment since it touched on their fiscal privileges (*DEP*, 7 June 1827).

1391

From Bishop Doyle (J.K.L.)

Carlow, 8 June 1827

My dear Sir,

I am induced to write to you on having seen in one of the newspapers that Mr. Goulburn and Mr. Croker,[1] the one the representative of Primate Beresford, the other of Trinity College, are ordered by the House of Commons to bring in not less than three bills[2] having for their object the further aggrandizement of the Irish Protestant Church. The last[3] of those three bills is intended, I presume, to facilitate the imposition of 'ministers' money' in cities and towns corporate in Ireland; for the law on this subject, as it now stands, admits in cases of alleged oppression an appeal to the Lord-Lieutenant in council. This weak defence of the people's property saved in the course of last year the inhabitants of Wexford from a permanent charge of some hundreds *per annum*;[4] and considering the character and influence of those who attempted the above rapacious impositions, I am inclined to attribute to them the present effort to amend the existing law after the manner in which the old vestry laws were amended last year.[5] This proceeding in the Commons accords with the tenor of the bill[6] lately introduced by Sir J. Newport and with the withdrawal of even that insignificant bill; it accords with the conduct of Mr. Spring Rice and those with him who threatened Mr. Goulburn when giving notice of the Irish estimate with opposition to the Education Societies, or rather, to the supplies destined for the army of the faith in Ireland,[7] and yet permitted these votes to pass without an effort either in public or private to induce the new Secretary[8] to vest the money in the Lord-Lieutenant with a view afterwards of distributing it impartially. It accords with the policy of those friends of ours who pretend to defer the intended arrangement respecting education until the reports of the education inquiry are all upon the table of the House,[9] though all of those reports which regard the education of the people have been long since printed. Whilst we witness those proceedings, those deeds and omissions on the part of the new Administration, it appears to me, and indeed to every person with whom I have conversed on the subject, that some strong representation of our feelings should be made to the Government through those friendly members of Parliament who have been so anxious lately that our body should continue in silence and suffering; nor do I think there is any person so well entitled to make such representations as you, who have taken upon yourself the responsibility of giving to the late Coalition[10] the sanction of our general approbation. It has from the beginning of the present changes been doubtful to me whether it were not better for the Irish Catholics to see Canning and the Grenvilles forced to join the Whigs in opposition, rather than to see the Whigs playing second fiddle to Canning, and both truckling to the Court and the Bishops; but as all are not as patient as I am in politics, nor all so averse to the building of buttresses to the oligarchy and the Church by accepting of Emancipation on Canning's principles, I have known how to be silent and to hold my own opinions without interfering with those of others but I am confident that the public would expect of you that you should do everything in your power, now that the Catholic Association is silent,[11] to save us from being swallowed alive by a cormorant Church without being able to emit a cry.

With the fate[12] of the unhappy Plunket before our eyes, and Wellesley getting worse and worse without one symptom of amendment in any department, with Goulburn and Croker called on by a Whig ministry to legislate for Ireland, with our people continuing to starve by thousands, are we to bear our sufferings untold, and not only to stay the indignation of our own people, to weaken the sympathy of foreign nations, but even make the Minister think that what some people call hope renders us insensible to neglect, injury and even insult?

SOURCE : FitzPatrick, *Dr. Doyle*, II, 30-1

1 John Wilson Croker (1780-1857), M.P. almost continuously, 1807-32; for Dublin University, 1827-30. First secretary of the admiralty, 1809-30; prominent opponent of parliamentary reform. See *DNB, Boase*.

2 On 31 May Henry Goulburn and John W. Croker were instructed by the Commons to prepare bills, one 'to amend the Acts relating to the Provision of Ministers in Cities and Corporate towns in Ireland', and another 'to amend the laws relating to the Union and Division of parishes in Ireland, and to make further provision respecting the establishment of perpetual curacies'. These bills were enacted on 21 and 23 June respectively as Acts 7 and 8 Geo. IV c. 34 and 7 and 8 Geo. IV c. 43. Only two bills were involved. The wording of the latter measure must have given Doyle the erroneous impression that it comprised two bills.

3 That 'to amend the Acts relating to the Provision of Ministers in Cities and Corporate towns in Ireland'. It proposed to transfer the power of applotting and collecting ministers' money in Dublin and all other Irish corporate towns from churchwardens elected by the parishioners to agents selected by the incumbents (*DEP*, 9 June 1827).

4 A petition from Wexford against this bill was presented in the Commons on 15 June 1827.

5 'An act to consolidate and amend the laws which regulate the levy and application of church rates . . . in Ireland' (7 Geo. IV. c. 72).

6 On 3 April 1827 leave was given Sir John Newport and Thomas Spring Rice to bring in a bill 'for amending the Laws for rebuilding and repairing Churches and for relieving the occupying Tenants of land in Ireland from the burden of Church Rates in certain cases'. This bill was withdrawn on 1 June 1827. A motion by Newport on

3 April 1827 asserting the injustice of requiring Catholics to contribute to the building and repair of Protestant churches was also withdrawn.

7 On 19 March 1827 in the Commons debate on the petition of the Irish Catholic hierarchy regarding education, Spring Rice and Sir John Newport condemned the Kildare Place Society, and Newport declared his intention of opposing the annual government grant to that body (*Hansard,* 1826-27, XVII, 1264, 1266). On 5 April 1827, Newport, supported by Rice, moved that 'a Select Committee be appointed to consider the Estimates . . . in so far as relates to the sums intended to be voted for . . . Charity and Education, and to report their observations . . . thereon to the House, as well as respecting the utility of the Establishments for which the same were intended to be granted'. The motion was defeated by 135 to 69.

8 William Lamb.

9 A reference apparently to the Commons debate on the petition of the Irish Catholic bishops respecting the education of the poor in Ireland which was presented by James Grattan on 19 March 1827. W. C. Plunket recommended that the discussion be deferred until 'the estimates, or the report of the committee of inquiry, were brought forward' (*Hansard,* 1826-27, XVII, 1264).

10 That of Whigs and Tories in Canning's administration.

11 See letter 1386, note 1.

12 See letter 1382, note 1.

1392

From Richard Newton Bennett

9 June [1827]

My dear O'C,

How could you neglect me[1] so? Had I the documents you promised I could finish my business by Monday. . . . I must wait for them. You will have this on Monday. Write that day and do not forget the *recommendation of the Catholics.*[2] As things now stand, that cannot be resisted even if it stood alone but, with other interests, must be all-powerful. So far for myself, now for the country. You need not have the least uneasiness. The Whigs are gaining strength and will be all-powerful. I threatened mildly, and a letter from N. Mahon this morning about Sir P. Bellew,[3] and throwing weight on my acquaintance with high people and wishing to know things were likely to go on. Mr. Brougham was quite glad I came over just now. He bid me assure you that everything was going on as well as could be expected but he [had] nothing to write and would rather tell me how matters were. I found fault with several things. He gave on answer to this, '*Oh, Lord Manners is playing the devil.*' He sent me to Lamb who received me most kindly and conferred quite confidentially. He said, 'Lord M. is watching every opportunity to embarrass us.' '*Tell Mr. O'C. I must for a time be worse than Peel* but when we can, we will do all the good we can. Beg of him to have confidence, though we cannot do much, or worse men will come.' Do all you can to inspire confidence and to give more time for trial. . . .

SOURCE : Fitz-Simon Papers

1 Bennett was in London for the purpose of seeking a judgeship in the colonies (see letter 1397) and was evidently hoping for a recommendation from O'Connell.

2 Bennett apparently hoped that a recommendation from the Catholics of Ireland would improve his chances of obtaining a judgeship in the colonies.

3 Sir Patrick Bellew (1798-1866), succeeded as seventh baronet, 15 March 1827; Barmeath, Co. Louth. M.P. for Co. Louth, September 1831-32 and December 1834-37. High sheriff, 1831. Created Baron Bellew, 1848.

1393

To the Knight of Kerry

Merrion Square, 9 June 1827

My dear Sir,

I send you under another cover a letter[1] I got from Dr. Doyle this morning. I send it as evidence of the state of the Catholic mind in Ireland—a subject which, I think, ought to interest *our* statesmen more than it seems to do. It appears to me that you would advance this object—I mean the acquaintance with the sentiments of the Catholics—by communicating the substance of Dr. Doyle's letter to our friends in the Cabinet. You will yourself perceive by this letter the very unpleasant state in which I have placed myself by the very action that I have taken in procuring the suspension[2] of our claims in this session. It is not pleasant to be reproached with all that has not *been done* for this country, but what signifies my individual suffering? I myself readily admit that it is quite immaterial but it may serve to excuse me for any uneasiness at the present state of affairs.

The folly of allowing Lord Manners, Saurin and Gregory to continue their dominion of this wretched Country is not exceeded by its criminality. When the new administration[3] was formed there was at once exhibited a readiness on the part of many—very many of those who heretofore were most intolerant—to accede to what was hoped to be *the new order of things*. Why, in Dublin—in the stronghold of Orangism—the beggarly corporation—I had arranged matters in such a way that if I got any assistance from the new Government there would be at this moment a strong and an *avowed* party in support of Emancipation and liberal measures. Take another instance. The guild of Merchants wished to address Peel, Lord Eldon, &c. They three times attempted to hold a meeting for that purpose, but all their leading men shrunk from the *invidious* task, and there was no chairman to be found to preside. Well, the declaration of war by Lord Manners in the case[4] of Sir Patrick Bellew was no sooner known than the bigots rallied, and yesterday there was a very numerous meeting[5] and violent partisan addresses. What does Mr. Canning mean to do for Ireland or with Ireland? To leave all the old *warriors* in office! There never yet was a game so completely thrown away as this is. Ireland *could* have been, and may still be, brought to perfect unanimity on the subject of our claims and the support of the new Ministry. I say *perfect* with just such a grain of Irish allowance as would qualify it into an exception so trivial as to be of no consequence whatsoever.

Lord Norbury has been at length *bought off* the Bench by a most shameful traffic.[6] What a dolt that man must be—if there be any such—who wonders at the state of Ireland, which has had its Chief Justice of the Common Pleas in the hands of a sanguinary buffoon for more than twenty years, and has its Equity distributed by the irritable, impatient, bigoted and occasionally even between man and man *influenced* Lord Manners. You will perceive that I am writing to you in the strictest confidence and with a view to show how necessary it is to change the system and how easy it would be to do so. Pray excuse me for being so troublesome, but indeed our indignation is boiling over. What a pitiable fall is that of Lord Plunket.[7]

The worst feature in the entire is the knowledge thus forced on the Irish people of the inveterate hostility of the King and of many of the Royal Family. This is exceedingly dangerous and ought to have been concealed, but I see that existing circumstances have *forced out* the mischievous truth. Depend on it that Ireland will be lost in spite of all our efforts unless the administration will assist us to alter the system.

SOURCE : FitzPatrick, *Corr.*, I, 145-7

1 See letter 1391.

2 See letter 1386, note 1.

3 That of Canning.

4 Sir Patrick Bellew was recently refused a commission of the peace by the Irish lord chancellor allegedly because he was a member of the Catholic Association (*DEP*, 9 June 1827).

5 A meeting of the Dublin Guild of Merchants, held on 8 June 1827, for the purpose of voting an address to Wellington, Peel and Eldon (*DEP*, 9 June 1827).

6 Norbury, an octogenarian, was induced to resign as justice of the common pleas by being advanced to the peerage as Viscount Glandine and earl of Norbury, with special remainder to his son and a retiring pension of £3,046 (see *DNB*).

7 See letter 1382, note 1.

1394

To Richard Newton Bennett

Merrion Square, 11 June 1827

Private

My dear Bennett,

Nothing could be more unsatisfactory than the letters I got on the day of your departure and the ensuing day from the Knight of Kerry and Lord Duncannon. I expected to have been *before now raking* the present administration and it is with reluctance that I keep upon terms with them. I scarcely *could* do so but for a lucky rumour that Doherty is to be Att[orne]y-General and Wallace[1] Solicitor [-General]. This rumour has reached me from a high and confidential quarter. I enclose under cover to Dawson[2] two other letters for you. The one to Brougham I hope will please you. The other for Blake[3] I think you ought to deliver as speedily as possible. You do not know how much he may serve you.

I have just got your note. I am greatly alarmed at what Mr.

Lamb said to you, 'that for a time he would be worse than Peel'. It is just as I prophesied. He has taken up the notion that in order to show his *candour* and *liberality* he will patronize men of the Orange faction. This is just the mistake that most excellent man, Charles Grant,[4] fell into. That faction is to be sure exceedingly fortunate. They generally have such secretaries as Peel and Goulburn but when they have a more liberal secretary, *his candour* to our enemies makes him a more useful patron to the Orangists than a decided no-popery man could be. It is however idle to expect anything from Mr. Lamb. That one sentence shows it. My confidence, I candidly own to you, is worn out or rather trodden to rags. Why was there ever anything so beastly outrageous as Lord Manners' conduct about Sir Patrick Bellew's commission of the peace?[5] I most heartily wish you were provided for—and then I believe we must begin the fight. I will tell you why I am so angry, simply because it *was* and yet perhaps *is* so easy to make this country *unanimous*. I could have this city *all* liberal. I tell you that in twenty-four hours I could find instruments to manage the Corporation. I do not say this lightly. There is not a single county in Ireland but could in the same way be *arranged*. We could have a petition from everyone of them in favour of Emancipation and the new Cabinet. I would beat Dawson with Protestants in Derry if the administration pleased to aid me. I could do it either with or without appearing as they pleased, but it is idle to talk. That one phrase of Mr. Lamb's shows what flimsy materials the new Cabinet is composed of. I have already had my head nearly broke for, as they say, suppressing the public voice.[6]

I cannot for a day or two send you the other paper in a satisfactory way but before Friday it *shall* go to you. Is there anybody else you would wish me to write to?

All this will at once show you that it would be quite impossible to say one word about myself to anybody. You perceive that it would be quite indelicate in me to allow it and in the present posture of affairs it may injure you personally to take any *such* part. Give up therefore all idea of that kind. I need not tell you that I am deeply anxious for you and therefore say whether there is any other channel in which you think I could move for your benefit. . . . Tell me whether Brougham, etc., are aware of Lefroy's incapacity. The cases from last circuit are decisive upon that subject. *Murphy* v. *Redden*[7] alone would prevent any English law officer from ever getting on the bench.

Young-v.-Lord Bantry[8] was another instance of most impertinent ignorance on his part. Think you there would be any use in writing on these subjects to *anybody*?

SOURCE : NLI, MSS 837

1 Thomas Wallace, K.C. (born c. 1766), son of James Wallace, Called to the Irish bar, 1798. M.P. for Yarmouth, 1826-30; Drogheda, October 1831-32; Co. Carlow, 1832-35.

2 Alexander Dawson.

3 Anthony R. Blake.

4 Charles Grant (1778-1866), M.P., 1811-35; chief secretary for Ireland, 1818-21. President of board of trade, 1827-28; president of the board of control, 1830-34. Secreteary for the colonies, 1835-39. Created Baron Glenelg, 1835. See *DNB*.

5 See letter 1393, note 4.

6 See letter 1386, note 1.

7 Unidentified.

8 *Recte* case of *Nugent* v. *Lord Bantry*, an action of ejectment on the title of lands known as ' The Point ' near Bantry, Co. Cork. It was tried at the spring assizes of 1827 before Serjeant Thomas Lefroy when a verdict was apparently given in favour of the defendant, Bantry. The case was appealed by the plaintiff, Nugent, on the ground of misdirection. At the retrial before Justice Richard Jebb, a verdict was given in favour of Nugent, on whose behalf O'Connell appeared.

1395

To his wife, care of Miss Connor, Tralee

Merrion Square, 21 June 1827

My heart's darling,

. . . Darling, I have dined for the last four days between nine and eleven at night but instead of interfering with my health it makes me really grow fat. We did an immense deal of business yesterday and I was especially in one case exceedingly triumphant. Did I tell you that the Knight of Kerry promised me as from Lord Lansdowne my patent of precedence? I am to get it as soon as the Chancellor[1] goes away, perhaps sooner. I should know that if I had time to call on Mr. Lamb, which I do not expect to be able to do before Monday. He, Mr. Lamb, has I know expressed his surprise that I did not call on him sooner. But I could not get one moment to do so. What chance is there that I should call on Mr. Lamb or anyone else while I have not time to write to my own darling heart's Love? I have just had an offer of a special retainer for Longford which I believe I shall accept.[2] . . . I do *so* hate to be away from my family but it is my own fault and I at least and solely deserve this and more punishment, and indeed it is a severe punishment to me, but I repeat, I deserve it for flinging away my money in handfuls and then going to such expense in building and, to crown all, making a reversionary purchase. Darling, if however I had the consolation to know that you were in good health I would not care for anything else. I much fear from your letters that you are not even so well as you say, and, alas, you admit that you are not quite well. I am so hurried that I am obliged to get White[3] to write to Rick[4] about the last *Courier* which contains an atrocious libel[5] upon me. I can write only to you, sweetest, and I must run to court in order to make up the time I spend in writing. . . . I hope I shall hear from you this day again although, darling, I would not deserve it if I was not so hurried by that abominable Baron Smith.

SOURCE : Fitz-Simon Papers

1 Lord Manners.

2 See letter 1403, note 2.

3 Robert White, a family friend of O'Connell, otherwise unidentified. Apparently he married the widow of James O'Donnell, Sackville Street, Dublin.

4 Rickard O'Connell, his brother-in-law.

5 In denying the (Dublin) *Morning Register's* report that O'Connell was about to receive a patent of precedency, the *Courier* of 18 July 1827 declared that the idea was a 'revolting absurdity'. It described O'Connell as 'the loud tongued brawler of the Catholic Association —the furious demagogue of thirty years', accused him of sedition and treason and declared he had escaped the penalties for his crimes only because in him 'the lawyer predominated over the rebel' (see *DEP*, 21 July 1827). On 17 August 1827 the grand jury of Kerry found true bills against the proprietors of the *Courier* for a libel on O'Connell. O'Connell's counsel offered to abandon further proceedings if the author of the article were given up (*DEP*, 21 Aug. 1827). Some disapproval of O'Connell's proceedings was expressed by the *Dublin Evening Post* as being calculated to undermine the liberty of the press (*DEP*, 28 Aug. 1827).

1396

To Richard Newton Bennett

Merrion Square, 23 June 1827

My dear Bennett,

It was in consequence of the existing state of Catholic affairs and the extreme difficulty of managing the discontent of the Catholics at the *letting* loose of Lord Manners by *our friends*[1] that made me substitute my letter[2] to Mr. Brougham for any other document. Believe me that I feel the utmost anxiety as well on *public* as on *private* account for your success[3] and that I would not be more solicitous for my brother if he were in your situation. I spoke to my friend Blake and he wrote on Sunday last to Wilmot Horton on your behalf. I believe you will find that he wrote *most zealously*.

You will have perceived by the Catholic proceedings that *your opinions* respecting the *present* administration and in particular of the energy of our new Secretary[4] have not been thrown away. I heartily thank you for giving me hopes which I acknowledge I did not *before* entertain. I am therefore now determined to continue the experiment[5] but if it does not *result* in Emancipation, all is idle.

Mr. Lamb is not aware of the facility of making the Dublin Corporation perfectly liberal. If you could suggest that facility to him I would undertake to bring the matter about. A petition from the Dublin Corporation in favour of liberal principles would be new and most important in its effects throughout Ireland, but if you get any opportunity of *this* kind, warn Mr. Lamb against *all* the protégés of Goulburn and let him know emphatically that Goulburn was the only secretary in Ireland who excluded *on all occasions* every man having the semblance of a liberal opinion. Let Mr. Lamb beware of *all* those whom Goulburn recommends. I mention these things to you because I know your cautious discretion and that if you cannot use them discreetly you will bury them in complete oblivion. In fact Mr. Lamb will either manage Ireland for good or be managed himself for the purposes of the old faction. Lord Manners is disposed to play and is playing the devil. No less than six new King's counsel and Perrin[6] passed over. Edward Scott! ! ![7] Schoales! ! ![8] Tickell! ! ![9] *inter alia*. But this is merely crowding the inner Bar least by possibility any Catholic should get even the benefit of the existing laws. No matter for us.

Let me hear from you and give me whenever you can with perfect truth a *legible* passage favourable to the views of this administration towards Ireland—one to make use of privately.

SOURCE : Connolly Autograph Collection

1 Manners excluded Sir Patrick Bellew from the commission of the peace allegedly on the ground of his being a member of the New Catholic Association (see letter 1393, note 4). At a Catholic meeting on 23 June 1827 an address to Bellew was adopted condemning Lord Manners for this exclusion (*DEP,* 26 June 1827).

2 See letter 1394.

3 In obtaining a judgeship in the colonies (see letter 1392, note 1).

4 No reference to Lamb's appointment as chief secretary for Ireland appears in press accounts of the New Catholic Association at this period.

5 That is, Catholic support for Canning's administration.

6 Louis Perrin (1782-1864), son of Jean Baptiste Perrin, Leinster Lodge, Athy, Co. Kildare. Called to the bar, 1806. Attorney-general, April-August 1835; justice of the king's bench, 1835-60. M.P. for Dublin city, May-August 1831; Co. Monaghan, 1832-35; Cashel, January-August 1835. See *DNB.*

7 Edward William Scott (c. 1783-1834), son of John Scott, Co. Wicklow. Called to the bar, 1807. K.C., 29 June 1827. Assistant barrister, Co. Fermanagh.

8 John Schoales (born c. 1768), son of Arthur Schoales, Londonderry. Called to the Irish bar, 1792. K.C., 29 June 1827. Assistant barrister, Queen's Co.

9 Edward Tickell (died 1863), 10 Clare Street, Dublin. Called to the bar, 1803. K.C., 29 June 1827.

1397

To the Knight of Kerry

Merrion Square, 24 June 1827

My dear Sir,

I am impatient to hear what you think of *the train* in which I have been able to place Catholic affairs.[1] It would have been impossible to do more, and to have attempted it would risk a disturbance. Besides, I could not convince myself that more silence would be useful. How could I expect to convince others? I showed your last letter to some persons discreetly and, of course, at my own suggestion. The effect was right good, and I could now answer for it that Ld. Anglesey[2] would be well received by the Catholics as Lord-Lieutenant if he would take any one occasion to declare publicly that he is *not* our Enemy. I mean by this merely a disclaimer of enmity even without any pledge whatsoever of friendship. What I said of Lord Anglesey at the Catholic meeting was greatly misreported.[3]

I gave the Sheriff Elect[4] of Dublin a letter of introduction to you. I would wish that he should find me useful to him through my friends. He is one of those through whom even I could *convict* the Corporation of Dublin. I would, of course, want the assistance of Mr. Lamb, but then the result would be most powerful Irish support to the Administration. I told you before, and I repeat, that with an honest Chancellor—who of course *ought* to be Plunket—with a neutral Lord-Lieutenant —that is, a *real* neutral, not as Mountain Mahony[5] called it, '*a mutual friend at the other side*'—and with Mr. Lamb, I would forfeit my Head if we did not un-Orange Ireland and make the Protestants content and good and the Catholics devotedly loyal; for our disposition truly leans to loyalty. The game is in our hands and Mr. Roose, the new Sheriff of Dublin, would help us very powerfully to play it. Perhaps I deceive myself but I have the vanity to believe that I could *manage* this Corporation easily. The Orange faction in Ireland could be made to crumble like a Rope of Sand. It, in fact, *is* a Rope of Sand, but Government patronage has twisted it into a Rope of Steel and then used it to manacle us poor papists. But let the Government force be taken from the twisting machine and a Rope of Sand Orangism will be again.

There is a most particular friend of mine—a Mr. Bennett of this Bar—in London looking for a judicial seat in the Colonies. He has hopes of being made Chief Justice of Ceylon. I got Blake to write warmly to Wilmot Horton for him. Doherty wrote at my instance to Mr. Canning. I wrote in the strongest terms I could venture upon to Mr. Brougham. I most anxiously wish that you could speak to Lord Lansdowne for him. If there be nothing inconsistent with your present relations with the Marquis, to do it will be conferring another obligation on me. I could not be more anxious for my brother than I am for Mr. Bennett. He has been at all times the decided friend of Civil and Religious Liberty, and his promotion would give the greatest satisfaction to all that part of the Catholic body in Dublin who have been working for Emancipation, that is, the really influential portion of the Catholic community. I know you will kindly give all the assistance in your power. But allow me to add that it seems to us all excessively strange that all the *bad* men are still continued in office in Ireland and that neither you nor Rice nor Sir John Newport are in any official situation. I do not say this because of my individual regard for you but more especially because your and their elevation would be so honest an earnest of the intention of the Government to substitute friends for enemies and no longer to patronize bad passions.

SOURCE : FitzPatrick, *Corr.*, I, 147-9

1 At a Catholic meeting in Dublin on 16 June 1827 under the chairmanship of William Burke Kelly, O'Connell, speaking of Canning's ministry, declared, 'I would beg of every Irishman, whether he dwell in . . . a palace . . . or . . . lowly cottage, to give that Administration his ardent and warmest support.' At the same time, however, he urged preparations for simultaneous meetings of Catholics to be held all over Ireland before the opening of the next session of parliament since, 'We ought not to throw ourselves into the hands of any administration' (*DEP*, 19 June 1827; see also *DEP*, 21 June 1827).

2 Henry William (Paget) (1768-1854), first marquis of Anglesey (created 1815). Lord-lieutenant of Ireland, 1 March 1828-6 March 1829, 23 December 1830-26 September 1833.

3 At the above Catholic meeting, O'Connell demanded, according to the *Dublin Evening Post*, 'Will anyone dare to charge us, as the Marquis of Anglesey did the Old Association, with bearding the Parliament or the Administration?' (*DEP*, 19 June 1827).

4 David Roose.

5 James Mountain Mahony.

1398

To Thomas Spring Rice, M.P.

Merrion Square, 25 June 1827

Private

My dear Sir,

I have been writing to the Knight of Kerry and to others on the facility of *non-oranging* Ireland, of getting rid of *all* the lay opposition to a liberal system and of perhaps some of the clerical. Strange as it may seem I know that the thing is quite practicable and there is nowhere that a beginning would be more easy and more useful than in Dublin. Mr. Lamb can have *this* corporation at his beck. But if he wishes to do that he must not fetter himself with any of Goulburn's nominations. *That* patronage was used to encourage the Orange party and to promote the spirit of bigotry by rewarding it. If Mr. Lamb directs *his* patronage the other way he will be still more successful because it is more comfortable for any man to live amidst the good wishes than the curses of his neighbours. The Catholics are so numerous and meet their avowed enemies at so many points in private and in public that I repeat it is very easy to tempt the orange partisans to become the champions of liberal policy. I introduce these obvious topics to lead to practical results—the use to be made of the patronage of this *our* administration. For example there is the Paving Board. The vacancies in that body would purchase the management of half the Dublin Corporation. They have no principle—not the least. Give them a practical hint on the subject of their interest and a high mettled pack never went off more merrily on a drag than they will. Amongst those fittest to manage the Dublin Corporation is a Mr. Hickman Kearney.[1] I believe you know him—he is married to a sister of Sir John Franks. He it was that threw out the bills of indictment[2] against me and I therefore can speak from experience of his capacity to counteract the feeling of bigotry. He is now a candidate for one of the vacancies at the Paving Board, and if you think it right to have the plan of *converting* this corporation carried into effect this would be a fit occasion to assist in enlisting him. I throw this out to you from the excess of my anxiety to realize so exceedingly useful a plan as that of concession to the Catholics founded on the concurrence of the Irish protestants. The harmony which would result from such success is the most desirable thing imaginable. . . .

SOURCE : Monteagle Papers, NLI 13368

1 Hickman Kearney (died 1851), appointed commissioner of the Dublin paving board, 1828. Married 1802 Ann, daughter of Thomas Franks, Ballymagooley, Co. Cork.

2 See letter 1144, note 2.

1399

To the Knight of Kerry, 25 June 1827

Extract

'He [Hickman Kearney] has a deal of the Wellesley interest but it would be his business and his wish to make himself useful to the new administration. He has more power in managing this Corporation than you can have any notion of. I know it practically, for he is a very particular friend of mine. He was foreman of the Grand Jury that threw out the Bill of Indictment[1] against me, and he would throw out the anti-Catholic petition for the new administration if they deem it right to direct their patronage that way.'

SOURCE : FitzPatrick, *Corr.*, II, 74n

1 See letter 1144, note 2.

1400

From the Knight of Kerry to Merrion Square

London, 26 June 1827

My dear O'Connell,

A writ will be moved on Friday on my acceptance of a Lordship of the Treasury. I am sure you will concur in the propriety of my taking office. The hostility of Tories suggests to any friend of Ireland to cling closely to the Ministry which has ousted them and which will grow stronger from day to day, and from the establishment of adequate strength in them I augur every practical good to Ireland. Though this will transpire in three days I resolved to anticipate it in your case. It has been tendered without the slightest application on my part directly or indirectly.

SOURCE : O'Connell MSS, UCD

1401

From John Hancock

Lurgan, 6 July 1827

Private

My dear Sir,

On my return here I sent for the parish priest of this and

the adjoining parish and stated to them the necessity of having affidavits made as to the intended processions of Orangemen on the 12th July, but such is the state of terror in which these miscreants with their arms in their hands hold this whole country that both these highly respectable gentlemen declared it would be impossible to get any person to make any affidavit on the subject of these processions as, if made, it would be a sure mode of drawing down the vengeance of the Orange faction on whoever would attempt to make such affidavit. I have done all in my power to inspire confidence in the reverend gentlemen but they seem to think it too dangerous a service for them to volunteer any affidavits.

I have requested them to communicate by letter with you this day's post.

SOURCE : O'Connell Papers, NLI 13647

1402

To his son John, Clongowes Wood College

Merrion Square, 25 July 1827

My dearest child,

I write this letter that you may have it to show to Mr. Kenny,[1] so that you may be ready to start from Clongowes at the earliest possible moment. Mr. White[2] shall be at the last day of the examination with a jaunting car to take you to Naas [en route to Limerick and Derrynane. O'Connell says he knows John does not like travelling with White so he has told White to be very kind.]. . .

SOURCE : Fitz-Simon Papers

1 Peter Kenney, S.J.

2 Robert White.

1403

To John Primrose, Jr., Hillgrove

Merrion Square, 26 July 1827

My dear John,

[Re bills of exchange drawn and request for money.]

Tom Fitzgerald[1] is complaining that he has not had one cask of butter. You know I ought not to treat him badly. I implore of you to be rigid with my tenants on this point. I am quite content to make it worth their while to do what I ask.

Are my sheep alive or dying of the rot? Pray, pray do not leave me as I am about them. It is useless to buy other sheep whilst that disease continues. I beg of you to look to this. You were in Waterford at the time it ought to have been attended to and there is little chance of anything being done in your absence. It is not creditable to us to be overcome by what I presume could be conquered or, if not, the sheep should all have their throats cut and be cast on the sea. You perceive that nobody else but me has such a persevering affliction to complain of.

I go off this day for Longford where I am specially retained.[2] I believe I shall not be in Tralee as I have two special retainers for Galway.

SOURCE : O'Connell Papers, NLI 13645

1 Butter merchant, Cork.

2 In the case of *Robinson* v. *McGaver*. The plaintiff was seeking 'to break a will'. The verdict favoured O'Connell's client, either Edward or Thomas McGaver, a parish priest.

1404

To Edward Dwyer

Limerick, 3 August 1827

My dear friend,

I beg leave to enclose £1 being my August gale of the new Catholic rent. I persevere in making a monthly payment from the conviction that the most useful thing that can be done for the Catholic cause is such perseverance. If every Catholic who could afford it would give something every month, there would soon be established an abundant fund for all useful and legal purposes. I rather regret that I have not made my monthly subscription lower, and in future I shall make it only one shilling for myself and one from each of my family. I will do this in the expectation that every member of the association in Dublin will make his monthly contribution of one shilling, and if this plan be adopted by the more wealthy classes and one penny a month collected from the poorer, there will be a most ample fund formed not only to protect the 40s freeholders but also to promote education and to fulfil all the patriotic [? aims] of the New Catholic Association. There is indeed another protection equally imperative with that of the 40s freeholders, I mean that of persons persecuted for not sending their children to fanatic schools.

This protection to all classes of persecuted can be afforded only as the result of steady and persevering exertions. A sudden burst of charity or sympathy may produce a transient support, but like all violent efforts it will soon exhaust itself and be succeeded by apathy. . . . We want collectors. All the Catholic Rent wants is collectors. It would be cruel to disturb the prospect that now exists of procuring collectors by giving an excuse to many to forego the persevering exertion which the office of collector requires. The County of Clare met yesterday, not as Catholics but as 'friends of civil and religious freedom'.[1] The chairmen[2] were both Protestants. Amongst other things the New Catholic Rent was placed on a basis of permanent collection. Believe me it requires only one County to begin and the rest of Ireland will speedily follow the example. Let us not however interrupt the experiment[3] which is now making to procure collectors.

Let me implore of my friend Mr. Lawless not to interfere[4] with this experiment. I do strongly hope that if I were able to attend in my place tomorrow I would convince Mr. Lawless that it is better not to attempt a disjointed effort, not to make an experiment which cannot in its nature be *continuous* and above all things not to make it at this time of the year when Dublin is drained of the far greater part of its wealthy inhabitants. . . .

For my own part I trust I will not be accused (although indeed there are persons more than enough ready to accuse me) of arrogance when I say that no person *can* know more of the details of the collection of the Catholic Rent than I do, and that my firm conviction is that the measure proposed would be highly injurious to that fund as it certainly would derange and in all probability defeat the permanent and persevering plan which I have in view. . . .

. . . I cannot and will not commit myself with any plan which interferes with the only resource which is left to the Catholic clergy for their own support and the sustentation of the sick and indigent poor, poor who fall almost exclusively on the funds of the Catholic clergy. . . .

Besides being, in my humble judgement, quite ungenerous

to interfere with the ordinary resources of the clergy[5] and of charity, it would also, in my humble opinion, be very ungrateful. The Catholic clergy have individually contributed to our funds. Poor as they are they have not only almost universally contributed to these funds but they have actually contributed as much as, if not (and this is my recollection) much more than, the wealthy classes of the Catholic laity. Would it therefore not be cruel of us to obtrude in any way between the Catholic clergy and these, their almost only resources! Let me not be told that they will consent to our doing so. Perhaps so, but the more ready they are to make such a sacrifice the more scrupulous should we be not to resort to the indelicate and unfeeling plan of interrupting any part of their small income.

. . . I beg of you to have this letter read . . . especially that it may convey to my friend Mr. Lawless my most earnest entreaty to withdraw or at least to postpone the discussion, and if I fail in persuading him to do so, then to implore of the meeting not to adopt Mr. Lawless' proposition without giving me an opportunity personally to state my objections to the measure, . . . although of course I respect the motives of Mr. Lawless as much as those of any other individual. . . .

SOURCE : Dublin Diocesan Archives

1 At the Catholic meeting in Dublin on 16 June 1827 (see letter 1397, note 1) O'Connell proposed that the Catholics should in future petition parliament for 'freedom of conscience for all denominations in these realms'. He added that he would 'drop the term Catholic Emancipation and henceforth seek for universal liberty' (*DEP*, 21 June 1827).

2 Thomas Steele and Hewitt Bridgeman.

3 Apparently a reference to O'Connell's resolution in the New Catholic Association on 17 July 1827 in favour of forwarding a circular letter to the Catholic clergy of Ireland, requesting that they renew their exertions for the collection of the Catholic rent (*DEP*, 17 July 1827).

4 Jack Lawless believed that the old system of collecting the Catholic rent had proved 'Barren and unproductive' (*DEP*, 26 July 1827) and was too slow to meet the emergency of relieving the forty-shilling freeholder (*DEP*, 7 Aug. 1827. In the New Catholic Association on 21 July 1827, he carried a resolution in favour of holding a simultaneous Sunday collection throughout all the Catholic chapels in Ireland for the purpose of providing a fund for the immediate relief of the freeholders. He claimed that the bishop of Waterford and clergy of Tipperary supported his scheme, and he moved that a deputation be appointed to wait on Archbishop Murray to secure his support (*DEP*, 24, 26 July 1827). At an extraordinary

and, according to Lawless, packed meeting of the association on 24 July 1827 O'Connell had Lawless's resolution rescinded. He accused Lawless in offensive terms of attempting to dictate to the clergy through the bishops, claimed he would deprive the clergy of the subscriptions of their flocks and added that in any case, 'He disliked . . . collecting at the chapel doors' (*DEP*, 26 July 1827). Lawless was given leave to have his motion again discussed in the Association on 4 August 1827. O'Connell's above letter, was read during this meeting at which Lawless agreed to abandon his motion (*DEP*, 7 Aug. 1827).

5 Lawless had been at pains to stress that the clergy should deduct from the receipts of the proposed collection the average amount of their own Sunday takings (*DEP*, 26 July 1827). Referring to the above point in O'Connell's letter, he declared, 'I am surprised that O'Connell, after a declaration so explicit . . . should again fall into the error that I contemplated an act of . . . injustice to the Catholic Clergy' (*DEP*, 7 Aug. 1827).

1405

To John Primrose, Jr., Hillgrove

Limerick, 5 August 1827

My dear John,

I believe you know that I intend to go to the Galway assizes which will commence the 16th inst. . . . I write by this post to Kean Mahony to beg the *loan* of Mr. Flaherty.[1] If you could, as Mrs. O'Connell tells me you can, get permission from Mr. Fitzgerald[2] to assure Kean that he or his assistant will say Mass every Sunday and holiday at Castlequin it will be probably an inducement to Kean to comply. Set about it therefore, I implore at once.

. . . I suppose you have no money for me. Derrynane absorbs everything. I wish for my part to sell off or otherwise disengage myself of that rascally hooker[3] which is rendered unserviceable at the only moment I really wanted her by the mere neglect of getting her papers. The fellow should not have been allowed to take possession of her without her papers. The sellers have *now* no interest in troubling themselves about her. This and my unfortunate sheep plague me a good deal. I hope you have got rid of them or got them cured. . . .

[P.S.] Has Tom Fitzgerald got any butter from my tenants? Will you take the trouble to send Jack Connell round to the tenants again on this subject? It is one on which I am peculiarly anxious.

SOURCE : O'Connell MSS, UCD

1 Rev. Edward [O']Flaherty.

2 Rev. Edward Fitzgerald (died 1866), P.P. of Cahirciveen, 1825-45; Rathmore, 1845-51; Kilcummin, 1851-59.

3 See letter 1254.

1406

From Henry Rooney[1] to Limerick

10 Moore St., Dublin, 8 August 1827

My dear Sir,

I beg leave to address you on the subject of the wanton outrage[2] offered to my poor father's remains at Howth on Saturday last, . . . I am anxious . . . to request your advice as to the course I should pursue for if the law has provided any redress for outrages of this description, surely this is a case in which filial duty commands me to avail myself of it for the insult offered to the ashes of the best of fathers! His funeral was numerously and respectably attended. Rev. Mr. Murtagh[3] and Rev. Mr. Glynn[4] attended it. . . . When the corpse was deposited in the grave Mr. Glynn proceeded to repeat the De Profundis, neither he nor Mr. Murtagh in canonicals, no prayer-book, nothing in their external appearance to mark an official character. . . . A Rev. Mr. Irwin,[5] who I understand is acting as the deputy of Mr. Smith, the Rector,[6] one of the sons-in-law of Archbishop Magee, came up and intimated to Mr. Glynn . . . that he should desist. Mr. Glynn at once complied. One of the Howth fishermen . . . immediately cried out, 'I will say it,' and proceeded audibly and distinctly to repeat the De Profundis, Lord's Prayer and Hail Mary. When he concluded, Mr. Glynn, apprehensive of a disturbance, led Mr. Irwin away, saying to him, 'Sir, you had better leave this.' Providentially, the bystanders, I believe, were not aware that the deceased was a Catholic as the body was brought direct from the hearse to the grave and deposited there without being brought round the churchyard as is customary when a Catholic is interred for I believe our clergy do not countenance that custom now. The people conducted themselves throughout with the greatest decorum and forbearance, not the slightest symptom of disposition to riot or resistance. . . . You must recollect my poor father; he was the Treasurer of the Catholic Rent in St. Mary's Parish. . . .

SOURCE : O'Connell Papers, NLI 13647

1 Henry Rooney (born c. 1799), second son of Thomas Rooney, Moore Street, Dublin, and Anne Marlay.

2 The account in the *Dublin Evening Post* of 7 August 1827 accords with that in this letter.

3 Probably Rev. John Murtagh (died 11 Jan. 1872), curate of Pro-Cathedral parish, Marlborough Street, Dublin. P.P. Kilcullen, Co. Kildare, c. 1835-72.

4 Rev. Joseph Glynn, administrator of Pro-Cathedral parish, Marlborough Street, Dublin, 1824-31.

5 Rev. Arthur Irwin (c. 1797-7 Feb. 1861), prebend of Howth, 1832-47; dean of Ardfert, 1847-61.

6 Rev. Charles Smith (c. 1801-5 Aug. 1842), prebend of Howth, 1827-32; precentor of Kilmacduagh, 1833-42. Married 17 February 1827 Elizabeth, third daughter of Archbishop Magee of Dublin.

1407

To his wife, Derrynane

Limerick, 9 August 1827

My heart's darling,

Mr. Canning is dead. There is another blow to wretched Ireland. No man can become of vital importance to her but he is immediately snatched off by one fatal accident or the other. The will of God be done. Rice left this in half an hour after the intelligence had arrived. He, however, took time to write to me to assure me that it was *impossible* to form a no-popery administration and he expects that the Marquis of Lansdowne will be premier. If so we shall be still better off but do I hope it? Alas, darling, I can scarcely venture to do so. . . .

I wrote to Kean Mahony about Mr. Flaherty and am anxiously expecting his answer. You *must* have a priest. The house cannot remain without one. . . . I am so delighted at your being satisfied with the place [Derrynane]. I wanted to make it comfortable to you, my heart's darling love. I saw yesterday Miss O'Shea,[1] Maurice's flame. She is really a sweet creature, greatly improved since I saw her last. Mrs. Howley,[2] her aunt, the widow of old Mr. Howley and a very sensible steady woman, says that her brother, General Roche,[3] showed her documents to prove that he was worth eighty thousand pounds. I really am convinced she would not say so if the fact were not literally true. She is to meet him in Dublin in September and she is most anxious for the match. D. O'Connell of Kilgorey told me that she, Mrs. Howley, wept and laughed at the pleasure and delight of her niece forming such a connection and she, who is his only surviving relative, will leave no stone unturned to bring him to bear. If he be really worth £80,000 and has the interest of his niece at heart, he ought surely to advance £20,000 at present and that would enable me to make an adequate settlement on Maurice. In short, I am in greater spirits on this subject than I was but we must be cautious.

SOURCE : Fitz-Simon Papers

1 Unidentified.

2 Catherine Howley, widow of John Howley (1750-1825), Rich Hill, Co. Limerick.

3 Sir Philip Keating Roche, K.C.H. (died 1829), son of Philip Roche, merchant of Limerick, related to the famous Limerick banking family of Roche. Knighted, 1816. Lieutenant-colonel in the British army. Lieutenant-general in Portuguese army; realized a large sum of money in the Peninsular War. Left his fortune to two nieces provided they took the name of Roche and did not marry an Irishman or a Spaniard. They married Englishmen.

1408

From his wife to Galway

Derrynane, 15 August 1827

My own love,

It must have surprised you to have received two letters from me since I heard of the dreadful loss poor Ireland has sustained by the death of poor Mr. Canning, so totally silent on that subject and on politics in general. The fact is, love, my mind was so engaged about our dear Maurice I could not think on any other subject. I can now, thank God, look forward with a strong hope that all will be well and my dear child's happiness secured by his union with Miss O'Shea, of whose amiable disposition and engaging manners you give so flattering a description.[1] I hope I shall hear from Maurice before he leaves Tralee. This letter will, I trust, meet you in Galway. I am fond of that town. It is the only place you are thought of or complimented as you should be, and I hope, darling, it is there you will have your action[2] against the *Courier* tried. Do not bring it to this odious county. Is there, love, any chance that the Marquis of Lansdowne will succeed Mr. Canning? There is no minding the paper reports. You probably will hear something certain on the subject from either Rice or the Knight of Kerry. God forbid that odious Peel or Wellington should again hold any station in the Government. Canning is indeed a severe loss. Poor man, what he must have suffered during his last illness, but it does not appear that he was attended by any clergyman. I hope your letter tomorrow will give us some hope that poor Ireland has still a sincere friend at the head of government. Mr. O'Flaherty arrived here yesterday and gave us Mass this morning. He is looking extremely well and, as usual, gay and good. Charles Connor, White[3] and Phry Moynihan[4] also came here yesterday. We are now a large party. . . . I much fear this bad summer will do a great deal of harm to the harvest that was so promising everywhere. Your crops were very promising but the steward is beginning to *croak* about them. You have the best potatoes in the country. . . . Kate told me she gave you in her letter a full description of this house. Between us both, love, you must be quite well acquainted with the improvements that have been made in it during the last nine months. It is indeed truly a most comfortable and convenient house.

SOURCE : O'Connell Papers, NLI 13651

1 See letters 1407, 1552.

2 See letter 1395, note 5.

3 Robert White.

4 Humphrey Moynihan, son of Humphrey Moynihan and Catherine (Kitty) O'Connell. Nephew of O'Connell. Died at Rouen, France, 28 March 1841.

1409

From Lord Rossmore to Merrion Square, redirected to Cork

Private

Cortolvin Hills, Monaghan, 19 August 1827

My Dear Sir,

The letter you favoured me with to London I showed to Mr. Canning, to the Duke of Gloucester and two other persons whose political principles I knew. They expressed very 'great satisfaction at the sentiments it contained and declared it a most interesting document'. Some days before its arrival, I had written a letter to Mr. Canning of a very strong nature, pointing at the necessity of tearing up the Ascendancy faction by the roots in this country. Thinking it is calculated to advance the cause of civil and religious liberty in Ireland, I am inclined to allow a gentleman in London to insert it in one of the English papers; it would make the whole more interesting if your letter[1] to me was published along with it as it bears me out in my assertions that the sentiments of the Irish Catholics were moderate, etc. Pray send me an answer to this as soon as possible; direct to me Isle of Arran, Salt Cotes, North Britain.

SOURCE : O'Connell MSS, UCD

1 Not extant.

1410

To Denys Scully, Kilfeacle, Co. Tipperary

Derrynane, 3 September 1827

My dear Scully,

When I saw you at Dublin some time ago you told me you would require some extension of the period for the payment of the bills I got discounted for you at the Hibernian Bank. Let me know precisely which and how many of those bills it will be your convenience to get *extended*, that is, send me a list of them by dates and precise sums. We must for these things make our arrangements beforehand. . . .

. . . I need not say that it would be much preferable not to want this species of accommodation but, although I say *that*, I am perfectly willing to procure it for you if you desire.

SOURCE : Scully Papers

1411

To John Primrose, Sr., Hillgrove, Cahirciveen, 4 September 1827, from Derrynane

Requests that his gun be forwarded 'as our grouse shooting is at a stand till my gun arrives'.

SOURCE : O'Connell MSS, UCD

1412

To Denys Scully

Derrynane, 19 September 1827

My dear Scully,

I received your letter which is perfectly satisfactory. We can settle for the December bill when you come to town. The fact candidly is that your own conversation made me apprehensive that it would not be your convenience to be so punctual. I ought however to have recollected that you very wealthy gentlemen are in the habit of affecting to want money.

SOURCE : Scully Papers

1413

To Richard Newton Bennett, Dublin

Derrynane, 26 September 1827

Confidential

My dear friend,

. . . I would look upon your obtaining a situation (*which* you *ought* to take) a proof that the present Administration have the good sense and the courage to act honestly by Ireland. I have as yet seen no one symptom of any such sentiments. There are to be sure some individuals in that administration perfectly free from guile and too honourable themselves to believe in the existence of duplicity. Such I unequivocably believe Mr. Lamb to be. Besides, indeed, his rank and station in society place him on a superior level. But all the acts of the Administration convince me that they are determined to give us good words as long as these can delude, but their acts, *their acts*, are unequivocal. They have made Joy attorney-general, a more bitter enemy than Saurin because *smoother* but, in fact, a virulent anti-Catholic partisan. Alexander,[1] Chancellor instead of Plunket. The Orange faction unchecked at [? tempo] and in the North generally. Gregory in full power at the Castle. The Trenches in full pay and patronage at the Custom House as well as in Connaught. Lord Wellesley manifestly treacherous to the new ministry exerting much more power than when he affected to be liberal. The system unbroken in upon in any one branch or department. The Hills and the Blackers and the other [*Dublin*] *Evening Mail* patrons as strong and influential as ever. What confidence can I, my dear friend, have in this administration! I want nothing from them for myself. I repeat it to you. My patent of precedence would be an act of justice because if I had been a Protestant or professed any or all the thousand and one modes of faith amongst which you good Protestants may and have your right to choose, if I had but made any such profession I may be as insincere as I please, and I would have been twelve years ago a King's Counsel, and do you, my dear Bennett, think that I will enter into any *capitulation* with any administration for that act of justice? If indeed any ministry were so absurd as to condescend to wish to *manage* me, they never could do it by means of my personal interests. My object is to make one step at least in the amelioration of mankind by carrying Emancipation. This measure would reconcile Ireland to England. If it is not carried soon, these countries will certainly separate. I see the growing materials of separation. Emancipation may blight them for centuries. Without it there is a moral impossibility to continue the connection although the disastrous struggle will be delayed by us who *now* possess influence, but come it will. But I am writing on matters of prophecy instead of replying to your letter. Do you know that your letter makes me despair of the Administration even for the reasons you think ought to inspire hope? I have only further to add that in my opinion the appointment of Lord Anglesey[2] is very likely to be popular.

You will see, my dear Bennett, how impossible it is that I should empower you to do anything with this ministry *for me*. Not that my confidence in your intelligence and perfect fidelity is at all diminished, but simply because I have nothing to ask for or to treat about for myself personally. If they do me justice they shall have all the merit—if merit it have—of doing a spontaneous act of justice. If I see them acting *honestly* towards Ireland, they will find me an active partisan.

. . . I would have you write to Burdett in the meantime and, if you choose, I will also write to him complaining of the way in which you have been treated and putting forward your right to Catholic gratitude. I will also write as you please to Brougham and to Spring Rice. There is nothing I can do for you that shall remain undone, but you feel how impossible it is for me to bargain with an Administration who are to this hour piddling with me as to a mere act of justice. Anything, however, that I can *possibly* do to forward your views I certainly will do.

SOURCE : NLI, MSS 387

1 Sir William Alexander (c. 1761-1842), a native of Scotland. Master in chancery, 1809-24; chief baron of the exchequer, 1824-31; knighted, 1824. Contrary to O'Connell's information, Alexander never became lord chancellor.

2 It had for some time been rumoured that Anglesey was to succeed Wellesley as lord-lieutenant (Canning to Wellesley, 12 July 1827, *Wellesley Papers: The Life and Correspondence of Richard Colley Wellesley, Marquess Wellesley, 1760-1842 . . .*, 2 vols. [London 1914], II, 202-3). He was appointed successor to Wellesley on 1 March 1828.

1414

From Richard Lalor Sheil to Cahirciveen

30 September [postmarked 1827]

My dear O'Connell,

Your letter dated the 26th did not reach me till the 29th. We should not hide from ourselves, the public mind is beginning to cool. The reason is, I think, this: when Peel and Dawson and our decided antagonists were in office, the Catholics were exposed to perpetual affronts which kept their indignation alive. The priests, especially, were held in constant ferment. But now that Lord Lansdowne is in,[1] we say to each other, 'what a pity that our good friends in the Cabinet cannot do us any service!' and, convinced that they cannot, we 'take the will for the deed'. In this view it would be almost better for us to have our open enemies than either our lukewarm and impotent advocates in power. I admit that there are counteracting considerations; still the effect in paralysing the Catholics is, I think, justly deduced. It behoves us therefore to make double exertions and I shall not, you may rely on it, be deficient in my efforts. With respect to the delegation[2] I have no doubt of its usefulness but I fear that I shall be unable to relinquish my profession for four weeks which I should be obliged to do. As to the petitions on behalf of the Dissenters,[3] they do not seem very anxious for *our* co-operation and I own I think our question is of such paramount moment that we should not ally it to any other. Our great object should be to bring the priests into efficient and *systematic* action. This is my plan and I shall do all in my power to rouse[4] them by waking them to a sense of the affronts which the parsons now studiously put upon them. Out of the Churchyard Bill[5] much valuable poison may be obtained.[6] Lord Plunkett has supplied us with plenty of hemlock from his Burial enactments.[7] I do not believe that Plunket has thrown *cold water* on your patent of precedence. It is no part of his character to act with duplicity. He has neither the *good manners* nor the *bad heart* of Iago. As to your *authority,* I question it much. I don't like Plunket because he is offensive in his intercourse in private life *but* I cannot believe that he would be base enough to do you a wrong. His declarations in the House in your regard must shut his mouth, if he were vile enough to be inclined (which I do not believe) to insinuate against you.

My opinion as to your patent of precedence is that with your private fortune, your great professional income, your rank at the Bar, and with the *country at your back,* you may be very indifferent about having this additional *plume* in your helmet for it is no more.

SOURCE : O'Connell MSS, UCD

1 Lansdowne became home secretary in July 1827.

2 Probably a reference to the ' mission to England '. See letter 1444, note 1.

3 At a meeting of the Catholics of Clare on 2 August 1827, O'Connell had supported a resolution in favour of the Catholics petitioning specially for the emancipation of the English dissenters (*DEP,* 11 Aug. 1827).

4 At a Catholic meeting in Dublin on 22 September 1827, Sheil declared his intention of having a central committee appointed to correspond with all the parishes of Ireland. ' We have ', he declared, ' admirable materials in our hands. In every parish in Ireland there is a Parish Priest and a Curate. The Clergy of Ireland constitute a sort of intellectual aristocracy, and supply the place of an aristocracy of rank or wealth in which we are deficient ' (*DEP,* 25 Sept. 1827).

5 An act passed in 1824 (5 Geo. IV c. 25) which allowed non-Anglican clergy to officiate at burials of persons dissenting from the Established church, subject to the permission of the local Church of Ireland clergyman. If refusing permission, the clergyman was obliged to state his reason for the refusal in writing. It had long

been customary to allow Catholic clergy to officiate at Catholic burials.

6 On 29 September the association appointed a committee to procure free Catholic burial grounds (*DEP*, 29 Oct. 1827).

7 Plunket had sponsored the 'Churchyard Bill'. See letter 1119 note 7.

1415

From Jeremiah McCarthy, 62 Dawson St., Dublin, 3 October 1827, to Derrynane

Concerning bills of exchange.

SOURCE: O'Connell Papers, NLI 13647

1416

From William Hart, 3 October 1827, to Derrynane

Concerning money payments.

SOURCE: O'Connell Papers, NLI 13647

1417

To Richard Newton Bennett, Dublin, 14 October 1827, from Derrynane

To leave for Dublin soon where he hopes to meet Bennett.

SOURCE: NLI, MSS 837

1418

To Rev. W. L'Estrange, Clarendon Street, Dublin

Derrynane, 17 October 1827

My dearest friend,

I am glad to find that you are seriously engaged[1] in getting Cathoic burial grounds. You may recollect that when this subject was first started I published an opinion on this point in the newspapers.[2] I now repeat the substance of that opinion. First, it is perfectly legal for any sect of Christians to have separate burial grounds. The Quakers have almost always had them.

Secondly, the Catholics have a kind of pre-eminent right to this privilege. At Common Law, when the Catholic religion was part and parcel of the constitution, the Catholics had undoubtedly this right. It has not been taken away by any statute whatsoever.

Thirdly, there is a vulgar error which attributes this right to merely unenclosed churchyards. They are equally legal whether enclosed or not.

Fourthly, it is advisable to have a chapel adjacent to each burial ground but it is not necessary. The legal right is not affected thereby, but the vicinage of a chapel affords a more legitimate opportunity of celebrating the burial service with suitable solemnity and religion.

Thus you will find no legal obstacle whatsoever to the plan of Catholic burial grounds. I will be in town in time to draw the necessary deeds from any person inclined to sell the land to the Burial Committee whoever they shall be. This measure will take away a large quantity of plunder[3] from a very vile class, the parsons of the Law Church. . . .

P.S. This Ministry are doing nothing for Ireland.

SOURCE : Dublin Diocesan Archives

1 See letter 1414, note 6. In the new Catholic Association on 15 September 1827 L'Estrange had raised this matter in a vigorous speech (*DEP*, 18 Sept. 1827).

2 The opinion appeared in the *Dublin Evening Post* of 20 September 1823 and was published by John O'Connell in his *Life and Speeches of Daniel O'Connell*, 2 vols. (Dublin 1846), II, 449-50.

3 In churchyard burial fees.

1419

To Richard Newton Bennett

Derrynane, 19 October 1827

My dear Bennett,

I am quite at a loss to know what I am to do about you.[1] I have not sufficient knowledge of facts respecting the precise state of the present Administration to enable me to decide what species of letter I should write to Mr. Rice. . . . It is my intention to call on Mr. Lamb immediately after my arrival.

I will not say one word to him of myself but I will endeavour to learn how the land lies in every particular. The nature of my letter on your behalf to Mr. Rice will depend in a great measure on the information I then receive. . . . In fact I see at present very little reason to confide in the present Administration. They have taken tolerably good care of themselves and *as yet* none at all of Ireland.

SOURCE: NLI, MSS 837

1 See letter 1397.

1420

From the Knight of Kerry

London, 24 October 1827

Private

My dear O'Connell,

I do not wish to write to you whilst politics are vague, but on important points I feel the fairness of putting you in possession of authentic information. Hart[1] is appointed Irish Chancellor. I believe no two persons go further than you and I in wishing that it were Plunket. And for myself I cannot even conjecture what adequate grounds exist in any quarter for delaying that most desirable arrangement but it seems they do exist in an authoritative degree and we have only to seek the next best characters. Everyone knows Hart to be an eminent equity lawyer and I know that he has actually stipulated that he is to have no politics, that he is to be a mere equity judge and to know no man's religion. I think your term erroneous (and I know you will forgive me for telling you so) in Alexander's[2] case. Though 74 he is in great mental vigour and, as I saw him picking up a Picci in Regent Street the other day, I presume also in other vigour, and he is a most agreeable gentleman. Hart is not too old for you, and I do hope that those who think right on our affairs will conciliate him and thereby vex those who think wrong. . . .

SOURCE : O'Connell MSS, UCD

1 Anthony Hart (c. 1754-1831), a native of St. Kitts, West Indies. Vice-chancellor of England, April-November 1827; lord chancellor of Ireland, 1827-30; knighted, 1827. See *DNB*.

2 Sir William Alexander.

1421

To his brother John

Tralee, 25 October, 1827

My dear John,

My brother-in-law Rick O'Connell is anxious to get out his youngest son, my namesake, to India as a *cadet* in the Company's[1] service. I am writing for him to the Knight of Kerry and I beg you will give him the strongest letter you can pen to Spring Rice. The Knight of Kerry used to get cadetships while he was in opposition. . . . Rick would prefer an ensigncy or commission in the Marines if that could be procured. You may, therefore, throw *that* in. Write as soon as possible.

SOURCE : Monteagle Papers, NLI 13368

1 The East India Company.

1422

To his wife, Derrynane

Listowel [Co. Kerry], 25 October 1827

My darling Love,

. . . He [Maurice] also gave up the *yacht* or pleasure boat cheerfully, for both which concessions, darling, we ought to be obliged to him and to pray for him. . . . James[1] and I came on here. We were four hours and a half *posting* from Tralee here. . . . I will write you a line from the Association Rooms on Saturday and you will hear of me through the newspapers. I suppose you will not *require* of me to write to you as the newspapers will tell you so much about me. . . . I left poor Betsey O'Connell in certainly a very precarious way. She has not as yet seen a clergyman. I spoke to Rick[2] on the subject and hope he will suggest *it* to her. We had a sensation made in Tralee by Arthur Blennerhassett,[3] the eldest son of Sir Robert, coming publicly into the sessions court and taking the oaths as a Catholic. It is a shame and a sin for the Catholics not to countenance his wife.[4] I asked him and understood from him that she is pregnant. You cannot imagine how his conversion annoys the bigots. . . .

SOURCE : Fitz-Simon Papers

1 Probably his man-servant.

2 Rickard O'Connell, husband of Betsey.

3 Arthur Blennerhassett (1794-1849), Blennerville, Co. Kerry, succeeded his father as third baronet, 1831. High sheriff of Kerry, 1820.

4 Sarah (died 1866), daughter of John Mahony; married July 1826 Arthur Blennerhasset, eldest son of Sir Robert Blennerhasset, second baronet.

1423

To his wife, Derrynane

[Catholic] Association Rooms [Dublin],
Past 4, Saturday, 27 October 1827

My darling Love,

I travelled all night to be here at this meeting[1] and here I am in perfect health and spirits, that is, darling, *considering*.

I arrived before seven this morning and found your lonely bed, oh, how lonely! But, darling, it is my own fault, my own extravagant fault. How I hate my own extravagance. Indeed I am severely punished for it. For it is cruel to me to be absent from you and my sweetest darling Kate. How I doat of her the sweet angel. . . .

We had a large meeting and the rent is £51. I made various *excellent* speeches and was *well* received. . . .

SOURCE : Fitz-Simon Papers

1 Of the new Catholic Association on 27 October 1827. It was mainly concerned with procuring Catholic burial grounds (see letter 1414). O'Connell also urged at the meeting that Lord Plunket be made lord chancellor of Ireland (*DEP*, 30 Oct. 1827).

1424

To his wife, Derrynane

Corn Exchange, 30 October 1827

My darling Love,

. . . We have had a meeting this day and I spoke for an hour and a half—*a great speech*. . . . I rose about six, worked till eleven, then went to the Custom House till three, and then to this meeting. But though I am busy my heart is lonely. I *want* my own own sweet darling Mary and I bitterly regret my cruel extravagance and folly which has separated us for the present. I laid out a foolish deal of money at Derrynane to practise the economy which we are now suffering under. Blessed be the great God. I am keeping very regular accounts and I will always mention to you the money I give Julia[1] for house expenses. I gave her this week already £5. I wish you would enter in a book the sums I give Julia. . . . We will then easily calculate what saving is made by your staying at Derrynane. It will console us in our absence from each other if that absence enables me to pay off debts and begin to accumulate my Kate's fortune.

SOURCE : Fitz-Simon Papers

1 Maidservant.

1425

To his wife, Derrynane

Merrion Square, 6 November 1827

My darling Heart,

I am writing to you in my gown and wig after coming in from court. I [? visited] the Chancellor[1] this morning. Sheil and I went together in Ellen's carriage. The Chancellor is a dry, snuffy, meagre Englishman, not half so ugly as Lord Manners and certainly not *so genteel*. He smiled and looked civil and shook hands with everybody. I perceive that the bad part of the Bar are not on the whole pleased with him. Not a word as yet about my patent of precedence. I believe we must do without it. But it is too early to judge.

. . . I will send down Lady Morgan[2] and Scott[3] and the two magazines this week. . . .

SOURCE : Fitz-Simon Papers

1 Sir Anthony Hart.

2 Probably *The O'Briens and the O'Flahertys: A National Tale*, 4 vols. (London 1827).

3 Probably *Chronicles of the Canongate* (Edinburgh 1827).

1426

To his wife, Derrynane

Merrion Square, 8 November 1827

My darling Love,

. . . Darling, put down against Julia[1] £5 for house expenses, £3 to the cook for wages and £5 for *old* bills, caps and something else since you were in town, and £1.10.0 for some extras. . . . Ellen Fitzsimon and Betsey are here. I did not ask them but of course I cannot turn them away. We, however, as yet live very cheaply. The Ballinamona turkeys' eggs and *partridges,* the carriage horses—Fitzsimon's—are here but he gets oats from his tenants at Glencullen and buys hay and straw. I would be most happy to have my sweet children here but that I am practising rigid economy in order to have the delightful society of the ever loved mother of those children. I have reduced everything to system and I look forward to complete ease. . . . There is little doing by others, but your husband has as much to do as if all the courts were crowded with causes. There is scarcely anything in the King's Bench, in the Common Pleas nothing. The Master of the Rolls[2] and the Chancellor[3] are at daggers drawn upon the subject of the appointment of a secretary. More cause of wrangle to the Lads! I rise at five, work till half after eight, then take my *shower-bath.* I have it placed like a sentry box near the small back room. The stairs are just placed as if they had been intended for the purpose of serving as a ladder to fill the barrel of my shower-bath. It is a great *shock* these cold mornings but it is delightful when over. I look as healthy after it as if I were young again. Darling, I am in great working spirits. . . .

SOURCE : Fitz-Simon Papers

1 Maidservant.

2 Sir William McMahon.

3 Sir Anthony Hart.

1427

To his wife, Derrynane

Merrion Square, 10 November 1827

Darling Love,

. . . Tell me, darling, whether there are any tradesmen in

the house and if your buildings in the yard, I mean the laundry and dairy, are finished. I wish they were out of hands as well as the office. It would be a pleasant study when the people are not about the place and we must be in a litter till all is finished. . . .

There is but little business in the Hall. However I am doing as much as ever and saving daily. I believe I am doing as much if not more than any other man in the Hall. . . .

SOURCE : Fitz-Simon Papers

1428

To his wife, Derrynane

Merrion Square, 13 November 1827

My darling Love,

. . . Maurice is beginning to work. He is in perfect health and good spirits and does not I believe receive any letters from the quarter you may apprehend. . . .

I am pressing *them* [Ellen and Betsey] to finish the two novels that I may send them off. I will read them myself at Derrynane. Is it to be Derrynane Abbey? Your son proposed to call it Mary's Abbey. I believe it would be a description of *the fact*. . . . I like the present Chancellor[1] well. I think we have got a treasure in him. My Chancery business has already increased considerably.

SOURCE : Fitz-Simon Papers

1 Sir Anthony Hart.

1429

To his wife, Derrynane

Monday, 19 [and 20] November 1827

My dearest darling,

I never was more afflicted by an accident than I was on Saturday evening when I found it was too late to write to you. I was detained in court till half after four and at the Association till six, at which hour the post office *now* closes. . . . Charles Connor is gone down this evening. He has a notion of being priested below. If Dr. Egan[1] thinks him fit to be ordained he will remain a curate in Tralee and *so* attend to Ellen[2] and the family. I believe William Neligan will take James[3] as an apprentice. We must have poor Ellen back to Derrynane. Could not Capt. Leyne[4] give us some assistance? . . . I gave Julia[5] already this week £5 and am to give her £2 more tomorrow. Set down £7 against her. Ellen, Betsey and Fitzsimon[6] are still here. We live as cheaply as possible. You would laugh at us if you were in spirits.

Tuesday the 20th

. . . I find that I owe more money than I thought, but with the blessing and aid of God it shall all be paid. I never enjoyed better general health. I rise at a quarter after four and work hard all day. The shower-bath is a great treasure to me. I enjoy the dressing after it of all things, and I care little for the shock. It preserves me, I am convinced, from cold. Are the tradesmen yet out of the house? Do not send them away till all is finished. Let me know if the out-offices in the yard answer the purpose. . . .

SOURCE : Fitz-Simon Papers

1 Bishop of Kerry.
2 Ellen Connor.
3 James Edward Connor (1814-73), attorney, youngest child of James Connor, Tralee, and nephew of O'Connell's wife. Married 1827 Anne, daughter of Jeremiah Lynch, Kilcullen, Co. Cork.
4 Richard Leyne, brother-in-law to the Connors.
5 Maidservant.
6 His daughters and son-in-law.

1430

To his wife, Derrynane

Merrion Square, 29 November 1827,
5 in the morning

My own Mary,

I sit down to write to you as the watchman calls five. I got your scolding letter and, indeed, I deserve that scolding for allowing this day week to pass without writing to you. . . . Darling, time flies swiftly with me. I rise at four, think of that. I then work till nine. By the by, I fancy I shall soon be able to rise before four because I daily feel how much less sleep is necessary for me now that I have totally given up wine. I never felt myself so well in my life as I do since I ceased to taste it. I am so cool and pleasant when I wake at night. The instant the clock, which is twenty minutes fast, strikes nine I shave, and having everything ready I run and take my shower-bath and dress in the little room, the schoolroom. James has a fire ready in it and everything comfortable. I then go to breakfast with my spirits quite cheered and indeed as much refreshed as if I had lain in bed till that hour. I eat a voracious breakfast, then work till half after ten. I am always in court before eleven, and, Darling, I go to bed soon after nine. I am in bed by half after nine. . . . I am very, very busy. This has been a noble term with me. I have received more than £720 of the old currency in this month and near £700 of the present currency. I can tell you candidly it never was *so much wanting*. You perceive by the return of expenditure that I have been able to apply the far greatest part of my receipts in reduction of former demands. Charge Julia with £2.5.0 more. Ellen and Fitzsimon are, after all, but of little additional expense. They dine out frequently and we live with the greatest moderation. I like Sir Anthony Hart exceedingly. I was before him yesterday in his chamber for Hodgins who ran away with Miss Walker.[1] Saurin was at the same side. The Chancellor strongly condemned the conduct of Lord Manners in the business and in the course of the day again more than once in other causes said that Lord Manners was *quite wrong*. I will apply for my patent without delay. *I think* I will get it, at least I will bring the matter to *a point*. I will write to Spring Rice and the Knight of Kerry about it. Indeed I am just going to write to the former. Darling, since I finished the last page I have written a long letter to Mr. Rice about my patent. I will bring the matter to a point. They shall either do me justice or have no excuse for postponement. Give my tenderest love to my own ever loved Kate and to sweet Danny. . . .

SOURCE : Fitz-Simon Papers

1 This law case is unidentified.

1431

To Thomas Spring Rice

Merrion Square, 29 November 1827

Private

My dear Sir,

I am ashamed of giving you trouble on my own account when you are so occupied by matters of importance, but I am everyday made to feel more and more the injustice which is done to me and my clients by the promotion of my juniors to the inner bar and the neglect to give me what I think my *due* precedency. Last week Mr. North, my junior by many years, taunted me with his station. Yesterday in Chancery Mr. Leslie Foster asserted his superior station most unpleasantly. My vanity makes me think too that an act of justice to me would be taken as a kindness to the Irish people.

I have a notion of appealing to the Chancellor on this subject by letter. I *know* that Chief Justice Bushe and *all* the judges of his court, especially Judge Burton, will strongly support my claim. So will Lord Plunket and the judges of his court and *at least* two of the Barons, I believe indeed three. In short all the judges except McClelland and I really do not like to think that he *could* befriend me.

I should take this step but that you told me at Limerick to make no movement in this country but to leave the matter to my friends. You were good enough to add that I had friends who would not neglect it. I am quite ready to continue to follow your advice if you still recommend the same course, but the pressure of business accumulates upon me. I believe I can with perfect safety assert that in general business I have done *more* this term than any other man in the Hall, certainly as much, and if I had my natural rank I think—but that is prophecy—that my business would be increased in quantity as it certainly would in quality.

Sir Anthony Hart gives the greatest satisfaction. He is an excellent *tradesman*, knowing his business perfectly well, patient, excellently tempered and most anxious to do *all* his duty. The system of favouritism has already disappeared. We actually breathe a new atmosphere in the Hall, and the little knot on whom alone Lord Manners smiled are reduced to the melancholy state of depending on their own resources for success.

As to myself, unless the Chancellor will consult the law judges, he cannot know *my claims* to precedency because my want of it as well as the *supposed* hostility to me of Lord Manners has prevented my having the same business in Chancery which I have in all the other courts. Let me do Lord Manners the justice to say that he never treated me badly in his court but the clients were afraid to employ me there.

My claim for precedency extends to be placed next after the first of my juniors who got a silk gown for his merits—Mr. Wallace.

SOURCE : Monteagle Papers, NLI 13368

1432

To his wife, Derrynane

Merrion Square, 30 November
[and 1 December] 1827

My darling Heart,

. . . Darling, the term is over and blessed be God I never had so good a term. But I wanted it sadly, indeed more, much more than I had any notion. I never looked so attentively into my own affairs and if God spares me a couple of years of health, we will be the better of it. I will tell you in the morning the amount of this month's earnings. But the matter is to save as much as possible to clear off in the first instance and then to save, but the first great object is to *clear off*. . . .

Saturday, 1 December

Darling, I have just totted up my actual receipts of the past month of November and you will be glad to hear that I received from the 1st to the 30th, both inclusive, no less than 703 guineas, that is £738.3.0 of the present currency and within a few shillings of £800 of the old currency. I never got in one month near so much, that is within £50 or £60 of so much although the Hall was never so slack of business as it is at present. So much for money. You will see in the papers an account of a great meeting[1] with the Lord Mayor in the Chair. It looks well, darling, and if followed up will lead to good results. Some of the Orange party join heartily. They little think how it will forward the cause of Emancipation to have the English understand that all parties are unanimous in the conviction that Ireland is miserable. That is, after all, an obvious but a precious avowal. Darling, I really do expect Emancipation this sessions. I think indeed that it is almost impossible that they should be able to postpone it longer. If they do, they are the greatest set of rascals the world ever saw. The triumph of the liberals in France[2] is also of use to us. . . . My shower-bath agrees with me famously. I can give you no idea of the refreshing and cheering effect it has on me. It is, to be sure, cold and unpleasant while one is suffering under it but that is over in a few seconds and I feel the benefit of it all day. It is so well contrived that it makes no kind of *splash* or wet. . . .

SOURCE : Fitz-Simon Papers

1 A meeting in Dublin on 29 November 1827 under the chairmanship of the lord mayor, Edmond Nugent, 'for the purpose of coming into resolutions relative to the formation of a Ship Canal from Dublin to Galway'. Among the attendance were Lords Cloncurry and Killeen, Sirs Samuel O'Malley and Charles Morgan and three M.P.'s—Henry Grattan (Dublin city), James Grattan (Co. Wicklow) and James S. Lambert (Co. Galway). O'Connell addressed the meeting (*FJ*, 30 Nov. 1827).

2 In the recent French elections.

1433

To his wife, Derrynane

Merrion Square, 4 December 1827

My darling Heart,

. . . The winding up of tradesmens' and labourers' accounts, etc., require my attention as well as business of other kinds. . . .

We give Lord Fitzwilliam a grand dinner on Tuesday the 18th. The aggregate takes place on Monday the 17th. . . .

Sweetest love, I am most anxious to be with you and yet my affairs are so deranged that I do not know what to do. Nothing but economy amounting to parsimony *can* wind them up. It is bitter to me to tell you this but it is necessary. If my health, which, thank God, is perfectly good, continues and that I could apply my entire Bar income for eighteen months or so to the reduction of all my debts, *that* would pay them off and leave me free the rest of my life. My income is now a fine one, upwards of £7,000 a year, but it is run away with by debts and engagements. If the month of November had not been as productive as it was, I should be *badly off* indeed. Darling, forgive me for croaking. It is with a bleeding heart I do it but it is necessary that you should know the exact state of my affairs. . . . There is no occasion, thank God, to despair, but there is every occasion to be *more than prudent*. Last winter was dreadfully expensive. I had an establishment of six horses, etc., but we will talk of this when I go down. In the meantime, I am leaving no stone unturned to lighten the load and I am daily making it more light. On Saturday I gave Julia £2.15.0 and I am to give her a cheque for £10 this day. . . .

SOURCE : Fitz-Simon Papers

1434

To his wife, Derrynane

Merrion Square, 6 December 1827

My dearest love,

. . . My time is now more closely pressed upon because I dined yesterday at Sheriff Roose's with the Lord Mayor[1] and a city party. . . .

I had this morning a letter from our darling Maurice that does the greatest credit to his head and heart. He will ever be my dearest treasure. Darling, pray for him that he may be also pious while he is yet young and not like his father, giving his youth to everything sinful and reserving only the remnant of life to attempt atonement. Betsey and Nell and *her* husband are quite well. My shower-bath continues to be delicious to me. . . .

SOURCE : Fitz-Simon Papers

1 Edmond Nugent.

1435

To Denys Scully, 6 December 1827

States that Scully does not owe him any money.

SOURCE : Scully Papers

1436

To his wife, Derrynane

Merrion Square, 8 December 1827

My darling Heart,

Since I wrote last I have been very well and very busy, bustling all day and sleeping soundly all night with my heart warm with the fondest love for my wife and children and filled however occasionally with *pecuniary* anxieties. How bitterly do I regret that I was not sooner more vigilant and attentive. There is in fact but one resource and that is strict and unremitting economy. . . . I have borrowed much money since I came up and so cleared my way for the present, and I am now labouring to make provision for the money so borrowed. What I want is to keep *all* my income for that purpose. One or, at the utmost, two years of my present economy would clear off all my debts and accumulate Kate's fortune. My duty would *then* be performed because all the rest would be easy. But, darling, why should I tease you with these croakings and yet into what bosom should I pour my sorrows but yours? To whom should I look for comfort, consolation and assistance but to you? However, darling, with the blessing and assistance of God all will yet be well.

. . . The old Marquis[1] is going. His friends are very anxious to get for him some tribute of popular applause at his departure but I do not agree. He did nothing for the Catholics. As to myself he was remakably inattentive to me except when he ordered me to be prosecuted.[2] He did the same favour by Sheil.[3] He it was that procured the Algerine act.[4] In short, he deserves nothing from the Catholics. Do you not think so, darling? I have as yet heard nothing further as to my patent. I wrote[5] to Spring Rice as I told you but am as yet without an answer. I will write to the Knight this day or tomorrow on the subject. I will also personally apply to the Lord Chancellor. In short, the rascals may refuse me but they shall not neglect me altogether.

SOURCE : Fitz-Simon Papers

1 By this time it was widely known that Anglesey would succeed Wellesley in the viceroyalty.

2 See letter 1144, note 2.

3 In the New Catholic Association on 19 January 1827 Sheil delivered a lengthy speech concerning certain lessons which the Catholics

ought to learn from the memoirs of Wolfe Tone. He described Tone as 'chivalrous, aspiring and enthusiastic' and declared that 'the supporters of ascendancy ought to look pale in turning over the Memoirs of Tone' which, he added, he would recommend 'to the nocturnal vigils of the Cabinet'. He also reminded his audience that 'a fleet . . . with fifteen thousand Frenchmen . . . ought to awaken reflections of which scorn should not constitute a part' (*DEP*, 23 Jan. 1827). On 19 February Sheil and Michael Staunton, editor of the *Morning Register*, were indicted, the one for uttering, the other for publishing this speech which the government construed a seditious libel (*DEP*, 20 Feb. 1827). Wellesley strongly advocated this step (Reynolds, *Emancipation Crisis*, p. 121). On Canning's becoming prime minister, however, the proceedings against Sheil were dropped (see *DNB*, s.v. 'Sheil, Richard Lalor').

4 The act suppressing the Catholic Association in 1825.

5 See letter 1431.

1437

From Thomas Spring Rice

Harley Street [London], 8 December 1827

Copy

Confidential

My dear Sir,

I have been absent from town for a vacation of 4 holidays or your letter of the 29th should not have remained so long unanswered.

I need not tell you that nobody regrets more sincerely than I do the disqualification imposed by law on the grounds of religious belief. . . . But *I confess I should most strongly deprecate any public appeal to the Lord Chancellor as being in itself a course so unusual as to have a tendency rather to impede than to further your object.*[1] . . .

I am truly pleased to have your account of the estimate formed of the Lord Chancellor by yourself and by the Bar. . . .

SOURCE : Monteagle Papers, NLI 13368

1 A patent of precedency. A few days later Thomas Spring Rice wrote to the lord chancellor of Ireland what is obviously a letter in support of O'Connell's claim to a patent of precedency (an undated copy of the letter is in the Monteagle Papers, 13368).

1438

To Thomas Spring Rice

Merrion Square, 11 December 1827

My dear Sir,

I should not have given you the trouble of another letter but that I cannot submit to be so entirely mistaken as I find I am. I did not allude to any *public* appeal to the Chancellor respecting that justice which ought but, of course, will not be done to me. I intended nothing but that species of private application by letter which is the usual course in England and which was suggested to me as such by Mr. Blake, the Chief Remembrancer. I now regret I ever thought of it.

It is indeed well that the individual character of Sir Anthony Hart serves to mitigate that system of exclusion which is almost as effectually in action now as ever it was. We have a little also of the grace of hypocrisy to mitigate that system but beyond these advantages—such as they are!—the change of administration has not reached this country for any one useful purpose. Our enemies were at all events sincere, and they deserved respect on that account.

SOURCE : Monteagle Papers, NLI 13368

1439

From Thomas Spring Rice

Harley St. [London] 14 December 1827

[Copy]

Confidential

My dear Sir,

I confess your letter has given me some pain and disappointment. The best answer I can give and one which I think will make you feel some regret for the tone you have adopted, is to inform you that at the very moment when you expressed so much of bitterness of feeling towards me and others and suggested so much more, I was actively, zealously and I hope usefully employed in advancing your object. It was just then when in conversation and correspondence I had gone beyond what was prudent and possibly what was becoming, that I find myself and my friends the object of reproach and of contumely. . . .

When you spoke or, rather, when you wrote to me informing me of your idea 'of appealing to the Chancellor' and of supporting your claims by reference to the judges, how could I guess but that such was to be a public application? On that supposition I answered you. . . . In the highest and most efficient quarters I have been sedulous on your behalf. . . .

SOURCE : Monteagle Papers, NLI 605 D&E

1440

To his wife, Derrynane

Merrion Square, 15 December 1827

My own sweet Mary,

Another short letter. Short, darling, but sweet. The triumph of the Rev. Mr. Maguire[1] is complete.[2] Victory crowned us with laurels. Only think, the jade was not with child at all! We had a verdict with the full approbation of the judge. My heart is light, for all the Bar declare that your husband made the best speech he ever made. The Bar applauded at the end of my speech.[3] They were silent when Mr. North[4] concluded. . . .

SOURCE : Fitz-Simon Papers

1 Thomas Maguire, D.D. (1792-1847), nephew of Patrick Maguire, coadjutor bishop of Kilmore. Parish priest of Drumreilly, 1818-25; Ennismagrath, 1825; Ballinamore, 1835-47. Also dean of Kilmore. See *DNB*.

2 Rev. Thomas Maguire was tried in Dublin on 13 December 1827, charged with having seduced Mary Anne McGarrahan of Drumkerrin, Co. Fermanagh Damages of £500 were sought. He was acquitted by a jury composed of Catholics and Protestants, O'Connell and Sheil being his counsel. According to O'Connell and the *Dublin Evening Post,* the case was fabricated by Maguire's enemies (*DEP,* 13, 15 Dec. 1827). On 11 February 1828 a motion was granted to have the verdict set aside (*DEP,* 12 Feb. 1828; see also . . . *Judgment given on a motion to set aside the verdict obtained by the defendant in the case of* McGarrahan *v.* the Rev. T. Maguire [Dublin 1828]; also, H. I. Comus [pseud.], *The Nymphs of Drumkerrin . . . an Humourous Poem with a Portr. of Miss A. McGarrahan* [Dublin 1827]). There is additional background information concerning this

affair in J. Roderick O'Flanagan, *The Bar Life of O'Connell* (Dublin 1875), pp. 138-51.

3 It took more than three hours to deliver. The *Dublin Evening Post* said that the newspaper reports 'can convey no idea whatever of the energy, the critical acumen displayed . . . and the burst of eloquence which electrified the audience' (*DEP*, 15 Dec. 1827).

4 John Henry North was counsel for the prosecution.

1441

From Michael Hickey[1]

40 Jervis St. [Dublin], 15 December 1827

Sir,

. . . I have heard with feelings of genuine pleasure and delight the proposed measure of establishing a model school[2] in Dublin as the foundation of a system of national education. I hail it as the forerunner of numberless blessings to my native land. I trust the hand of Providence will assist you and your fellow labourers in accomplishing this great national undertaking.

Ideas have occurred to me respecting the most suitable site for the proposed model school. Some distinguished individuals and those whose opinions on education deserve the first consideration in this country have expressed an opinion that Kildare Place is a very desirable situation on the ground that it would be attacking the Bible Gentry at their headquarters. This I must confess is a very cogent reason for recommending Kildare Place, but many overbalancing considerations, I respectfully submit, present themselves in favour of the north side of the city. I will make bold to assert that no part of the Archdiocese of Dublin or the country at large has greater claims to the blessing of having the model school established in it than the north side of the city of Dublin. If an extremely numerous and poor school population, an almost total want of free school education and the being a prey to the baleful and destructive influence of nearly forty fanatical and proselytizing establishments form grounds for claim, the appendix to the little worth that accompanies this letter will show you that there are thirty-six of these establishments in Dr. Murray's united parishes[3] to which upwards of a thousand Catholic children are attending. A few facts will illustrate the want of Catholic education in this part of the city. I have known children to go from the North Strand to the monastic establishment in Hanover St. East[4] and to Rev. Mr. Flanagan's[5] school in Meath St. I know children at present under ten years of age going at this inclement season from near the North Wall to the Rev. Mr. Young's[6] school at Phibsborough. I know several going from Britain St., Moore St., and the neighbourhood of Marlborough St. to Hanover St. schools and even to Kildare Place schools. Doctor Murray's Education Society[7] since its establishment this time twelve months has done wonders. It has five schools superintended by efficient masters and attended by between six and seven hundred boys. These schools are crowded to excess. Still they are unable to stem the torrent of proselytism pouring in upon the people in this part of the city. Nearly a hundred Catholic children are attending the Protestant free school of St. Mary in King's Inn St. I know of no situation where a model school would more advance the sacred cause of our holy religion and of Catholic Education than King's Inn St. It is a large tract of waste ground back of Dominick St. It is with[in] five minutes' walk of six of these schools I have mentioned. It is also the centre of the residences of upwards of six thousand poor Catholic little ones, one fourth of which are not adequately provided with education. Kildare Place has very few if any of these claims to induce you to adopt it for the situation of the model school. It is for the most part surrounded by the habitations of [a] wealthy and respectable portion of the community. The monastery schools, Hanover St., are sufficient to educate the male school population from Grafton St. to Ringsend and there are female schools in Baggot St.[8] and Townsend St. I think, Sir (to use an expression which you will readily recognize), that I have made out a good case to prove the preponderating necessity and consequently the wisdom and utility of having the model school established in the north side of the city.

SOURCE : Dublin Diocesan Archives

1 Unidentified.

2 In the New Catholic Association on 8 December 1827 O'Connell recommended that £1,500 be appropriated for establishing in Dublin a model school in opposition to the proselytizing establishments which he claimed were in operation there (*DEP*, 11 Dec. 1827). Resolutions to this effect were carried by O'Connell at the aggregate meeting on 19 December, one of which recommended that 'such model school should be constituted on such a plan as to be capable of extending scientific education to the poorer classes of Ireland

as suggested in the late letter of the Rt. Rev. Dr. Doyle' (*DEP*, 22 Dec. 1827). O'Connell laid the foundation stone of this new school (of the Irish Christian Brothers), known as O'Connell School, in North Richmond Street on 9 June 1828.

3 Presumably the Pro-Cathedral and St. Andrew's (Townsend Street chapel) parishes.

4 The school of the Irish Christian Brothers in Hanover Street East, founded 1812.

5 Rev. Matthew Flanagan (died 1856), curate in St. Catherine's, Meath Street, 1809-27; P.P. St. Nicholas Without, 1827-56. Educated St. Patrick's College, Maynooth; ordained, 1809.

6 Unidentified.

7 The Education Society to establish Free Schools for the Doctrinal, Moral and Useful Instruction of the Poor, formed in Dublin at the close of 1826 under the patronage of Archbishop Murray. It had as its president Lord Cloncurry and as its vice-presidents Lords Dungannon and Killeen and Sir Thomas Esmonde.

8 Maintained by the Sisters of Mercy.

1442

To his wife, Derrynane, 20 December 1827, from Merrion Square

Instructions to Mary concerning her coming journey to Dublin.

SOURCE : Fitz-Simon Papers

1443

To his wife, Derrynane, 22 December 1827, from Merrion Square

Sends detailed instructions concerning her journey to Dublin.

SOURCE : Fitz-Simon Papers

1444

To his wife, Derrynane

Merrion Square, 24 December 1827

My darling Love,

. . . I got your letter a while ago and read it with great disappointment. I did hope you would not wait for a second bidding to come off to me. I bitterly regret your delay because

I believe I *must* go to England for ten or twelve days. They are furious for a mission[1] and you will admit that without me there can be no effectual step taken. Really, darling, the fact is that I would not go only I scruple preventing so much good to the Catholic religion as I think the mission calculated to produce. That is my *only* motive and I go very much against my will, but I will not go unless Lord Killeen and one or two influential priests belong to the party. We must leave this on the evening of Sunday the 6th of January. . . . Darling, I still hope you *can* come up before I set off. My last letter was urgent though I did not then know of the mission. . . . Darling, I am fretting between my sense of duty and my happiness in your sweet society. . . . I hope you have not kicked away my last letter as you did the first. I thought of nothing all day and all night but of your alacrity to start at a moment's notice. But perhaps your health does not admit of it. If so, sweetest, do not deceive me. . . .

SOURCE : Fitz-Simon Papers

1 The idea of a mission to England to combat anti-Catholic popular prejudices there was moved by Andrew Carew O'Dwyer in the New Catholic Association on 22 December 1827 (*DEP*, 24 Dec. 1827). At the Catholic meeting on 24 December O'Dwyer declared that such a mission would 'unweave those webs of calumny and deceit of which the Bible and Tract Missionaries have been the dishonest artificers' (*DEP*, 27 Dec. 1827). O'Connell declared himself 'convinced of the complete utility of such a measure' (*DEP*, 29 Dec. 1827) and carried a resolution in its favour on 24 January 1828 in the Fourteen Day Catholic Association. The resolution was criticized by Lord Killeen, Thomas Wyse and Jack Lawless (*DEP*, 26 Jan. 1828). O'Connell had already declared that he would go on the mission only if Lord Killeen and 'two or three clergymen nominated by Dr. Murray' were to accompany it (*DEP*, 27 Dec. 1827). The mission does not appear to have ever set out.

1445

To Thomas Spring Rice

Merrion Square, 24 December 1827

Private

My dear Sir,

I thank you very much for your letter of the 14th inst. I do *indeed* regret that I wrote so hastily and if I mention why I felt hurt, it is to *excuse* not to *justify* my peevishness. In fact I should say *palliate* rather than *excuse*.

When the new administration[1] was formed I received a cart-load of letters urging forbearance on the part of the Catholics. My own judgement coincided with the advice of so many influential persons and I therefore exerted myself for that purpose. The result was such that although I distinctly disclaim any merit on that account, yet I received many, very many letters of thanks, I think one from you in which you say 'the conduct of the Catholics is beyond all praise.' Mr. Brougham wrote to me on the same subject and in his letter he *volunteered* a distinct promise 'that I should immediately get a patent of precedence'. I have that promise but, of course, I shall never make use of it. If it were indiscreetly made, it shall never rise in judgement against the eminent man who wrote it.

Lord Eldon in the debate on the Catholic bill on the 17th April 1821 held out a distinct hope that he himself would give patents of precedence to Catholic barristers. He published that speech in a pamphlet, and if you wish to refer to Hansard's *Parliamentary Debates,* volume 46 at fol. 311-312, you will find the use he made of this topic to show that it was *no grievance* to Catholics not to be able to hold the office of King's Counsel.

Thus fortified I felt it a duty I owe to my clients to procure for them that advantage. I do not think I should be honest if I did not make such an effort in their favour. I was actually taking steps for that purpose when I happened to meet you in Limerick and there I consulted with you. You[r] answer, which I mentioned in my last letter, made me give up the idea of putting forward my claim. Three months elapsed and there the matter rested and would have since rested if my friend Mr. Blake[2] had not suggested to me to address the Chancellor on the subject. I would not do so without consulting you. Your answer certainly surprised me—that you should think me capable of a bullying public address to a judge.

Let me add there were other matters connected with the government of this country of real importance that *terrified* me at that time. You know well and I am sure you deplore that Mr. Lamb has done nothing, that although Lord Wellesley spoke the Catholics fair, all his countenance was given to the enemies of Irish tranquillity. Nay, the *knowledge* I have of the readiness of the Orange corporations to be *influenced* into liberality. Add to these circumstances the strong expectation of that party from Lord Anglesey[3] *whom they will surround*—that is, Gregory and his party at the Castle—the Attorney General,[4] an eleve of Saurin and his party at the Bar, and on the Bench, the entire established church of course.

With nothing done at present and with such prospects before us, I allowed my selfishness perhaps to get the better of my judgement and exclaimed against what probably is inevitable as if it were designed. I could say more and give more details of the causes that made my cup of bitterness to overflow but *indeed, indeed* we are fated to a bad futurity in Ireland if *the system, the system* be not changed and speedily. . . .

Allow me to assure you most solemnly that I am most grateful for your exertions on this subject. I beg and, allow me to say, insist that they will not be persevered in beyond the ordinary and measured recommendation. I wish to show you how deep is my regret by wishing to be under another obligation to you.

It is painful to me, to be sure, to have nothing to return but my cordial gratitude for your kindness to my friend Kearney.[5] . . .

SOURCE : Monteagle Papers, NLI 13368

1 Probably that of Canning, formed in April 1827.

2 Anthony Richard Blake.

3 Anglesey succeeded Wellesley as viceroy on 1 March 1828.

4 Henry Joy.

5 Hickman Kearney.

1446

From Rev. Cornelius Scully[1] to Merrion Square

Cove [Co. Cork], 26 December 1827

Dear Sir,

Enclosed I beg leave to send one guinea (which I understand is the usual retaining fee) from the parishioners of the Great Island of Cove. They are endeavouring to defend themselves against law proceedings actually undertaken against them by the executors and legatees of the *late* Rev. Dr. Atterbury[2] of this Island for tithe arrears due over six years. Should the executors, etc., of Atterbury succeed in their present most unjust and oppressive proceedings, we may all in this quarter bid adieu to peace or order. I am convinced the ferment which should in such an event be excited would end in nothing less than blood, rebellion and finally in the total ruin of our now peaceable and amenable people. . . .

SOURCE : O'Connell Papers, NLI 13647

1 Later P.P. Ballyclough, Mallow, from before 1836 until his death in 1858.

2 Unidentified.

1447

From Thomas Spring Rice

London, 27 December 1827

Private

My dear Sir,

The old proverb tells us of storms that clear the air and I am certain that between two minds of firmness, candour and good feeling an occurrence like that which has taken place in the present instance will always lead to good and not to evil.

Forget the whole transaction and only allow me to remember it as leaving a gratifying impression of the spirit and feeling which is manifested in your last [letter]. . . .

SOURCE : Monteagle Papers, NLI 605 D&E

1448

To Bishop Doyle, (J.K.L.)

Merrion Square, 29 December 1827

My Lord,

The public papers will have already informed your lordship of the resolution[1] to hold a meeting for petition in every parish in Ireland on Sunday, the 13th of January.

I should not presume to call your lordship's particular attention to this measure or respectfully to solicit your countenance and support in your diocese, if I was not most deeply convinced of its extreme importance and utility. The combination of national action—all Catholic Ireland acting as one man

—must necessarily have a powerful effect on the minds of the ministry and of the entire British nation. A people who can be thus brought to act together and by one impulse are too powerful to be neglected and too formidable to be long opposed. Convinced, deeply, *firmly* convinced of the importance of this measure, I am equally so of the impossibility of succeeding unless we obtain the countenance and support of the Catholic prelates of Ireland.

To you, my Lord, I very respectfully appeal for that support. I hope and respectfully trust that in your diocese no parish will be found deficient in activity and zeal. I intend to publish in the papers the form of a petition for Emancipation, which may be adopted in all places where no individuals may be found able and willing to prepare a proper draft. . . .

SOURCE : FitzPatrick, *Dr. Doyle*, II, 52-3

1 At a Catholic meeting on 19 December 1827 it was resolved that the Catholics of Ireland should meet simultaneously in their respective parishes on Sunday, 6 January 1828, to petition parliament for unqualified Emancipation and repeal of the vestry and sub-letting Acts (*DEP*, 24 Dec. 1827). The day was later deferred to 13 January, and an address to the Catholic clergy and laity was drawn up in support of the project (*DEP*, 29 Dec. 1827). The Sub-letting Act was passed in 1826 (7 Geo. IV. c. 29). It subjected tenants who sublet without their landlords' consent to severe legal disabilities. It was originally sponsored by Sir Henry Parnell (R. B. McDowell, *Public Opinion and Government Policy in Ireland, 1801-1846* (London 1952), p. 74).

1449

To Bishop MacHale,[1] *31 December 1827*

Essentially the same as O'Connell's letter to Bishop Doyle (J.K.L.) on 29 December 1827.

SOURCE: Cusack, *Liberator*, p. 518

1 John MacHale (1791-1881), a native of Tobbernavine, Tirawley, Co. Mayo; lecturer in theology, St. Patrick's College, Maynooth, 1814-25; titular bishop of Maronia and coadjutor bishop of Killala, 1825-34; archbishop of Tuam, 1834-81. See *DNB*.

1450

From Thomas Spring Rice

Whitehall, 15 January 1828

Confidential

My dear Sir,

I apprehend I date from Whitehall for the last time[1] and that the meeting of parliament will see me on my old bench. I came here in hopes that I might be of service to Ireland and, when that hope ceases, I shall quit office without at least the consciousness of having done or omitted any act that could compromise the great interests to which I am pledged.

. . . A Tory and exclusive government cannot certainly claim any sympathy from me, should such a *monster* be formed as I consider is most probable. But even then, if despair were in our hearts, my word would be still the same, that the Irish Catholics should be calm in their strength and moderate in all their determinations.

Attempts will be made, I have no doubt, to goad and irritate but the quarter they come from should be our safeguard and protection. . . .

SOURCE : O'Connell MSS, UCD

1 It probably was. When the duke of Wellington became prime minister on 22 January, Spring Rice quitted the post of undersecretary for the home department (which directed the Irish administration), a post he had held since July 1827 under Canning and Goderich. He remained a backbencher until Grey took office in 1830.

1451

From Committee formed at the Waterford Meeting to Merrion Square

Waterford, 25 January 1828

Dear Sir,

The work of persecution still proceeds in this quarter but we are glad to have it in our power to inform you that instead of breaking down the spirits of the people, it has only tended to produce a manifestation of patriotic feeling. . . . By public advertisement a meeting was this day convened to devise some means for relieving one hundred and forty human beings who are just evicted from their habitations on the lands of Lismethane within the immediate precincts of Curraghmore demesne for one year's rent due only on the 1st of last November. The motives of this conduct on the part of the Beresfords are amply developed in resolutions adopted at the meeting. . . . Money to the amount of £*140* was instantly raised by way of loan to be repaid by the New Catholic Rent. . . . Our object in doing this is to produce effect and to convince the Ascendancy men that we are determined to stop at no sacrifice in order to keep the people together and particularly to protect those noble fellows who at the late election broke down the power of the Beresfords. We hope that you will . . . use your influence . . . with the New Catholic Association in procuring us this sum to enable us to keep faith by refunding to those honest and patriotic people the respective sums which they have advanced.[1]

The meeting as well as the contributors of this money consisted principally of the middle and humbler classes of society. . . .

[Signed by]

[Rev.] John Sheehan	Pierce Power PP	Daniel Dunford
Thomas Carroll	John Fitzpatrick	W. [? Wall] RCC
Roger Hayes, Chairman	John Brick RCC	[one other illegible]

SOURCE: NLI, MSS 5243

1 On the back of this letter is written: 'Committee of Revenue, 3 Feb. 1828. Resolved that Mr. Dwyer do remit Roger Hayes Esq. One hundred and forty pounds mentioned in the within for the relief of the 40/- Free Holders. [Signed] Daniel O'Connell, Domk. Ronayne, James Sugrue.'

1452

From Charles Phillips

Sheriff's Court, Saturday (c. mid or late February 1828]

Dear O'Connell,

The place whence this is dated must excuse this scrap of paper. I am sitting beside Brougham who gives me the cover and waiting till his case is over as I am in the next. I write hastily in consequence of an anonymous letter which I got yesterday stating—but I will enclose the letter itself, which will speak for itself. . . .

B— desires me to say he has received McDonnell's[1] letter and is considering the best way of noticing the subject in Parliament, but is of opinion that going to Lamb[2] in the first instance is not the most prudent plan. I say this by his desire as I know nothing of what it means, but I suppose it alludes to Eneas' sentence[3] which I deeply regret. He is a good fellow and far too honest for the day he lives in. I did not expect that Vandeleur and Burton would ever have agreed to such a sentence. I saw Dawson[4] a day or two ago. He seems to me a man of mind and principles well calculated to do honour and service to Ireland.

I am glad to see by the papers that you hold your course in the *courts* in spite of all opposition. Long may it be so. Mrs. P. begs to join me in kindest regards to Mrs. O'Connell and all your circle. Remember me also to Finlay and Walshe.[5] I hear North is here but have not seen him. In fact, I am become a mere mechanic working hard and, thank God, getting work enough to do, but I still have recollections which I wish I could get rid of, for no man can now benefit Ireland, at least no man that can, will.

My case is called on—again excuse this,

Ever yours,

C. Phillips

SOURCE: O'Connell Papers, NLI 13647

1 Eneas MacDonnell.

2 William Lamb, chief secretary.

3 In the court of king's bench on 11 December 1827 Eneas MacDonnell was found guilty of libelling Charles Le Poer Trench, archdeacon of Ardagh, in the *Weekly Register* on 21 October 1826 in the course of a controversy at Ballinasloe over pressure being put on Catholic tenants to send their children to certain Protestant schools (*FJ*, 11, 12 Dec. 1827). The same court on 18 January 1828 found him also guilty of a similar libel against Walter McDonough (*FJ*, 19 Jan. 1828). It sentenced him on 12 February to one year's imprisonment for the libel on Trench, to a further six months' imprisonment for the libel on McDonough and to enter into recognizances for £500 to keep the peace (*FJ*, 13 Feb. 1828). An order for MacDonnell's release on grounds of ill health was made on 5 September (*FJ*, 6 Sept. 1828). A fund was raised to sustain him. Some Catholics

mistrusted him and with reason, for he was moving politically to Toryism (Inglis, *Freedom of the Press*, p. 187).

4 Probably Alexander Dawson, M.P.

5 Unidentified.

1453

To the Knight of Kerry

[postmarked 27 February 1828]

[No salutation]

Lord Lansdowne has gone out of office[1] not only with honour unsullied but with character exalted. He has been steady and consistent and affords *stronger* grounds to hope that the next change—if we live to see it—will place him at the Head of the Government. His *whole party* certainly deserve the public confidence and amply justify that confidence. The others—the Liberal Tories—are miserable creatures. I am exceedingly glad to find that you do not commit yourself to the Sub-letting Act.[2] It is just the very worst and vilest piece of legislative folly and injustice that ever was promulgated. Sir H. Parnell and Spring Rice have wisely put themselves forward to protect Goulburn from bearing the odium of that Bill. It ought to be called An Act to render it impossible for a labourer to become a farmer, to prevent a farmer from becoming a gentleman, to prevent a gentleman from acquiring Property, to purchase an estate. It is the worst of the Penal Code, and a hypocritical Penal Law to boot.

SOURCE : FitzPatrick, *Corr.*, I, 154-5

1 As a result of Goderich's resignation on 8 January Lansdowne ceased to be home secretary and was succeeded by Peel on 26 January.

2 See letter 1448, note 1. Feeling against the act was widespread. At 'a numerous and highly respectable meeting of magistrates, gentlemen and freeholders' at Tralee on 27 March it was decided to petition parliament for the repeal of 'this obnoxious and abominable statute' (*DEP*, 17 April 1828).

1454

From Lord Shrewsbury[1], to Dublin

Sidmouth, 7 March [1828]

Sir,

I beg leave to forward to you my subscription [£50] in testimony of the sense which I entertain, in common with every individual Catholic in the Empire, of the eminent services of Mr. Eneas McDonnell in the great cause of civil and religious liberty, a cause in which it is an honour to be a martyr.[2]

SOURCE : Dublin Diocesan Archives

1 John (Talbot), sixteenth earl of Shrewsbury (1791-1852), succeeded to the peerage, 1827. Married 1814 Maria Theresa, first daughter of William Talbot of Castle Talbot, Co. Wexford.

2 See letter 1452, note 3.

1455

To the Knight of Kerry

22 March 1828

[No salutation]

This great work[1] is a species of practical Emancipation. It emancipates the Catholics of Dublin, and the Liberal Protestants also, from the odious monopoly of the Bank of Ireland. In fact, it is the only useful and practical plan I ever knew the Catholics establish.

Its directors, too, are men as incapable of trick or fraud as either of us.

This Establishment operates in two ways: first, directly by accommodating the Catholics and Liberal Protestants who would be rejected by reason of political or religious dislike or difference; and secondly, by inducing the Bank of Ireland to be more liberal and less *restrictive* lest the business should accumulate to the rival Establishment. You could not inflict a deeper injury on the Shareholders at large or upon the least part of the Dublin commercial population than by forwarding the Bill[2] I allude to.

The Marquis of Lansdowne is turning out 700 families in Kerry.[3] We shall have bloody work next circuit!

SOURCE : FitzPatrick, *Corr.*, I, 155-6

1 The Hibernian Bank, established 1824. An open breach had occurred between its directors and a section of its shareholders, the latter claiming that the promoters had been guilty of a breach of faith as, at the time of the bank's establishment it had been understood that it would enjoy the right of note issue. (F. G. Hall, *The Bank of Ireland, 1783-1946* (Dublin 1946), pp. 138-9, 143-4).

2 The unsuccessful Hibernian Joint Stock Company Bill introduced into the Commons by Viscount Ennismore and the Knight of Kerry on 17 March 1828. Its effect would have been to dissolve the bank. It passed its second reading on 1 May only by the speaker's casting vote and was not proceeded with.

3 In 1875 the then marquis of Lansdowne owned 95,000 acres in Co. Kerry valued at £9,500 annually, much of it being mountainous.

1456

To the Knight of Kerry, 28 March 1828[1]

O'Connell writes that the bill with which the Knight has been entrusted would have the effect of dissolving the Hibernian Bank, and he ask him to decline giving it support. He detailed various conveniences which the Hibernian Bank gave to the people and pointed out that it possessed all the 'advantages of competition as contrasted with monopoly'.

SOURCE : FitzPatrick, *Corr.*, I, 155

1 This calendared version is based on what FitzPatrick says of the letter.

1457

To the Knight of Kerry

Merrion Square, 29 April 1828

My dear Sir,

It has just been suggested to me that those who seek to destroy the Hibernian Bank have asserted that the decided support I gave that Establishment arises from motives of personal interest. It, to be sure, does afflict me to have any person base enough to make any such suggestion, and I throw myself on your kindness to contradict that report should it reach you. I empower you to contradict it in the most direct terms. I solemnly assure you it is totally false. I have, indeed, 32 shares[1] in the Company, and that gives me this interest in the concern that I am quite convinced I should be able to dispose of this stock in a few years if the Company be allowed to proceed in its present course. But other interest I have none, and the circulation of a report that I have only proves to what falsehood the assailants of the Company are capable of resorting. I wish the discussion[2] could be postponed for another week as this report has roused me and I think I could within the week procure strong public support for this Company.

We are in tremulous expectation of the result of the Catholic debate,[3] expecting that the English will give us fresh grounds to hate them. Heaven knows there were enough before. Believe me, there is an *under swell* in the Irish people which is much more formidable than any sudden or *showy* exhibition of irritation. I have no doubt that if the present system is persevered in for twenty years, it will end in a separation brought about in blood and confiscation.

SOURCE : FitzPatrick, *Corr.*, I, 156-7

1 The nominal capital of the bank was divided up into 10,000 shares of £100 each, an amount of £25 being paid up on each share (Hall, *Bank of Ireland,* p. 139).

2 The Commons debated the Hibernian Joint Stock Company Bill (see letter 1455, note 2) on 22 and 24 April and then adjourned further discussion to 1 May.

3 On Sir Francis Burdett's motion that the Commons go into committee on the Catholic question. Intended for 29 April, the motion was in fact not made until 8 May and was passed 272-266 on 12/13 May.

1458

To John Primrose Jr., Hillgrove

Merrion Square, 30 April 1828

My dear John,

[Deals with bills of exchange and routine business matters.]

. . . [Dr.] Barry[1] proposes to buy the materials of the old house at Carhen. I think that is my best way to dispose of the buildings there. . . . I do not mean to make any lease of any part of lower Carhen save building lots until the town *gets on.* . . . I hope the painting of the woodwork is over at Derrynane. . . . I think the *bunnion end* next to the sea should be weather slated as soon as the good weather sets in. The best way would be to give Harris[2] lime and slate and a lump sum for doing the work. . . .

SOURCE : O'Connell MSS, UCD

1 Dr. James Barry, Cahirciveen.

2 Unidentified.

1459

From the Knight of Kerry

London, 13 May 1828

My dear O'Connell,

I consider it almost certain that something practical must soon result from our triumph in numbers and still more in argument in the late most important debate.[1] I endeavoured to give effect to the *terrors* of your Association.

SOURCE : O'Connell MSS, UCD

1 See letter 1457, note 3. The Knight of Kerry contributed at some length to the debate on 8 May.

1460

To Richard Newton Bennett

Merrion Square, Tuesday, 27 May 1828

Most Confidential

My dear Bennett,

I cannot see you today. I am exceedingly *pressed*. I wanted to say a good deal to you. Everything is in confusion at the other side but as yet—that is on *Saturday last*—no approach made to our friend.[1] Write to me as soon after you get to London as you *know* anything or say that nothing is to be known. Spring Rice's letter today to '*a friend*'[2] is not satisfactory. See *B*[3] as speedily as possible. *I confide* much in your discretion. Should *we* be able here to do anything, which indeed is not now probable, you may make a *pledge* for me but recollect the Catholics must press forward. The manner and matter of the pressure may be regulated and there can be no adjournment of the cause. I do not know what more to say to you. Use your discretion if any emergency arises but use it *discreetly*. You know how I confide in you. But in *sad, sad* truth the Whigs behaved badly to their friends when last in office. Plague on that policy that courts enemies and neglects friends. I fear it is British Whiggery.

See Blount, the English Catholic Secretary, from me and tell him that the 'Securities' will produce an immediate rupture between the English and Irish Catholics. If his *Catholic Journal* be not muzzled on that infernal subject[4] we shall be at open war. Tell him I *must* lead in that war. Eneas,[5] the pious Eneas, is raving on the subject. Jack Lawless is mad with delight at a good row. Coppinger[6] grins a ghastly smile at the prospect of a good quarrel with the English Catholics. See Blount privately. Tell him I would not *write this* because I only wish you to speak it. I *do* write bitterly and in the extreme of hurry.

SOURCE : NLI, MSS 387

1 Unidentified.
2 Unidentified.
3 Henry Brougham.
4 At a meeting of Catholics at the Corn Exchange, Dublin, on 26 May O'Connell called attention to the latest available number of Blount's *Catholic Journal,* deploring the inclusion in it of recommendations that 'securities' should accompany any emancipation measure. He went on to propose the removal of the paper from the Corn Exchange rooms. Lawless, while agreeing with O'Connell about 'securities', expressed disapproval of such a step (*DEP,* 27 May 1828).
5 Eneas MacDonnell.
6 Stephen Coppinger.

1460a

From Primate Patrick Curtis

Drogheda, 27 May 1828

My dear Sir,

I should have had the honour of answering your letter of the 22nd inst. sooner, but that I was absent from home, on duty, when it arrived. It reminds me of the advice given to the Catholics of Ireland by the late general meeting of that body, to hold a simultaneous meeting on Sunday the 15th June, in order to petition His Majesty the King and the House of Lords.

You earnestly recommend this measure and express a wish that you preserve enough of my confidence for successfully pressing it on my consideration as a matter of great importance. I really believe it to be so, relying full as much or more on your opinion than on my own or any other, and I shall accordingly give it all the concurrence in my power.

But even though I should differ from you in opinion on this or any other subject, it would by no means diminish the confidence and esteem that you so well deserve and possess in my mind and as far as I know, in that of every good Irish Catholic.

It may not, however, be unreasonable to add that I think simultaneous Catholic meetings should only be held on very rare and momentous occasions and never used or appealed to for the purpose or in the style of intimidation of which we are so often publicly accused, while we utterly disavow and condemn it.

SOURCE : *Morning Register,* 30 May 1828

1461

From Henry Grattan, Jr.[1]

20 Bentinck Street [London], 19 June 1828[2]

Dear Sir,

You will read the fate and failure of my motion.[3] I tried all I could but in vain. Government is incorrigible. The opinion of the Solicitor-General[4] was thought good law in St. Stephen's; *quaere,* will it be so thought in the Orange North?

I hope the Catholics will not fall *into the trap* of Securities and Veto. These words should be banished from their mouths. In my opinion the simultaneous meetings should be held but in a more solemn and effectual and general manner than the last. The Dissenters' dinner[5] yesterday was a grand triumph for us. Nothing could be better. Their support of emancipation bordered on the spirit of chivalry.

SOURCE : *Irish Monthly,* XIV (1886), 231-2

1 Henry Grattan, Jr. (1789-1859), M.P. for Dublin City, 1826-30; Meath, 1831-52. Married October 1826 the only daughter of the late

Philip Whitfield Harvey and thus became proprietor of the *Freeman's Journal* which formed part of his wife's inheritance. He remained proprietor until 1830.

2 The *Irish Monthly* erroneously dates this letter as 19 *January* 1828.

3 An amendment proposed by Grattan on 16 June to the (Irish) Malicious Injuries Bill (enacted as 9 Geo. IV c. 56) for the purpose of giving greater protection to Catholic churches and officiating clergymen, but the solicitor-general replied that existing law gave adequate protection (*FJ*, 20 June 1828).

4 John Doherty.

5 On 18 June a public dinner was held in the Freemasons' Tavern, Great Queen Street, London, to commemorate the act (9 Geo. IV. c. 17) repealing the Test Acts which had received the royal assent on 9 May. The duke of Sussex presided at the dinner.

1462

From James Macartney[1]

21 June 1828

Sir,

Having heard that you lately expressed at a public meeting[2] enlightened and philosophic opinions on the subject of anatomical dissection,[3] I take the Liberty of enclosing for your perusal a lithograph of a declaration which has been signed by 133 individuals who are anxious for the promotion of a science which makes no distinction of sect or party. The document lies in my museum for the purpose of being signed by all who may approve of it.

SOURCE : O'Connell Papers, NLI 13648

1 James Macartney (1770-1843), born at Armagh; at age ten joined Charlemont's volunteers; started United Irishmen branch at Armagh, 1792; student, Royal College of Surgeons of Ireland, 1793-96; befriended several United Irishmen, including Tone; qualified in London, 1800; elected to chair of anatomy, T.C.D., 1813; a pioneer of research in and teaching of anatomy. See Alexander Macalister, *James Macartney, M.D., . . . a Memoir* (London 1900).

2 Unidentified.

3 Until 1832 the only human bodies legally available for anatomical dissection were those of executed murderers. The deficiency was made up by 'resurrection men' who surreptitiously disinterred recently buried corpses from the various cemeteries around Dublin. Macartney was leading a campaign to amend the law. *Hansard* (3rd ser., X, 378) reports O'Connell in the Commons on 15 February

1832 as follows: 'He hoped that somebody would dissect him when he was dead. He had endeavoured to be useful while he lived and he should wish to be so after death.'

1463

From Joseph Michael J. G. Hamilton to Merrion Square

Annadale Cottage, [Phillipsburgh Avenue, Fairview, Co. Dublin], Friday [27 June 1828]

Countryman,

I offer you the use of the printing press on wheels which my boys worked in different places during the Waterford election, which headed the procession on the day of triumph and on which the accompanying 'Freeholders Charter Song' was printed for gratuitous circulation. Messrs. Dwyer and L'Estrange told me this day to call on Mr. Scott[1] but when I went to Earl St. I found he had started for the scene of action.

Having heard that your adversary, Mr. Sheehan,[2] is in Clare, I think it may be to tease you upon the *Point of Honour,* and send you some pages of a new edition of the *Royal Code*[3] in which your name is mentioned as well as those of your son[4] and Mr. Bric.

I believe Mr. F.[5] will only poll one day and petition, relying on mere disqualification as in the case of Wilkes;[6] in that case you can return to the scratch again and again if you cannot take your seat conscientiously under the Dissenters Act which some assert you can do.

The anecdotes of Themistocles, Aristides, Pulfio and Varenes, in the 30th and 31st pages of my *Reflections upon Duelling*[7] were written in the spirit which dictates this letter from a man whose humble energies would volunteer in your good cause.

[P.S.] I have the leading banner, with the palm of victory and the key of the County which I carried at the head of the procession in Waterford. The key is the same which Mr. Stuart wore when he spoke from the balcony after the chairing. It was I who invested him with it. If you want the press let a carpenter come for it.

SOURCE : O'Connell Papers, NLI 13647

1 Richard Scott, attorney, election agent to O'Connell in the famous Clare election. On 24 June O'Connell had announced his intention of going forward as a candidate against Vesey FitzGerald.

2 Probably Remigius Sheehan (died 1847), a Cork attorney, and lapsed Catholic, who in 1824 succeeded Timothy Joseph Haydn as an editor of the *Dublin Evening Mail*. He was proprietor of the *Star of Brunswick* which he established around 1828 to combat the Emancipation movement. The *Morning Register* of 28 August 1828 stated that he and his brother Thomas, joint proprietor of the *Evening Mail,* were the first Catholics since the Relief Act of 1793 to receive the freedom of the city of Dublin.

3 *Extracts from Various Works of Joseph Hamilton* (Dublin n.d.).

4 Maurice.

5 William Vesey FitzGerald.

6 John Wilkes (1727-97), the celebrated agitator elected for Middlesex.

7 *Extracts from Various Works of Joseph Hamilton* (Dublin n.d.).

1464

From John Barclay Sheil, M.D.

London, 34 St. James's St., 29 June 1828

My Dear Mr. O'Connell,

We are all delighted here in the prospect of your success. All the Catholics of London are enthusiastic in their wishes for your return.[1] Your plan of operations has absolutely paralysed the ministerial bigots. . . .

SOURCE : O'Connell MSS, UCD

1 As M.P. for Co. Clare.

1465

To Cornelius MacLoghlin, Dublin

Ennis, 5 July 1828

My dear friend,

The cover[1] of this will announce to you a cheering fact. It is that there is in parliament a man, one of whose greatest consolations in life is that he can truly call himself

Your attached and sincere friend,

Daniel O'Connell

SOURCE : *Irish Monthly*, X (1882), 717

1 This meant that O'Connell was franking the letter, that is, exercising the right of free postage which was accorded to members of parliament from the time of being declared elected. MacLoghlin had subscribed £100 to O'Connell's election expenses (*FJ*, 27 June 1828). According to an unidentified issue of the *Limerick Chronicle*, O'Connell franked his first four letters to the duke of Wellington, Lord Eldon, Peel and Goulburn, announcing to them his return for Clare (*Times*, 16 July 1828).

1466

From Edward Dwyer to Ennis

Corn Exchange, Dublin, 5 July 1828

Daniel O'Connell, Esq., M.P.

My dear Sir,

I have no doubt but that I am right in attaching these delightful consonants to your name.[1] What an era? I never expected to have such a pleasure during the natural period of *my* life. You can have no idea of the enthusiastic feeling which pervades every rank in the city on this momentous crisis. Our receipt of rent this week exceeds two thousand pounds. It is determined 'and justly' that there shall be a procession on your entering the city, a *proclamation* goes forth tomorrow calling upon the people *not* to illuminate but they shall be gratified with a procession. The Committee would wish that you would acquaint me with the hour on Wednesday at which you could with convenience meet the horsemen 4 miles from town. *That* once known, we can easily arrange for the *chariots* and *infantry*. . . .

SOURCE : O'Connell MSS, UCD

1 As M.P. for Co. Clare. The *Freeman's Journal* of the same day reported the gross poll on the fourth day of voting (3 July) as 1,820 votes for O'Connell and 842 for FitzGerald. The final state of the poll on 5 July when O'Connell was declared elected was O'Connell, 2,057, FitzGerald, 982 (*DEP*, 8 July 1828).

1467

From Anthony Marmion

19 Downing Street, London, 5 July 1828

Dear Sir,

Since you declared yourself a candidate for the representation of Clare, I wrote both to O'Gorman Mahon and John Lawless not only as to the course which should be pursued in managing to have a liberal Protestant candidate (if your force would permit it) over Vesey Fitzgerald on the poll, your name of course standing first, which is of more importance to our purpose than if there were 100 liberal Protestant Members ret[urne]d for Ireland, but also to acquaint them with the feelings and opinions of that body of Englishmen on whom you can alone rely for countenance and support in your arduous undertaking; and this body is composed of the Radical Reformers. Several opportunities have been lost of uniting the Catholics of Ireland with the Reformers of England, and although it has been frequently asked at the Association, who are the Reformers of England? I say they are the great mass of the people; it is true they do not meet as in 1816-17-18-19, but the principle has sunk deep in their minds. . . . In 1817 when the Reformers held out the hand of friendship, imploring them to join them in one common effort for reform, the Catholics shrunk from the offer.[1] In 1819 and during the Queen's prosecution the Reformers again appealed to the Irish nation and were again refused.[2] . . . 'our Deputies in 1825'[3] [likewise refused their support to the Reformers]. This then is the favourable moment to bring about the consummation. You have declared yourself a radical reformer, and in that declaration is buried all differences which have existed between us. . . . It will be necessary for you to throw off all intercourse with either and both parties and rely with confidence on the people. . . . [Mr. Hunt, Mr. Richard Ronayne of Cork,[4] Sir Charles Wolseley,[5] myself and others will support you.] But the imbeciles of the Catholic Associatiton here and the Whig aristocracy of Ireland, with Lord Rossmore at their head, are frightened to death at your declaring yourself a Radical Reformer . . . and consequently Rossmore and his party retreated from the meeting[6] rather than put Mr. Hunt's resolution which went to pledge the Reformers to support you on the ground that your election was not an Irish but a National question. Your experience of 1825 will convince you that such milk and water men can neither serve you nor the cause of Ireland. . . . It will be necessary if you are returned for Clare (of which I suppose there is little doubt) that the popular excitement manifested in Ireland shall be followed up here. If there is a meeting of the people on the day on which you arrive here and that 50,000 or 60,000 should convey you down [to] the House, this would have a most imposing and paralysing effect on Ministers, etc. This display is only to be done through Mr. Henry Hunt. . . . I write at the suggestion of Mr. Hunt [but you must reply to me at once or to Ronayne]. . . .

SOURCE : O'Connell Papers, NLI 13648

1 See letter 680. It is not known if and how O'Connell replied.

2 The occasions on which these happenings occurred have not been identified.

3 The deputies sent to London by the Catholic Association in February 1825.

4 Richard Power-Ronayne, Dellaughten, Co. Waterford (near Youghal, Co. Cork); married 1811 Mary, eldest daughter of Nicholas Power, Snowhill, Co. Kilkenny, and added the additional surname of Power.

5 Sir Charles Wolseley, seventh baronet (1769-1846). Imprisoned on charges of sedition and conspiracy, 1820-21. Elected to Middlesex Reform Committee together with Jeremy Bentham and Sir Francis Burdett, 1821. See *DNB*.

6 Of the Committee of Friends of Catholic Emancipation at the Crown and Anchor Tavern, London, on 2 July in support of O'Connell's candidature. Lord Rossmore, in the chair, declined a resolution from Hunt as 'foreign to the purpose for which they had assembled'. It was eventually put but defeated by a three-to-one majority. Still dissatisfied, Hunt pressed, eventually with success, for Rossmore to leave the chair, and after the termination of the meeting, he and his fellow radicals stayed on in the room (*Times*, 3 July 1828).

1468

From Edward Dwyer to Ennis

Corn Exchange [Dublin], Sunday, 6 July 1828

My dear Sir,

. . . I have a second letter from Mr. Quin[1] by which it appears that your return was announced in London *on*

Thursday last.[2] He asks *officially* to receive the earliest information of the time when the Member for Clare may be expected to arrive in London in order that the Committee[3] may be enabled to prepare a reception for him suitable to the glorious occasion. . . . I omitted to mention that Mr. Quin's application was in consequence of a resolution to that effect moved by Lord Rossmore, seconded by Sir Wm. Brabazon, Bart.[4]

James Sugrue appears to [be] most active in the Committee at the Crown and Anchor. I advised him to send a remittance[5] as soon as possible and I would arrange to have a vote of thanks given to him for his exertions. It would tend to reinstate him in the minds of the people after the Hibernian Bank affair.[6]

SOURCE : O'Connell MSS, UCD

1 W. Quin, secretary of the Committee of Friends of Catholic Emancipation.

2 A false report. The latest news from Clare in London on Thursday, 3 July, was dated 29 June (*Times*, 3 July, 1828). The *Times* of Saturday, 5 July, reported in error that Vesey FitzGerald had withdrawn from the election.

3 See letter 1467, note 6. O'Connell did not in fact go to London until the 1829 session of parliament.

4 Sir William John Brabazon, second baronet (1778-1840), Brabazon Park, Co. Mayo. M.P. for Mayo, 1835-40.

5 At this meeting, £265.10.0 had been collected (see letter 1467, note 6).

6 James Sugrue was one of the two signatories of a petition presented to the Commons on 1 May in support of the bill (see letter 1455, notes 1 and 2) designed to dissolve the bank (*Commons Journal*, LXXXIII, 291).

1469

From Lord Rossmore

London, 11 July [1828]

My Dear O'Connell,

. . . I have just been informed that Peel is to [? be made a] Peer immediately, that Daly[1] is not for some time, for fear of a defeat in Galway.

In the morning it was stated by high authority that the Duke and Peel would not long remain united. The business in

Clare has bothered them. Opinion here is six one way, ½ dozen the other on your validity.[2]

Brougham to be Chancellor of the Exchequer. The above I have all from right good authority. I have had a right set of men here [about one word missing] for talent, exertion and independent principle.

I am now going to give you a hint which all your friends here agree in. They do not think the time is arrived for its being necessary that a man should declare himself a Reformer. He may do so hereafter but they think it injures the cause greatly *here at present* and prevents them from being of the use they otherwise could. Hearing all this I did not think proper to withhold [? it]. I see you are to attend at Du[?ndalk] on the 16th[3] and as I know some there are of that way of thinking.

There never was so fine [? firm] a movement made as that in Clare.

SOURCE : O'Connell MSS, UCD

1 James Daly, M.P. for Co. Galway.

2 On his right to take his seat in the Commons since he was not prepared to take the oaths objectionable to Catholics.

3 At a dinner in his honour in Dundalk by the Louth Independent Club on 14 July (not 16). On this occasion O'Connell declared, 'I am now, I ever shall be, a Radical Reformer' (*MR*, 16, 17 July 1828).

1470

From John Foster[1]

Knaresborough, Yorkshire, 13 July 1828

Sir,

Will you permit a Protestant to congratulate you on the success of your election, and at the same time offer you some desultory remarks thereon?

You are aware of the bitterness of the London Press against the justice of the Catholic cause; you are also doubtless aware that such an array of rancour and falsehood is daily exhibited against the Catholics as is viewed with pain and disgust by hundreds of sincere and conscientious Protestants.

But, notwithstanding your knowledge of the London press, it can hardly be supposed you are acquainted with the country newspapers which excel their brethren in London both in dullness and malignity.

The interference of the Catholic priests at the late election from the Co. of Clare is now the subject on which they wish to agitate the public mind, forgetting that in England the most complete agitators at every contested election are, beyond any matter of doubt, the clergy of the Church of England.

Why do you not, then, throw this notorious fact in their teeth? But assertions are not arguments. I will therefore refer you to one case, *viz.*, the last election for the County of York which, by-the-by, was *not a contested* one[2] but which was as much or more distinguished for blind and bigoted zeal as any election I ever read of.

But I will give you names and particulars. You there saw in every man's hat of the Tory party, probably amounting to 50,000, a card with 'No Popery' and 'The Protestant Cause' printed thereon; and when Lord Milton rose to address the electors from the hustings there was a regular organized party came forward to prevent his lordship from being heard, headed and led on by the Rev. T. S. Read[3] of Sand Hutton, nr. Thirsk.

At Bramham near Wetherby the Rev. B. Edmonson[4] gave an entertainment to all the Blues (the Tory colour) in his neighbourhood, distributing at the same time his own illiterate and abusive publications. Nay, the parsons all over this great county were the most conspicuous and violent partisans; and I cannot do better than close this account by referring you to a newspaper of that period, and which I send herewith, giving particulars of the proceedings in this town, headed by our own vicar, the Rev. Andrew Cheap.[5]

Permit me to say to you what I before said to Mr. MacDonnell, you must by all and every means enlighten the English mind. Englishmen are violent against you from sheer ignorance; they are ignorant both of your religion and their own.

SOURCE : *Dublin Evening Post*, 17 July 1828

1 Unidentified.

2 The candidates were Viscount Milton and William Duncombe.

3 Rev. Thomas Cutler Rudston-Read (1762-1838).

4 Unidentified.

5 Rev. Andrew Cheap (1775-1851), son of Thomas Cheap, Bloomsbury, Middlesex. Rector of Elrington, Yorkshire, 1809-41.

1471

From Sir John Sinclair

133 George St., Edinburgh, 13 July 1828

Private

Sir,

[Writer suggests that the Emancipation issue could be solved by an annual Indemnity Bill, 'and I was thence glad to see, in one of your speeches, that you entertained the same idea.' He says he had spent nearly thirty years in Parliament.]

SOURCE : O'Connell Papers, NLI 13648

1472

From Charles Sharpley,[1] *Ballinamore* [Co. Leitrim], *18 July 1828*

The writer says he is a Catholic and the treasurer of the Catholic Rent. He wishes O'Connell to send £10 to Mr. R. O'Beirne[2] of Carrick (-on-Shannon) for the legal defense of fifteen Catholic men arrested on account of their protesting an Orange procession in Ballinamore on 12 July. He thinks the matter worthy of the Catholic Association's notice. He praises Mr. Acheson O'Brien[3] as 'an excellent and liberal magistrate' and describes local Orange activity: 'From the earliest period of Orangeism they have had their procession unmolested here until July 1826 when a sanguinary and unequal contest took place between a well armed body of Orangemen and a number of unarmed young lads. Last year the magistrates prevented an Orange walk. This year a number of Orange Delegates met in this town and [the] result was they declared their intention to have a great display on the ensuing 12th and the country people as fully determined to prevent them.'

SOURCE : O'Connell Papers, NLI 13648

1 Merchant.

2 Probably Roger O'Beirne, woollen merchant.

3 Capt. Acheson O'Brien.

1473

From James Feeny[1] *to Merrion Square*

Sligo, 21 July 1828

[No salutation]

. . . On tomorrow we are to have a meeting at our chapel to arrange a public dinner for you of which you will get due notice. . . . I beg the favour of a line to say the day you will be here[2] that we may go some miles from town to meet you. I hope when you come here you will be able to form a Liberal[3] club in this county which, God knows, is much wanting. . . .

SOURCE : O'Connell Papers, NLI 13648

1 Baker, Market Street, Sligo.

2 O'Connell arrived in Sligo on 30 July for the assizes. He attended a public dinner there on 31 July. As a protest the Orange Society held a dinner on the same evening (*MR*, 13 Aug. 1828). At the Catholic Association meeting on 2 August O'Connell claimed to have founded a Liberal club during his visit to Sligo (*DEP*, 5 Aug. 1828).

3 The establishment of Liberal clubs on a national basis seems to have been first advocated by Thomas Wyse after the Clare election. The rules drawn up for their organization envisaged the extension throughout the country of a network of country and parish clubs controlled by the Catholic Association. Members joining the county clubs, which were responsible for directing the parish clubs, were to pay a subscription of thirty shillings a year. The parish clubs were to consist of 'the principal gentry, clergy, churchwardens, and such of the respectable farmers as can read . . .' They had for their object 'keeping every man in constant readiness for future elections, maintaining the registries, inquiring into and giving information of any persecution of freeholders, . . . promoting good order, perfect subordination to the laws, political knowledge, and liberal feeling' (Thomas Wyse, *Historical Sketch of the Late Catholic Association of Ireland*, 2 vols. [1829], app. xxv, clxx-clxxi; for an account of the later development of the club system which came to play an important part in the O'Connellite and liberal political machines of the 1830s, see Macintyre, *The Liberator*, pp. 88-90).

1474

To the Knight of Kerry

Friday [17 April 1829 (see letter 1555a)]

My dear Sir,

I have heard *something* which convinces me that Mr. Vesey FitzGerald *ought* to be seen without delay by some friend of mine who could pledge himself to my willingness and that of the Catholics to atone to him for our conduct and to express our sense of the magnanimity of his. The sooner the better—the sin of ingratitude is heavy on us just now.

SOURCE : O'Connell MSS, UCD

1475

From Aubrey William Beauclerk[1]

12 Chester St., Grosvenor Place, London
[c. mid or late July] 1828

Sir,

Though I have not the honour of being personally acquainted with you, . . . I feel I have a sort of right to congratulate you on your recent success in the County of Clare, and hail you as the first Roman Catholic representative of Ireland *since the Union*. My mother was half-sister to Lord Edward FitzGerald. This connection, with the prospect of a large estate in the County of Down at the death of my G. Father,[2] gives me a privilege of sympathizing with the wrongs of that ill-fated country, more particularly as no one can feel more indignation at them than I do. Your triumph will at least destroy that absurd idea entertained in this country by the ignorant that the people of Ireland themselves are lukewarm in the cause of Emancipation when they thus see a whole country leagued together to throw off the yoke of oppression and determined in the face of their landlords to assert the rights of freemen. . . . The whole fabric of bigotry and oppression must soon crumble to the ground in spite of the prayers and wailings of Eldon and Peel or the rage and fury of Orangemen. . . . Most sincerely do I wish you success in your next step which I conclude will be the House of Commons, though I confess I have too poor an opinion of the majority of that House to hope they will be true to those principles they have pledged themselves to. I trust I may be mistaken, time will show. . . . In India where any district has been much oppressed by the government and their prayers of redress not listened to, they have with one accord refused *passively* to pay *rents* or taxes. This they have often found the only receipt for their wrongs. I think Ireland might adopt that receipt with success, if other measures should not succeed. A general combination to that effect till their wrongs were redressed would bring a speedy cure, I am convinced. Excuse *this* hint, to *one* so much better able to see all the bearings of the case than myself.

SOURCE : O'Connell Papers, NLI 13647

1 Major Aubrey William Beauclerk (1801-1854), St. Leonard's Forest, Horsham, Sussex, son of Charles George Beauclerk and Emily Charlotte, second daughter of William Ogilvie by Emily Mary, formerly dowager duchess of Leinster. M.P. for East Surrey, 1832-37.

2 William Ogilvie (1740-1832), Ardglass Castle, Co. Down, a Scottish schoolteacher in Ireland who became tutor to the children of the first duke of Leinster and married the duke's widow in 1774.

1476

From Patrick Molony[1] *to Merrion Square, redirected to Sligo*

Jail St. [Ennis, postmarked Limerick,
30 July 1828]

Sir,

[The writer complains that O'Connell's agent, Mr. Scott, refuses to pay him £23 for porter, wine and cider supplied during the Clare Election. He describes having a row with Mr. Singleton of Quinville, ' who attempted to take a man of his from me by force when I was about to poll him '. When he called Singleton a liar and a scoundrel, Singleton called on the High Sheriff to commit him to prison. He asks O'Connell to direct the election committee to pay for the liquor.]

SOURCE : O'Connell Papers, NLI 13648

1 Grocer and wine merchant.

1477

From the Cartwright Monument Committee to Merrion Square

6 Alfred Place, Bedford Square [London],
1 August 1828

Sir,

I am instructed by the Committee appointed at a public meeting[1]—Sir F. Burdett, Bart. in the chair—for conducting the subscription to erect a monument[2] to the late Major Cartwright, to request that you would have the goodness to favour the Committee by giving your name and countenance to so desirable an object. . . .

You, having in your late address to the freeholders of Clare and on various other occasions declared yourself a radical parliamentary reformer, I have only to observe, from the Committee, that it would be beneficial to that cause to erect a monument to him . . . besides being the only thing of the kind heretofore attempted to commemorate such principles. . . .

There is now a fund of about £600 . . . which is too small to accomplish anything worthy . . . and they therefore hope that *you* will . . . forward the subscription in Ireland. They are led to suppose that America will not be backward in assisting to preserve the memory of him who resigned his preferment in the Navy rather than draw his sword against her opening independence. *The venerable and patriotic Lafayette[3] has already subscribed £20.*

I am instructed also to request that you will be good enough to give the Committee information as to the time when you purpose being in London as a public meeting of the subscribers and others is in contemplation.

[Then Cleary sends his personal congratulations to O'Connell for his work for Emancipation and to the electors of Clare. A native of Ireland he sees these events with pride.]

[signed] Thos. Cleary, Hon. Sec.

SOURCE : O'Connell MSS, UCD

1 Probably that held at the Crown and Anchor Tavern, London on 20 June 1825 (*MC*, 21 June 1825).

2 The subscription had been opened shortly after Cartwright's death

in 1824 and by the time of Burdett's Crown and Anchor Tavern meeting had reached £500. It was a young Irish sculptor, Patrick Macdowell (1799-1870), whose design for the monument (a seated statue of Cartwright) was selected. Owing to the insufficiency of the amount subscribed, however, Macdowell did not carry out the design himself but allowed it to be executed by another sculptor who was ruined by the commission. Eventually the monument was erected in the garden opposite Cartwright's residence in Burton Crescent, London (Frances D. Cartwright, *The Life and Correspondence of Major Cartwright,* 2 vols. [London 1826], II, frontispiece, 290-8; *DNB*, s.v. 'Cartwright, John', 'Macdowell, Patrick').

3 Marquis de Lafayette (1757-1834), the celebrated French general and political leader.

1478

To Rev. William Shepherd[1] *at Daniel Gaskell's Esq., Lupsett Hall, nr. Wakefield, Yorkshire*

Merrion Square, 3 August 1828

My dear Sir,

Your letter of the 15th of July has remained unanswered merely because I am compelled to give so many franks to others that I had not one for myself. . . .

I have always cherished your valuable exertions in the cause of civil and religious liberty as a consolation amidst the evils which your nation had inflicted and *was* inflicting on mine. I trust the good men of both countries will soon become too strong for the common enemy. In plain truth it is time they should for that enemy has had a sufficiently long career and has done abundance of mischief and to spare.

It is with pride and pleasure that I tell you of the improved state of the Irish peasantry. Only think for one moment of an entire circuit all over the island without as yet one execution. The attempt to proselytize the children of the Irish Catholics by the means of education has produced a reaction in favour of education of the most beneficial nature. There is scarcely one parish in Ireland without a school on the most improved plan and the rising generation of the Irish are beyond any comparison the people in Europe amongst whom the greatest number of readers are to be found. It is astonishing by what moral magic the Catholic clergy have collected from the poorest people on earth the means for building and supporting so many schools, and you concur with me in the certainty that a reading people are not likely to continue in a state of depression. Let me turn prophet and tell you that both you and I *will* see a great and salutary political alteration worked out in both countries by means of the political and moral excitation at present at work in Ireland.

I believe you are right in your conjecture and that Wellington is about to lower the flag of intolerance. I believe so for more reasons than one. We annoy his Irish friends and are likely to give them still more annoyance, and all Europe is now in a state which may shortly make it essential for the safety of the British Empire to combine the strength of all the people. They cannot expect to have us until they determine to do us justice, aye, and carry that determination into effect.

SOURCE: NLI, MSS 5759

1 Rev. William Shepherd (1768-1847), Unitarian minister and author. He was the only non-paying guest at the dinner on 19 July 1819 in Dublin in honour of Devereux and South American freedom (see letter 778, note 7). See *DNB*.

1479

From Richard Lalor Sheil to Cork

Kilkenny, 6 August [1828]

My dear O'Connell,

I have just received a letter from Moore,[1] the poet, in which he informs me that on account of the part taken by the *Times* newspaper relative to Ireland, he has thought it incumbent on him to withdraw from all connection with that journal. This he wishes that *you* should *know* but, at the same time, is anxious that it should *not be publicly mentioned*. He desires me to communicate it to you. He regards your election as a most important and beneficial event.

I yesterday saw Lord Duncannon who says that Lord Holland has made parliamentary law his peculiar study and that he has *great doubts* as to the question of your admissability. He is far from being of opinion that you cannot sit.

Lord Duncannon told me that the King was very much disposed to put the Regal veto in the Bill for the repeal of the Test and Corporation acts, and that the Duke of Wellington had been under the necessity of exerting all his influence in order to obtain his assent. The great obstacle to our question is in the Palace.

SOURCE : O'Connell MSS, UCD

1 Thomas Moore (1779-1852). See *DNB*.

1480

From the Knight of Kerry

Valentia [Co. Kerry], 30 August 1828

My dear O'Connell,

If it be not inconsistent with your [? policy] to give me a *toties quoties* lease of the lot of ground which you have assigned to Mr. Neal[1] at Renard Point, I would endeavour to effect a very improved landing place there with reference not merely to the ferry but for the establishment of fish *salters*, as they are called, to give a market which does not at present exist for our fishery.

I am taking measures to fix hereabouts a better class of fishermen but there is no existing demand for fresh fish and it will require houses to be built for the carriers. Such a landing place would facilitate the conveyance of sand to the large tract of coarse ground in your College lands and it would be further my object to improve the ferry considerably for cattle as well as passengers by additional buildings and conveniences.

SOURCE : O'Connell MSS, UCD

1 Neal (O'Neill), Renard Point, Cahirciveen, Co. Kerry, fish salter. Renard is the place from which the ferry crosses to Valentia Island. O'Neill's descendants still live at Renard Point.

1481

From Lord Clifford

[c. 15 September 1828]

Dear Sir,

On my return to Ugbrooke[1] I was agreeably surprised on finding a letter from you. Mr. Chester[2] had mentioned in the letter I received from him in July last that he had hoped to have been able to procure a frank from you, that he had not succeeded as you had left town. This naturally suggested the anomaly of a Roman Catholic commoner's being Member of Parliament, having a right to frank his letters while that privilege is withheld from English Roman Catholic peers, being members of the Upper House. I am much gratified that the remark I made has been the means of my being favoured with a letter from you, and which claims my best thanks for the honourable mention you [? made of] English Roman Catholic peers [? who will], I trust, emulate the example of those who are gone before them by their strict adherence to the religion of their ancestors, their loyalty to their King and their attachment to the Liberties and Constitution of their country.

I cannot express the pleasure with which I perused your statement of the present state of Ireland. What a contrast is the peaceable conduct of the Catholics to the sanguinary threats of their enemies! I rejoice that Providence has chosen you to direct their peaceable and constitutional efforts, to obtain an equality of rights and privileges with their fellow subjects. It is impossible that a steady perseverance in such principles should not at length induce Government to grant their just claims. [Two lines illegible] the meetings which are taking place in [one or two words illegible] parts of the country. However well [? conducted and] peaceable they may be at present, taking into consideration the agitated state of the public mind, circumstances may occur to render them dangerous.

I well remember the discussion which took place when you were in London respecting the 40s. freeholders; it was clearly understood that Emancipation was to be conceded before their case could be taken into consideration. On political questions there must ever be difference of opinion. No one could then anticipate the services they might be enabled [? to re]nder the body.

As to securities, I can assure you no [? proposals] relating thereto have been made to [? the] English Catholics. They are ignorant [nearly two lines illegible]. We have given and are still willing to give any test of our civil allegiance. What more can be required of us? As to spiritual matters, we disclaim any interference, leaving them to the decision of the proper judges, our ecclesiastical superiors.

SOURCE : O'Connell Papers, NLI 13649

1 Ugbrooke Park, Devon, seat of Lord Clifford.

2 Unidentified.

1482

To Rev. Michael Slattery[1]

Derrynane, nr. Cahirciveen, 2 September 1828

Rev. Sir,

I beg you will at your earliest convenience write to me to enable me to contradict what I presume must be a calumny on the good people of Tipperary. It is said that at one of those public meetings to make peace between contending factions of which we all so much approve, the noted Kirby,[2] who is charged with the horrid crime of murder and has not [? surrendered] himself for that, had the audacity to appear in the midst of the honest and worthy men to whom I am so deeply indebted for taking my advice. Our cause is too sacred and too holy to allow it to be tarnished by the society of men who are stained with crime. The great Catholic cause of Ireland is the cause of virtue and honesty. The great God of heaven will not allow it to prosper if we associate with murderers or criminals of any kind.

There must be no drunkenness, no debauchery, no riots, no secret meetings, no illegal oaths, no Whiteboy outrages. Above all, there must be no murders. The hand of every good man must be always raised against murderers and the vengeance of God is directed against them. I hope and believe the people will listen to my advice. If they but knew how sincerely I love Ireland and how anxious I am for the liberty of the Irish people, they would follow the good and wholesome counsel I give as if it were a command. Let them but obey this advice for one space of twelve months or two years and within that time, with the assistance of good men, we will put down the vile Orange faction. The only men who can assist me for this purpose are the *good, honest, religious* men. I will not accept the help of any others. They must be *sober, industrious, attentive to their religious and moral duties* or I will not consent to their being collectors of Catholic Rent or even paying it or in any manner joining us. The men I want to contribute to that sacred fund and to help me to keep the country quiet and to put down Orange oppression are the steady men who are good sons, good brothers, good husbands. Surely there are enough of the people of virtue and true religion to put down all delinquents of every description.

Let me have the happiness to hear that this report about Kirby is false. I am quite sure it is but I want the sanction of your authority to contradict the base falsehood.

We are striving for Ireland and for religion. We must be joined only by men who cherish religion and hate every species of crime.

SOURCE : Cashel Diocesan Archives, 1828/1, p. 6001

1 Rev. Michael Slattery (1785-1857), a native of Co. Tipperary. Professor of philosophy at Carlow College, 1809-15; P.P. of Cashel, 1815-33; president of St. Patrick's College, Maynooth, 1833-34; archbishop of Cashel, 1834-57. See *DNB*.

2 Unidentified.

1483

To Lord Cloncurry

Derrynane, 4 September 1828

My dear Lord,

I know you will excuse me for writing to you anything I think useful to Ireland. If you agree with me you will zealously assist, if not, you will forgive the trouble I give you, out of regard for my motives.

The Orange faction is endeavouring to beard the Government; that seems quite plain. Their ostentatious display of their peerage strength in the Brunswick Club[1] is manifestly made in order to terrify the Government of Lord Anglesey and to encourage the friends of bigotry in England, where there are many, and some in the highest station. It would be, indeed, quite idle to conceal from ourselves that the great enemy of the people of Ireland is his most sacred Majesty!! It is but too obvious that the pimps and parasites who surround the throne have an idea that their power is connected with the continuation of abuses in Ireland. They are miserably mistaken, and they would be much more secure by doing us justice; but it is with the fact we have to do, not with the theory. The fact, then, is most unfavourable and the Saurins and Lefroys are only struggling to give their friends in the Ministry and men near the throne a notion that their party in Ireland is strong enough to continue misgovernment with impunity. This is obviously the object of the recent and continued display of Orange aristocracy.

In the meantime, what are *our* friends doing? Alas! nothing. They, the Orangeists, have their peers coming forward with alacrity, openly and with ostentation. They have their Marquis[2] at their head—more than one marquis. We have scarcely any symptom of sympathy from the higher order of Protestants. There is, indeed, a Duke[3] who you say, and I believe you, means well; but allow me mournfully but not reproachfully to ask you of what value are his intentions? What a glorious opportunity is he not letting slip to serve Ireland and to exalt himself; but above all things, to serve Ireland. I know that there is a declaration being signed in favour of Emancipation; a paltry declaration it is—just enough to serve as an excuse for *doing* nothing. I want to see something *done*. The Orangeists are *doing* and so are the Catholic Association; and we are doing so well that we can afford, after all, to go on without being encumbered with other aid. But, although we can *afford it,* we shold much desire not to let things remain as they are.

The assistance of Protestants generates so much good feeling and such a national community of sentiment that I deem it more valuable than even Emancipation itself. I tell you frankly what I think ought to be done but what I fear will not. I think the Duke of Leinster and every other Protestant peer friendly to the principle of freedom of conscience should avail themselves at once of the formation of the Brunswick Club and come forward and join the Catholic Association. There is in Ireland no neutral ground; whatever is not with us is, in reality, against us. The time is come to take an active part in struggling to preserve the country from the bigots.[4]

SOURCE : FitzPatrick, *Corr.*, I, 164-5

1 The Brunswick Constitution Club of Ireland was founded at a meeting in Dublin on 15 August 1828. The club had Lord Longford as president and some twenty noblemen as vice-presidents. Eight of its founding members were M.P.'s. Its object was the preservation of ' the integrity of our Protestant Constitution '. Preparations were made at this meeting to establish a fund for the extension of the club throughout the country (*DEP,* 26 Aug. 1828). Within a few weeks O'Connell was expressing alarm at the rapidity with which

Brunswick clubs were springing up all over Ireland (O'Connell to Edward Dwyer, 3 Sept. 1828, *MR*, 8 Sept. 1828).

2 Either the second marquess of Donegall or the second marquess of Ely. Both supported the foundation of the Brunswick Constitution clubs.

3 Duke of Leinster.

4 The conclusion of this letter has been lost.

1484

To Edward Dwyer[1]

Derrynane, 8 September 1828

My dear Friend,

As more than a month must elapse before I reach Dublin I beg of you to call the attention of the Association at its next meeting to the subject of the other provincial assemblies which ought to take place this vacation. Connaught I know will do its duty, notwithstanding the mistaken attempt of a few gentlemen to control the resolution of the Association requiring 'the pledges'.[2] Leaving therefore Connaught to itself, let us see what can be done in the other provinces. . . .

SOURCE : Dublin Diocesan Archives

1 This is a public letter published in the *Morning Register* of 12 September 1828 but the first paragraph, because it provides a footnote defining the 'pledges', is being published.

2 At an extraordinary meeting on 4 August the Catholic Association called on all candidates for parliament to pledge themselves publicly (1) not to support the administration of Wellington or Peel until Emancipation had been unconditionally granted, (2) to try to repeal the Sub-letting Act and (3) to support parliamentary reform, particularly an extension of the franchise and shorter parliaments. The meeting called on all members of the association to oppose candidates who would not give these three pledges. It demanded from candidates for Co. Galway the additional pledge that they try to 'open the now unjustly closed Borough of the town of Galway' (*MR*, 5 Aug. 1828).

1485

To Pierce Mahony, Merrion Square N.

Derrynane, 17 [and 19] September 1828

My dear Mahony,

I write as you desire by the return of the post but there is a delay interposed from Monday till Friday at this time of the week [*sic*].

I thank you most sincerely for sending me Mr. Horton's book[1] and letters.[2] I wish that my reply may enable you to suppress the publication of his book. I conjure you for his sake to suppress it if possible. I really believe him to be an exceedingly well intentioned man and should be sorry he exposed himself to the contempt and ridicule that would follow such a publication. But he is literally mad as any man in Bedlam to suppose that the Catholics as a body would consent to be emasculated by way of Emancipation. What! He would not allow us to vote upon any question relative to the Protestants, the Catholics or the Dissenters. You yourself do not seem aware of the extent of his notions. Consider only this—we are not to vote on anything affecting the *emoluments* of the Protestant Church. The Corn question directly and immediately affects those emoluments because a corn bill, by making corn dear, increases those emoluments, and the repeal of a corn bill, by making corn cheap, would lessen those emoluments. . . . The security proposed by Dean Swift actually to emasculate the male Catholics was wisdom compared to the dream of Mr. Wilmot Horton. . . .

I differ with him on every proposition. I totally deny his theory of over-population. I see with my own eyes that the greatest part of Ireland does not contain one-tenth of the population it could and ought to support in comfort. He relies on the Emigration Committee[3] witnesses—Mr. Dixon,[4] the agent of Sir Thomas Chapman,[5] a man that knows just as much of political economy as one of my hounds, and there is another learned Theban on whom he also pins his faith—Mr. Bodkin[6] of the County of Galway. Well, well, after that one is not surprised at the romance of the Emigration Report.[7]

With regard to the approbation of Lord Kenmare, he certainly for honourable intention cannot be exceeded but his retired habits render him a stranger to the Catholic population and the calibre of his mind is not likely to render his opinion valuable. Amiable he is and respectable but you are aware that he has no *public* weight whatsoever.

Poor Mr. Blount, how I pity him if Mr. Horton's book shall appear! The English Catholics are running just the same course that was run by the Catholics in Ireland. There was a division between the aristocracy and democracy. The latter separated and set up 'a committee' of their own which became the only powerful body. Just so in England there is a popular Catholic association forming but for the silliness of its leading members, it would already be the potent machine. Let Mr. Horton's book be published and make a sensation, which I really think it will *not*. My opinion is that it will be totally disregarded, but if it makes a sensation it will either cause Blount to be expelled from his office of Secretary or it will organize and so strengthen the popular association that the peers themselves must soon do as they did in Ireland—give in their adhesion to the democratic party.

There is another position of Mr. Horton's which I utterly deny. I totally deny that any man is a knave or a fool who thinks the Catholics can expect Emancipation without securities. This is his wholesale mode of disposing of that question. Now I know not in which class he may rank me but this proposition I am thoroughly convinced of, namely, that an Emancipation bill *cannot* pass accompanied with *securities*. Mine is directly the converse of the proposition of Mr. Horton. I have at my side the experiment of 1825, at which time I am convinced we should have had Lord Liverpool compelled to grant Emancipation if I had not foolishly acceded to the securities called 'the Wings'. In fact we were carrying the Emancipation bill not by reason of the political wisdom of the Ministry but from the apprehension entertained of the resentment of the Irish nation in consequence of the suppression of the Catholic Association. The course I should have taken was to have kept up that salutary apprehension and I could easily have done so but, instead of *that*, I listened in an evil hour to the suggestions of Mr. Plunket, etc., who said that if we conceded 'the Wings' by way of security, we should certainly carry the bill. Now, it would have been impossible to obtain a public sanction to 'the Wings', so I gave mine and succeeded. I was the only man, I believe, who could succeed in causing a perfect silence to reign amongst the universal Catholic body. I procured for this purpose public tranquillity. The Ministry saw that I had appeased the storm, they considered that the danger was passed and the House of Lords scouted our Emancipation bill. Nay, Peel and Wetherell, the Attorney-General, actually taunted me with having betrayed popular rights in order to attain the objects of my personal ambition.

I was deceived once but I should indeed be more than insane, I should be indeed 'a knave or a fool' if [I] were to be deceived in the same way again.

We shall never be emancipated but as we were relieved in 1778, 1782 and 1793, that is, when it becomes *necessary* for the English Government to do something for Ireland. I am endeavouring to create that necessity by obtaining a control over the Irish Members of Parliament. If I had fifty county members obliged to attend constantly and to vote against every ministerial measure, *I do think* I should soon be disarmed by having Emancipation granted besides the power which is obtained by having the people perfectly tranquil in every county in Ireland and at the same time publicly united in legal exertions to carry the measure. I do think *the necessity* for Emancipation is nearly created already by the state of Ireland, and the aspect of foreign affairs is so unfavourable to England—England has so completely fallen from her *'high estate'* that unless our ancient allies, the Turks, should defeat the Russians, or some other *untoward* event shall speedily happen, believe me, believe me that Emancipation is at hand without the rotten reed of 'Securities' to lean upon. England wants Ireland at present and therefore we may be emancipated.

As to the Clare Election that raises a question upon which there will be naturally diversity of opinion. . . . It is the commencement of practical reform in Parliament. Mr. Horton as a Tory thinks it is property which should be represented, not men. I differ with him. His notions are fit for the ancient ladies of the present day. They are passing fast into disregard and only sustained by a standing army. The young mind as well as young blood of the British dominions is strongly tinged with democracy. The democratic principle is making a silent but steady progress, and the mere jobbers in politics of the school to which Mr. Horton belonged will soon be like excellent boats on this coast when the tide is quite out and that they be on the naked strand.

I perceive a new word in *his* letters to you and yours to me. You beg I will not 'reclaim' against this plan of securities. You may readily believe me that, as far as personal influence is concerned, no man possesses more over my mind and *very, very* few half so much. I would do at your request as much as I would do for any other person living. I know and I have already felt and most highly value your friendship. I am not only pleased with it but proud of it. As far, therefore, as I can go I will, that is, I will not 'reclaim' against this plan as long as it continues even in partial obscurity, and I really expect that will be always. It is so monstrous that I cannot bring myself to believe that even the proverbial stupidity of the honourable House [of Commons] would suffer it to be gravely stated. But if it makes any way, I must, indeed I must 'reclaim' against it in the most unmeasured terms. . . .

Observe the totally unconstitutional nature of this proposal. Any county or borough that elected a Catholic would have only a half representative. . . .

My opinion is so fixed upon it that I infinitely prefer our present state to such an emancipation. We are now aggrieved, we should then be dishonoured. . . .

I should indeed infinitely prefer to see Mr. Horton sitting by his former colleague, Mr. Peel, and voting against us altogether. He is honest in his vote for us. *That* is pretty certain, and yet how could the brother-in-law of Lord Kenmare vote otherwise? . . .

I was unable to finish my letter by the first post. I scarcely can persuade myself to finish it now—19th September—but I hold in readiness enough to blow the project of Mr. Horton to atoms.

Heaven help his head. He talks of dividing the Catholic body. What, when the old Orange lodges are revived, when two new ones are *being* constituted—the York Club—and the Brunswick, alias Bloodhound Clubs! At such a moment as this Wilmot Horton to dream of dividing the Catholic body —poor man!!!

. . . I intend to be in Dublin more early in October than usual. I will then work with you upon my case[8] for the Committee. Think you that there will be a sessions in November?

Do you know that nothing ever pleased me more than the conduct[9] of Mr. Dawson! He has done a great deal of good. You have seen that I hailed him cheerily and I think delicately.[10] . . .

SOURCE : Rathcon Papers

1 This book does not appear to have been published unless it was *Protestant Securities Suggested* . . . (London 1828). In it Horton argues for the qualified Emancipation that O'Connell ridicules but says almost nothing about over-population and makes no mention of Dixon or Bodkin.

2 Unidentified.

3 On 15 February 1827 the House of Commons appointed a select committee to consider 'the subject of Emigration from the United Kingdom'. Horton was appointed a member of the committee.

4 Hugh Dixon.

5 Sir Thomas Chapman, second baronet (1756-1837), Killua Castle, Co. Westmeath.

6 John Bodkin. Probably John James Bodkin (1801-82), Kilclooney and later of Quarrymount, Co. Galway; M.P. for Galway town, 1831-32; Co. Galway, 1835-47.

7 The select committee presented three reports (February, April and June 1827) which were published: *Report from the Select Committee appointed to inquire into the expediency of encouraging Emigration from the United Kingdom*, H.C. 1826-27 (88) (237) (550) V, 1, 2, 223.

8 On 22 July 1828 the Commons accepted a petition controverting the election of O'Connell for Co. Clare.

9 On 12 August at a public dinner in Londonderry to celebrate the erection of a monument to the city's resistance to James II, George Robert Dawson, M.P. for the county and hitherto a determined opponent of the Catholics, came out in favour of Emancipation. Dawson was a brother-in-law of Robert Peel.

10 In a speech at the Munster grand provincial dinner at Clonmel on 26 August (*FJ*, 29 Aug. 1828).

1486

From Thomas Fitzgerald, Cork, 18 September 1828, to Derrynane

Concerning bills of exchange. 'I will send this day by . . . Sullivan Casure[1] [liquor to Derrynane]'.

SOURCE : O'Connell Papers, NLI 13648

1 Patrick O'Sullivan, Eightercua, Waterville, Co. Kerry. His family had the soubriquet 'Casure' (the Gaelic for hammer). He was O'Connell's piper. O'Connell's son Maurice erected a tombstone to his memory at Ballinskelligs, Co. Kerry.

1487

To Michael Staunton

Derrynane, 20 September 1828

My dear Staunton,

The enclosed[1] reached me by post. I think it will be an act of humanity to give it insertion, heading it with an article to the effect that you got it from me to publish, with an expression of hope that other newspapers would insert it so as to give the parties interested a chance of learning intelligence of value to them. The deceased was probably a relation to Bradley King, the Orange Alderman. If you think so, call on him *from me* and show him the enclosed letter, telling him that *we* at least are superior to our enemies in civility and disposition to do a service.[2]

SOURCE : FitzPatrick, *Corr.*, I, 166

1 Unidentified.

2 FitzPatrick writes: 'Staunton, instead of publishing the letter, waited on Sir Abraham Bradley King, who seems to have been pecuniarily interested in its contents' (FitzPatrick, *Corr.*, I, 166, n9).

1488

To Michael Staunton

22 September 1828

[No salutation]

I have seen my letter[1] to Hunt and am greatly obliged to you for your attention to it. It is the best printer's job I ever saw. There are no white snails in it. I wrote that letter not for Hunt but for the dormant reformers in England, Bentham,[2] Bowring, &c. The Law Reform is now my grand object. You should give it *more* lifts. Everybody should help to get rid of the present most vexatious, expensive, cabalistic and unintelligible system of law proceedings. It is a disgrace to civilized society to have scoundrel judges acting most despotically over lives and fortunes without the possibility of control or punishment. I think I do not exaggerate when I say that no man since the days of 'the Sainted Alfred' was ever half as useful as I shall be if I can abolish the present nefarious and abominable system and introduce a code of Common Sense both in its mode of proceeding and in its rules and enactments. Help me to do this as you have already helped me to emancipate the Catholics. The which we have done, for it is done.

SOURCE : FitzPatrick, *Corr.*, I, 167

1 His public letter to Henry Hunt from Derrynane, 9 September 1828, published in Staunton's *Morning Register,* 18 September 1828. In this he declared: 'I am, I ever have been, I ever will be, a radical reformer.'

2 Jeremy Bentham (1748-1832), the celebrated political philosopher and radical reformer. See *DNB*.

1489

To Lord Cloncurry

Derrynane, 24 September 1828

My dear Lord,

I am not going to inflict another long letter upon you, but since I wrote and sent off my last letter I saw a speech of Sheil's[1] at the Association in which he calls on the Duke,[2] Lord Charlemont and on you by name to join us for Ireland. I wish to clear from your mind all suspicion that he and I are *thus* acting in conjunction. I do assure you solemnly we are not; and his having concurred with me is only another evidence of the deep conviction the Catholics now entertain that they are either opposed or deserted by the Irish Protestants. This is to me a most painful subject. Why should I not grieve, and grieve to my heart's core, when I see Lord Rossmore active and Lord Cloncurry dormant?—when I see Lord Rossmore the most popular of the Irish peerage, and the Duke of Leinster the least so? It is vain to accuse the people of rash judgements. They know their friends, not from the wishes and intentions of those friends but from their actions and exertions. It would be easy, indeed, for the Duke to resume his natural station. He would be received with the loudest acclaim. He is, however, in principle or for want of thought, a Unionist; and the time is come when every honest and sensible Irishman should be preparing to compel the Repeal of that measure. But *we* must do this *alone*. Protestant assistance will be given us when the difficulties are over and that success is approaching.

I do not ask you for a declaration of your concurrence in the opinion that Protestant patriotism in Ireland is at the lowest ebb. You would have long since done much for Ireland if you could have found Protestant co-operators. This defection is the more to be regretted because it leaves so much alive the religious prejudices of the people—those fatal prejudices which have been so long the destruction of this wretched country. For my part, the only sensation which remains in my mind is that which creates the determination to exert myself *doubly* for ' Old Ireland '.

SOURCE : FitzPatrick, *Corr.*, 167-8
1 On 18 September (*MR,* 19 Sept. 1828).
2 The duke of Leinster.

1490

To Unknown

[27 September 1828]

Copy of Extract

There is, you say, a jealousy of me for having employed another solicitor on the petition[1] beside Mr. Scott. Heaven help us, what a precious set we are! How ready to tear out each other's eyes, but surely the persons who fret themselves on this subject and abuse me ought to wait till they heard me. I never showed Mr. Scott any slight and I am incapable of doing so. He was the volunteer agent at the election and I am as much obliged to him and indeed more so than if he was my agent, not merely on such an election as this was but upon an election where I had the usual corrupt interest. No man was ever better served than I was by Mr. Scott, and it is not possible for any man to be more grateful to him than I am. I therefore neither intended nor showed him any kind of discourtesy by having at the same time an English agent in the person of my most particular friend, Pierce Mahony, especially as our measure[2] of profound secrecy in its nature became instantly necessary on the security being given—a measure which, by having been effected secretly, and before any human being in Ireland knowing it, will probably alone defeat the petition should it be persevered in. If it be persevered in, Mr. Scott will be still the Irish Agent, having abundance of business to do in Ireland to support the election whilst Mahony and his English partner act in London. . . . My friend Mahony was then in London. He is the very best parliamentary agent

I ever knew. It is of the utmost importance to have a parliamentary agent who knows *all* the members as well as *all* the ways of the House. The Kilkenny petition[3] against Doherty was lost by reason of the packing of a vile committee. No man living could do that against Mahony. He regularly attends the parliamentary sessions and has carried more difficult acts of parliament than any other Irish or English solicitor ever did. . . .

A parliamentary agent is essentially necessary as much so as the Irish election and petition agent Mr. Scott holds both the last situations—and it is a great kindness in him to hold them. My friend Mahony fulfils the duties of the former. . . . I have written this detail that no person at the Association, . . . should have it in his power to say that I behaved badly to my friend, Mr. Scott, to whom I feel many, many obligations in public as well as in private.

SOURCE: Rathcon Papers

1 See letter 1485, note 8.

2 Unidentified. This matter concerns the Clare election, now being controverted.

3 Read to the Commons on 22 November 1826 (*Commons Journal*, LXXXII, 19) and determined in John Doherty's favour on 26 February 1827 (ibid., p. 227).

1491

From Lord Duncannon

Bessborough [Co. Kilkenny], 27 September 1828

Private

Dear Sir,

It is with very great regret that I offer any opinion adverse to yours upon a subject with which you are so conversant, but as I entertain a very strong opinion on one point I am sure you will wish me to state it fairly to you. I allude to the pledges.[1] Now in one of these pledges I entirely concur, that of requiring a distinct assurance from every Irish representative that they will oppose any government that does not make the Catholic a Cabinet question. In the other resolutions I differ from you, not because I object to the subjects alluded to or undervalue their importance but because I think the first of such paramount consequence that the mixing any other matter with it weakens the first pledge and gives a loophole to those who may be inclined by this means to avoid the whole. It appears to me you have now brought the Catholic question to that point that it must be successful unless it is marred by some unfortunate and unexpected circumstance. The acknowledged union of every Catholic, the improved feeling in England, the disgusting violence of the Brunswick Clubs have placed you in a position that could not have been contemplated. The Duke of Wellington, though not positively pledged unless the Catholics by unnecessary violence find him the means, will not easily extricate himself from what his speech fairly conveyed. Add to this that he sees a determination in Ireland to be represented only by those who will oppose him or any other minister that does not make the Catholic question a *sine qua non*. No minister can look on such a state of things with indifference, but you will pardon me when I say that in my opinion, if he was called on to name the means of relieving himself from some of the difficulty, he could not devise a more likely one to meet his wishes than raising in his opponents' ranks a question like Parliamentary Reform. I would require a *positive* and *distinct pledge* from every Irish member to oppose any government that does not make the Catholic question its object but I would do this simply and in such a way that it could not be evaded. I feel this so strongly that I cannot help stating my opinion to you and begging you to give it a further consideration. Whether you agree with me or not, you will I know do me the justice of believing that I am actuated only in stating my objections to you by an anxiety to forward the Catholic cause, and by a conviction in my own mind that the introduction of other matters must injure that cause.

SOURCE : O'Connell MSS, UCD

1 See letter 1484, note 2.

1491a

To Patrick Costello, care of Edward Dwyer Esq., Catholic Rooms, Corn Exchange, Dublin

[Cahirciveen, 28 September 1828]

[first part of letter missing] persuade the other Kilkenny men to be well tempered. I am more afraid of Finn's[1] violence than of any body else. The 'bloodhounds' are unanimous, why should we be divided?[2]

Believe me always to be,

My dear Costello,

Your ever faithful and sincere

Daniel O'Connell

SOURCE : Archives Department, Manchester Public Libraries

1 O'Connell's brother-in-law, William F. Finn.

2 On 20 September the Catholic Association decided to hold the Leinster provincial meeting in Mullingar (*MR*, 22 Sept. 1828). It had been thought that it would be held in Kilkenny. At a meeting there on 21 September Finn spoke vigorously, and it was decided to send a protest delegation to the Association (*Leinster Journal*, 24 Sept. 1828). The problem was solved by a compromise (see letter 1492, note 1).

1492

To Edward Dwyer

Derrynane, 1 October 1828

My dear Friend,

I am delighted that the Leinster *Row*[1] has been compromised. I was greatly terrified about it.

. . . I also send as a parcel my draft of the address to the people of Tipperary. Get my friend, Mr. Staunton, to attend personally to the printing of it. I am sure he will do it at my request. By printing it as I drew it the Association will not be responsible for its contents. All its offences will fall on my single head.[2]

. . . Churchwardens have been appointed in this barony and I will in a post or two send you the *return*. This letter is not to be read in the Association.

I think Mr. Lawless was quite right at Ballybay.[3] If the Chapel had been in the town he should have gone there at all hazards but as it was not he was quite right and the people decidedly wrong. I also think that he ought not to be recalled. He should proceed through the Counties of Monaghan and Down and the opposition to him will, I should expect, totally cease. If it were necessary to recall him it would be a great triumph to the *bloodhounds* of all description. I am sorry to see that some members of the Association omit to call the Brunswickers by their appropriate name of 'Bloodhounds'. That name, if properly flung at them, will go near to be their destruction. No man or at least few men will like to hear themselves called by the name of the 'Bloodhound' and thus very many will be deterred from joining these clubs.

I think Mr. Lawless should be left on the subject of his mission to his own discretion, so that if he deemed it right to stop short he should communicate privately with the Association and procure an order to desist.

I doat so much on this place. I so much love to be here that I can scarcely tear myself from it. I have had several visitors. Mr. Rosson,[4] the English Catholic agitator, spent a few days with me. I have had Prince Pukler Muskau!!![5] and I expect Lord Nugent. But I must be off for Kilkenny. We shall of course see you there. 'The Triumph to neither party' is exemplified in the decision and the public are certainly served by the double meeting.

SOURCE : O'Connell Papers, NLI 13645

1 A problem had arisen as to which place would be most convenient for the Leinster provincial meeting of the Catholic Association. Eventually it was decided to hold it in Kilkenny on 15 October and then to adjourn it to Mullingar on 29 of the same month (*FJ*, 26 Sept. 1828).

2 The address, dated 30 September 1828, was in due course published in Staunton's *Morning Register* of 7 October 1828.

3 The finance committee of the Catholic Association on 5 August instructed John Lawless to tour the northern counties to organize the collection of the Catholic rent (*MR*, 6 Aug. 1828). On 23 September Lawless, according to his own account, proceeded from Carrickmacross, Co. Monaghan, towards Ballybay. After seven miles he found he had before and behind his carriage at least 250,000 people. The multitude pressed him to go into Ballybay town, an Orange stronghold, but Lawless persisted in terminating his journey at the Catholic chapel a mile and a half before the town (Lawless to Dwyer, undated, *MR*, 26 Sept. 1828).

4 John Rosson, barrister, 11 King's Bench Walk, Temple, London, an energetic member of the English Catholic Association.

5 Prince Hermann Louis Henri Puckler-Muskau (born 1785); a celebrated traveller and adventurer who toured England and Ireland, 1828-29; a relative of the Bonaparte family and a major-general in the Prussian service. Supposedly the author of *Tour in England, Ireland and France: By a German Prince*.

1493

To Nicholas Purcell O'Gorman

Derrynane, 1 October 1828

My dear O'Gorman,

I had the pleasure of receiving your letter by the last post containing a resolution[1] of the Catholic Association of Ireland expressive of the wish of that body that I should draw up an address to the people of the County of Tipperary in order to induce them to desist holding large meetings. I beg you will be so good as to communicate to the Association that I feel greatly honoured by that patriotic and illustrious body making any demand on my time or exertions. I consider their request as a command. . . . I have accordingly prepared the draft of an address to the people of Tipperary and transmit it along with this letter. . . . I am solely responsible for the sentiments contained in my address. . . .

I am quite convinced, however, that the people of Tipperary will desist from holding large meetings the moment they learn that such meetings do not any longer obtain the approbation of the Catholic Association. . . . We will thus protect and preserve the people from . . . uselessly risking the public peace and putting in danger the approaching success and triumph of the Catholic cause. . . .

SOURCE : Dublin Diocesan Archives

1 Of 23 September (*FJ*, 26 Sept. 1828).

1494

To Edward Dwyer[1]

Derrynane, 14 October 1828

My dear friend,

I send under another cover a letter which reached me from Yarmouth with £5 Catholic rent.[2] I enclose you in this letter eight guineas being Catholic Rent for this parish, Kilcrohane. This is the third or fourth remittance from this remote parish. This sum includes one pound each from Messrs. Roger[3] and Eugene[4] O'Sullivan of Berehaven, and also one pound from our Catholic Rector[5] who has already contributed no less than £3 to the Clare election fund. Where do the Catholic Clergy get all the money they give to charities and for patriotic purposes? Their incomes do not amount to anything like the one hundredth part of the revenues of the Clergy of the established Church, and they contribute in exactly the inverse ratio to the building of schools and places of worship and to all public and private charities with the clergy of that Church. And for this, amongst other causes, the Rev. Parsons are now basely recommending to the minor bloodhounds to shed Catholic blood.

Having been appointed at the Munster provincial meeting[6] one of the persons whose duty it is to report to the Catholic Association the state of the Collection of the Catholic rent in this county, I beg to announce that I shall be able to make my report on my arrival in Dublin. I trust that every parish in this county will have sent up its contribution before the close of the present year.

Will you be so good as to give notice in my name of a motion of thanks to Mr. Lawless for the manner in which he performed the duty[7] confided to him by the Catholic Association of Ireland.

[P.S.] (private) I send no less than *five* letters to you by this post.

SOURCE : Dublin Diocesan Archives

1 This letter, apart from the postscript was written for publication, was read to the Catholic Association meeting of 16 October and appeared in the *Morning Register* of the following day. Even though it comes within our definition of public letter, it is being published because it contains items of special interest and because its postscript was not published.

2 From the Catholics of Yarmouth per Rev. Joseph Tate.

3 A relative of O'Connell but not clearly identified.

4 Later of Westcove House, Caherdaniel, a relative of O'Connell; at this time (1828) sub-agent to David Roche who was land agent for the Hartopp estate.

5 Rev. Denis Teahan, P.P. of Kilcrohane (Caherdaniel).

6 In the New Chapel, Clonmel, Co. Tipperary, on 25 and 26 August, James Scully in the chair.

7 See letter 1492, note 3.

1495

From Eugene McCarthy[1] *to Merrion Square, redirected to Kilkenny, redirected to Merrion Square*

Killury [Co. Kerry], 19 October 1828

Dear Sir,

Your letter of the 6th of October dated Derrynane had not reached me until the evening before your departure for Tralee. The people of Killury felt greatly disappointed that you had not honoured them with your advice what they were to have done relative to the tithe-lease of which I had sent an exposé in a letter directed to Derrynane Abbey. Perhaps you would have now more leisure to satisfy them in that particular.

SOURCE : O'Connell Papers, NLI 13648

1 Unidentified.

1496

From John Finch[1]

Home's Hotel, Dublin, 24 October 1828

Dear Sir,

Herewith I present you with the printed report of the last Annual Meeting of the British and Foreign Unitarian Association, and as a member of that, as well as of the Irish Roman Catholic Association, I respectfully request that at your next meeting you will read that Resolution in the Report (the 11th) respecting the Catholics and that you will move that it be entered in the minutes of your society.[2] At the same time I would beg leave to suggest the propriety of the Catholic Association holding correspondence with the Unitarian, as they have pledged themselves to mutual co-operation with the Catholics in the great cause of civil and religious liberty. Should not the Dissenters and the liberal members of the established church (for there are great numbers of these in England) hold simultaneous meetings for the purpose of petitioning at the same time as they are held by the Catholics? Whenever I can be useful to the good cause of universal civil and religious liberty in Liverpool, pursued among the Unitarians in the peaceful manner it has been by the Irish Roman

Catholic Associations, you may command and will most cheerfully receive the best services in [my power]. . . .

[P.S.] Private. Could not an union with the Unitarian Association be brought about by means of the excellent Dr. Drummond[3] of your city?

SOURCE : O'Connell Papers, NLI 13648

1 Unidentified.

2 Whether O'Connell did make such a motion has not been identified.

3 William Hamilton Drummond, D.D. (1778-1865), a native of Larne, Co. Antrim; moved to Strand Street, Dublin, 1815. Poet and controversial writer on religious topics. See *DNB*.

1497

From Richard Lalor Sheil to Merrion Square

Saturday [postmarked 25 October 1828]

Private

My dear O'Connell,

I have but time to write to you that although the Brunswickers had a majority in Kent[1] yet we had the preponderance of rank and wealth and also an immense body of the people. The meeting was not the result of genuine interest in the question but was produced by the most extraordinary exertions of the clergy and of a few of the nobility. It is manifest that *apathy* upon the measure prevails through the mass of the people. The voice of the *nation* will be silent. I saw nothing to dishearten. . . . Between acclamations and hostings scarce one word I said was heard. I never witnessed such an assembly. The ferocity of the Brunswickers exceeded even my conceptions of faction. But they do not represent the people who are really indifferent to the whole affair.

SOURCE : O'Connell MSS, UCD

1 There was a meeting of gentry and freeholders at Pennendon Heath, Kent, on 24 October to petition against emancipation. To qualify himself to address it, Sheil had purchased a small freehold in the county (see *DNB*, s.v. 'Sheil, Richard Lalor').

1497a

To Edward Dwyer, Corn Exchange

28 October 1828

My dear friend,

I enclose you a cheque for £100. There will be your draft on me for £274 due on the 30th. You *must* make up the difference until Friday when I return. Draw on me for that difference with interest at four months and I will accept the bill on Friday.

SOURCE : NLI, MSS 17070

1498

From T. I. S. Shannon,[1] Ennistymon, Co. Clare, 3 November 1828, to Merrion Square

Claims expenses for work done in the Clare election which Mr. Scott refuses to pay him. He says he had incurred the displeasure of his cousin and landlord, Corny O'Brien,[2] for inducing tenants of Corney O'Brien and Stackpool[3] to vote for O'Connell.

SOURCE : O'Connell MSS, UCD

1 Unidentified.

2 Cornelius O'Brien (1782-1860), son of Henry O'Brien, Birchfield, Co. Clare. Attorney, 1811. M.P. for Co. Clare, 1832-47, 1852-57. See *Boase*.

3 Probably Andrew Stackpoole, J.P., Ballyalley, Ennis.

1499

From Edward Dwyer to Merrion Square

Committee Rooms, 5 November 1828

My dear Sir,

A number of gentlemen attended here this evening consisting of Counsellors Fogarty,[1] Dwyer,[2] and Brady;[3] Messrs. Costello,[4] Ford,[5] etc. They objected strongly to my forwarding the circulars with respect to the Provincial Bank,[6] giving as reasons that it would in the first place be contrary to the rules of the Association to forward any letter as from the body without first having a resolution passed to that effect. Secondly that it would be injurious to the Bank. The letters are ready to forward.

SOURCE : O'Connell MSS, UCD

1 Probably Philip Fogarty, 57 Denzille Street, Dublin. Called to the bar, 1822. Later assistant barrister for Antrim.

2 Probably James Dwyer.

3 Probably J. C. Brady.

4 Probably Patrick Costello.

5 Probably William Ford.

6 The circulars have not been identified. They presumably related to the crisis through which the bank was passing as a result of the 'runs' on its branches at Carlow, Clonmel, Limerick, Waterford and Wexford (*FJ*, 4 Nov. 1828). On 6 November the pro-Catholic *Morning Register* praised the bank for having surmounted the crisis by importing large quantities of gold sovereigns.

1500

From Thomas Steele[1] *to Catholic Association Rooms, Dublin*

Limerick, Wednesday 12 November 1828

My dear Sir,

I do myself the honour of sending you the *Limerick Evening Post and Clare Sentinel* of yesterday in which you will find an account, on the accuracy of which you may rely, of the circumstances which occurred on Sunday and Monday at Finough, Newcastle, and Rathkeale.[2] . . .

. . . As I acted upon this occasion as the delegate of the Catholic Association, I await the orders of that illustrious body.

In a speech which I made in this city on the evening when the congregated trades made me free of their guilds I called the Irish Catholics '*White Slaves*', and I should be glad to be informed by what other name they can be so justly described, if such acts as these are performed, I ought rather say perpetrated, under the sanction of the Government conveyed in '*Secret Instructions*'.

I have seen the Catholic this week obliged to fly from the bayonet, out of his sanctuary which had been profaned. . . .

SOURCE : O'Connell Papers, NLI 13646

1 Thomas Steele (1788-1848), son of William Steele, Derrymore, Co. Clare. Raised money for and joined revolt against Ferdinand VII of Spain 1823-24. Enthusiastic admirer and supporter of O'Connell. See *DNB*.

2 At the chapel at Finough, Co. Limerick, on 9 November, Steele, as delegate of the Catholic Association, assisted by three priests, Thomas Coll, Kelly, P.P., and Hogan of Ballingrane, succeeded in reconciling the two warring factions, the Longs and the Macnires, by investing their heads with the green ribbon of the Order of Liberators. On the return of Steele and Coll to Newcastle to address a meeting at the chapel there, three magistrates, the Rev. Mr. Geraghty, Major Bushe and Thomas Furlong informed them, allegedly on the authority of a viceregal proclamation and 'private instructions', that the meeting about to begin was illegal. Steele then called off the meeting while protesting, as a magistrate, to Bushe at the illegality of the interference. The next day Steele and Coll attended a chapel meeting at Rathkeale where resolutions were passed deploring the magistrates' action. Afterwards, 'while the Very Rev. Dr. Coll was subsequently addressing the people, Mr. James T. Massy of Clonarrold, a magistrate, passed through the crowd, climbed over the rails of the sanctuary, and in terms most insulting to the meeting, alleged that it was illegal and should not continue'. After Steele had got the people to withdraw, a heated discussion took place between himself and Massy (*Limerick Evening Post and Clare Sentinel,* 11 Nov. 1828).

1501

To Edward Dwyer

15 November 1828

My dear Sir,

As acting chairman of the committee to whom the question of 'exclusive dealing'[1] was referred I beg leave to insist upon the use of the rooms this day for the meeting of servants to procure information for that committee, and I am the more peremptory on this subject as there have been two meetings of the Association since we directed that advertisement to be inserted without the measure being brought before the Association if it were a bad one. On the contrary, it was virtually adopted by the Association when it authorized us to seek by advertisement *further* information.

I really would expect just this consideration and no more

that when it happens, and it happens but seldom, that I am obliged to absent myself from the committee, there should not be brought forward any measures without regular notice.

I therefore *claim* the use of the rooms this day and ever.

SOURCE : Dublin Diocesan Archives

1 The Catholic Association was asked on 6 November by a member, William Ford, to endorse the principle of refusing to deal with Orangemen and 'Brunswickers' (that is, 'exclusive dealing'), but O'Connell managed to get the matter referred to a committee which would investigate and report the following week on the operation of this principle by Orangemen especially in relation to servants (*FJ*, 7, 8 Nov. 1828). O'Connell reported on behalf of this committee on 13 November, saying it was intended to 'publish an advertisement in the newspapers calling on all persons who have been persecuted and aggrieved by this heartless practice to come forward' (*FJ*, 15 Nov. 1828).

1502

From Andrew Carew O'Dwyer[1]

Brussels [postmarked 13 December 1828; date illegible]

Private

My dear Sir,

. . . The clergy of *Holland,* who were comprised in the concordat[2] [about one word illegible] *take the payment from the government although a sum for their purpose has been voted in the decennial supplies.* It may be of use to mention to you but of course you will use the information with great caution and not make it public that there is a nephew[3] of the Duke of Norfolk (a son I believe of Lord Stafford) attached to the embassy here. . . . Cardinal [*sic*] Cappicini[4]—he signed the concordat on the part of the Pope.[5] He is now recovering his character amongst the clergy but he was suspected of being a creature of the King[6] in consequence of his *dining* occasionally with him, but the suspicion is wearing away and it is now said that he is here for the purpose of ascertaining whether the clergy is [*sic*] unjustifiably turbulent as has been represented to the Holy See and make complaints without cause. . . . I believe there is no doubt that a bill [in the British Parliament] for emancipation is really contemplated. Lord

Granard,[7] who is here, mentioned yesterday that to his knowledge the bill is *prepared*. . . . That was a very imprudent speech you made lately about *resistance* to disfranchisement.[8] As we extend our operations and assume a more permanent character as *legislators in Brunswick St.*,[9] we should more strictly keep clear of Wellington's fangs for he is a cold blooded and treacherous opponent. However, no one knows so well as yourself the length to what you can go with safety.

SOURCE : NLI, MSS 5243

1 This letter is preceded by a long though not fully extant account of suppression by the Netherlands government of freedom of the press because of attacks by newspapers on the anti-Catholic laws.

2 This provided for government control of episcopal appointments. At the Catholic Association meeting on 30 December 1828, O'Connell moved a vote of thanks to O'Dwyer for 'his very able statement of the Concordat in the Netherlands' (*FJ*, 31 Dec. 1828).

3 Probably Hon. George Sulyarde Stafford-Jerningham (1806-74), third son of seventeenth Baron Stafford. See *Boase*. He was not a nephew of the duke of Norfolk. O'Dwyer may have been confused by the fact that the future duke of Norfolk, now earl of Arundel, was married to a daughter of the second marquess of Stafford (Leveson-Gower family). Stafford-Jerningham entered the foreign office in 1825.

4 Francesco Capaccini (1784-1845), a native of Rome. An official of the papal secretariat of state from 1815; negotiated with the Netherlands the Concordat of 1827. Internuncio to the Netherlands, 1828-31, 1841-44; created a cardinal, 1844. See *New Catholic Encyclopaedia*.

5 Leo XII (1760-1829), elected pope in 1823.

6 William I (1772-1844). First king of the Netherlands from 1815; abdicated, 1840

7 George (Forbes), sixth earl of Granard (I) (1760-1837), created 1806 Baron Granard (U.K.); major-general, 108th Foot, 1808; lieutenant-general, 1813; general, 1830. Clerk of the crown and hanaper, 1806-07, 1815-36. Married Selina Frances, sister of first marquess of Hastings.

8 At a meeting of the Catholic Association on 2 December, O'Connell declared vehemently that he would never accept Emancipation if it should mean the disfranchisement of the forty-shilling freeholders, and he attacked the British government for its conduct about Emancipation in 1825 (*DEP*. 4 Dec. 1828).

9 This reference is obscure.

1503

From Lord Rossmore to Merrion Square

Drogheda, 21 December 1828, Sunday night

My Dear O'Connell,

Just as I was leaving town this day, a professional friend whom you know, but upon whose opinion I rest not much, called on me in consequence of Lord L. Gower's[1] answer to Col. Leslie[2] and the Monaghan magistrates.[3] The version he gave it was that it was unfriendly to me, that it implied advice to them under the authority of the Law Officers of the Crown to proceed against me for a libel, etc., to exasperate them no more, that my answer of date 6th November to their resolutions of date 30th October had revived their justification and legal authority to prosecute me for a libel on speech referred to them by them [*sic*]—that if they proceeded, I might be confined, fined £1,000, etc.

I had prepared a general contradiction and extinguisher to the dark insinuations[4] levelled of late about Turf transactions *cum aliis.* I wait your answer to the queries on the other side which pray send an answer to *by return of post,* and also enclose back to me the extract I enclose from the *Times.*[5] Pray don't delay one post.

[P.S.] . . .

Quere

1st. Was the extract from my speech of date 14th last July and sent with the resolutions of 30th October to the Lord Lieutenant libellous and consequently actionable? *Vide* extract from *Times* enclosed.

2d. If libellous, was time elapsed for taking such notice of it and did my publication of 6th November enclosed, revive it?

3d. By whom could I be prosecuted? Is it by the whole Bench of Magistrates or, if any declined, could any of the others proceed against me?

4th. Do you construe Lord Gower's letter to Col. Leslie as pointing out a mode of proceeding against me?

Vide remarks of the *Times* on O'G. Mahon, Lord Killeen and Lord Rossmore, would the Government attempt, or would the Ascendancy B—h [Bench] venture to make an example of me under such circumstances and in such times?

An answer—an answer—quick.

SOURCE : O'Connell MSS, UCD

1 Lord Francis Leveson-Gower (1800-57), second son of first duke of Sutherland; M.P. almost continuously, 1822-46; chief secretary for Ireland, 1828-30; secretary at war, 1830; created 1846 earl of Ellesmere. Assumed surname of Egerton only on 24 August 1833.

2 Charles Powell Leslie (died 15 Nov. 1831), Glaslough, Co. Monaghan; M.P. for Co. Monaghan, 1802-26; New Ross, 1830-31. Colonel, Monaghan Militia.

3 In London on 14 July Rossmore accused the Monaghan magistrates of having illegally usurped power by constituting a court martial in the county and of having acted as partisans in election riots. On 30 October the magistrates drew up resolutions complaining of Rossmore's attitude, a copy of which was sent to Leveson-Gower (*Times,* 17 Dec. 1828). On 6 November Rossmore wrote a public letter in reply (*FJ,* 12 Nov. 1828). On 21 November Leveson-Gower wrote in acknowlegment to Leslie, suggesting that action in a court of law was the proper remedy to the magistrates' grievance (*Times,* 17 Dec. 1828).

4 Unidentified.

5 Of 17 December 1828.

1504

From P. M. Murphy[1]

Navan, 26 December 1828

My dear Sir,

In the case of *Stanley* v. *Sir Thomas Chapman which I* brought before the Committee last Saturday,[2] I stated that the sum of five pounds had been advanced by the Rev. Mr. [O']Donoghue[3] of Summerhill to buy the poor man's cow and restore it to his family. . . . Perhaps you would have the further kindness to direct Mr. Dwyer to forward the money to Mr. Donoghue through the Rev. Mr. Burke of Athboy.[4]

SOURCE: NLI, MSS 5242

1 Patrick Mathias Murphy (c. 1800-62), son of Edward Murphy, Navan, Co. Meath. Called to the bar, 1827; assistant barrister, 1835-62; Q.C., 1841. See *Boase.*

2 Unidentified.

3 Rev. Patrick O'Donoghue (c. 1793-27 Oct. 1840), P.P. of Summerhill, 1826-31; Kilbride, 1831-40.

4 Rev. John Burke, P.P., Athboy.

Index of Persons

In this index no distinction is made between persons mentioned in letters and those mentioned in notes, or between a name mentioned once or more than once in a letter and its notes. Numbers in italics indicate that the person is either the writer or the recipient of the letter; a form of relationship after a name indicates relationship to Daniel O'Connell. All numerical references are to letter numbers.